SERVANTS ON THE SLOPES

Stories of Faith Over Failure, and the Miracle of Changed Lives

SKIP SCHWARZ

✝

SERVANTS ON THE SLOPES
Stories of Faith Over Failure, and the Miracle of Changed Lives

© Copyright 2016 by Grayson L. Schwarz

ISBN: 978-0-9971987-0-6

All rights reserved.
With the exception of short excerpts for critical reviews, no part of this work may be reproduced or transmitted in any form or by any means whatsoever without permission in writing from the author.

Cover photo: Courtesy of Gus Gusciora

Unless noted, other photos in the book are courtesy of the author.

For information or additional copies of the book, write:
SkiRev Press
P.O. Box 349 Hampden, Maine 04444

Or visit:
www.skirevpress.com

Printed in the United States of America.

Because of Easter

Acknowledgments

This book is my wife's fault. It began as a handbook on how to start ski ministries, but when my initial interviews in 1997 revealed that the Southern Baptists had this down to a science, I forgot about the idea. My wife, however, didn't. "When are you going to write that book?" she'd ask, only to get the brush-off. It was a dead subject for me, but not for her. From time to time, others also inquired. Finally, I recognized "The Voice" behind the voice(s). The idea of a "how to" book might be dead, but the stories of God working in the lives of those I interviewed were still very much alive. After finally deciding to write, my wife's unwavering support insured the book's successful completion.

Others have played an indispensable role in what you're about to read. For providing housing for my writing retreats, I'm indebted to Bob and Denise MacLeod, Gary and Holly Lovgren and Rev. James Smith, whose mobile home-away-from-home was the birthplace of this book. In addition, Rev. Scott Records of First Baptist Church, Bar Harbor, Maine, let me turn one of their Sunday school rooms into a writing room for my camping getaways at nearby Acadia National Park.

If ever a book was the result of a group effort, it's this one. For the past two years, I've been part of a writing workshop sponsored by the Edyth L. Dyer Community Library in Hampden, Maine. Led by Professor Adam Crowley, the skilled writers in this group provided perspectives I lacked, uncovered mistakes I didn't notice, and revealed misunderstandings I didn't see. Because of their encouraging honesty, this book is a much better read.

I'm also grateful to my editor, Professor Robin Morris. After making the decision to write in 2005, it was her offer to do the editing that served as a constant and unspoken encouragement.

In thinking about the printing, another blessing appeared in the person of Craig Chevalier. I met Craig and his family on the slopes of Loon Mountain and soon discovered these weren't your "run of the mill" church folks. Most notably, their desire to serve Christ led to a vibrant and growing ministry to the homeless in Manchester, New Hampshire. Craig found out about my book at the same time he was expanding his printing company, and generously offered to print the book at his cost.

PREFACE

Testimonies can be powerful. The personal experiences of others have changed my life, and I expect they've changed yours. In the spiritual realm, it's one thing to hear the phrase "God loves you," and an entirely different thing to see the results in a person's life. I once told the story of a famous person in the 1940's and '50's who became an alcoholic. He went to a Billy Graham crusade, accepted Christ's forgiveness and came home a different man. Inspired by the example of Louis Zamparini in Laura Hillenbrand's "Unbroken," a couple in my congregation also turned to Christ, their lives were changed and their marriage, saved.

I began collecting material for this book in the fall of 1997. Holed up in a friend's mobile home at the start of a badly needed sabbatical, I called other ski resort ministers around the country, interviewing them about their work and their lives. One after another, they shared what God had done in stories that soon replaced my exhaustion with inspiration. During one of those interviews, my wife walked through the door. Taking one look at me, she exclaimed, "I haven't seen you this excited about ministry since we came to Loon seven years ago." Those stories inspired me, and I thought they might do the same for you. As will become clear in the pages ahead, all of us are ordinary men, but as you're about to discover, we're serving an extraordinary God.

Ski resort ministries, the common thread in this book, are not well known. "I didn't know they had such a thing," is the response I hear most often, and it's understandable. Until those of us in this book started them, such ministries were unheard of at the resorts we served.

AUTHOR'S NOTES

Recorded and transcribed interviews are my primary source of information. Where memories fail, conversations are interpolated. The only dialogue I created—the campfire scene—was approved by the attributed narrator as similar to those that actually did occur. I have vetted all quotations for accuracy, occasionally requiring a healthy dose of humility by those interviewed. For this, I'm grateful, for without such transparency, you would be reading a very different book.

To protect the privacy of the survivors, I've changed the names and identifying information in the book's two major accidents.

CONTENTS

SKIP SCHWARZ

1.	Blindside	5
2.	Growing Up	16
3.	Fort Benning, Georgia	20
4.	From Army to Seminary	25
5.	It Started with a Call	30
6.	Easter	34
7.	Settling Down	38
8.	Cox Memorial	42
9.	Domestic Disaster(s)	45
10.	Strong and Kingfield	51
11.	Around the Country in Forty-Two Days	55
12.	Sugarloaf	58
13.	Going Downhill Successfully	61
14.	Summertime	65
15.	Leaving Sugarloaf	70
16.	New Hampshire	75
17.	The First Winter	78
18.	The Vision: At Least I got it Half-Right	83
19.	Encore!	86
20.	Ski Patrol	89
21.	Aftermath	101
22.	"You're Not Going to Believe This"	105
23.	Marcus	110
24.	Looking Back and Going Forward	115
	Photographs	121

DANN MASTERS

1.	"The Poorest Family in Town"	127
2.	Rev. Ritzinger	132
3.	The Call	137
4.	An Uncertain Future	145
5.	Eddie Malphrus	152
6.	When One Door Closes	157
7.	An Unfinished Work	162
8.	Angel Fire	165
9.	We're Not in Dallas Anymore	171
10.	Show Time	174
11.	Angel Fire Corporation	180
12.	Community Impact	183
13.	Dann the Man	187
14.	Accepting the unacceptable	193
15.	Family Matters	196
	Photographs	202

CONTENTS

STEVE HOEKSTRA

1. "The Cows Didn't Care If I Was Stoned." — 209
2. The Early Years — 213
3. Loveland and Beyond — 216
4. The Next Morning — 221
5. The Call(s) — 224
6. Late One Evening — 228
7. Vail — 232
8. RAAT Patrol — 236
9. A Life-Changing Friendship — 248
10. Making a Difference — 251
11. Community Servant . . . and Target — 256
12. Director of Special Ministries — 260
13. The Institute — 265
14. Aspen — 268
15. The Rest of the Story — 273
16. The "C" word — 278
17. State Staff — 283
Photographs — 290

BRAD LARTIGUE

1. "The Most Beautiful Fish." — 297
2. Growing Up A Man of Color — 301
3. BSU — 306
4. From Nerd to Athlete — 310
5. Taos — 314
6. Unforgettable Encounters — 317
7. Big Sky — 321
8. The Visit(s) — 328
9. Differences — 336
10. Mountain Employee — 340
11. Yellowstone — 346
12. ARLM — 352
13. The Winds of Change — 358
14. "One Killed on I-90." — 364
15. Missoula — 370
16. Released — 374
Photographs — 382

ENDNOTES — 387

SERVANTS
ON THE
SLOPES

SKIP SCHWARZ

Chapter 1 | BLINDSIDE

It would be the worst ski accident in my thirty years as a ski resort minister. The February day was cold and drizzly. Obscuring a thick blanket of steel gray clouds, a curtain of darkness descended with the setting sun. My phone rang.

"Skip, this is Janet [the supervisor of the mountain's First Aid Department]. We need you here...good, I'll explain when you arrive."

The car's headlights stabbed through the darkness as I turned off the highway onto the access road leading up to the mountain. Approaching the base lodge, the red and white flashing lights of a Life Flight helicopter, its engine quiet, lit up an otherwise empty parking lot—not a good sign. Stranger still were the blazing lights from the First Aid building, usually closed and dark by now. Entering through the waiting room, I noticed Mountain Ambassador Mac Jarvis sitting with a woman I didn't recognize. In the treatment area, an assortment of ski patrollers and medical personnel were finishing reports, replacing sheets on gurneys and putting equipment back in place. In a secluded corner of the room, the mountain's general manager and his second in command, rare sights in First Aid, talked quietly. Janet took me aside.

"We've got a fatality and two seriously injured: a man and his niece. The man's on his way to the trauma center with a TBI [traumatic brain injury] and the niece to the hospital with multiple injuries. Hers aren't life-threatening but his could be. To make matters worse, this happened in the morning, and we didn't find them until sweep. The wife had been looking for them since before noon. The third person was the girl's boyfriend. He's still up on the mountain with a broken neck. We can't move him until the medical examiner arrives. The mother doesn't know he's dead. She wants to go the hospital to be with her niece, but needs a ride, so if you could help I know she'd appreciate it."

Walking back into the waiting room, I introduced myself to the wife.

"I don't know what I'm going to do," Emily said hesitatingly, her eyes staring past me. Then, her composure returning, "They're taking Heather to the hospital, but my husband has the keys to the car."

"No problem," I replied. "I'll give you a ride."

During the hour's drive, I discovered that Emily and her family were devout Christians, actively involved in their church. Heather's boyfriend served on the staff of Young Life, a worldwide parachurch ministry to high school students. After dating for several years, the two of them were looking forward to getting married and would soon be announcing their engagement.

5

"I don't know what's happened to him," said Emily, referring to the boyfriend. "No one's telling me anything."

At that point, neither did I.

The week of Emily's visit was a particularly treacherous one for New England skiers. The weekend before they arrived, it rained, then froze, then rained, then froze. The resulting skiing conditions were not just difficult; they were deadly. With a nationwide annual fatality rate in the mid-thirties, it was the most lethal seven days in New England ski history. Five skiers died.

The morning of the accident, the family of four skied the easy trails—those that Emily enjoyed. Then, not wanting to hinder them from the more challenging terrain they preferred, she offered to wait for them in the lodge. Norman suggested they meet at 11:30—after they'd tested the skiing conditions—to discuss their plans for the day.

When 11:30 came and passed, and no family appeared, Emily was confused—this wasn't like them. Norman was so considerate that when they had skied together that morning, he insisted that she stay at the bottom of the bunny trail—the easiest trail on the mountain—until he first checked it out—the bunny trail!

By noon, a worried Emily approached the woman at the ski school counter to ask if any of the lifts were down, thinking that her family might be stranded somewhere.

"No, everything's running," the woman replied. "They probably just decided to take a few more runs." The woman wasn't worried. In all her years in the ski industry, no group had ever gotten into trouble. If a single person were missing, especially a child, her response would have been quite different, but not with a group. In addition, there was no phone at the counter, and normally she would have had a radio, but they were short that day, so she spent the day scurrying between the counter, the ski school office next door and the class lineups outside.

"If she's right," Emily thought, "and they're out there skiing while I'm sitting here worried to death, they're going to get a piece of my mind when they get back."

Emily didn't even think about searching for them. "If I'm ever late meeting you someplace," Norman once told her, "stay there and don't go looking for me. That way I won't have to go looking for you when I arrive."

Emily began talking to a family from Boston sitting at a nearby table. Time passed quickly as they became acquainted. After a while, the woman excused herself. When she returned some time later, Emily was busy removing the belongings that she had placed to reserve seats for her family's lunch.

"They haven't shown up yet?" asked the woman, surprised.

"No, and they were supposed to be here at 11:30. I don't know what could have happened to them."

Emily now felt the stabbing of a cold, chilling fear. "I started to pray," she told me later. "It was the only thing that kept me calm during that time. I just prayed and prayed and prayed."

"Did anyone call to report the family missing?" I later asked Daniel (Dan) Rann, the veteran patroller on dispatch that day. His reply surprised me.

"No, and it wouldn't have made any difference if they had. The day was drizzly and rainy. We get those kinds of calls all the time on days like that. The missing people are usually sitting in their condo in front of a warm fire watching TV, or in a bar taking a break to get out of the weather. It happens all the time. Furthermore, you don't go looking for groups of people because you know that if something's happened and there's been an accident, the others will either stop someone on the trail or go for help themselves.

"It'd be a whole different matter if it was a single person, especially a child, which is the most common scenario. In that case, you'd get a description of age, gender, what they were wearing, and it would be posted at the top and bottom of every lift. Also, an 'all-points bulletin' would go out. Everybody would be on the lookout for them—patrollers, lift attendants, *everybody*, but a *group* of people? And on a day like that? We wouldn't have worried."

Emily's conversations with the family from Boston and others mercifully helped pass the time. In between, prayer kept her fears in check. About 3 p.m., she again approached the woman at the counter, as she often had that day, this time to find out when the mountain closed. "3:45," the woman replied, and then added, "I'm leaving, so if they don't appear after that, why don't you call First Aid."

At 4 p.m., Emily glanced outside to see Mac Jarvis moving the ski racks off the snow for the grooming machines that would soon appear.

An Annapolis graduate and General Electric retiree, Mac joined the Ambassadors for his love of skiing and desire to help people. A stocky six-footer with white hair, his calm demeanor, quick smile and alert mind gained him instant respect, at least in normal circumstances.

"My family is missing," Emily said, concern and worry echoing in her voice. "I was supposed to meet them here at 11:30, and they never showed up."

"Have you checked with First Aid?" Mac asked.

"No, the woman inside didn't have a phone."

"There's one upstairs in the bar, follow me," he said, reassuringly.

Mac called First Aid himself. No, the family wasn't there, but ski patrol was dealing with something, why not give them a call.

"Dispatch, this is Mac. I've got a lady down here at the lodge and her family is missing."

"Get off the phone," shouted an angry Dan, "all hell is breaking loose up here."

Mac put the phone down and turned on his two-way radio. It crackled to life with news of sleds and trauma packs heading to the scene of several injuries and a request for Life Flight. Emily's worst fears were coming to life.

"Why don't we walk over to First Aid," suggested Mac.

Entering the reception area, Mac went up to Janet.

"I've got the mother of a missing family with me," he said.

"Okay, why don't you stay with her in the waiting room," said Janet solemnly, "I'll let you know when I've got something."

A little while later, Janet left the treatment area and walked up to them, "They're sending one down and have two criticals."

After Emily left them that morning, Norman and company took the lift to the top of the mountain heading for the more difficult trails. While skiable, many of them had hard, boilerplate surfaces. Finding the conditions more difficult than he expected, Norman stopped his little group and announced that he would lead them onto some easier terrain. Turning to ski off, he lost his footing and fell, sliding down the steep trail. The fall line took him toward Blindside, a narrow, ungroomed expert trail, closed and roped off that day because of the ice. As his niece and her boyfriend looked on in horror, Norman's body picked up speed and shot under the rope on Blindside. His initial attempts to regain control failing, he rolled himself into a protective ball. The moment of his concussion was obvious when his body suddenly went limp, taking on the appearance of a rag doll. With arms flailing, he plummeted out of sight. First his poles, then his skis and eventually even his boots came off before he finally came to a stop almost a thousand feet later. Rushing to his aid, Norman's niece and boyfriend skied down to the top of Blindside. Clicking out of their skis to walk through the woods, they crossed their skis and stuck them into the snow. Unfortunately, the ice on the trail was also in the woods. Almost immediately, their feet shot out from underneath them, sending them hurtling down the icy trail. The boyfriend's fall ended six hundred feet later when he crashed headfirst into the base of a large tree. Heather's path followed that of her uncle's, her battered body coming to rest just inside the woods, fifty feet above him. Miraculously, she was still conscious. It was 11 a.m.

At 3:45 that afternoon, having received their trail assignments, the patrollers left the warm comfort of their shack for afternoon sweep, the safety routine ensuring that no one is left on the mountain when it closes. With the patrol's snowmobile starting up in the background, they clicked into their skis and headed to their assigned trails. On weekdays such as this when staffing was slim (only seven patrollers that day), other employees help with sweep. On that day, ski school instructor Chris Turner was among them. It was an extra hour's pay and at the wages he was making, every bit counted. Glancing down a side trail, he spotted a lone ski jutting out of the woods near the entrance to Blindside. "Uh-oh," he thought. He skied down to his checkpoint and reported his find to Assistant Patrol Director James ("Dirk") Dirkson.

"It was good that Chris spotted it," dispatcher Dan said later. "It was getting dark, and if he had missed it, we would never have found them during sweep."

Dirk traversed to the top of Blindside and called dispatch.

"Dispatch, this is Dirk. I've got a lone ski at the top of Blindside. I'm going down to check it out."

"Roger"

Digging the sharp edges of his skies into the ice-covered trail, Dirk started down, calling into the woods as he went. Six hundred feet later, just off the trail to his right, he came upon a crumpled body at the base of a large tree. Below him, the trail's glassy white surface was dotted with skis, poles, and boots.

"Dispatch, this is Dirk. I'm on Blindside. I have a non-responsive male in the woods on skier's right about halfway down and equipment on the trail below me. I'm going to check it out."

Dirk started down again, still calling out, and was surprised a moment later when a female voice answered.

"Here, here! I'm over here!"

Dirk spotted her just off the trail on the right; her back propped up against a tree. A little ways below her another form appeared, face up, its legs extended over a little creek running alongside the trail. Dirk skied over and checked the man's breathing: it was light, and his pulse, weak.

"Dispatch, this is Dirk. I have a triple on Blindside: the unresponsive male in the woods on skier's right about halfway down, and toward the bottom, a responsive female, and unresponsive male, both on skier's right. I need three sleds, three trauma packs, and every patroller you can send. Call Life Flight. We're also going to need the extrication equipment and crampons."

What began as the end of a quiet day soon became a scene of frenetic energy. Dan ordered all patrollers to recycle and called the snowmobile to pick them up. Hearing first Dirk's call, and then Dan's over the mountain's radio net, employees responded like firefighters to an alarm. Ski school called and volunteered to finish sweep. The lift started up again and snowmakers, lift maintenance, and even administration personnel headed for the top.

After making his calls, Dan busied himself readying sleds and equipment for transport. "Whoever showed up took something down," he recalls. "Peter [the mountain's second in command] never ran a sled before, but he was available when I had one ready to go, so I showed him how to use the chain and off he went—a great skier—no problem."

Years of training and experience merged to produce a response as smooth as an oft-rehearsed routine, with a myriad amount of essential details addressed as if each patroller was following a prepared script.

"We're going to need the trauma pack from First Aid," said Dan.

"It's already on its way up," came the reply.

"It was amazing," said one of the patrollers afterward. "You practice and train and work with each other so long, and then something like this happens, and everybody knows what needs to be done without being told."

When Emily and I arrived at the hospital, Heather was still in the operating room, soon to be transferred to the Intensive Care Unit (ICU). I excused myself, and while I was gone, the state police officer assigned to the incident entered the waiting room. Emily questioned him about Heather's boyfriend and learned of his death, adding yet another horror to the day.

"How am I going to tell Heather?" She asked, visibly upset when I returned.

Wheeled into the ICU, Heather remained unconscious. The nurse said that the surgery went well, and they were going to transfer her to the nearest trauma center, better equipped to deal with her multiple injuries. Furthermore, with Norman there, it would be easier on Emily. When we went in to see Heather, she was drifting in and out of consciousness, unable to talk. Suggesting that we pray, I reached across the bed and took Emily's hand. "Lord, Heather could really use your hand of healing…"

I drove Emily back to the family's rented condominium to retrieve some personal belongings, and we continued to the trauma center, another two hours away.

Emily told me about her husband, Norman, and how he loved to share his faith with other truck drivers. His quiet, easygoing manner and compelling invitation to follow Jesus introduced several men to faith in Christ. Every year Emily and Norman purchased a case of Bibles. After taking a highlighter to verses describing God's plan of salvation and other key passages, Norman gave away the Bibles to any trucker showing an interest.

The time passed quickly as we talked. Before I knew it, we were walking through the trauma center's emergency entrance.

Finding Norman in surgery, we went to see Heather. Although still drowsy from the pain-killing medications, she was alert enough to ask about her uncle. After hearing he was in surgery, she then asked Emily about her future husband. The tears and embrace that followed begged for a privacy I quickly provided.

The swelling in Norman's brain posed the greatest threat to his survival. Surgeons immediately removed a portion of his skull to relieve the pressure and sent him to the ICU, where we joined him. Monitors drew their green, red, yellow, and white lines on darkened screens, the accompanying LED numbers measuring heartbeat, respiratory rate, blood pressure and the all-too-important intracranial pressure (ICP). With his eyes shut and swollen, his head encased in bandages, a clear blue breathing tube protruding from his throat and other medical necessities entering and leaving his body, Norman bore little resemblance to the man Emily had talked to just that morning.

In an empty waiting room near Heather, the nursing staff prepared a cot for Emily to spend the night. About midnight, I left for the long drive home. On my way out, I called the mountain's general manager from a payphone in the lobby, leaving an update on his voicemail.

Arriving back at 11 a.m. the next morning, Emily and I were sitting in a waiting room when the neurosurgeon entered. "I'm sorry," he said, "each brain injury is different, and we never know how they're going to turn out. In spite of the surgery, the pressure on Norman's brain remains dangerously high and shows no signs of lowering. The trauma was so severe that it would have made no difference if we had seen him sooner. Actually, the cold temperatures slowed down his bodily functions and protected him from further complications."

News of the swelling was disturbing, but having visited others with head injuries whose swelling always abated, I was sure the same thing would happen to Norman. I was relieved, however, at the doctor's second announcement. I would have never asked the question for fear of a far different answer, but knowing that the delay in finding Norman didn't affect his chances of recovery was good news. I wasn't even on the mountain that day, but because I worked there, I felt strangely responsible—even guilty—for the delay in finding him.

Late that afternoon, following a flight from the Midwest and a drive of several hours from Boston, Norman's brother Robert arrived. Emily's relief was visible in their embrace. After introducing us, Robert thanked me for looking after Emily. No longer needed, I bid my farewells and left for home. For the next few days, I expected to return daily for what I thought would be a long and drawn out recovery. It wasn't, and I didn't.

A short while after I left, the neurosurgeon, looking tired and defeated, approached Robert and Emily as they sat in the waiting room.

"I'm afraid I've got bad news. We've done all the tests, and there's no sign of brain activity." Following a few questions and a quiet discussion, the surgeon left. Robert, now losing a brother of over fifty years and Emily, a husband of thirty, dissolved quietly into tears. A few minutes later, regaining their composure, Robert suggested they go down to the cafeteria.

"You've got to eat," Robert responded over Emily's objections. She finally consented. Sitting in the cafeteria and picking at a bowl of chowder, Emily looked up at Robert.

"Norman said that if it ever came to something like this, he wouldn't want to be kept alive by machines. I've been with him for thirty years, but you've been brothers all your life. What do you think?"

"I totally agree," said Robert. "He wouldn't want it. Besides, he knows where he's going and at this point, he's probably eager to get there."

Emily was relieved. It felt good to have Robert's support. While the decision was legally hers, it belonged to both of them. His response was comforting.

Still, this was a big decision for Emily. Its burden remained. Her mind still reeling from the shock of the past twenty-four hours, she needed some reassurance.

"Please, Lord, give me a sign," she prayed.

After making reservations at a nearby motel, Emily was in a deep sleep when she felt a tugging on her big toe and bolted upright. "It was the way Norman always announced he was home when he came in late at night," she explained. "This time, he was standing at the foot of my bed. He looked much younger—like he did in his thirties."

"I'm in a good place," Norman said softly. "Everything's going to be okay."

"Norman, Norman!" She yelled, her voice waking her.

In relating the story some time later, Emily added, "You, Robert and Heather are the only ones I've told about this. I kept it to myself because I don't want people to think I'm crazy, but I know what I heard, and I know what I saw. After he left, I had a peace I didn't have before."

Following a light breakfast the next morning, Emily and Robert went over to the hospital to visit Norman and Heather and for a conference with the medical staff. The staff wanted to discuss Norman.

"We've run a complete battery of tests," said the presiding doctor, "and there's no indication of any brain activity. We need to talk with you about removing life support. How do you feel about that?"

"We were expecting it," said Emily. "We've talked it over and agree it's what Norman would have wanted. We'd like you to run the tests a second time just to make sure. Then, if they're still the same, Robert, Heather and I will need some individual time with him before you go ahead."

"Of course," said the doctor. Things didn't always go this smoothly, and his relief was visible.

The second round of tests produced the same results. At noon, following the family's visits, the hospital staff withdrew life support. With Emily holding his hand, Norman passed away at 4:01 p.m.

A few weeks later, I traveled to Connecticut to visit Emily and Heather.

Emily greeted me warmly, but it wasn't long before her anger surfaced, magnified by the indifference she encountered from the woman behind the counter.

"I told them they were missing, and nobody would listen to me," Emily said, the distress and frustration in her voice echoing the trauma of those five hours.

Prayers and Patrol

Following the accident, the National Ski Patrol honored the mountain's patrollers with awards and commendations for their response. Still, the worst tragedy in the mountain's history left many sober and reflective. A couple of months after the accident, a patroller at a party suggested I pray with the other patrollers. "I think they'd find it comforting," she said. I checked with the patrol director, who gave me the okay. On the remaining Sundays until the season ended, I showed up for morning sweep and offered a prayer for the day ahead. When the patroller who suggested the idea found out I was doing it every week, she was surprised. "I meant just once, not weekly," she said. That was the first misunderstanding.

Shortly after the next season began, one of the patrollers approached me after the Sunday morning prayer and asked if I couldn't make it more personal. That's easy, I thought, I'll just do what I do at the start of my church services and use a guided prayer, letting people silently fill in the blanks when it comes to sins they need to confess, problems they need to surrender, and blessings for which they're thankful. The second week I did this, as soon as I said, "Let's pray," two patrollers walked out. A few days later, the ski patrol director called me into his office, "I'm sorry," he said, "You're going to have to stop the prayers. People are complaining."

It took me a while to realize my mistake. I completely misunderstood the request to make my prayers more "personal." Too afraid of offending those whose beliefs were so different from my own, my prayers had become sterile and perfunctory. I prayed for things like safety on the mountain; that the guests would enjoy their day; that God would keep them safe and show them how they could be of help. What the patrollers wanted was for me to pray for *them*. For God's protection for *them*, that God would guide *them*, help *them* as they responded to wrecks and bless *them* with his joy and love in the day ahead. To the patrollers, I was the man with the "connection," whose words would at a minimum reassure them of God's love and at best, perhaps give them a good day.

As time diminished the impact of that fatal day, the need for my prayers would have eventually faded. Still, had I been open and honest enough to share my fears of offending them and ask them how they'd like me to pray, there's no telling how long the prayers might have continued or where they might have led.

In the Months Following

I stayed in contact with Emily following the accident, but it was awhile before I heard the sound of laughter at the other end of the phone. As one might expect, her road to recovery was neither easy, or quick, nor even complete. Her initial panic attacks have subsided, but she still gets nervous when a family member doesn't arrive when expected.

To Emily's credit, she maintained her faith and contact with her church. The church responded with a bountiful supply of love and support. When Emily didn't feel comfortable leaving her home for the woman's Bible study, they came to her. When she couldn't attend the services, church members brought her tape recordings of the morning's message. Youth from the church stopped by to run errands, and the men of the church took Norman's place in maintaining the home.

Heather's emotional recovery was somewhat faster, aided in part by marriage to her boyfriend's best friend. He had been interested in Heather for a long time but would do nothing to come between the two. Even as the newlyweds started their family, however, Heather began returning to the hospital for what would become many follow-up surgeries.

Never Again

While praying with patrol on Sunday mornings was temporary, another change at the mountain was permanent. Grimacing over Emily's torturous five hours of waiting, the mountain changed its protocol in dealing with missing persons. Today, a ski patroller stays with anyone reporting someone missing until that missing person is found. If a patroller isn't available, then it's a Mountain Host, and if a Mountain Host isn't available, then a mid-level manager is given the job. No one will ever again go through what Emily experienced.

Chapter 2 | GROWING UP

Many people assume that I became a minister at a ski resort because I was a minister (true) and loved skiing (false). Ours wasn't a skiing family. My childhood experiences with the sport consisted of examining two circa 1930 skis hanging in the garage of our San Lorenzo, California home. They belonged to my mother, who used them in the Italian Alps while studying art in Florence, Italy. Her marriage put a quick end to that sport. From our home in the Oakland Bay Area of California, ski resorts were both geographically too distant and, with my dad being a minister, financially prohibitive.

I took up skiing *after* starting a ministry at a ski resort. The idea occurred to me that if I was going to live and work at a ski resort, it just might help to know how to ski. Fortunately, I had a gifted and skilled instructor. She took our class of beginners and transformed our fear into confidence, and our trepidation into joy. I fell in love with the sport.

Dad, the Minister

Having met each other at a church young adult group, my parents began their sixty-six-year marriage in July of 1941. Dad was thirty-two and Mom, twenty-six. They moved to the Boston area, where Dad attended Andover Newton Theological Seminary. I entered the world in April of 1943. Following Dad's graduation, we returned to California where he served as a youth minister at a church in Los Angeles. My sister Christie was born a year later.

With the end of WWII, the Oakland Bay Area of California—like many other parts of the country—saw a flood of returning soldiers and war workers. Asked to start a church in the exploding bedroom community of San Lorenzo, Dad accepted the challenge and we moved north. A short time later, the birth of my youngest sister, Lynette, completed our family.

Beginning with seven families, San Lorenzo Community Church moved to a new site, obtained and remodeled a recently decommissioned Navy Quonset hut chapel, and eventually grew to eight-hundred-and-fifty members with a Sunday school of a thousand.

To say Dad was busy is an understatement. He'd be home for dinner, often complaining about his children's fighting at the dinner table, and then back to work. I was proud of his success and brag about it to this day, but it came at a cost. Hours spent at church weren't hours spent at home; evenings in committee meetings weren't evenings with his family; time spent listening to others wasn't time spent listening to us.

In the sixth grade, I arrived home from school to see medical personnel loading Dad into the back of an ambulance. Having survived a heart attack, he was on his way to the hospital and eventually, a quadruple by-pass surgery. Heeding the warning, he radically altered his diet, lost weight and ultimately lived to be ninety-seven years old.

To aid in his recovery, Dad received a six-month leave of absence, filling the time by pastoring a small church in a farming community in Northern California. The move made things easier for Dad, but not for his children. Torn from our friends and thrust into an insular community where long-time friendships were deep and newcomers rare, my sisters and I were the outsiders. Not surprisingly, these farm kids were tough. The girls, encouraged by the fact that I didn't fight back (how could I? I was repeatedly taught, "You don't hit a lady") treated me like a human punching bag. Fortunately, in the midst of one plummeting, there came a life-saving epiphany: "these are *not* ladies!" Whap! My flying fists quickly brought a long-overdue deliverance.

My bedroom was on the second floor of an old two-story home. During that physically and emotionally cold winter, I often crawled between a pair of cold sheets under a bundle of blankets and talked to God. From my earliest days, I learned that God created us, loves us, and is concerned about our lives—comforting thoughts to a scared and lonely twelve-year-old in a new and strange environment.

While our parents loved us and provided a stable and secure home, they were the products of their own upbringings and of their own times. Our quiet and reserved mother buried herself in her artwork not only because it was inherently rewarding, but also because the classes she taught and the paintings she sold contributed to the family income. The recent Great Depression with its over 20 percent unemployment and rampant poverty was still fresh in the memories of people like our parents, leaving an anxiety incomprehensible to us today. We frown upon workaholism these days for the unmet emotional needs it produces. In my dad's day, however, it was a virtue for the economic security it provided.

Dad once told me that they were raising me to be independent. In this, they succeeded, which was both a blessing and a curse. The blessing emerged much later in life, enabling me to survive two domestic disasters and start three ministries. The curse lay in the absence of close family relationships. In those teenaged years of impressionable immaturity, I remember vowing—with fists clenched—"I'm *not* going into the ministry—I want a family life."

Mom, the Artist

Growing up in the home of a preacher (and seminary professor) Mom skipped a couple of grades and graduated at the top of her high school class when only sixteen. She loved art, studied at the Boston School of Fine Arts and later in Italy. In selecting the lot for our new home in San Lorenzo, Dad saw to it that she had an artist's cherished northern exposure for her studio. Painting portraits, landscapes, making jewelry and dabbling in gold leaf, she collected numerous awards. It wasn't unusual to come home and occasionally find a model in her studio (not that kind).

Three childhood memories of my mother stand out. In the first, she was holding my hand as she walked me to kindergarten, four or five blocks away. After the second day, I was on my own (not a safety issue in those days).

In another memory, I was about nine or ten years old when, after punishing me for something I didn't do, Mom sent my sisters off to bed and sat down on the couch next to me. "I'm sorry," she said. "I know you didn't do it." I was shocked. Mistakes were something we kids made, and frequently at that age—they weren't something grown-ups made. I felt closer to her at that moment than at any other time in my life.

Lastly, one day I found card tables set up in the living room. Mother was hosting a group of women for an afternoon tea. While they were talking over tea and cookies, I kept coming out of my room and making a nuisance out of myself. Mom told me that if I interrupted them one more time, she'd take care of me when everyone went home. Of course, I continued, and when the women left, I heard footsteps in the hall of our single-story ranch home. As soon as she opened my bedroom door, I shot past her and ran out the front door. The chase was on, and she was right behind me. Down the sidewalk we raced. Soon, no longer hearing her footsteps, I glanced back. There she stood, in the middle of the sidewalk, doubled over in laughter.

My mother loved us, but she wasn't an emotional person. Her pleasant, quiet and reserved personality was neither demonstrative nor affectionate, something which was to affect me in unexpected ways many years later.

College

After moving to Spokane, Washington, I graduated from high school in 1961 and entered Pacific University, a small liberal arts college in Forest Grove, Oregon. Shortly after my arrival, a deep-rooted sin in my life unexpectedly surfaced. The Pledge Captain of the fraternity I hoped to join announced, "You've been rejected."

"Why?" I asked, surprised.

"Do you really want to know?"

"Of course."

"Well, everybody likes your roommate Ken, being class president and all. But when he found out you were *also* pledging, well… he told us you were stuck on yourself; that if we let you in he didn't want to have anything to do with us."

I was stunned. It's the kind of revelation that begs for a confrontation with the accuser, a confession, and a change in behavior. Lacking both the required maturity and desire to change, however, nothing happened. Looking back, I regard it as God's "shot across the bow," to get my attention, but it was wasted. I sailed blissfully on, selfish enough to continue hiding my own care packages from home while helping my roommates consume theirs. God would have to do better than that to get me to change. A few years later, he did.

I joined the college choir as a freshman, and the following fall managed their cross-country tour. One of the concerts I booked was at my dad's old church in San Lorenzo. After arriving, we had the afternoon free, and I went up into a vacant sanctuary. The afternoon light filtered through the blue plate glass wall in the back. Standing in the U-shaped pulpit, my hands resting on its sides and looking out over the empty pews, a surprising feeling came over me: *I belong here.* That's interesting, I mused. The feeling wasn't strong enough to fight, nor compelling enough to follow, rather it came as a simple announcement. Only later would it be seen for what it was.

Midway through my second year of college, I became a student radical long before the phrase conjured up images of politically motivated longhaired, pot-smoking hippies. Seeing things that needed changing on campus, I drew up a list and went to see the president.

"Well," he said, "you seem unhappy with many things at this university."

"I am," I replied.

"So, why don't you go somewhere else?"

Chapter 3 | FORT BENNING, GEORGIA

"Grace as a theological concept is interesting; as an experience, it's life-changing."
—ANONYMOUS

Following two semesters at Whitworth College in Spokane, Washington, my future remained a blank. As a junior, I had to select a major, but with no clear direction and after receiving a notice from my draft board, I decided to let Uncle Sam pay me to figure out my calling in life. I volunteered for the draft, spent the first six months in Basic and Advanced Infantry Training at Fort Ord, California, and then started officer training.

On a hot August day in 1964, two hundred and twenty-five new Officer Candidate School (OCS) students filed into the auditorium of the Army Infantry School at Fort Benning, Georgia. We took our seats in the tiered rows of plastic chairs with their fold-down Formica desktops, our curious eyes focusing on the stage below and the uniformed man behind the podium. After welcoming us, the Commanding Officer of the Infantry School continued.

"Take a look at the person on your left and on your right. On graduation day, one of you is not going to be here. You will either quit because the program is too hard, or you'll be sent back to the ranks because we've decided you're not leadership material."

A shaft of fear shot through me. What if they find out? I led coed groups in school and youth groups in church, but this wasn't school, and this wasn't church, and the group I was being trained to lead was definitely not coed. We're now talking about men, many of whom would be tougher and stronger than me, and even some who'd be older, and I was supposed to lead them? My concept of a "leader of men" was someone like a tall, strong and unflappable John Wayne of twentieth-century movie renown, or a brilliant, rough and driven General ("blood and guts") George Patton of World War II fame. I was neither of them. I started to feel like a soft and easygoing Robin Williams auditioning for the lead in a muscle-bound Arnold Schwarzenegger movie. Lured by the status, pay and responsibility of an officer, I neglected to process intellectually what was now revealing itself emotionally: I wasn't prepared for this job. Having embarked on it, I wasn't going to quit, but I was scared they'd discover what I already knew: I wasn't a "leader of men."

During our six-month course, everyone in our platoon of fifty men would be a squad leader four or five times, but a platoon leader and assistant only once. When serving in leadership positions, those over us and under us evaluated our performance, but only our tactical officer saw the evaluations.

I had no problem being a squad leader since I simply passed on the orders of the platoon leader—the same with the position of the assistant platoon leader. Two-thirds of the way through the course, however, my stomach tightened when I saw the list for the next three days: Platoon Leader—Skip Schwarz. No more conveying someone else's orders, I was now in charge.

The night before I took over, I called my squad leaders together. One of the leadership qualities evaluated was "initiative." If I could ace that, I thought, I might just make it.

"Okay men, here's what we're going to do," I said, enthusiasm masking my fears.

"First of all, we're going to spit-shine the floors of our rooms like we used to do. Secondly, I want cardboard inserts put back in the sleeves of the fatigue shirts hanging in our lockers so the creases will be sharp for inspections. Thirdly, I'm going to have some charts made up showing how we're organized and how everyone is progressing in their qualifications. Fourthly, it's been awhile since we've painted the stairwell, so I thought it'd look great if we did that again."

I expected my enthusiasm to be contagious. After all, whenever someone did this on TV or in the movies, people could hardly wait to follow. Instead, my ideas evoked a collective groan. "What?" "Are you kidding?" "Do we have to?" These ideas weren't new—we'd already done them at the beginning of the course when eagerness reigned. Our initial zeal, however, had long since fallen victim to sixteen-hour days of physical training, marches, running, classes and studying, not to mention the ever-present harassment ("Why are you looking at me like that, Candidate Schwarz? Is there something wrong with my looks, Candidate Schwarz? You don't *like* my looks, Candidate Schwarz? Drop and give me twenty, now! Too slow, Schwarz, make that forty!"). Now in our sixteenth week—two-thirds of the way through the course, eagerness had long since given way to exhaustion.

"Okay," I said to my squad leaders, "let me think it over. I'll get back to you in the morning."

After they left, I walked down the hall to the small meditation room located on every floor of the barracks. I used to go in there, pray, and come out with a smile on my face because Christians were supposed to be happy. Sitting down in a large vinyl upholstered chair, I pondered my options. I could either please the tactical officer, or please the men. With embarrassing clarity, I remember my decision: "The tactical officer keeps me in the program; the men don't, so I'll go after him and to hell with the men."

The next morning I called my squad leaders together and told them that my ideas were now orders. I expected reluctant compliance, but within the platoon there now arose a chorus of dissent. I tried to quell the storm with pep talks, but my intransigence guaranteed their failure. A strategy designed to keep me in the program now threatened to get me kicked out. I panicked. As stated in one of my evaluations, "he got on his horse and rode off in all directions at once." I responded to the men's anger with my own and by the time my three-day tour was up, I had successfully alienated the whole platoon. I'd walk up to a group, and they'd walk away. I'd sit next to someone in the cafeteria, and they'd move down a few feet. It sent chills up my spine. The only person who talked to me—because he had to—was my roommate. It was my first encounter with group rejection. My response? "If that's the way they want to be about it, then to hell with them, I don't need them anyway." Or so I thought.

One afternoon a couple of weeks later, we were out in the field on maneuvers. I went through the chow line, found a large tree, and sat down, propping my back against its trunk. After a couple of bites, I looked up. Walking across the field, tray in hand and heading in my direction was one of the two natural leaders in our platoon. Several years older than the rest of us, and a veteran of years of army life, Joseph Pojmanski had the maturity, experience, and personality that commanded respect. Seeing his rugged, bull-like features approaching, I knew what was coming. I'd seen him chew out men when they messed up, and my turn had come.

Pojmanski sat down next to me and opened the conversation with a comment about the field problem we were running, and I waited. Next, we talked about the weather, and I waited. Then we talked about home, a bit unusual since we weren't that close, and I waited. Ten minutes later, he got up and walked away without having said anything about the mess I had made as a platoon leader. There was no scolding, no reprimand, no chewing out—nothing! I deserved a tongue-lashing; I received a friendly conversation. I deserved rejection; I received acceptance. As I watched his back disappear across the field, an unexpected warmth flooded over me. To borrow the words of John Wesley, the eighteenth-century "Billy Graham" of England, "my heart was strangely warmed." That warmth was powerful, overwhelming and life altering. For the first time in my life, I *saw* my self-centeredness. "Putting myself first has brought me as close as I've ever come to hell," I remembered thinking, "From now on, others first and myself, second." In the years since, this change of heart and new direction has remained, even on those too-numerous occasions when I've strayed off course.

As I expected, the rest of the members of the platoon, with a couple of exceptions, followed Joe's example. They now talked to me; no longer moved away when I sat down and no longer dispersed when I approached. In the days that followed, however, I couldn't figure it out. What did 28-year-old

Polish Catholic Joseph Pojmanski do to provoke such a profound change?

Upon entering OCS, a doubt and a question plagued my faith. I wouldn't have admitted it, but I had a gnawing feeling that my faith might simply be the product of my weakness: that if I were "strong," I wouldn't need God. Never mind that such a distinction quickly disappears in any objective study of the lives of the greatest believers. Secondly, and theologically more serious, was the question: "what does the death of a man on a cross two thousand years ago have to do with me today?" As far as I could see, nothing.

Several days later, while still pondering what Joe had done, years of sitting in church on Sunday mornings unexpectedly paid off. A Scripture verse flashed into my mind.

"While we were yet sinners," said St. Paul, "Christ Jesus died for us." (Romans 5:8)

It was an epiphany. *I* was the person Paul was talking about—my self-centeredness placing me firmly in the category of "sinner." No more thinking I was such a good guy because of what I *didn't* do—because I never smoked, drank, swore, etc. No more thinking that God must be glad to have someone as good as me on his side (I still wince at that one). I was a sinner—pure and simple—the way I treated the men in my platoon left little doubt. However, the Bible says, "While we were *still* sinners, Christ died for us." In a flash, it came together—Christ gave his life for us—the greatest gift anyone can give—not as a reward for our good behavior, but while we were "*still* sinners"! We're offered something we don't deserve. Now it was clear: God used Joseph Pojmanski to show me his own—Christ's—forgiveness before I even knew I needed it. Paradoxically, I didn't even *know* I needed it until *after* I received it. It wasn't the normal sequence of seeing the light and asking for God's forgiveness; I didn't even *view* what I had done as a sin until *after* I was forgiven. "So *that's* the difference the cross makes," I thought, "and *that's* the forgiveness I received through Joe." There's a word in the Bible for what happened to me; it's called "grace," as in the well-titled hymn, "Amazing Grace."

In the years following, two regrets lingered: first, that I didn't apologize to the men. To their credit, they didn't demand it; to my regret, I never gave it. Secondly, I never told Joe how God used him. Twenty-five years later, with the advent of the internet I tried to find him, but failed. Then, fifty years later, I tried again. An internet search produced a couple of invalid addresses and phone numbers, followed by a notification. They had email addresses for a Joseph Pojmanski that I could access for a small fee. I received two addresses, none of which looked promising. Nevertheless, I emailed both. A few days later, I received a response.

"This is Joseph Pojmanski. I don't know if I remember you, but OCS comes to mind." That was in January of 2014. We've been in touch ever since, developing a much closer friendship now than ever existed fifty years ago.

In spite of my self-inflicted damage, I still managed to graduate from OCS. Since we weren't shown our evaluation forms, some might wonder how I knew of the comment written on mine about "getting on his horse and going off in all directions at once." Confession time: toward the end of the course, I was cleaning our tactical officer's office. No one was around, and the file drawers were open. I found my evaluations and looked at my leadership rankings. Much to my surprise and chagrin, when I took over as platoon leader, there was no need to worry.

I walked away from OCS with a Second Lieutenant's bars pinned on my uniform. What I left with on the inside, however, lasted much longer. The "I belong here" feeling in the pulpit of my dad's old church during my college years? Now with a message to share, those words became a calling.

Chapter 4 | FROM ARMY TO SEMINARY

Shortly before leaving Fort Benning in the spring of 1965, our OCS class marched into a large multi-purpose room to receive our "dream sheets." Soon to be commissioned officers, we were given two options: six months of active duty plus five-and-a-half years in the reserves, or a straight two years of active duty. We were also asked where we'd like to be stationed. There were no guarantees of course, that's why they called them "dream sheets." I wanted to go to Germany and knew I wouldn't be sent with a six-month commitment, so checked the two-year box. Then came an unexpected insight: if I signed up for two years and after six months decided I *didn't* like it, I was stuck. If, however, I signed up for six months and decided I *did* like it, I could always extend. Feverishly erasing my first choice, I checked the six-month box. Three weeks later, with Viet Nam heating up, that option disappeared.

The army sent me to Fort Lewis, Washington, and gave me command of a mechanized infantry platoon—fifty men and four armored personnel carriers. Leaning heavily on the experienced non-commissioned officers assigned to me, it was an easy job.

Another platoon leader in our company was Peter Danylchuk, a distinguished West Point graduate. Possessing the leadership skills and self-confidence that I lacked, Peter was a man I admired, and we soon became good friends and roommates, sharing an off-base lakeside apartment. The girl I was dating at the time lived in my hometown of Spokane, Washington, five hours away. An idea came to me while making plans to visit her on a summer's weekend.

"Hey Pete, how about coming home with me this weekend? I'll take out Mary, and you could go out with my sister Lynette—the two of them are friends—we'd have a ball!"

Pete paused for a moment, and then replied with his customary calmness, "Yeah, that would work."

And work it did. After the weekend, Pete and Lynette began corresponding, which I thought was great, because Pete would let me read her letters filled with news from home. Then one afternoon, walking into our condominium, I saw a letter sitting on the breakfast bar.

"Pete, you got a letter from Lynette—could I read it?"

"Nope," he said, smiling.

As of this writing, their next big wedding anniversary will be their fiftieth.

Discharged in Seattle, I ended up with a blue-collar job at Boeing. The plan was to save up money, finish college, and then on to seminary. That's exactly what happened, but not in that order.

Seminary

Bangor Theological Seminary, in Bangor, Maine, featured the "Bangor Plan," designed for people entering the ministry midway through life. With only two years of college, students could go through seminary and then finish their last two years of college while supporting themselves as pastors. I had been at Boeing for several months when, in a chance meeting with the parents of a recent graduate, I found out about the seminary. A couple of weeks later I was on my way to Maine.

My three years of seminary were both fun and formative. In the first category was our Old Testament class. Sitting next to me in the back row was a wiry native of Antigua named Arthur Davis. His ready smile and quick laugh made him popular and well liked. Our professor was Dr. Stephen Szickszai (pronounced "six-eye"), a 62-year-old Hungarian, who still spoke with a noticeable accent. Tall, with a crop of receding white hair crowning his round and cherubic face, Dr. Szickszai had been at the seminary so long and given the same lectures so often that he developed a unique talent. While sitting at his desk facing the class, he could take his long map poker and, without even looking, hook the correct map from the half-dozen rolled up over the chalkboard behind him. He would then pull it down and, still not looking, point exactly to the place he was talking about in his lecture. The third or fourth time he did this, a thought entered my mind. Nudging Arthur, I whispered, "Arthur, what if he pulled the map down and there was a Playboy centerfold on it?" We exchanged silent laughs.

The following Monday morning, we filed into Dr. Szickszai's class and, after taking our seats, bowed our heads for the customary prayer. Dr. Szickszai began his lecture. A few minutes later, he reached for the map poker, his eyes not leaving the notes in front of him.

Arthur turned to me. "Watch this," he said.

"What?" I replied, confused.

"Watch *this*," he repeated. Then it hit me. Looking at him in stunned disbelief,

"You *didn't*!"

He nodded slowly, a broad grin spreading across his face.

I looked to the front of the class just in time to see the map coming down. Suffice it to say the borders of the Holy Lands had markedly fewer curves than the barely-clothed beauty looking down upon us. A split-second of shocked silence gave way to an eruption of unrestrained laughter. Dr. Szickszai stopped lecturing. Looking behind him first casually and then with a quick double take, he studied the "map" he had just pulled down. Then he turned to the class and slowly, in his thick accent, "Vell, it looks like I got de booby prize."

Grade: "F"

On the serious side, I fell in love with the Bible at seminary, but not from any lecture or even by reading it. I knew that if I was to be an effective minister, I had to know it. The problem? It bored me to death. My dad was a minister, but our family never prayed or read the Bible together, and religious topics rarely came up. It was as if one's faith was private and you didn't express it by what you said as much as by how you lived. In some Christian homes, it's "you've got a problem? Let's see what the Bible says about it," but not in ours. My dad once mentioned that they made a deliberate decision to raise us in a "normal" and not a religious home so that we would find it easier to adjust to the world around us. I don't doubt the sincerity of their intentions, but I also know enough about human nature to recognize that their own backgrounds had an impact. The result? The Bible was in our home but rarely read.

Convinced I *had* to know the Bible if I was going to be an effective minister, I tried reading it, but repeated attempts produced the same results: I couldn't get beyond the first few words before my mind took off elsewhere. I remember sitting alone in the chapel late one afternoon, the sun streaming in through the stained glass windows, the Bible in my lap, trying again to read it. I couldn't. Gritting my teeth and forcing myself only made things worse. Finally, I gave up. It wasn't going to happen. I'd like to say I prayed and surrendered it to God, but in those days, I didn't even know about such a concept, so I just gave up. There's no way I could read or relate to that book.

Many students find themselves wanting to please and impress certain professors. For me, it was Dr. Szickszai. With his first exam coming up, I studied hard. I memorized all the names, dates, places, facts, and figures about the Old Testament period we were studying. I was ready—or so I thought. If the test had been a multiple choice or true/false, I would have done well, but it wasn't. It was an essay test, requiring a clear understanding of the subject—something not forthcoming from a superficial memorization of data. Oh well, I thought, I'll get a "C" on this one and ace the next. At the end of the next class, Dr. Szickszai handed out the blue exam booklets, grades marked on the front covers. I didn't expect an "A", and I didn't get an

"A." Nor did I get a "B," or a "C," or a "D." There, in bright red ink on the front of my booklet was the letter "F." I was stunned. Never before had I studied so hard and done so poorly. I remained glued to my seat as the classroom emptied, my eyes staring off into space. Finally, I stood up and trudged out of the room, shuffling down the stairs of the now empty building. Dr. Leslie Ziegler, a highly intelligent, tall, thin professor in her early sixties, started up the stairs, took one look at me and stepped back down onto the landing. "Skip, what's the matter? You look like a whipped dog."

I told her what happened.

"Well you know," she said, "the Bible isn't a collection of names and dates and facts and figures. It's a record of people's relationships with God." While it's much more than that, I never heard the Bible described that way before, and with those words came an epiphany: if the Bible is filled with people and their relationships with God, and *I'm* trying to have a relationship with God, then this is a book I can relate to. No longer containing dead and irrelevant history, its pages now reported on the lives of those who, like me, were seeking a relationship with God. To protect this new appreciation, I began a daily half-hour "quiet time," split evenly between prayer and Bible study. That half-hour would eventually grow to an hour-and-a-half and became as important in my relationship with God as communication is to any marriage. In studying the Bible, I learned about God and the person he wanted me to become, and my daily time with him anchored a relationship that was especially helpful twelve years later when the storms hit.

A short time after the above encounter, I saw Dr. Ziegler on campus and stopped to tell her how God had used her. A slight smile accompanied her self-deprecating response. "Well," she said, "God can use the devil, too, you know."

"Heart Knowledge"

The distance between a living faith and a dead faith is about twelve inches, roughly the distance between a person's head and their heart. Addressing this difference was a homeless man I met one day on the streets of Bangor. Midway through our conversation, he asked me what I was doing. I told him I was a student at the seminary.

"Up there on the hill?" He inquired, nodding his head.

"Yes," I replied.

"Humph…" he continued, "they got a lot of head knowledge up there; ain't got much heart knowledge."

His assessment was, unfortunately, accurate. When I arrived at the seminary, I quickly learned not to talk too openly about my relationship with Christ. Those who did were quickly marginalized. You confessed your sin in the liturgy of a church service; you didn't talk about God convicting you of covetousness, or lust, or greed, nor did you talk about personally experiencing his grace and forgiveness. To do so was to be regarded as one of "those"—the conservatives, evangelicals and fundamentalists whose simplistic faith just didn't cut it in the self-assured stratosphere of the intellectually elite.

Shortly after the conversation with my homeless friend, my name appeared on the schedule to lead a chapel service, a weekly event led by students or faculty. I incorporated my conversation with the homeless man into a message on the importance of a personal relationship with Christ. It was a futile effort. As a B and C student, my words didn't carry a lot of credibility among the faculty. Not that it would have made any difference. A few years later, they also rejected the same message from a straight A student, although with more controversy. The morning I spoke, the members of the faculty and administration took their customary places standing against the back wall of the chapel. As I progressed, their relaxed demeanors stiffened and their looks of initial interest soon gave way to somber tolerance. They didn't verbalize their disapproval, nor did they offer the usual words of encouragement given to students following the service. Their silence spoke volumes. The rest of the student body took it in stride—they'd heard me before on that subject—and a couple of my also-marginalized friends even sought me out to express their appreciation.

It was the last time my name appeared on the chapel schedule.

Chapter 5 | IT STARTED WITH A CALL

My career goal in seminary was to end up as the Senior Pastor of a large multi-staffed church. As a preacher's kid, I felt right at home in a church environment and had every confidence I could pull it off. Leading a freelance ministry to youth? I never thought of it. Starting ski ministries? You're kidding, right?

After three years at Bangor Theological Seminary, I left Maine and returned to California, living with my parents and finishing a major in psychology at Pepperdine University. After that, it was back to Maine. Simply put, I felt needed in Maine and didn't in California. People who could lead singing with a guitar were rare in Maine, and a dime a dozen in California. Just as important were relationships. I had far closer and more numerous friends in Maine than in my home state of California. Completing studies at Pepperdine in the summer of 1970, I contacted the Maine Annual Conference of the United Methodist Church and requested a pastoral appointment (in the Methodist church, pastors are appointed by the presiding bishop).

Faith-At-Work

A non-denominational ministry emphasizing relationships, Faith-At-Work had its origins in the Oxford Group of the early nineteen hundreds—the same group later giving birth to Alcoholics Anonymous. The Oxford Group and its subsequent mutations shared a common understanding: one's relationship with God started with a spiritual rebirth through surrendering one's life, past/present/future into God's control. Participants were encouraged to confess their sins and temptations to one another and develop a daily time of prayer and Bible study. Like its predecessor, Faith-At-Work was not a religion, but a movement. There was no membership roll and only a handful of salaried staff on the national level.

Asked to lead singing at one of their conferences, I was introduced to Maine Faith-at-Work while in seminary. What I saw, I liked—a lot. One's denominational affiliation meant nothing; one's relationship with Christ, everything. In small group gatherings, self-disclosure, honesty, and vulnerability were the rule ("what's said here stays here," became a mantra), and people shared how God was at work in their lives. Lay Witness Missions, sponsored by Faith-At-Work and various denominations, recruited lay people to travel at their own expense to churches around the country for a weekend of leading small groups and sharing their experiences with Christ. To this day, I remember the presentation of a Texas rancher.

"Outwardly, I wasn't hurting," he began. "I had a great family, was a very successful rancher and attended church, but inwardly my life was empty. Something was missing, and when I turned my life over to Christ, I found out what it was. Before Jesus came into my life, making money was my goal, and I became quite successful at it. When Christ came into my life, however, that no longer meant anything. I read where Jesus told the rich young ruler to sell all that he had and follow him, and I seriously wondered if that's what I was supposed to do. I prayed about it and asked God if he wanted me to give up everything *for* him or to continue *with* him. Shortly after that, a great business opportunity presented itself, and I took it as God's guidance to continue *with* him. Interestingly enough, since then I've contributed far more by continuing *with* him than if I had sold everything *for* him."

I became good friends with many "Faith-At-Workers," and kept in touch with several while finishing my studies at Pepperdine. Talking to one of them before receiving my assignment as a Methodist pastor, I said I'd be returning to Maine but wasn't sure about a job. Soon after that call, the Bishop appointed me to five small churches on the northern coast of Maine. Providentially, as it turned out, I neglected to tell my Faith-At-Work friends.

The Sunday afternoon of Memorial Day weekend in 1970 was warm and sunny in the backyard of my parent's southern California home. Stretched out in a lawn chair and reading a book, I heard the phone ring inside.

"Skip, this is Marilyn Hardy," the voice announced in her familiar monotone. Almost twenty years my senior, she had become something of a spiritual mother.

"I'm at the Faith-At-Work leadership retreat, and we're just finishing up. A couple of days ago we talked about starting a youth ministry in Maine. We wanted to do it, but couldn't think of anybody to lead it, so we dropped the subject. This afternoon in our closing prayer circle Bruce Larson [the National Director] asked for prayer requests. I mentioned your name, explaining that you had just finished your schooling and were looking for a ministry in Maine. 'Tell me about him,' said Bruce. 'He's a young man,' I replied, 'who just finished college and seminary. He plays the guitar, is good at working with youth and he's looking for a job.' Then Bruce said, 'You said he's good at working with youth and looking for a job, and two days ago we talked about a ministry to youth, but couldn't think of anyone to lead it. Could we be talking about two sides of the same coin here?' As soon as he said that," continued Marilyn, "it was as if a bolt of electricity shot around the room.

"That's why I'm calling. Is this something you'd be interested in? We haven't figured out the finances yet, but if you are interested, we'll go to work on them."

"Yes, definitely!" I responded.

The finances turned out to be a problem, but for them, not me. I had just finished *The Cross and the Switchblade* by David Wilkerson, a riveting story of a country preacher's ministry to the gangs of New York City. Repeatedly, when a financial need arose, he shared it with his church back in Pennsylvania. They'd pray, take up an offering, and either then or shortly after, the needed funds always appeared. The lesson was clear: where God leads, he provides, and if he could do it for Wilkerson, then he could do it for me.

Faith-At-Work's attempts to raise ten thousand dollars for the first year went nowhere.

"Let's forget about the money," I suggested, recounting Wilkerson's experiences. "If this is God's will, he'll provide. Let's just do it."

That was easy for me to say. I was single with no responsibilities and eager to get to work. My Faith-At-Work friends, however, were conservative, very responsible, and cared about me. The last thing they wanted to do was to call me into a ministry that failed because they couldn't raise the needed funds. I saw it as an issue of faith; they saw it as one of responsibility. Fortunately, they had a wise leader in Rev. Harry Starbuck, who proffered a suggestion:

"Look," he said, "if Skip is willing to step out in faith and take the risk, then why don't we do this: knowing it won't be enough, we'll give him as much support as we can and then together, we'll trust the Lord to provide." They did, and God did.

Experimental Youth Ministry

We called it "Experimental Youth Ministry" because our focus was on youth and we had no idea what we were doing. As it turned out, for the next three years I traveled the state of Maine with guitar and Bible, sharing experiences with Christ, leading retreats, preaching in churches, speaking at youth conferences, putting on seminars, providing leadership for high school and young adult groups and leading singing at conventions. Talented singers Bill Fisher and Marnie Darling, concert-level pianist Tom Davis, and even a troupe of Karate experts who illustrated Biblical principles by smashing concrete blocks, soon joined me. Riding the wave of the Jesus people movement of the early seventies, we were in high demand. Most invitations came from New England churches and religious groups, but our venues also included civic groups and public schools. I remember Bill Fisher joining me in a program for 800 students at a high school in Northern Maine. "We told them the assembly wasn't mandatory," the principal said. "If they don't want to attend, they can always go to study hall." The event was a tribute to Martin Luther King. Besides honoring him, we openly talked about Jesus and the difference he made in our lives (not likely to happen in today's public schools).

In February of 1971, I received a call for help. Living in Salem, Maine, Rev. Charles Reid ran a ministry to the poor and held church services in Salem's micro-church (maximum capacity 50). He also led winter services at Sugarloaf Mountain in the Richard Bell Interfaith Chapel, a large cedar-shake A-frame conveniently located in the base area parking lot of what was then Maine's largest ski resort. Sugarloaf would be hosting the World Cup ski races and Charles saw it as a great opportunity to share God's love with the thousands attending.

Charles and I put our heads together and came up with a twofold plan: we would blanket the base area with "Jesus People Papers" (think shopping papers filled with stories of Christ-changed lives) and hold daily "rap sessions" (discussions) in the balcony of the chapel. Providing the warmth and ambiance of a living room, Charles filled the balcony with couches and easy chairs. A table was set up for refreshments, and I put up posters in hotels, motels, restaurants, and stores. Our daily gatherings drew 20-30 young adults and college-aged students. I led some group singing—an acceptable activity in the era of folk music—and we opened our lives to each other through a series of increasingly more personal questions. People responded with stories of faith and doubt, victories and defeats, accomplishments and struggles. It was a relaxed environment, with generous helpings of laughter mixed in with the more serious moments, leaving me with feelings of satisfaction and gratitude. I wasn't the only one who felt that way.

It was well into spring, the snow long since melted and the sun bright and warm when I parked my car on the campus of Bates College in Lewiston, Maine, for a visit to the hospital across the street. Walking from the car, I looked up to see a tall, lanky runner in shorts and T-shirt heading toward me. I glanced at him as he ran past, and then heard a voice behind me,

"Are you Skip Schwarz?"

"Yes," I said, wheeling around in confusion.

"I was with you in the chapel at Sugarloaf during the World Cup. I just want you to know I've never felt closer to God in all my life."

Chapter 6 | EASTER

Maine's Sugarloaf Mountain was dark and chilly on Easter morning in 1971, with a heavy blanket of fog enveloping the base area. A guitar in one hand, a portable speaker dangling from the other and a canvas tote bag hanging from my shoulder, I climbed the steps from one graveled parking lot to another, focusing on a distant speck of light and the accompanying whine of machinery.

Drawing closer to the small building, my steps quickened in anticipation. "Hi!" I said to the gondola attendant standing before his bank of dials and switches.

"G' morning!" He replied with a smile, quickly turning back to his controls.

Earlier that spring, the phone rang in my office. "Skip, this is Charlie Reid, Easter is coming up, and I'm going to have to be away. Could you possibly do the sunrise service at Sugarloaf?" Easter, for most ministers, is one of the two busiest weekends of the year. For me, however, leading a freelance ministry to youth, it was down time.

"Sure," I replied excitedly, "I'd be glad to."

"Good. The service is in the lodge at the top. You'll be taking the gondola up. We've been running around 150 people. I'll take care of the publicity and arrangements. The service starts at 5 a.m., so you'll want to be at the gondola by 4:15 to allow time to set up."

"You ready?" asked the gondola attendant, standing by the egg-shaped gondola car. After I got on, he handed me the speaker and guitar, then returned to his control panel. He flipped two switches, and then a third. The whine of the motor increased and the overhead cable turned, closing the gondola door and launching my car into a darkened, fog-filled sky. Unable to see anything, I imagined myself welcoming the congregation to an Easter fog-rise service.

After completing the mile-and-a-half climb, the gondola eased into its mountaintop nest, its doors opening onto a concrete platform. Equipment in hand, I disembarked from my slow-moving pod and climbed the thick, worn wooden stairs into the warmth of a well-lit pentagon-shaped building, its glass windows providing a circular panorama of the mountains and valleys below.

"Oh good," I thought, seeing clear sky through the windows, "no fog-rise service."

As I was setting up, a movement caught my eye. I turned to see a ski patrolman in his early thirties, clad in a red jacket with its identifying white cross, carrying a thermos and making his way toward the east side of the building. He nodded as he passed by. A few seconds later his voice pierced the silence: "I've never seen *that* before."

I walked over to the window and followed his gaze downward. Illuminated by the pre-dawn light, a panorama of puffy white clouds lay below us, stretching endlessly to the horizon. For air travelers, the sight wasn't unusual, but this one was stunningly different. Multiple snow-capped mountain peaks jutted through the clouds like tips of icebergs emerging from a billowy cotton sea. "I've been here for five years," he said, "seen two or three hundred sunrises—never one like this."

A few minutes later, the sound of boots on stairs announced the first wave of worshippers streaming through the doors in their heavy coats and skiwear. Anticipating a scenic view, they made their way to the windows, their initial gasps and exclamations ending in awe-struck silence. After absorbing the view, and with senses satisfied, they migrated to the wooden benches. People were still coming in when I introduced myself and led everyone in practicing the morning songs. With such an eclectic group, no one knew all the music, so this practice time provided a measure of familiarity to what for some would be a very unfamiliar experience.

After the last person took their seat, I introduced myself, welcoming them with excitement in my voice and a smile on my face. Directing their attention to the call to worship in their bulletin, I continued a centuries-old tradition with a loud and vibrant,

"He is risen!"

"He is risen indeed," the people responded, some still turning in their bulletins to find the words.

"Oh c'mon," I chided, "I know it's early, but you can do better than that." And then, turning up the volume,

"He is risen!"

"He is risen indeed!" They shouted back.

"Ahhhhh... much better! Our first hymn is 'Christ the Lord is Risen Today.' Let's stand as we sing together..."

Practicing the songs and their second chance at "He is risen, indeed," paid off, for their singing was livelier than I expected. Following an opening prayer, I continued.

"Our next song is 'Because He Lives,' written by Bill and Gloria Gaither during a particularly difficult time in their lives. While Bill was recovering from mononucleosis, a split developed in their church. They and others were the targets of false accusations and mockery. Surprisingly, in the midst of Bill's illness and the emotional turmoil at church, Gloria experienced God's peace, and from that peace came this song.

"Shortly after the song was published, another couple was dealing with their own trials, this one the life-and-death struggle of their newborn son. He was born with an untreatable condition that could either disappear in the next several days or take his life. The parents prayed. Nothing happened. Their church prayed. Nothing happened. Their friends and relatives prayed. Still, nothing happened. Finally, after several agonizing days, they realized their prayers were misguided. Before his death, Jesus prayed for God's will and not his own. Acknowledging that God loved their child more than they did, their prayers changed.

"'Lord, you know what we want. We love you and trust you, so we surrender him into your hands. He's yours, to take him into your presence or to give him into ours.' Upon finishing, they felt the lifting of a tremendous weight; in place of their desperation came an unexpected calmness. They were sitting in the waiting room the next day when their doctor entered, an uncharacteristic smile on his lips.

"'We just got the test results. He's turned the corner. He's going to be all right.'

"'Of course, we're glad he was healed,' said the mother in a church service a few weeks later, 'but we had surrendered him into God's hands. We were prepared for it to go the other way, and if it had, it would have been okay.'"

My congregation remained silent, their eyes fixed while their minds went to experiences beyond my knowledge. One woman dabbed at her eyes with a handkerchief, and a man lowered his face into his hands.

I picked up my guitar. In place of the exuberance of our first hymn, the singing was now somber. Its volume, however, increased when we got to the chorus:

"Because he lives, I can face tomorrow because he lives, all fear is gone. Because I know he holds the future, and life is worth the living just because he lives."

The rest of the message consisted of stories of people whose faith in Christ dramatically changed their lives. There was Nikki Cruz, leader of the feared New York gang The Mau-Maus. After hearing, "Jesus loves you and will never stop loving you," Nikki slapped one-time country preacher David

Wilkerson in the face and spat out a warning.

"If you ever talk to me about Jesus again, I'll kill you!"

"'Yeah, you could do that,' Wilkerson replied, 'You could cut me up into a thousand pieces and lay them in the street, and every piece will still love you.'[1]

"Nikki later accepted Christ's love, and when he did, his own gang members became his first converts. He went on to become an evangelist with a ministry to millions and a life story chronicled in the book, *Run, Baby, Run.*"

The absolute stillness and riveted eyes of those before me indicated we were on the same page. Not only was I receiving their solemn attention during the serious moments, but also their laughter at the occasional humorous asides. The connection we were making was almost magical. No longer strangers, we were like friends and family united in an understanding born of years of shared experiences. Never before had I connected so strongly with any group as I was with this one, nor would I ever again in my fifty years of ministry.

We wrapped up by singing the popular Easter hymn, "He Lives," and as the words went from their eyes to their hearts, each verse came out more loudly than the one before.

I closed with a prayer, suggested that they get acquainted with those standing around them, and wished them the greatest Easter they've ever had.

As I was packing up, several people—more than I expected—came forward to thank me for the service. Their firm grips, direct eye contact, and words of appreciation gave evidence of lives deeply touched. It would be awhile before I discovered how deeply.

In a morning still very young, the highway leading down from the mountain remained deserted. Moved by the morning's experience, I asked myself what the churches of Maine were doing to minister to the thousands of tourists and vacationers flooding the state. Not much, I thought. A few open up for the summer months, and that's about it. Somebody should do something for all these people, I concluded. Nine years later, somebody did.

Another Easter passed before I again saw Rev. Charles Reid. We were attending a conference when he came up to me during a break. "Skip," he began. "I thought you might be interested. At our Easter sunrise service this year, over eleven hundred people showed up. We had to have five services back to back to accommodate everyone."

Chapter 7 | SETTLING DOWN

In the summer of 1972, I was a twenty-nine-year-old bachelor with no serious relationships in the past and no girlfriend in the present. Wrapped up in an exciting youth ministry, I had little time for a social life and, relating primarily to college and high school students, little opportunity to meet someone my own age. That was about to change.

"You should come—it'd do you good," said Connie. Labor Day weekend was coming up, and she was inviting me to join her and a few others from our young adult group on a hike up Mt. Katahdin. I hesitated—there was a lot of work to do—well, not a *lot*, but for a workaholic, any work was appealing. "Oh come on—it'll be fun to have you. When was the last time you took a break?" Well, she had me there.

"Okay," I said, yielding to her motherly persistence.

Two carloads of us arrived at the state park around nine in the morning. As we waited for Connie and the girlfriend she was bringing, we stored our gear in the wooden bunkhouse. Its front door opened into a common area with a long wooden picnic table stretching from side to side. Beyond the table sat a large stone fireplace, its insides blackened from use and an ash-covered grate nestled at the bottom. Doors on either side of the common area led to the bunkrooms—five bunks on each side. The girls claimed the one on the left, so the rest of us headed to the right.

Dust rose as Connie's car pulled into the forest clearing. She got out, and with her, an unknown and pretty face. I rushed over to help them unload their car, making sure to introduce myself in the process. On the way up the mountain, I positioned myself next to this attractive stranger, anxious to get to know her. We talked sporadically at first, and then more consistently as our lives connected in a deepening conversation. We talked all the way up the mountain, all the way down the mountain, and until two the next morning. I called it "love at first talk."

If there's any such thing as a "nesting instinct" in the male species, this girl just triggered it. The next afternoon I gave her a ride home and immediately fell in love with her two-year-old daughter from a previous marriage. The thought of an "instant family" was becoming attractive. We saw each other frequently for the rest of the month, and if the relationship wasn't serious to begin with, it quickly became so. I felt as if I had found my "soulmate." A couple I was close to knew each other only two weeks before entering into a long and happy marriage. Encouraged by their example, I was convinced:

God had just found a wife for me. She was divorced, and while I didn't know the details, I was certain I could provide the needed security and stability to ward off any fears of a reoccurrence. Her church involvement gave evidence of her faith, and I looked forward to adopting her two-year-old daughter Lori. We met in September, were engaged in October, and married in November. Days before the wedding, not wanting me to marry under any false pretenses, she took me aside.

"In my last marriage," she said, "I was the one who filed for divorce, not him."

Unfortunately, my emotional needs obscured the red flag she was conscientiously waving. It proved to be a costly oversight.

Instant Family

Both my new wife and I paid a price for our rush to the altar. The scars of her broken marriage and my ignorance of the emotional needs of women collided like atoms in a centrifuge. Arguments often ended in explosions of frustration punctuated by tears and threats of divorce on her part and anger and mental preparations for a return to the single life on mine. Sometimes I'd have the presence of mind to interrupt the mounting anger with a direct appeal for assistance: "God," I'd say, "We're getting nowhere and could really use your help." Interestingly, answers always appeared. On more than one occasion, we experienced "divine interruptions"—an unexpected phone call or a knock on the door providing us with a much needed cooling-off period from which we emerged with new understandings leading to reconciliation.

Being a dad was a challenging adjustment with a two-year-old, but also rewarding and at times humorous. One morning I heard a strange animal-like scream coming from the upstairs of our bungalow. I stood at the foot of the stairs as my daughter descended.

"What was that?" I asked

"I...I... flush da kitty down da toilet."

Rushing upstairs, I found our half-grown and soaking-wet cat sitting in a puddle of water in front of the toilet, licking herself dry. Years later, when Lori decided to pursue a career working with animals, I couldn't help but wonder if there was a guilt-induced connection.

"You're Not Hearing What She's Saying"

As Bob Dylan sang in the 1960's, "the times, they are a-changing," and by 1973, they changed for me. Shortly after our marriage, the speaking and musical invitations for Tom, Marnie, Bill and our Karate for Christ team began declining. Our ministry had run its course.

Tired of driving thirty-six thousand miles a year and ready for a change, I allowed Experimental Youth Ministries to die a natural death. In the fall of 1973, I received a part-time appointment as youth director for a large church in the capital city of Augusta, and a full-time appointment as pastor of the neighboring United Methodist Church in Hallowell, Maine. The couple who advised the youth group were long-time friends, and the high school kids were a great group, among them a bright, beautiful and bubbly cheerleader. The church in Hallowell was a large, white, two-story New England style building set against a gently sloping hillside and topped with a spire not quite as high as the disappearing tops of nearby century-old oak trees.

Six months after our move to Hallowell and a year-and-a-half after the wedding (amusingly, not the seven or eight months expected by some), our daughter Leanne was born. I remember the day quite vividly, though not for the expected reasons. It was a sunny Saturday morning in early March. I drove my wife to the hospital. Before leaving, I cornered the doctor in the hallway, "how long do I have?" I asked.

"There's no rush," he said. "It should be quite a while."

Relieved, I informed my wife I was going back to the church to make the necessary arrangements to be with her all night and even the following day if necessary. Someone once told me that witnessing the birth of their child was the closest thing they ever had to a religious experience, and I was looking forward to it with great anticipation.

Returning to the church, I ran off the bulletins and secured a colleague to take the next morning's worship service if necessary. A Faith-At-Work retreat was going on at our church and after sharing the news of the impending birth, I instinctively grabbed my guitar to help with the singing. After a few songs, one of the women said: "Don't you think you should be getting back to the hospital?"

"Yeah, I guess so," I replied. It had only been a couple of hours, and the doctor said I had plenty of time, so I felt little urgency.

Upon entering my wife's room, I found it empty. Puzzled, I went to the nurse's station.

"Oh, she's in the delivery room,"

"What?!" Quickly sizing up the situation, a nurse threw me a surgical gown and hat and pointed to the set of double doors at the end of the hall. Running, I burst through the doors and into the delivery room…twenty seconds too late.

The twenty-second gap between Leanne's birth and my appearance ignited several explosions in the months to come. My wife was angry because I *wasn't* there, and I was angry because she didn't acknowledge I *wanted* to be there. Finally, months later during a marriage enrichment weekend held at the Methodist campground, there came an epiphany. Couples received a list of questions to discuss by themselves, and my wife and I left the lodge. No sooner were we outside than we got in another argument over the now months-old issue. My wife ran into the woods crying, leaving me frustrated and angry. A moment later, an older colleague, tall, slim, with a receding crop of graying hair, came up to me.

"Skip, we couldn't help hearing what was going on." He paused briefly before continuing. "You're not hearing what she's saying."

"What?" I asked, unsure if I heard him correctly.

He repeated himself, this time slowly and deliberately.

"Ohhhhhhhh," I thought.

I walked toward the woods just as my wife was emerging.

"Honey, you must have felt very much alone when you were giving birth, and I wasn't there."

"Yes, I did."

"And it must have made you pretty angry that the one person you were counting on wasn't there for you."

"I was so angry...."

The subject never came up again.

Chapter 8 | COX MEMORIAL

Fulfilled by the family life I had yearned for since childhood, my years at Cox Memorial United Methodist Church in Hallowell were some of my happiest. People's relationships with Christ blossomed and flourished. While few entered the ranks of God's family for the first time, the faith of those who already knew Him came alive. Responding to the emphasis on "heart knowledge," they learned to trust God in the practical areas of life, experiencing the small miracles that carry their own power.

Togus Pond

It was encouraging to see the church filling up, so when summer came, I was surprised to be looking at suddenly empty pews. Where'd everybody go? It didn't take long to find out. Besides the normal absences due to summer vacations, many of my flock were summering at nearby lakes—close enough for necessary trips; too far for Sunday services.

What would Jesus do, I asked myself—preach to a bunch of empty pews or...?

I looked up a church family living on Togus Pond (lakes are called "ponds" in Maine) and paid a visit.

"What would you think about having services here at the pond?" I asked.

"You mean outdoor services?" The wife asked, surprised.

"That's what I was thinking."

"That would be wonderful," she responded excitedly. "Let me check with the others." She called back a few nights later.

"I checked with our Fish and Game Club; people love the idea! We can use the area next to the Club landing. We'll close the landing during the service, and club members will provide refreshments. When can we start?"

Two weeks later on a sunny summer's day, I made the half-hour drive from my church in Hallowell to Togus Pond. The tires of my little brown Subaru crunched on the gravel road that twisted and turned under a canopy of pines, maples, and birches. Pulling into a grassy clearing ringed by birch trees, I saw several picnic tables, one of them covered with the promised refreshments. People arrived carrying folding chairs, lounge chairs, beach chairs, and campstools. Transportation was just as varied. Kids would ride their bikes, an older teen might arrive on horseback, and parents would arrive on foot, in cars, on motorcycles, or by boat. Most attended other churches the rest of the year, but for some, this was their only "church." The group was never large—attendance averaging in the thirties, but we were close. Since everyone on the lake already knew each other, the social dynamics were similar to a family gathering, with smiles, easy laughter and the latest tidbits of local news: "Did you hear what happened to Julien when he went out in his boat yesterday?"

Prison

Following his conversion in the driveway of Tom Phillips—the CEO of Raytheon Corporation—life changed for Charles Colson, a former lawyer and the hatchet man for President Richard Nixon. He surprised the Watergate prosecution by voluntarily pleading guilty to a crime for which he hadn't been charged: obstruction of justice. Subsequently imprisoned, his incarceration combined with his new faith gave birth to a new love: prisoners and their families. The result was Prison Fellowship, now a worldwide ministry. My interest in prison ministry piqued after reading his best-selling book, *Born Again*, and I started holding weekly Bible studies at the Maine State Prison, then located in Thomaston. Only about a half-dozen men participated consistently, but over a two-year period, we became close.

Several years later, competing in a 10K race, I was in a dead heat for last place with another runner. I shuffled along at a snail's pace while he would alternately run and walk. About the third time he passed me, he turned around, "aren't you Skip Schwarz?" It was one of the men from the Bible study. "So what are you doing with yourself these days?" I inquired.

"I've got a church."

"You what?"

"I've got a church about a half-hour away. After my release, I went to seminary and became a pastor. I've been there about three years now."

Besides the state prison, I'd occasionally visit prisoners in the county jail. One afternoon I was in a man's cell trying to explain to him the meaning of the cross. I wasn't making much progress until an idea flashed into my mind.

"How much time are you doing?" I asked.

"Six months for breaking and entering."

"What would you think if someone came into your cell, said he was serving your time for you, and you could go free?"

"That'd be great!"

"Well, that's what Jesus did for you on the cross."

He paused, then his eyes widened in understanding.

The Third Degree

My parents stressed the value of education and of helping people, so it shouldn't be surprising that all three of their children ended up with doctorates in the helping professions. My oldest sister worked as a lawyer in a public defender's office and my younger sister acquired her Ph.D. in family counseling while working with her husband in their counseling practice. With no desire to teach, an academic Ph.D. held no interest, but when seminaries started offering a professional doctorate for pastors, I jumped at it. Signing up through Boston University's School of Theology, I started their Doctor of Ministry (DMin) program in January of 1978. Specially designed to enable ministers to complete the degree without leaving their jobs, the program consisted of professor-led, monthly two-day gatherings at a centrally located church. Additional requirements included writing a project paper (the DMin equivalent of a thesis), and attending two on-campus summer courses. It was the project paper, however, that would change the direction of my life and ministry for the next thirty-five years.

Chapter 9 | DOMESTIC DISASTER(S)

It was a clear and chilly March day. My car's tires thumped across the concrete seams of the Augusta Memorial Bridge on my way to the hospital. Thinking of the life-threatening issues faced by the patients I was about to visit, my mind drifted. "How do I get off being so lucky?" I thought, "I have a great ministry, a wonderful wife, and two beautiful children. I am in good health and haven't lost any family members to death or disease. Everything is going so great—why me?" It was the first time I ever asked that question. Within a few weeks, it would be the last time.

The Dining Room

Located between the sunlit living room and equally sunny kitchen of our single-story ranch parsonage, the dining room, of all the rooms in the house, held the most memories and heard the most laughter. Its east window flooded the room with light during the morning hours, an overgrown bush blocking the west window from doing the same in the afternoon. An old mahogany dining room table almost filled the room, leaving just enough space for the dishes and table linens stored in a sideboard against the wall. A linen runner with two candlesticks graced the sideboard, and on the center of the table sat a basket of large gold and silver pinecones. Opposite the entrance from the kitchen, an opening led into the living room and just to its left, a door led to an unfinished basement. Our family of four gathered around the table for dinner every night—a tradition held almost sacred. Hot dishes of food sitting on the table added more than one kind of warmth, especially coming home on a cold winter's night after not seeing the girls all day. At mealtime, our two daughters, ages four and seven, vied for my attention, telling me stories from school and playground.

"So," I would say to our four-year-old, "you were playing on the monkey bars?"

"Yes," she replied, grinning from ear to ear. "It was fun!"

"They let you play on *their* bars?" I replied.

"What?" She responded hesitatingly, her face scrunched in confusion.

"They let you play on *their* bars!"

"Whaaaaat?"

"The *monkeys*—they let you play on *their* bars."

"Daaaaaaaad!"

I enjoyed seeing my girls laugh, and if constant teasing didn't do the trick, then a quick pinch to their side under the table was bound to produce the sought-after squeal, together with the not-too-serious, "quit playing at the table," reprimand from Mom.

The dinner hour was helpful in other ways. Before having a family, I could afford to be a workaholic. With a family, I couldn't, and my daughters unknowingly kept me in check. When I didn't spend enough time with them, I noticed they fought with each other at the table.

Sometime Later…

The sideboard was empty of the dishes and table linens it once held. Empty, too, were the bedroom bureaus, closets, kitchen drawers and cupboards of the small house. Our family once lived there, but no more. Of all the rooms, the dining room held the most painful memories. I recalled entering it one morning the previous spring. Tiny specks of dust floated on rays of sun streaming through the window, at least that part of it not blocked by my wife of five years. While our marriage started roughly, each succeeding year brought fewer conflicts and more harmony—a welcome relief. The worst was behind us, or so I thought.

We stood in the dining room that day, exchanging the minutiae common to people whose lives are intertwined. Then, during a pause in the conversation, she looked up and calmly stated:

"I don't want to be married anymore."

This was not the emotionally charged threat of divorce common in the first months of our marriage. This time, her measured tone had a stinging note of finality.

"What did I do?" I asked, stunned. Surely, I must have done something, and whatever it was, I could make it right.

"Nothing."

"How can I change?"

"It's too late."

It took a little while for the shock and numbness to subside. When it did, a pulling pain in my chest moved the word "heartbreak" from metaphor to reality. Not long afterward, I saw the movie *Tootsie* with Dustin Hoffman. The movie starts with his divorce and shows him walking down the street relaxed and calm as if nothing had happened. Well, I thought to myself, there's one screenwriter who doesn't know his subject matter.

I went into denial. This was a test, I said to myself. We're going to work through this, come out stronger, and have a wonderful ministry to people going through rough spots in their own marriages. Even as my emotions began their roller coaster ride, I knew in my heart that we were going to make it.

Finally, after some coaxing, my wife agreed to go to counseling. Good, I thought to myself, now we can start getting things back on track.

"Are you committed to the relationship?" asked the counselor.

"Yes," I responded resolutely.

He turned to my wife.

She answered quietly, but with the same resolve. "No, I'm not."

Leaning forward and clasping his hands together, he continued, "I'm sorry," he said, "in that case there's nothing I can do."

Following my wife's announcement, the dining room turned into a very quiet place, as did the whole house. Gone was the kidding, the joking, and the fun, replaced now by arguments in spite of our joint attempts to quell them for the sake of the girls. My emotions swung like a pendulum from optimism to depression to anger. Meals—on the few occasions we now ate together—were quiet, the conversation perfunctory. Hot food still appeared on the table, but its warmth was gone. And the door leading down to the basement? It now hid a secret: an angry fist-sized hole in the wall. As soon as I put it there, the frightened tears of my four-year-old implanted a "never again" resolve.

A few months later, my wife secured an apartment and moved out, taking our daughters with her. These were the days before the popularity of shared custody. She was a good mother, and I wasn't going to put our kids through a custody battle. More honestly, I didn't see how I could care for them by myself. She promised I could see them whenever I wanted and kept her word.

For the longest time, I had no idea why she was divorcing me, and she wouldn't say. The little bit I knew about her own family provided some understanding. More importantly, however, was my own unwitting contribution. It was to take me twenty years to recognize that she needed much more affirmation and reassurance than I provided. My sin was not one of commission, but omission. Compared to what she needed, I *had* done "nothing."

And where was God in all of this? I've never expected my faith to protect me from the hardships and sufferings of life. Nor did I think God was causing the divorce as part of a plan for my life that I couldn't see at the time. The Bible is clear: God hates divorce (Malachi 2:16). The fact that God can bring good out of our suffering shouldn't be confused with the mistaken belief that he caused the suffering in the first place.

The time I spent with God every morning kept me grounded. In the midst of an emotional hurricane, God helped me with both the anger and discouragement. One Sunday morning before the service, I was feeling particularly depressed. Then, stepping into the pulpit, I looked out over those in the pews. In any congregation, there are always those with whom one has deeper relationships than with others. That morning I saw a sight I had never seen before, nor would ever see again. In a congregation of a hundred, every single person I felt close to was present that morning. The message? "Hey, I haven't forgotten you."

God also helped with the anger. Whenever it reared its ugly head, I'd ask his forgiveness. The anger would go away, only to return. I'd repeat the confession, and it would go away only to return, albeit not quite as intensely nor as quickly. Along the way, I discovered something: when deeply hurt, forgiveness isn't just a decision, it's a process. While decreasing in frequency and intensity, the anger kept returning for two years until God sent someone to take it away for good: my estranged wife. We were talking one day when she confronted me with it, and in her confrontation came my deliverance. All that time, I thought I had been hiding it from my daughters, but that was an illusion. When it finally disappeared, their relief was visible.

God also helped me when I thought I was losing it. My wife had been gone for a while when one morning, clad in pajamas and bathrobe, I sat in the living room, realizing I needed to get ready for the day. A friend would soon arrive to give me a ride to a conference we were attending. I had to get dressed, to shave and shower, but I just sat there in the living room chair unable to move. I couldn't understand why. Finally, I said aloud, "I will now stand up and walk to the bathroom." I did. Then, "I will now get my shaver out of the medicine cabinet." I did. This is stupid, I thought. Cut the drama, but I couldn't, and the only way to accomplish those mundane tasks that morning was to talk myself through each one of them. Things didn't return to normal until after I was dressed. Am I losing it? My ride that morning was a minister friend who specialized in counseling, and as soon as we got under way, I told him what happened. "Am I having a nervous breakdown?"

"No, you're not. It sounds like your brain is simply overloaded; dealing with more stimuli than it can handle comfortably, so it's reverting to the most elemental way of getting something done."

"How will I know if I *am* having a nervous breakdown?"

"For you, that would only occur if you were dealing with several major stressors at once. Our mind is like a pressure cooker. As long as we get rid of the pressure, there's no danger. You're a person who finds it easy to share what's going on inside you, so you're not likely to build up the pressure necessary for a breakdown with just the divorce. If, however, you had other serious issues such as losing your job or a life-threatening illness, then, even with all your sharing, there could well be more on your plate than you could handle, and you'd be a prime candidate." I breathed a sigh of relief, and that morning's bizarre script never repeated itself. Some would call my timely meeting with a colleague whose gift is counseling a coincidence. I regard it as a loving God looking out for one of his hurting kids.

Christmas Eve

In the midst of getting ready for the church's Christmas Eve candlelight service, I heard a knock at the door.

"Grayson Schwarz?" inquired the uniformed sheriff's deputy.

"Yes?"

He handed me an envelope.

My wife didn't intend to serve papers on me the day before Christmas, and was sincere in her apology, but I regarded them as a gift. Months of uncertainty were now over, and I could start looking for someone else. A couple of months later, when the divorce went through, I began dating a girl I met years before when she was in the youth group I was directing. She was a beautiful high school cheerleader and homecoming princess with a bubbly personality. Now twenty-one years old and a recent college graduate, I saw her as God's reward for what I'd just been through. Fairy tale ending, here we come! Granted, she was fifteen years younger, but another minister in the area married a girl fourteen years younger, and they appeared to be very happy (they've since divorced). After dating for three months, she wanted to get married right away. Fearful of a repeat of my previous marriage, I suggested we wait a year. We compromised at nine months. As our wedding day approached, however, conflicts arose stemming in part from our age differences. Worried, I sought counseling from a colleague who knew both of us. It would have been better if he hadn't. Caught up in his own joy over our upcoming marriage, he dismissed our concerns and reassured us—to his later regret—that we didn't have anything to worry about. Nine months after we started dating, we were married.

Instead of the marital bliss I was expecting, I soon discovered I had gone from the proverbial frying pan into the fire. Still wounded from the rejection of my first wife, I was now facing a torrent of rage from my second. A counselor said her anger was coming from something far deeper than a twelve-month relationship, and I'm sure he was right, but that knowledge didn't give me the resources to cope.

Following one particularly intense eruption, I went into our bedroom. Sitting on the floor with my back against the door and tears running down my cheeks, I pulled the phone down from the nightstand and called my dad in California. After hearing what was happening, his response was immediate: "You've got to get out of there."

It took a few minutes to regain my composure, and then I called my district superintendent. My congregation had stood by me through one divorce and now, filled with embarrassment and guilt, I wasn't going to put them through another. I asked for a new assignment. He called back the next day to tell me of a group of three small churches in western Maine. Eight months after marrying, I moved, and within the year, she filed for divorce.

This new marital failure hit me like the second of a one-two combination in a prizefight, sending me reeling against the ropes. Angry with myself for the foolish decision to marry two women too quickly and feeling a disgrace to my calling, I responded with self-loathing. At the time, I didn't see it—after all, I'm a guy; what do I know about feelings—but the members of my DMin group noticed it quickly. Disturbed by what they were hearing, several of them stayed after an evening session to continue our discussion on divorce in the Bible and promptly unmasked the emotional roots of my hostile rhetoric. After initially rejecting the term "self-flagellation," I realized they were right.

The Vision

Shortly after hearing of my new pastoral assignment, I was driving over an I-95 overpass near my home in Hallowell. Without warning, a vision flashed into my mind. I saw myself going from one small church in Maine to another for the rest of my pastoral career. A resounding "NO!" Emblazoned itself over the scene. From that point on, pastoring a local church lost its long-term appeal. I didn't know yet what I *would* be doing, but a career as a church pastor no longer motivated me and its rewards no longer enticed me.

Chapter 10 | STRONG AND KINGFIELD

"It seems that God goes out of his way to choose the most unlikely candidates. God sees your potential, even when you don't. He sees you for what you will become in the days ahead."
—GREG LAURIE

The afternoon sun streamed in through the living room windows of the Methodist parsonage in Strong, Maine. Representatives from the Strong, Kingfield and Salem United Methodist Churches sat around the room. Between us, an old-fashioned braided rug covered the hardwood floor. Interviews normally precede appointments in the Methodist church, and I began mine with a brief biographical sketch, concluding with my first divorce and stating that I'd probably be going through another. To my relief, they accepted the news without any questions. The interview was going well, but as it progressed, I had a gnawing feeling inside. Should I tell them or shouldn't I? Realizing they'd find out anyway, and surprising them at the last minute could result in some justifiable anger, I took a breath and interrupted the conversation.

"Before we go any farther, you need to know I'm feeling called out of the pastoral ministry into something else. I don't know what it is, but I would only be here two or three years at the most."

There was a slight pause and then the conversation continued as if I'd just given a weather report. I relaxed.

The representatives from the two larger churches, Strong and Kingfield, had always wanted their own full-time ministers instead of sharing one. Previous pastors lacked either the experience or the time to make that happen, but here I was with the experience and, sans family, with the time. "Let's do it," I suggested. We came up with a three-year plan.

Turning Strong and Kingfield into full-time ministries would take all of my available time and energy. There was no room for distractions, so I promised God to forego a social life for two years and throw myself into my work. Coming on the heels of two divorces, that wasn't a hard decision to make. The thought of another relationship scared me as much as the challenge of growing the Strong and Kingfield churches excited me. The only downside, I soon discovered, was the gut-wrenching loneliness.

The Answer to a Prayer Never Prayed

The week between my first Christmas and New Year's in Strong saw bright blue skies and temperatures in the high twenties. One morning I glanced out the window to see the tops of normally bare branches bending under a blanket of new snow, the sun turning the ground into a carpet of shimmering crystals. Gazing at the Christmas gift from my congregation leaning up against the wall, I had an inspiration. Heading for the kitchen, I made a thermos of hot chocolate, packed some cheese and crackers, threw everything into a small backpack and laced up my new cross-country ski boots. Grabbing the skis and poles leaning against the wall, I hurried outside onto the gravel driveway, pausing to take a deep breath of the needle-crisp, pine-tinged air.

A stone's throw away, a snowmobile trail—one of several such trails crisscrossing our small town—disappeared into the woods. Recalling a visit to a family's small summer cottage on a nearby pond, I now had a destination. This trail went right by their place, and five miles was the perfect distance for the maiden trip on my new skis. Exhilarated, I stepped into the skis, clicked the metal toe clips over my boots, and started out.

Pole—push—lunge, pole—push—lunge, I glided forward, the fish-scaled bottoms of my skis zipping on the packed snow. The trail was fairly level with only a few small hills, and I maintained a smooth and consistent rhythm as tree branches flew by on either side. After what felt like only a few minutes, I looked down on my destination: a cabin perched on the edge of a pond, its roof and deck covered with snow.

Clipping out of my skis and walking onto the deck, I slung my pack onto the picnic table, brushed the snow off one of the wooden deck chairs and pulled it up, propping my feet on the bench. Enveloped in the peaceful, frosty silence with a cup of hot chocolate warming my hands, I munched on the cheese and crackers. A few feet away lay the pond, its frozen surface covered with snow, an occasional evergreen showing off among the forest of bare branches ringing the pond's perimeter. After several minutes, a chilling yet gentle wind interrupted my daydreaming to remind me that the temperature was still below freezing. Re-packing the thermos, I donned my pack and carried my skis to the top of the rise for the trip back.

Upon returning home, I was clicking out of my skis when there came a jolting realization: I had a ball, all…by… myself. Until then, such fun would have only occurred in the company of another, yet I just had the time of my life all…by…myself. Never in my wildest dreams did I think it possible, but with that brief trip, something deep inside me changed. Dragged back into the single life kicking and screaming, I was now, much to my surprise, happy being alone—a contentment that would remain for years to come. No longer did I need to share my life with someone. Gone forever were the nights of crying myself to sleep. If my lot in life was to remain single, that was no just acceptable, it was now preferable. In the years to come, loneliness would occasionally brush the surface of my emotions, but never again plumb their depths. I had just experienced a little-talked-about aspect of God's goodness: *God works wonders for those he loves.* (Psalm 4:3)

A New Direction

When not busy with church responsibilities, I spent the next year wondering about my future. If not pastoring a church, then what? At the same time, I was searching for a subject for the required project paper for my DMin. Then I remembered my thoughts while driving home from the Easter sunrise service at Sugarloaf: why isn't the church doing something to reach out to tourists and vacationers? *That* could be my subject. Perhaps I could encourage others to start outreaches to this forgotten group. Soon after, I was attending a conference and mentioned the concept to a colleague. "That's a great idea," he replied. "Have you ever thought about doing something like that yourself?" Then, a short while later, one of the members of my DMin program commented, "It's a great topic to write on. Have *you* ever thought about such a ministry?" Well, I hadn't, but I certainly was now. Perhaps there's a reason my Kingfield church was only twenty minutes away from Sugarloaf Mountain.

If I was going to start another ministry, I needed help. At the next Maine Faith-At-Work conference, I took a few minutes during dinner to tell the hundred-plus people about the new direction my life was taking and invited those who'd like to explore the idea with me to meet during our free time. Between thirty and forty showed up. After telling my story, I solicited their feedback. It was reassuringly positive, even enthusiastic. I announced the formation of a Backup Team, similar to the one that supported me in my youth ministry a decade earlier.

With Kingfield and Strong excited about having their own full-time ministers, attendance and giving surged. We met our goal in two years instead of three. The Strong church called their own pastor and I moved to Kingfield, the weaker of the two.

Services at Sugarloaf

The Kingfield church didn't have any housing available, but they did have a small, unused chapel, which we remodeled into a parsonage. As I settled into my new home, responsible now for only one church instead of two, it wasn't the Kingfield church that was on my mind.

With the ski season drawing near, I approached the church's governing board. The Richard Bell Interfaith Chapel would provide the perfect location. Would it be okay if I started holding Sunday services at Sugarloaf? The Board was less than enthusiastic. Not wanting me to take any time away from them, they approved my request with the condition that I hold the services on Sunday afternoons, a time normally devoid of their own activities.

With five thousand skiers at Sugarloaf on any given weekend, not to mention their non-skiing family members, I had high expectations. Showering the area with posters, I thought to myself, "If only 10% of them attend church... sure hope we don't run out of room." There was no need to worry. At our first service on December 5, 1982, I looked out on a massive crowd of about twenty. It was then that the truth hit: people don't go to ski resorts to go to church; they go to ski! Local residents and second-home owners made up most of my congregation and, except for Easter, only an occasional skier came off the slopes. While certainly a reality check, the numbers weren't discouraging. The few who attended were consistent, and when I put out feelers about turning Sugarloaf into a full-time ministry, they responded positively.

As spring approached, I kicked into high gear. If I was going to start my new ministry that summer, there was a lot to do. Navigating the United Methodist bureaucracy, I received an enthusiastic endorsement from the first two of the three required boards. I now wrote to the last, the Board of Ordained Ministry, requesting a special appointment to my new ministry. I wasn't asking for any funding, just their moral support, so I didn't anticipate any problems. I also called a meeting of my supporters from Faith-At-Work. I needed their confirmation on the timing and their approval of my initial plans for the ministry. They gave both. Winters would be at Sugarloaf and summers in campgrounds. Acadia National Park and Baxter State Park— Maine's largest— were the most likely prospects. If local churches caught the vision, we could even end up with outreaches to every campground in the state. We scheduled another Backup Team meeting for June to elect officers, establish guidelines, decide on a name and become a non-profit. Plans for a campground ministry that summer were still incomplete when my next DMin gathering made them irrelevant.

Chapter 11 | AROUND THE COUNTRY
IN FORTY-TWO DAYS

With summer approaching, I felt a growing uneasiness. I knew absolutely nothing about recreational ministries. A regular church—it felt like home, but ministering in a campground? I was clueless. And at a ski resort? I didn't even ski! Hearing of my feelings of unpreparedness at the next DMin meeting, colleague and friend Jack Grenfell spoke up.

"Why don't you find out where those ministries are presently happening and go visit them? You could tour the country and put your findings into your project paper."

"What a great idea," I replied. "I'll do it!"

Research produced nineteen ministries, a number that would grow to twenty-five during the tour. The next few weeks revealed how little I knew about the bigger picture, including the discovery of a denomination—the Southern Baptists—who had over three-hundred-and-fifty people involved in resort ministries around the country.

With the blessing of my Backup Team, on July 6, 1983, I packed my little brown 1976 Subaru with camping gear and left on a six-week, nine-thousand-mile journey that would leave its mark on my life for the next thirty-plus years.

Campgrounds and Ski Resorts

Expecting to start summer ministries in campgrounds, I had a special interest in those on my list and visited both individual and multi-campground ministries. When I discovered A Christian Ministry in the National Parks, I realized I could forget about starting a ministry at Acadia National Park. They were already there.

Of the ski ministries I visited, I discovered a variety of approaches. Pocono Area Leisure Ministry built on-mountain shelters for visiting chaplains to lead short fifteen to twenty minute services. In California, Tahoe Resort Ministries enlisted the help of local clergy and laity to provide outdoor services at most local ski areas. In Vail, Colorado, Rev. Don Simonton, besides holding services for skiers on the slopes, came up with a revolutionary idea for the churches in a community of prohibitively expensive real estate: all meet under one roof. Vail Interfaith Chapel was born.

Summer Outreaches

Attending a Billy Graham crusade in a South Carolina stadium in the early eighties, I watched as hundreds of people left their seats and walked down onto the grassy field in response to Graham's invitation to accept Christ. A lump rose in my throat thinking about the dramatic changes that were about to occur in so many of their lives. "I'd give anything to be able to lead people to Christ like that," I mused. I'm no Billy Graham, and never will be, but being used by God to lead others into that same life-changing relationship is something I've always coveted. It was also the goal of the summer evangelism projects I visited.

Sponsored by both Campus Crusade for Christ (renamed "Cru" in 2011) and Inter-Varsity Christian Fellowship (IV), summer evangelism projects consist of groups of students securing full-time jobs and then spending evenings and weekends in sharing their faith with the summer population.

Both Cru and IV projects employ several ways of telling people about Jesus. Entertainment is a guaranteed draw, with the Gospel shared publicly through concerts, puppet shows, and street singers, or privately as project members engaged onlookers in conversation. While visiting the IV project on Cape Cod, I joined the others in breaking up into pairs and heading toward a local baseball game. We approached spectators gathered on a grassy rise overlooking the playing field and struck up conversations with the hope of talking about Jesus. I was teamed with a college coed, and the first people we approached were two high school girls. When my partner mentioned IV, one of them excitedly volunteered that her sister was active in the group. We concluded our animated conversation with an invitation for them to join us for dinner at the project house. We then turned our attention to a couple and a small boy sitting on a blanket, the family golden retriever prancing around them. The dog was a good conversation starter, and everything was going fine until my partner mentioned that she was involved with IV. As soon as the word "Christian" left her lips, it was as if the two of us ceased to exist. They immediately stopped talking to us and even looking at us, as if we had just disappeared, which we soon did. My partner and I split up and after a couple of unsuccessful attempts at talking with others; I took a seat on the bleachers to enjoy the game. Sitting next to me was a middle-aged man and his young son, and we started talking. He was a college professor. Upon discovering I was a minister, the talk soon turned spiritual. He admitted to having a "superficial" relationship with God. Having once believed quite strongly, he told me; he went through a painful experience that caused him to lose his faith. In the presence of his son, he offered no details, and I didn't press. The next day I sent him a note thanking him for his openness and telling him of my prayers for his re-connection with the God he once knew so well, and who still loved him so much.

While visiting Cru's project in the music capital of Branson, Missouri, a student related how God led him to share the Gospel with a well-known entertainer. After the concert, he went backstage where a worker pointed him to the singer's dressing room. The student knocked on the door, and when it opened, he explained that he felt God was leading him to share a message with the performer. Invited in, the student proceeded to share about God's love, the purpose of Jesus' death and resurrection, and the eternal life available through faith in Christ. When he finished, the two of them knelt on the floor and Noel Paul Stookey, of the folk-singing trio Peter, Paul and Mary, became a follower of Jesus.

A year or so later, I was in the chapel at Sugarloaf when Stookey, who lives in Maine and owned a condominium on the mountain, came to set up for a concert that evening. I introduced myself and asked him about the above encounter.

"At that time in my life, I was wondering if life made sense or if it was just a big compromise. I said to myself, 'I'll allow a couple of months for an answer, and if one doesn't appear by then, I'll conclude that life is just a compromise.' It was toward the end of that time that he knocked on my door."

Interestingly, all the project directors I visited pointed to the same source for ninety to ninety-five percent of their conversions. It wasn't the hundreds they entertained with concerts or the scores of strangers they talked to on the streets (my oldest daughter amusingly called the practice "street-walking for Jesus"). Instead, it was the project member's own coworkers. Simply put, friendships change lives. This is nothing new. The Billy Graham Evangelistic Association discovered that nine out of ten of the unchurched who became followers of Jesus did so because of their friendships with Christians.

It was good that I paid a lot of attention to summer evangelism projects. For the next seven summers, I'd be leading them.

Chapter 12 | SUGARLOAF

While preparing for my cross-country tour, the Board of Ordained Ministry of the United Methodist Church responded to my request for a special appointment: denied. I was stunned. Their letter explained that our ministry's goals (leading vacationers to Christ and mobilizing local churches to reach out to them) were incompatible with those of the Maine Annual Conference. Translation? "Your ministry is new and untried, and we don't feel comfortable with it." Committees are comprised of people. Sometimes they're creative and open to new ideas and sometimes they're not. I just happened to be dealing with the latter. A follow-up letter said they'd entertain my request for a leave of absence, but pointed me to the rule that started, "The exercise of ministry shall be *limited* to the church in which the individual's membership is held..." That was clear. If I continued as a member of the Kingfield church, I wouldn't be allowed to minister at Sugarloaf. Well, that's one way to get rid of me, I thought. Hurt, and all too sensitive to rejection after two divorces, I resigned from the denomination.

Now a denominational orphan, I went looking for a new home. Feeling a theological kinship with the American Baptists, I made an appointment with their Executive Minister. After telling him about Sugarloaf and my desire to become an American Baptist, I went on to describe my two failed marriages. Instead of a welcome, I received a warning:

"Don't do with denominations what you did with your marriages."[2]

A few years later, our summer ministry worked with the Southern Baptists. Impressed with their emphasis on resort ministries, I considered joining them. That lasted as long as an appointment with one of their leaders. After an hour-and-a-half drive to his office, I took a chair near his desk.

"So what do you think?" I asked, pitching the thought to him.

"You *could* become a Southern Baptist, but because you're divorced, you wouldn't receive any financial support."

At that point, I wasn't looking for money. Our ministry at Sugarloaf was now in its fourth year and doing well. But I didn't need any more rejection. I stopped looking.

In the Beginning

Starting a ministry is not unlike building a home. You need plans. The first year at Sugarloaf we had organizing meetings to frame the house and then planning retreats the next two years to finish the construction. We experimented with the times of the services and even tried meeting on a Saturday evening. That was a mistake. People sitting in the warm chapel after a day of skiing and a good meal quickly found a degree of comfort I hadn't expected. Seeing more eyelids than eyes, I quickly returned to Sundays (I later old people that at my Saturday night services, the "peace of God" descended upon my congregation).

Housing

Lacking the money for a long-term lease at Sugarloaf, I was always uncertain about housing. The first winter I commuted from the home of a friend in Kingfield, and then moved into a donated condominium at season's end. With the next ski season approaching, "Ma" Judson, the beloved four-foot-ten grandmother and owner of Judson's Motel, offered me the use of the small, vintage mobile home behind her establishment. Since she hosted our potluck suppers and church meetings in the motel's dining room, it was a convenient location. In following years, condominium owners John and Audrey Nickerson and real estate developer Peter Webber supplied my housing. Peter owned several condominium complexes and gave me a place to stay rent-free between seasons and at a heavily discounted price during the season. One winter King Cummings, the chairman of Sugarloaf's board of directors, let me use his home while he escaped to Florida. I paired up with friends to rent a home another winter, and we shared a small cabin at the bottom of Sugarloaf's access road for my last two years.

Learning to Ski

It didn't take long to realize that if I was going to be ministering at a ski resort, it might help to know how to ski. The ski school was offering a week long beginner's clinic of twice-daily classes. At the age of forty, I donned my first pair of ski boots. I clearly remember the last day of classes. Our instructor took us to the top of the mountain. We followed her past a sign pointing to Narrow Gauge, accompanied by the black diamond of an expert trail. *That* got our attention. She then stopped just above the pitch of the headwall, the trail's steepest part. The definition of fear: looking down the headwall of Narrow Gauge when you're just learning to ski. "You can do it," she said, reading our minds. "I wouldn't have brought you here if you couldn't. All you have to do is follow me and stay in my tracks. Where I turn, you turn." One of those rare instructors with the gift of instilling confidence, we believed her and followed her down like a line of ducklings. While we kept our eyes glued to the tracks ahead of us, she gently made her way from one side of the trail to the other; each turn a few feet lower than the last one. With the last of us joining her at the bottom of the headwall, she turned to her brood, "Now look at what you just did," she said, nodding upwards. Feelings of relief turned to pride as we followed her gaze. It was good no one wore helmets in those days. Mine would have broken from the inside.

When Silence Isn't Golden

Good things were happening spiritually among our little flock at Sugarloaf, and there was an air of expectation. Through countless prayer fellowships, Bible studies, book studies, men's breakfasts, potluck suppers and church parties, we were becoming a community. Still, our small numbers led to a problem. My Backup Team, now reconstituted as "Vacationland Ministries" (VM), provided about fifty percent of our income. Without them, the ministry at Sugarloaf would never have left the launching pad. However, even with VM's help, our income consistently fell below our bare-bones budget, and I was to blame.

Inspired by George Mueller, a nineteenth-century missionary who supported his London orphanage solely by praying about their needs, I decided to do the same with church finances. There was, however, one important difference: everybody knew George ran his orphanage that way; nobody knew I was running the church that way. The results were predictable. It took a couple of years, but after cashing in my Methodist retirement fund and maxing out the limit of my credit card, things came to a head in the summer of '85. I was either going to have to scrap my self-imposed silence or get a job, perhaps both. Then there arrived in the mail the latest newsletter of Last Days Ministries, a ministry led by Melody Green following the death of her then-famous husband, singer/speaker Keith Green. In remarks aimed at increasing openness within the Christian community, she pointed out that the Bible tells us to bear one another's burdens, and that couldn't happen if we keep those burdens to ourselves. I had my answer.

At the next Backup Team meeting, I confessed, telling people what I had been doing and revealing my financial predicament. Others besides the Backup Team needed to know. A letter from our treasurer to those on the mailing list of both VM and Sugarloaf brought an immediate response. The generous outpouring that followed delivered me from debt and taught me a valuable lesson. In the nearly thirty years of ministry that followed, every need I shared was met.

Chapter 13 | GOING DOWNHILL SUCCESSFULLY

No longer preoccupied with financial worries, I turned my attention to our worship services. The Easter Sunrise and Christmas Eve Candlelight services each drew great crowds, but comparatively few showed up for Sunday mornings in the chapel. I wondered—is there a way of combining the reason people come to Sugarloaf—skiing—with worship? I wasn't interested in the fifteen to twenty-minute services I discovered on my cross-country tour. How can you get to know people in that limited time? Used to leading hour-long services followed by a social hour, I was looking for a more complete worship experience and especially interested in building a sense of community. But there was a problem—standing on the snow in Sugarloaf's frigid temperatures for longer than ten to fifteen minutes would turn any congregation into Popsicles. So who says we have to stand still? What about taking a service and dividing it into stops along the trail? Since people come to ski, what better way to combine the two! I was excited. Besides providing a nearly complete worship service, breaking it up would maintain people's attention, give us time to become acquainted and, of course, they'd be skiing, which is what they came to do in the first place. I bounced the idea off some friends, and they loved it. Nancy Marshall, the mountain's Assistant Director of Communications thought it was a great idea. "You're going to wear your robe, aren't you?" she asked. I hesitated. The only time I ever wore my black pulpit robe was in Hallowell, and then only because the women's group had bought it for me. "Everybody will notice you," she exclaimed. "Yeah," I thought to myself, embarrassed at the very thought, "That's what I'm worried about."

Sugarloaf's general manager agreed to supply both the necessary signage and even a complimentary half-day lift ticket for those who needed one. Since we'd all be downhill as opposed to cross-country skiers (snowboarding hadn't yet appeared), Nancy suggested calling it "Downhill Worship." Our meeting place would be in the mountain's base area adjacent to the most popular chairlift. The mountain affixed a large sign on a nearby tree, and we were ready to go. Only one question remained—the robe. I *would* feel foolish wearing one, but Nancy had a point: it would attract a *lot* of attention. Besides good advertising, there was a practical benefit: it would help keep my flock together as they followed me down the slopes. "Well," I finally concluded, "If I'm going to feel like a fool, I guess there's no better cause than this one."

As expected, the robe attracted attention—lots of it. In the beginning, I received shouts of "congratulations!" from those who confused it with a

61

graduation gown, and more than one skier thought I was a judge. It turned out to be a great conversation starter. One Sunday I was riding up the chairlift with a college girl from Massachusetts. "What's that all about?" she asked, referring to the robe. I explained, told her about the service, and invited her to join us. "What the hell," she said, "Might as well."

Some correctly pegged me as clergy, which resulted in at least one amusing incident. I was walking down the hall in my condominium building one Sunday afternoon when I saw a ski instructor—a woman in her early thirties—walking toward me.

"Skip," she said, stopping as I approached. "You're going to want to hear this. One of the kids in my class came up to me this morning,

"'Miss Julie, Miss Julie!' the boy shouted. 'Something really bad must have happened!'

"'Why do you say that?' I asked.

"'Because there was this priest and a whole crowd was around him, and he was praying—somebody must have died!'"

Then there was the day I *didn't* want to be recognized. After finishing the service at mid-mountain, with robe flapping in the breeze, I was flying down Tote Road, a long intermediate trail. Toward the bottom, the trail dips abruptly in several spots, resulting in a series of lips. I love skiing fast and was having a ball, catching a bit of air going over the first rise. Then I crested the second and froze. Gazing downward, a row of skiers stood along the entire width of the next lip, completely blocking the trail. Seeing a four-foot gap between two of them, I quickly set my skis toward the opening. Just then, the guy on the right, facing across the trail, moved forward. The four-foot gap became three-and-a-half, and then three and then—whish! My black-robed shoulder brushed his chest as my razor-sharp skis sliced over his own. Stopping at the bottom, I looked up. "Are you okay?" I shouted. Apparently he was, for he started talking about God and Jesus Christ, mentioning their names loudly and with great feeling. Everybody was now staring down at the black-robed figure below. Exit our hero, praying that they thought I had just graduated.

While only a handful joined me for our first-ever Downhill Worship service, we had a great time, word spread, and it wasn't long until the warmer months of spring brought crowds of thirty, forty and in later years even fifty.

"You've got the only church I know of that's going downhill successfully," quipped a friend.

Not Your Normal Church Service

I'd begin our Downhill Worship services at Sugarloaf by asking people where they were from and how long they had been skiing. It gave us a way to become acquainted and helped me choose the morning's trails. In those beginning years, our Sunday service would follow different routes. With beginners, we'd stick to the easy trails and with experienced skiers, the more challenging. One Sunday when I asked "how long have you been skiing?" a man in his thirties named John evoked a chorus of laughter by responding, "What time is it?" Easy trails that day.

In researching the needs of vacationers, I came across "aesthetically rewarding experiences." Think sunrises, sunsets, beautiful views, breathtaking scenery and tranquil surroundings. At a ski service, this means peaceful settings and beautiful scenery. At Sugarloaf, upon reaching the top of the mountain, we skied away from the noisy chairlift, over to a quiet and secluded location surrounded by views of mountains and valleys stretching to the horizon.

"Take a look around you," I'd say, pointing to the panorama extending before us. "The Bible tells us that the God we worship is a personal God who wants to be involved in our lives. Don't you think the One who has created all that you see before you is capable of resolving the problems you're facing? As we start our time together, I invite you to take those concerns and silently surrender them into his hands. Let's pray." Following the same format, we then confessed our sins and gave thanks for our blessings.

At our next stop, I delivered a short message, and at the last stop asked people what requests they had of God and what they'd like to thank him for, combining both into a closing prayer. As people left, I handed each a self-addressed envelope containing a response form and inspirational literature. The response form solicited prayer requests and offered literature to those who were spiritually searching or wanted to accept Christ. The form also contained opportunities to receive our newsletters and make a financial gift. While some assumed the whole purpose of the envelope was simply financial, I was more interested in establishing an enduring connection than anything else. In later years, we also took a group picture, providing free copies.

Our unique Downhill Worship service had a life-changing effect on at least one person. Due to his infidelity, John's ("what time is it?") marriage was in serious trouble. It might have stayed that way if he hadn't met Bill and Louise. In their fifties and married only a few years, the couple enjoyed a relationship striking in their unabashed love for each other. Bill was a talker to begin with, and it was a rare conversation that didn't include such statements as, "I love that woman. She's such a beautiful person—everything about her! She's smart and kind and loves people so much. I am truly blessed." Louise would often be within earshot, her face glowing. Their marriage was, to put it mildly, a bit different from John's, and his desire for a similar relationship tugged at his heart.

John hadn't planned to attend our service that day, coming only to accompany his good friend Gary. At our first stop, when I encouraged people to surrender their concerns into God's hands, John later told me that his response was simple and to the point: "make my marriage like Bill and Louise's."

As John recalls, "God's words that day lay heavy on my heart during the long trip home to Massachusetts." This story would have turned out much differently were it not for John's forgiving and gracious wife. The two of them worked through the hurt and pain, ending the year with a closeness never before experienced. At year's end, reflecting on the dramatic change in his marriage, John wondered, "if the Lord can do this with my marriage, what can he do with my life?" Upon accepting Christ's forgiveness and turning his life over to God's control, John became actively involved in his church. In the years to come, he held leadership positions in his own church, in several other ministries and then became part of Eastern European Outreach, leading short-term mission trips to Russia and the Baltic states. As of this writing, he and his wife have been married over forty years.

Coming to Faith

In addition to John, others accepted the life-changing message of the Gospel. During one month, we had four people decide to become followers of Jesus, one of them ending up in seminary.

The Bill and Louise we mentioned above were already active in their home church when they began attending our services. One day Bill, a weekend ski instructor, offered to give me some tips. As we rode up in the chairlift, the talk turned to church, and I asked him if he had ever accepted Christ.

"Well, no, I don't think I have."

"What's stopping you?" "I don't know," he said, becoming unusually silent, "I'll have to think about it."

Before turning out the lights that night, Bill turned to Louise and told her of our conversation. After some discussion, they reached a conclusion. Taking each other's hand, they bowed their heads and entered the relationship that God yearns to have with all of us.

Chapter 14 | SUMMERTIME

Whenever we've received a great blessing in our lives, there's a natural desire to share it. A person who has recovered from a lifetime of alcohol addiction through Alcoholics Anonymous (AA) will have a natural desire to introduce other alcoholics to AA. It's not surprising, therefore, that ever since experiencing Christ's forgiveness, I've wanted to lead others to him. To that end, I've studied how people become Christians and how to share the Gospel most effectively. For the curious, the word "gospel" comes from the old English word "godspell" meaning "good news" or "glad tidings." As it's used today, it pertains to the life, death and resurrection of Jesus Christ and more specifically, to the uniquely Christian doctrine that eternal life comes through faith in Christ's justifying work on the cross and not by our good deeds. According to the Bible, heaven is not—as most people think—a reward for good behavior; it's an inheritance given to members of God's family. If it were the former, sending Jesus was a colossal waste of God's time, because we don't need Jesus to be good (a fact borne out by the lives of many non-believers). Instead, we enter God's family through faith, and the resulting relationship so overwhelms our life that—as Jesus explained to a religious leader of his day—it's like being "born again" (John 3:1-21).

At first, I ignorantly looked for the "magic recipe" in introducing people to Christ, but soon discovered it wasn't that simple. We're not talking about baking a cake or making a casserole, but changing people's lives—infinitely more complex and resistant to anything smacking of a "one size fits all" approach. We're also walking onto an eternal stage under God's direction, not ours, and I soon realized that changing people's hearts was God's job, not mine. Eventually, I discovered an approach that may not work for everyone but has served me well. When I want to talk to others about Jesus, I simply ask God to provide the opportunity. Interestingly, when I ask, the opportunities come, and when I don't, they don't.

Martha's Vineyard

While Sugarloaf's world-class golf course would eventually draw a respectable number of golfers in the summer, the mountain remained primarily a winter resort, becoming a virtual ghost town after the snow melted. Summers would be spent elsewhere, and I planned to start campground ministries around the state. Then I received a call that ended those thoughts.

"Skip?" asked the voice at the other end of the phone line. "This is Doug Whallon [the New England director of IV]. We have a group of students recruited for a summer project on Martha's Vineyard, but no one to lead it. Would you be interested?"

Located forty-five minutes via the Woods Hole ferry from Cape Cod, Massachusetts, Martha's Vineyard is a summer playground for coastal residents of Massachusetts and neighboring states. With a cost of living significantly higher than the national average and housing almost double, the island draws many of the rich and famous, the Kennedy clan perhaps the most well-known. In 1984, it was home to eight thousand year-round residents with a summer population of over sixty thousand.

Doug began recruiting and ended up with sixteen students, half of whom were Mennonites (think "Amish Lite"). Mennonite dress ranges from that of the "plain people" whose attire is simple and whose women wear a lace head covering, to our students who dressed modestly, but more like the general population. Raised in loving and healthy families, exhibiting traditional values and an unbeatable work ethic, these students stood out for their simple, old-fashioned wholesomeness. In all the time we were together, there were no displays of petulance or selfishness. Instead, there was an abundant supply of kindness, compassion, smiles and laughter. Altogether, they left such a positive impression on me that to this day, I still pulse with joy whenever meeting a Mennonite.

In the summers of '84 and '85 on Martha's Vineyard, I was "Dad" to our sixteen project members. We connected over nightly suppers, prayer and Bible studies, singing together, talking to strangers about Jesus, playing beach volleyball, hosting cookouts and seeing God change people's lives. After bonding with them and collecting a treasure-trove of memories in those ten weeks, saying goodbye was always difficult.

My experiences on Martha's Vineyard and in summer projects elsewhere were both rewarding and revelatory. The friendships made them rewarding, and seeing how people came to believe in Christ made them revelatory. I made two discoveries about the latter.

Friendships Make a Difference

During our three-day orientation, my sixteen students in Martha's Vineyard quickly became family. They were a group of highly motivated, mature young adults with a strong faith and the desire to share it. Local church members threw open the doors of their homes and hearts, initiating relationships that for some have lasted to this day. Our housing arrangement also provided some unexpected benefits for the hosts, as our project members had a powerful influence on the youth in those families. One family had a rebellious teenage daughter at the beginning of the summer and quite a different young woman at the end. Cooperation replaced rebelliousness; joy replaced sullenness, and communication, silence. "Thank-you for giving my daughter back to me," wrote the girl's mother.

Tom, a teenage member of Eldon's host family, invited Eldon for a walk. It was a clear and warm summer day when they walked from behind their home into a field of tall hay-like weeds. After a few minutes, they came to a small patch of ground containing several plants.

Without speaking, Tom uprooted the plants—worth a couple of thousand dollars today—throwing them helter-skelter into the surrounding weeds. With their clusters of seven spear-shaped leaves, Eldon didn't have to ask what they were. Still silent, Tom turned and started walking back to the house. Halfway back a hand rested on his shoulder.

We were out on the streets one night in Martha's Vineyard when I saw a young man in his early twenties. Well-tanned with a full head of black hair and mustache, he was outside the bar he managed, smoking a cigarette and leaning against the wall. I struck up a conversation, got to know him, and he responded with interest when I told him what I was doing. A friendship soon developed. I made it a point of stopping into the bar to a consistently warm welcome and enjoyable conversation. On more than one occasion, he showed up at our evening suppers at the church, his girlfriend accompanying him. We lost touch when I returned to Sugarloaf, but a year later, I was running a summer evangelism project in Camden, Maine, when he called.

"Skip, this is Jeff Parker. Would you come down here to the Vineyard and baptize me?"

Much to the delight of both of us, we've recently re-connected. He's still actively following the Lord and involved in ministry, including developing technology that will enable smartphone users to download Scripture and church info on their smartphones from a specially printed business or gift card.

Dale, a project participant, was working as a waiter when a waitress came up to him and asked, "Why don't you help me?" Thinking she was talking about clearing the dishes from the tables, which he had already done, he responded,

"Help you do what?"

"Help me find God."

They talked often over the next few weeks, and Dale answered many of her questions. While she didn't come to faith by the time he left, she was much farther down that path than when he arrived.

One day, I was driving along an old, well-used coastal highway near Camden when I saw a young man hitchhiking. I pulled over to pick him up. A short, thin man in his early twenties with black hair and a small, black beard, we starting talking and I soon discovered that he worked at the same restaurant as Dale, knew him well, and spent winters working for friends of mine at Sugarloaf. Raised in a Christian home, he had strayed away from his faith and succumbed to alcoholism. "I've got to stop running," he said. The next day he joined us for lunch and that Sunday—for the first time in six years—for church services.

David

After two years in Martha's Vineyard, IV began moving their summer projects from recreational to urban areas. By that time, our ministry was ready to sponsor its own. Our first was in Camden, Maine and the next four up the coast in Bar Harbor. It was during one of these summers that I experienced the second principle of spiritual rebirth: "God encounters" add up. Studies of those who come to faith reveal that it's not through a single dramatic event, but most often a series of encounters with other Christians that finally compel a change. Imagine an old-fashioned scale, much like the one held by the iconic statue of blindfolded justice. On one side of the scale, representing an individual's resistance to God is a weight, its heaviness determined by that individual. The other side of the scale receives weights representing God's attempts to reach us. First, God adds one small weight, and then another, and another. Depending on the size of the counterweight, at some point, the scale may well tip.

After hitting the streets one night in Bar Harbor, we returned to a church lounge for a time of singing and sharing. I encouraged team members to bring anyone they met on the streets to this wrap-up time and that night we met David from Wisconsin. A young man in his mid-twenties, David was on a two-week vacation from his factory job back home. As he proceeded to tell us, this vacation was turning into something quite different than he expected.

On the first leg of David's cross-country bus trip, he sat next to a man who, for the next five hours, talked to him about the Bible. This was new territory for David, a non-practicing Catholic. Getting off the bus in Bar Harbor, David looked around for his motel. Standing nearby, a girl noticed his confused look and asked if she could help. When he mentioned the name of the motel, she responded, "Oh, that's right down the street. I'll be glad to show you." While they walked, the girl turned to him. "By the way, do you know Jesus Christ as your personal lord and savior?"

"How did you answer?" I interjected.

"I didn't know what to say," David responded.

The following night Dave was walking around town when he met Becky, one of our project members. "Before I knew it," Becky said, "we were talking about the Holy Spirit, and I thought, 'I've got to get him back to Skip!'"

After hearing his story, I turned to Dave. "Do you think God's trying to tell you something?"

"Yeah," he said slowly, a far-off look in his eyes.

We met in my office the next morning and went over the basics of becoming a Christian. I pointed out that to become a follower of Jesus is not only to accept his forgiveness, but also to set our hearts on pleasing him. He and his girlfriend were living together, so we talked about the implications of accepting Christ on their relationship. David understood, and we prayed.

Back in Wisconsin, David and his girlfriend went their separate ways. He started attending a weekly Bible study at a Baptist church, Catholic Mass on Sundays, and on Saturday nights, took his Bible to the local roller skating rink to tell kids about Jesus.

It's interesting to note that neither the man on the bus or the girl on the street will ever know the part they played in the birth of David's faith, but without their encounters, we wouldn't have had ours. To those whose hearts are open—as was David's—the accumulated weight of "God encounters" will always tip the scales.

Chapter 15 | LEAVING SUGARLOAF

Rev. Gary Rolph, the pastor of Pemi Valley Church in the popular White Mountains of New Hampshire, called me in the spring of 1987.

"Skip, I've just recently moved here and could use your input on how to reach out to vacationers and tourists. Could you come, take a look around and give us some ideas?"

I drove over and surveyed the area. The more I looked, the more excited I became, not for Gary and his church, but for me. Compared to Sugarloaf, the Lincoln-Woodstock area was teeming with opportunity. Not only were there three ski resorts in the vicinity (Loon Mountain, Cannon Mountain and Waterville Valley) the area also offered numerous summer attractions such as campgrounds, a water park, and Clark's Trading Post with their famous bear shows. In addition, nature's provisions of waterfalls for viewing, forests for hiking, mountains for climbing, and lakes and rivers for fishing, swimming, kayaking, and canoeing made the area a popular summer destination. Unlike Sugarloaf, Loon Mountain was open during the summer and fall, ferrying thousands of visitors to its breathtaking mountaintop views. While the mountain was busier in the winter, the whole area was busier in the summer. With both a vibrant winter *and* summer population, the thought of moving excited me. I pitched the idea at our next Backup Team meeting, but received a "thumbs down." Sugarloaf wasn't ready for a change in leadership. It might be a good thought for later, they told me, but not now. While disappointed, I knew they were right, and appreciated their check on my impulsiveness. I stored the idea for future reference.

Loving the challenge of starting something new, I never imagined a lengthy stay at Sugarloaf. I'd come, establish a ministry, then go elsewhere and repeat the process. Sometimes I wondered how I'd know when it was time to leave, but when that time finally came, there was little doubt.

Joyce

In 1988, our summer ministry in Bar Harbor opened a bank account at People's Heritage Bank. I became acquainted with their staff, noticing one teller in particular. Joyce Morgan was blonde, soft-spoken, with a beautiful face nestled in a bed of feathered blonde hair, à la Farrah Fawcett. We became acquainted over deposits and withdrawals and toward the end of the summer in a more personal way. "You're not dating?" I asked, "why not?"

"Oh, you've got to kiss a lot of frogs before you meet a handsome prince," she responded.

"You just wait," I answered mischievously, "One of these days…"

I was on a mission. Whenever entering a store selling greeting cards, I'd head right for them. After a couple of months, I found it. On the outside was the picture of a frog with the words, "One of these days," and on the inside, showing a suitably attired prince, "Voila! Prince Charming!" I sent the card to the bank, attention Joyce. From that time forward, the all-female staff always signed my deposit receipts "the ladies in waiting."

As the next summer approached, I was torn. After seven years of no romantic involvements, should I or shouldn't I? Given the disastrous endings of my last two relationships, my attraction to Joyce triggered feelings of fear. Still, she was available, beautiful, and her quiet gentleness had a magnetic appeal. Our communication at that point was superficial, but it was also fun. To date or not to date—that was the question. I went back and forth, attracted to her on the one hand and scared to death on the other. Indecision was my passenger as I drove to Bar Harbor that summer.

A couple of weeks after my arrival, I was out for a morning run when I met the bank's manager walking to work. We stopped to talk.

"The girls really enjoyed your notes over the winter," he said.

"Yes," I replied, "that was fun."

"It seems to me someone ought to get a date out of this."

"Oh, she will."

Uh-oh, I thought. I've just committed myself. He's going to go back to the bank and tell Joyce I'm going to ask her out (which is exactly what he did).

I showered, changed and drove to the bank, both nervous and excited. Walking up to her teller window, I smacked my hands loudly on the counter in front of her and declared, "Well, I guess you and I've got a date!" It's safe to say that those first words to her in over nine months carried all the romantic charm of a traffic summons. Stunned and speechless, it took her a minute to regain her composure before accepting. I left the bank happy; not quite believing that, after seven years, I was actually going out on a date. It must have been my suave approach.

I took Joyce to the University of Maine at Orono's performing arts center where we laughed our way through Tim Sample's program of Downeast Maine humor. On the way back, I pulled into a Dunkin' Donuts. Over tea and decaf, we dove into our first deep conversation. From my marital history, there was one thing I had to know, and the sooner, the better. "So, how did you and your father get along?"

"Pretty good. When my parents divorced, I went with him. He worked as an itinerant carpenter, and we traveled the country together. He had a good sense of humor. From time to time he became 'Lord Epping,' and I was 'Lady Buffwaffington.' He'd put a quarter in his eye as a fake monocle and grab a stick to use for a cane, and we'd sit at a card table sipping tea and talking to each other in English accents. We were closer before he remarried, but still keep in touch."

Whew! That was a relief. A good relationship with Dad equals a good relationship with husband. If we end up getting married, I'm not going to be catching hell from the unconscious transference of her hurt or anger.

The sharing went deeper. As we opened up to each other things were going well—actually, *too* well. It was like the joy of skiing down a freshly groomed trail at forty-plus miles an hour and all of a sudden becoming air born. Scared, I needed to get down and fast. Still on the subject of my divorces, I declared adamantly, "I'm never getting married again!" While taking the statement in stride, Joyce later confided thinking to herself, 'who's asking?' My emotional safety net now deployed, our conversation continued for the better part of an hour.

Because any participant wrapped up in a new romantic relationship wouldn't be able to concentrate on much else, our summer projects had a standing rule against dating. Consequently, except for an occasional lunch, Joyce and I put our relationship on hold for the next ten weeks. Then, after everyone left and before I had to return to Sugarloaf, we made up for lost time with day trips and picnics, a return trip to the University of Maine to see Noel Paul Stookey, and evening dinners and movies.

When winter arrived, Joyce came up on weekends and stayed with my secretary Sandi, learning how to ski and becoming an instant hit with my friends. Skiing was new to Joyce, but Sandi promised to help. On a bright and sunny Saturday, Joyce donned her pink ski pants and pink jacket. Sandi helped her into a pair of ski boots, onto a set of skis, and started her down the bunny slope. She forgot only one thing. "How do I stop?" yelled Joyce, quickly picking up speed. "Fall down!" Shouted Sandi.

In comparing Joyce to my first two wives, God's hand was clearly visible. My desperate emotional need to be married drove those first two marriages. This time, there was no such need. I was perfectly happy being alone. If anything arose to end this new relationship, I could easily return to the single life. Time revealed Joyce to be a gift from God. Her appearance came as a pleasant surprise, making the next chapter of my ministry possible and introducing me to a marital happiness I never expected.

With Joyce in the picture, the thought of staying at Sugarloaf raised several questions: for starters, housing. Searching for a place to live every season was okay as a bachelor but wasn't going to work with a wife. Something needed to change, and something did, but not as I expected. First, there were the rumors.

Questions about my sexual orientation shouldn't have been surprising. I was single, with no dating life and my roommates were all guys. When I grew up, same-gender roommates were expected. Today, they're cause for suspicion. When leaving a chapel board meeting one afternoon, a friend sided up to me and shaking her head, said quietly, "the rumor's going around that you're gay." I was angry. Thinking about Joyce, I shot back, "Yes, and I suppose if I get married they'll be saying I'm bisexual." Rumors weren't the only thing happening; I also managed to get myself kicked off the Chapel's board of directors.

Our ministry and the Catholics who used the chapel were fortunate not to have to worry about the upkeep of a building. An independent board of directors, of which the Catholic priest and I were both members, took responsibility for the upkeep and improvements to the chapel, and charged our two religious bodies only a nominal rent. In the spring of 1990, the chapel board made plans to renovate the sanctuary, including carpeting the hardwood floor. I suggested a sound system. Acoustics were great with the hardwood floors, but I knew from experience that the carpet would make a noticeable difference. The board's chairwoman didn't think it was necessary. Short and trim, blonde and bright, a bundle of energy and highly active in the community, she was very much a take-charge type of person, outspoken to a fault. Over the years, I noticed that if you disagreed with her, she took it personally, and you quickly became "the enemy." Normally, I'd go along with whatever she wanted just to keep the peace, but not this time. I knew I was right about the acoustics and rebelled at the thought of keeping quiet for fear of offending her. Instead of backing off, I continued to bring it up. Then, without telling me, she called a special meeting of the Board and kicked me off. The Catholic priest also lost his seat, even though he rarely attended. Stunned, and not knowing how far this was going, I prepared for our ministry's eviction from the chapel. Fortunately, it never came to that.

Confirmation

Rumors of my sexual orientation, banishment from the chapel board and my deepening relationship with Joyce got me wondering: should I be thinking about leaving? I mulled it over for a few days and then went to see close friends John and Audrey Nickerson, a retired couple and two of the founding members of our ministry. I admired Audrey's close relationship with the Lord and valued her counsel. When I broached the subject of leaving, her response was both surprising and confirming.

"It's interesting that you should bring it up," she said thoughtfully. "Last night I was thinking about that very thing and told John that maybe it *was* time for you to leave." That's all I needed to hear. I submitted my resignation in the spring of 1990, effective the end of August. After seven years, the Sugarloaf ministry had a capable and gifted Board, and I was confident they could weather the change and find a suitable replacement.

Where to go from Sugarloaf? Remembering my visit to the White Mountains of New Hampshire, one ski area stood out: Waterville Valley. Thanks to the press generated by the frequent appearance of the Kennedy's from Massachusetts, Waterville Valley's popularity soared. Having performed a wedding for one of their management team, I even had a connection.

During an end-of-season après ski event at Sugarloaf, I was mingling with friends when one of them said to me, "I understand you're leaving."

"Yep," I replied.

"Where will you be going?"

"I was thinking of Waterville Valley."

"If I were you …['pay attention to what he says,' flashed the unbidden thought]… I'd think about Loon Mountain. Waterville has reached its peak, but Loon is still expanding. Also, Waterville Valley caters to the rich crowd while Loon is much more of a family mountain."

That's all well and good, I mused, but I'm heading for Waterville Valley… or so I thought.

Chapter 16 | NEW HAMPSHIRE

On a sunny weekday in April of 1990, I settled into the driver's seat of my little white Subaru hatchback and drove down Sugarloaf's access road, the start of a four-hour trip to Waterville Valley, New Hampshire. Turning off I-93 in New Hampshire, I followed the two-lane highway terminating twenty minutes later in the small resort community. I decided to do some exploring before visiting my friend and headed for the town center, a large three-story U-shaped complex housing retail shops and offices. A grassy courtyard complete with gazebo occupied the middle of the horseshoe, opening up to a small pond just beyond the perimeter. Following a brief walk-around, I returned to my car and headed up to the mountain and the ski resort's administration building. I hadn't made an appointment, so was pleasantly surprised to find my friend occupying his small office. He greeted me warmly and motioned toward a chair. After catching up on his life since leaving Sugarloaf, I mentioned my desire to start a ministry at Waterville Valley.

"Well Skip, we could certainly use you," he replied, "but frankly, I don't think you'd get any support from management. The town library (a small stone church-like building) closes on Sundays, and I suggested to our general manager that we use it for church services. He wouldn't hear of it—dismissed the idea without even considering it." He paused, thoughtfully. "Now if I were you," he continued, "I'd talk to Phil Gravink over at Loon Mountain. We attend church together, and I think he'd be receptive to the idea."

Shaking his hand and thanking him for the suggestion, I walked back to my car. Remembering the words of my après-ski friend brought a smile to my lips—I might be going to Loon after all.

Loon

Louise Watson, Phil's administrative assistant, greeted me warmly. A petite, older lady with white hair, she possessed the warmth and charm of everyone's favorite grandmother.

"I'd like to talk with Phil Gravink," I announced. "Is he available, and if not, can I make an appointment?"

"Well, I think he is," Louise responded. "He had a meeting scheduled with the Forest Service, but they stood him up, so you might be in luck. Let me check." Then, "he'd be glad to see you: go right in."

Tall, trim, a narrow face sporting a salt-and-pepper mustache below bushy eyebrows and receding gray hair, Phil rose from behind his desk, a warm smile accompanying his outstretched hand.

"Skip Schwarz," I said, gripping his hand and returning the smile. Covering the walls of his office were award plaques and pictures of him with the politically famous. Closer to his desk hung a photo of Cornell's rowing team.

"Well," he said, "What can I do for you?"

"For the past seven years, I've had a ministry at Sugarloaf," I began. "The time has come to move on, and I'd like to start a ministry here at Loon."

"Okay," said Phil thoughtfully, "why don't you tell me a bit about yourself and what you have in mind."

"I grew up in California where my dad was a Congregational minister…" I went on to tell of my tour in the Army, college, and seminary, my churches in Hallowell, Strong/Kingfield and the calling into recreational ministries that landed me at Sugarloaf.

"We started a church at Sugarloaf comprised of locals and second homeowners," I said, "and 'Downhill Worship'—a church service divided into three stops going down a ski trail. We averaged in the twenties, with forty or fifty showing up in the spring. Our Christmas Eve and Easter sunrise services were both popular, drawing a few hundred at each. I'd like to do something similar at Loon, starting a church in the community and providing chaplaincy services for your guests and employees. I'd be available for counseling and glad to visit any guests who might end up in the hospital."

Phil asked about finances and appeared relieved when I said that we'd be self-funded, asking only that the mountain make a financial contribution. There followed some other questions about our ministry at Sugarloaf and how I came to choose Loon, a story I enjoyed sharing. He wanted to know what we'd need from Loon, and I mentioned a ski locker, ski passes, the donation, and help with advertising. A half-hour after walking into his office, he stood up.

"Well," he said, smiling slightly, "I'm cautiously optimistic. I'll need you to prepare a formal proposal to present to our senior staff along with a list of references for me to check. I'll call you as soon as I know something."

A few days later, my phone rang: "When do you want to start?"

Loon approved my written proposal, agreeing to make an annual contribution and provide advertising, a ski locker, and two season's passes. When telling other ski ministers of Loon's response, their shocked reactions and stories of far different experiences increased my gratitude for Phil. My record at Sugarloaf helped paved the way, but to most general managers even that would have meant little. As with any business, ski resorts exist to make money. Against that backdrop, the idea of a ministry appears irrelevant at best and distracting at worst. Being a man of faith, however, for Phil the word "ministry" carried an inherent value. Close to several ministers and seeing them comfort the bereaved, help people get along with each other, mobilize assistance for the needy and support those in emotional crises, Phil regarded me as a help to both guests and employees. My colleagues, however, received a far different response from resort managers who, absent Phil's faith and church involvement, were doubtful, suspicious and even hostile to the idea of a ministry.

In interviewing Phil for this book, I discovered that my proposal wasn't as much of a slam-dunk as I thought. While opposition faded after I arrived, in the beginning, some of his own Board members were against the idea.

"What are we doing," asked one of them with barely concealed mockery, "running a faith-based mountain?"

"No," replied Phil, patiently. "We're simply providing an amenity for our guests that will make us more attractive to them."

Another Board member was talking with Louise, Phil's administrative assistant.

"What's he coming here for, to fleece our wealthy guests?"

"Well actually, at this point he doesn't know how he's going to support himself. He's just got faith that God will provide, and you know what?" She said, giving him a grandmotherly pat on the arm, "I believe he will."

Thanks to Phil, I now knew where I was going after Sugarloaf. What I didn't know was how I'd support myself—correction—how I'd support *us*, for Joyce and I would marry at the end of the summer. I *thought* I knew what I'd be doing at Loon—starting a church with an outreach to the mountain—just like Sugarloaf. As it turned out, I was only half-right.

Chapter 17 | THE FIRST WINTER

As a single man, I could live in a tent, but that wasn't going to happen with a wife. At Loon, we'd need a regular income and housing. I didn't want to end up in a homeless shelter. That, however, is exactly what happened.

Now operating under the name "Vacationland Ministries," my Backup Team would continue the support they provided at Sugarloaf, but as a married man, I needed much more. Then I heard that the American Baptist Churches were launching a campaign to start two thousand new churches by the beginning of the next millennium. Contacting Rev. Jim Smith, in charge of new church development for the American Baptist's of New Hampshire, and the future Chairman of our Board, I asked if one of those new churches could be Loon. Yes, it could. With Jim's help, the American Baptists promised four years of decreasing seed monies, providing not only the needed funding, but also giving me—after all these years—a denominational home. Now our only need was for housing. I was thinking of getting a part-time job when I received a call from Rev. Gary Rolph.

"Skip, I'm serving on the Board of Lincoln-Woodstock Housing Opportunities (LWHO), and we've secured a grant to purchase a home to use as a homeless shelter, but we don't have anyone to run it. Would you and Joyce be interested? You'd be living in the house, so your housing and utilities would be covered, plus there's a salary of $10,000 a year."

My pumping fist almost hit the ceiling.

Jayne's House

Named after a former owner, "Jayne's House" provided four bedrooms and a shared bath for its guests and a private bedroom and bath for us. We weren't as busy as expected, so some clients stayed for long periods, giving us the chance to know them quite well. Three stand out in my memory.

The Geezer

We affectionately nicknamed him "The Geezer." In his early sixties, he stood about 6'2" with thinning black hair topping an oval face. His hawk-like nose looked down on a set of teeth whose survivors had never seen a dental office. At over two-hundred-and-fifty pounds, he sported a well-developed paunch dutifully hanging over the front of his belt. He was quiet and often appeared preoccupied, but was responsive and pleasant to talk to. He was also free of the more noticeable mental issues plaguing some of our guests. Among my favorite memories were our coordinated attacks on Joyce's freshly baked bread. Butter-melting hot, with a mouth-watering smell and soft, doughy texture, it wasn't unusual for the two of us to finish off a loaf within minutes.

A pleasant person to have around, The Geezer became such a part of our lives that when we rented a home of our own a couple of years later, he took us up on our offer to sublet the small basement apartment. He didn't talk much about personal issues, but when he first arrived, he mentioned that he and his son hadn't spoken in quite a few years. It was gratifying, therefore, to hear that when he left us a couple of years later, he moved into his son's home in Maine.

Linda

I heard a knock at our front door. "I'm Linda. The town said you could give me a place to stay for a while," she said in a near whisper. Standing before me was a small, frail woman in her late thirties of light, almost anemic complexion with straight, brown hair falling to her shoulders. She held a small suitcase in one hand and a large garbage bag of belongings in the other.

"Of course, come right in," I responded, helping her with her things. Joyce appeared, and taking in the familiar scene, greeted her warmly.

"Can I get you something to eat?" She asked.

She looked like she could use some nourishment, if not physically, then at least as a possible antidote to the despair in her eyes.

"No, thanks… I don't eat much."

Joyce began to worry, "I don't doubt that," she thought to herself.

"And your name is?"

"Linda"

"Okay, Linda—how about something to drink? Coffee? Tea? We've got Coke and Diet Coke."

"I like Diet Coke," she answered.

Sitting down at the kitchen table, Joyce started filling out the required client questionnaire.

"Are you on any medications?"

"No, just laxative," Linda replied, confirming Joyce's fears.

The next day, Linda was sitting in the living room, crocheting a blanket. "Oh, I see you can crochet," said Joyce, "that looks nice, is it a gift?"

"No, it's for my baby."

She certainly didn't look pregnant, and Joyce squelched the next natural question, waiting until the following day.

"So, how long have you been pregnant?"

"About three years."

Faced with Linda's anorexia and other mental issues, both Joyce and I felt helpless. We provided a safe and comfortable place for her to stay, and what food she was willing to eat, but as with others we occasionally served, her needs far exceeded our provisions.

Marty

Marty was probably the kind of person LWHO expected to be helping when they opened Jayne's House: normally responsible, but temporarily victimized by financial circumstances beyond her control. In her late forties and with nowhere to go following knee surgery, she was taken to Jayne's House. Short and slender with long dark hair, Marty had an innate respectability at odds with the unkempt and poverty-laced stereotype of the homeless. Like Joyce, she was quiet and reserved, and the two of them soon became good friends. She stayed with us about a year, eventually securing a full-time job as a home health aide and saving up enough to move into her own apartment in a town north of us.

We stayed at the homeless shelter for two years before securing our own housing for the next six. Then, in the fall of 1998, we purchased a home of our own. The price was low, but we had a lot of work to do on it since it used to be a homeless shelter. They called it "Jayne's House."

Downhill Worship—Take 2

A meeting with Loon's marketing director brought a change in the format of our Downhill Worship service. "The base area isn't going to work as a meeting place; it's too congested. Sugarloaf's base area is pretty spread out, but not ours." Then, after pausing for a moment, "What would you think about starting from the top?"

"Where?"

"You could meet on the deck of the Summit Café."

"Oh… hey, that'd be great," I replied. "People could stay inside and keep warm until the service starts." Then, with a grin, "and you'd sell a lot more hot chocolate."

The mountain's sign shop produced sandwich board signs that I put up in front of both lodges and near the Summit Café. Plastering the base areas with posters on Friday nights (and taking them down on Sunday afternoons), I donned my robe for our Sunday services, and it was—literally—downhill from there.

In the winter of '93-'94 the media discovered us, helped in no small part by the North American Ski Writer's convention held at Loon in January of '93. Organizing the event was a good friend of mine, Alice Pearce. Writers are always looking for stories, so she distributed a list of attractions in the area, our service being one of them. Several writers talked to me, including two from the British Broadcasting Corporation (BBC) who asked to interview me after the service. Waiting with them in a hotel function room looking up onto the slopes, Joyce announced my appearance. "Here he comes," she said, pointing to a distant black robe flapping in the breeze. Ministers in England are called "vicars," and are noted for their staid conservatism and formality. The two Brits could hardly believe what they were seeing. "That's the Vic?" They exclaimed.

Later that spring, the BBC asked Loon to provide a picture of me skiing with my guitar on my back (something I never do). They got the idea from a caricature of me appearing in the back pages of a ski magazine. The mountain had closed a few weeks earlier, but there was still some "mashed potato" snow remaining—just the kind I hated. Loon collected the mountain's photographer, grabbed my friend Danny to drive the snowmobile and sent us up. After dropping off the photographer below a small rise in the trail, Danny drove me up a few hundred feet. I took a couple of awkward runs in the super-soft snow with the photographer clicking away. Then, an inspiration: giving my poles to Danny, I brought my guitar around front, pointed my skis downhill and started singing at the top of my lungs, "Amazing grace…" interspersed with shouts of "Repent! Repent!" I came to a stop just below the photographer. "That was great," he said, "it was all I could do to quit laughing long enough to take the picture."

"Just my luck, that's the one you'll use," I responded with mock annoyance. I was right. They blew it up into a 2x3-foot portrait that hung in the Summit Café for years and now hangs on the wall of our family room.

It wasn't just the print media that paid attention to us. We appeared on ESPN-1, ESPN-2, WLBZ-TV out of Boston, and toward the end of my tenure, Public Broadcasting radio. While fun to talk about, I never regarded such publicity as very important. At the time, it was, "Yep, that and a $1 will get me a cup of coffee." Consequently, I never bothered finding out when the programs aired and since we didn't have a TV, never watched them. My parents in California however, did have a TV, and as dad was surfing the channels one day, my face suddenly filled the screen. "Mother, Mother," he called out, "Come here, Skip's on TV!"

Many of those who attended our winter services did so frequently, enabling the building of a family-like atmosphere. In the winter of '99-00, Jerry and Roe (short for "Rosemary") Lavoie joined our group and became instant "regulars." A man who loves people and enjoys helping, Jerry became my chief assistant, passing out bulletins and envelopes, and taking the group picture at the end of the service. Because of his presence, Joyce felt comfortable backing out of the winter services when a couple of upsetting ski accidents sealed her decision to quit the sport. Not only did Jerry and Roe attend, but they also introduced many of their friends to our services and people like Rob Turunen, and the Edingtons joined us regularly. Together with others such as the Leavers, Philbricks, Reids, Walter Protas, Tim White and Gregg Reynolds, my winter congregation soon felt like family.

Chapter 18 | THE VISION: AT LEAST I GOT IT HALF-RIGHT

Having started a seasonal church at Sugarloaf, I envisioned a year-round church at Loon, with the mountain as our *raison d'être*. Since guests and employees would provide little in the way of support, the church would carry the primary financial burden. Unfortunately, I forgot one detail: a seasonal church such as Sugarloaf is one thing; a year-round church, with its standing committees, Sunday school and youth programs, was another. I was no longer called to lead a year-round church, even if it was at a ski resort. Forgetting this at the time, I started holding services for the locals. We attracted a small group that disappeared our first summer when they sensed that my heart was with the ski ministry and not with them. Distracted by an exploding summer ministry, I didn't have time to dwell on my church's demise, and it wasn't until years later that I realized the cause.

Sermon on the Mount

Approaching my first summer at Loon, I wondered what I'd be doing. Ministering in campgrounds was a possibility—there were several in the area. Then I discovered the mountain had an "all you can eat" pancake breakfast at the Summit Café on Sunday mornings, attracting a couple of hundred people. Perhaps some of them would like to attend a church service. Securing Phil Gravink's approval, Joyce and I painted the town with posters advertising our "Sermon on the Mount."

"How do you do that?" joked Loon's ski patrol director a couple of summers later.

"Do what?" I responded.

"Deliver a sermon on horseback?"

Grabbing my guitar and bulletins, Joyce and I hopped on the gondola for our first Sunday service, arriving a half-hour early. It was a clear and sunny morning with temperatures in the mid-seventies. We made the rounds of the crowded picnic tables and people hunched over plates of eggs, sausages, and pancakes, getting to know them and telling them of the approaching service. With ten minutes to go, I yelled out, "Church service in ten minutes—right down this trail," repeating the announcement five minutes later. When starting time arrived, we had quite a crowd…of four. A couple from Florida joined us. Not a thrilling beginning, but I shrugged it off—par for the course in a resort area. The next day I reported to Joel Beaudin, my contact person on Loon's Senior Staff, reassuring him that the turnout wasn't discouraging. A few days later, he called.

"Skip, this is Joel. I thought you'd like to know we were talking about you at senior staff today. We decided to offer a complimentary gondola ticket [$8.50 at the time] to all those wanting to attend the church service. And if they want to stay afterward and take advantage of everything up top, that's fine, too."

"Wow!" I replied, shocked. "Can I advertise that and put it on our posters?"

"Of course."

Joyce and I wasted no time putting up the new posters. After moving us to the most scenic spot available, Loon installed log seating and a small speaker's platform. In future years they would add a sound system, replace the logs with benches and even pave the pathway, making it more comfortable not only for us but for the increasing number of couples desiring the breathtaking view as a backdrop for their weddings.

Attendance skyrocketed, averaging over a hundred that first summer. After occasionally running out of seating space, we added a second service the following year. Word spread among tour companies that Loon was offering free tickets for a gondola ride, and tour busses began disgorging their passengers fifty and sixty at a time. Attendance kept increasing and by our fourth year, crowds of two hundred were common. Then everything changed.

In need of capital for an expanding summer program in 1995, the mountain began charging for the church ticket. While still a fraction of the cost of a regular ticket, the impact was predictable—the tour buses stopped coming, and as the price continued to rise over the years, attendance declined proportionately, leveling off in the high double digits.

While the elation accompanying large crowds waned, the pleasure of those services remained, exciting for their unpredictability. Old friends, new friends, visitors from out of state and out of the country, couples I married some years before, musically gifted people sharing their talents, pastors, whole youth groups—every week brought surprises. A few years after we started, a thirty-something-year-old music teacher from Haverhill, Massachusetts, showed up with her mother and informally adopted sister "Doc" (Dr. Cinthia Proano). Lingering after the service, Ruth Cranton volunteered to provide special music for our services. From then on, she and "Doc" would drive up from Massachusetts several times a summer, sometimes joined by her mother and sister and, on Columbus Day weekends, by several girlfriends for a traditional girl's getaway. Joyce and I reciprocated by visiting them at least yearly, and we soon became good friends.

Rain always made things interesting at our outdoor services. We'd stay at the bottom if it was raining at the start of the service, but occasionally mother nature held off until we were all comfortably—and dryly—seated. One of our regulars, Jim Cummings, thoughtfully donated fifty large umbrellas, so we were always prepared. My standard line when God turned on the water works was, "Okay, folks—no extra charge for baptisms. You Catholics, Presbyterians, Methodists and the like can leave after you've been sprinkled, but our Baptist friends who believe in total immersion? You've gotta stay!" One Sunday, I had no sooner read a passage in the Bible about thunder than a crack of lightning flashed across the darkening sky accompanied a split-second later by the distant sound of kettledrums. The heavens opened, and everybody dashed up to the Summit Café. After we were safe and dry inside, a little boy, recalling me reading about the thunder, looked up at his father and asked, "How did he make it do that?"

Chapter 19 | ENCORE!

In the third year of our ministry, Joyce and I had just left the homeless shelter to rent a place of our own when it happened. My failure to establish a local church, along with the scheduled decrease in denominational funding, resulted in a financial crunch. My salary was the last thing our ministry paid (my decision) which made me the first to feel the shortage. Discouraged, one evening I sank into a moment of self-pity. "Here I've got three degrees, and I can't even pay my bills," I lamented to some close friends. While Joyce and I were current with monthly payments, there just wasn't anything left over for the inevitable emergencies, so a car in need of repairs sat motionless in our driveway. I knew in my mind that God would provide, but my emotions lagged far behind. In the Bible, the psalmist writes, "I waited patiently for the Lord…" (Psalm 40:1). I was waiting all right, but it *wasn't* patiently. Fortunately, it also wasn't long.

I ducked into the small, single-room "Clothing Closet" operated by the town of North Woodstock. An older woman sat in a chair behind a card table, pulling articles of clothing from the mound of bulging trash bags surrounding her and placing them on hangers. While she worked, her husband dragged in two more bags. My mind flashed back to Sugarloaf. With affluent skiers and low-income workers, there was a built-in supply and demand for good used clothing. We put up a clothing collection box and gave the keys to a nearby church-sponsored thrift store. In the years that followed, the collection box at Sugarloaf provided literally tons of clothing for the needy and thousands of dollars for the ministry helping them. The sight of this woman surrounded by those bags kindled a thought: why not? I called a carpenter friend and a clothing collection box soon appeared at the entrance to Loon Mountain. We turned over the keys to the couple running the Clothing Closet, feeling good about the increase in donations that would soon descend upon them. Everything was going smoothly until the husband had a heart attack, requiring his wife's full-time attention. With no one left to run the Clothing Closet, the town closed it down, presenting us with a problem: what to do with the donations that were still coming in.

I drew up a list of needs and costs and ran it by our Board. They gave their approval, pending receipt of the necessary funds. A letter with the same information went out to those on our mailing list, and the money appeared. We were going to open a thrift store. After renting a small space in a local strip mall, and with the help of volunteers from Pemi Valley Church, Encore! Thrift Shop opened for business on November 30, 1993.

Starting a business is not unlike becoming a parent. It invades your life with new demands, joys and challenges. This "baby" was very demanding. There was always clothing in need of sorting, cleaning, repairing, pricing, sizing, tagging, and hanging.

Six months later, having outgrown our small space, we moved into a storefront two-and-a-half-times larger. Then, two years later, we doubled that area by expanding into an adjoining unit.

With the store's opening, Joyce went from managing a homeless shelter to managing a thrift store. She was better than me at dealing with an all-female staff, so I left employee management in her hands and concentrated on picking up furniture, cleaning shoes, fixing electronics, ordering supplies and keeping an eye on the finances.

The thrift store helped both the community and our ministry. The public received good used clothing and furniture at affordable prices and every year, those in need received thousands dollars' in help through monetary gifts and free merchandise. In addition, thanks to the two thousand hours donated every year by our volunteer staff, the ministry's financial pressures disappeared, never to return.

Sometimes, when God blesses, he doesn't stop. I was sitting in my office in the back of the store at the end of 1999 when the phone rang.

"Skip, this is Alan [our landlord]. Are you sitting down?"

"Yes, why?"

"I've been talking to my accountant. He suggested we give away all our property in the mall to a non-profit and take a tax write-off."

After initially offering to "give us" the ten units and their 20,000 square feet for a six-figure price, "Tell you what, we'll let you have it for $65,000, and you don't have to give it to us until you sell some units."

"Okay," I said, both excited and tentative. I'll have to run this by my Board, but we've got a meeting in just a couple of weeks. I'll give you a call."

I emailed the good news to our Board members. Word spread among the mall's commercial tenants, and one of them approached me wanting to buy his large unit, only to back off several days later. I arrived at our Board meeting excited by the potential windfall.

"I've taken a look at the figures," I announced to the Board members, "and between what we'd be paying out in expenses, and what we're taking in for rent, we'd be breaking even."

With that assurance, I expected an instant acceptance of Alan's proposal, but that's not what happened.

"I'd be willing to take the property if he wanted to give it to us outright," said the Rev. Jim Smith, "but I don't think we should pay him anything. If he wants to give it to us free and clear, we'll take it, but not with any strings attached." The other two Board members concurred. Afraid that we'd lose the donation, I was devastated. I called Alan from our meeting and sadly told him of the Board's decision.

"Let me talk to my partner," he replied. "I'll get back to you." A few minutes later, "Okay, we'll do it."

A week after the signing, the people who initially told us they were interested in buying their unit, only to back off, called again. The deal was back on. We agreed on a price and signed the papers. Wondering about the effect on our balance sheet, I began by running the figures without the sale and was stunned: we weren't anywhere *near* breaking even. Instead, we were losing a thousand dollars a month. When factoring in the sale, however, we *were* breaking even. For the longest time, I couldn't figure it out. It wasn't until writing this chapter that the likely answer emerged. I drew up the first balance sheet shortly after the initial request to buy that unit. When they withdrew the offer a few days later, I neglected to recalculate the figures. I call it "God-ordained ignorance." None of us would have pursued Alan's offer if we knew we were losing a thousand dollars a month.

Over the next thirteen years, we ended up selling off the properties and disposing of the proceeds. Ten percent of the receipts went to our ministry and the rest—about a quarter of a million dollars—went for everything from fuel and rent assistance to missionaries in need of vehicles, to the local crisis pregnancy center in need of an ultrasound machine.

A few years later, a second unit adjoining our thrift store became available. We took down the wall and expanded yet again, now occupying as much retail space as some department stores. With more space for merchandise, sales continued to increase. Expenses such as condominium fees, property taxes, labor costs and store supplies consumed two-thirds of our income, but that still left a full third for the support of the ministry, providing the greatest share of its budget.

After many years managing the thrift store, Joyce wanted to pursue her jewelry-making business, so we turned over the reins to our long-time friend Linda McIntyre. Linda brought in her extended family and added her creative touches to a job she'd been requesting for years ("If you ever need a replacement, I'm available!"). Her husband Scott took over my moving duties. Capable of hoisting heavy queen mattresses in a single hoist, he didn't need any help from my aging muscles. New faces appeared to take over my other store responsibilities, leaving me to respond to the occasional crisis and keep an eye on the finances. Blessed by Linda's energetic leadership and a great staff, sales continued to rise steadily in the years to come.

Chapter 20 | SKI PATROL

If my ministry at Loon was going to include visiting accident victims, the natural starting point would be an injured skier's first contact: Loon's ski patrol. I needed to know them, and they needed to know me.

The smell of old wood and ski wax greeted me upon entering Loon's decades-old ski patrol shack (since replaced). To the left, two long picnic tables sat surrounded by empty chairs. A couple of red jackets hung from pegs on the wall, their owner's helmets tucked into the wooden cubbyholes above them. Dark blue plywood lockers lined the left half of the back wall and on the right, a window-like opening for the dispatcher, who sent patrollers to the scenes of accidents by either keying his mic or shouting at them through the open window. Two patrollers sat in a cast-off stuffed chair and sofa. A cold, black wood stove protruded from the right wall, an empty net hanging over it. When the temperatures fell, the net would hold pairs of wet gloves drying over the stove's heat.

I introduced myself to the dispatcher and the two patrollers and, as they filtered in from their assignments, the other three on duty. These were the weekday full-timers, their more numerous part-time counterparts showing up on weekends and holidays. A group of caring professionals highly committed to their job, they were also a tightly knit group, and remain so to this day.

A patroller's wages guaranteed that money wasn't their motive (a study on skipatrol.net called ski patrol "One of the worst paying jobs in America"[3]). For many, the attraction is the group itself, which has remained consistent over the years. As of this writing, I've been away from Loon for two years, but on a roster of fifty, there were only four names I didn't recognize. "We're tight," said one of them, clearly an understatement. Another thing that impressed me was their concern for those they treated. On more than one occasion, they'd go out of their way to check up on a seriously injured skier, even visiting them at the hospital.

I didn't admire the patrollers because they were perfect, and they'd be the first to reject such a label. Back then, their parties would start out mild and then frequently end up on the wild side when their beverage of choice entered the hot tub of opportunity. Joyce and I ensured a great time simply by leaving early. I remember raving about one such party, telling everyone how much we enjoyed it. Word got back to the host, who called me a couple of days later, sounding perplexed.

"When did you leave?" He asked.

"Around 9 o'clock."

"Oh, okay," he said, satisfied.

They invited us to a toga party. I'd never been to one before, but it sounded like fun—everybody donning swimsuits and wrapping themselves with a sheet or something. And that's what happened—well, almost. Everybody had the sheet, but later on in the party, the blonde girlfriend of one of the patrollers revealed that not everyone had the "other part."

"I *think* we'd better leave," I told Joyce as the pocket cameras started flashing.

Besides the parties, the language could be an issue. The words flying around the patrol shack in those days would make you think twice about introducing a child into the environment. Since then, following a few marriages and their numerous two-legged consequences, things have improved considerably.

After getting to know Loon's patrol, I volunteered for afternoon sweep. I was looking for ways to be of help, and they often needed people on weekdays, so it was a good fit. Two or three times a week I'd leave my office for the five-minute drive to Loon, change into my ski gear and hop a lift for the summit.

The Social Scene

As chaplain to the mountain, my ministry to the employees consisted primarily of befriending them and lending a listening ear. When I got home, to keep track of the important things in their lives, I'd make notes of our conversations and pray for them accordingly.

I attended Loon's employee parties and the patrol's social functions, soon discovering that people open up much more easily in a relaxed social setting than at work. The patrollers would gather in each other's homes for parties, at a lake home for the annual summer get-together, and in the mountain's bars after work.

As much as I liked the patrollers, we didn't have a lot in common. Not only was I twenty to thirty years older than most—a significant difference itself—but they shared a common mastery of a sport I was still learning. Most were experts who had skied since childhood while I was an intermediate who didn't start until he was forty. They're always following the Boston Red Sox, Celtics, and New England Patriots while I rarely pay attention to any of them. They love the outdoors, and I'm more of an indoor person. These differences didn't keep me from loving and admiring them, but they did prevent the natural bonding that occurs among those with common interests.

There was another reason for my discomfort at patrol social functions. The patrollers had a good balance between work and relaxation. I, on the other hand, was addicted to work and didn't know the meaning of relaxation. One day after sweep, a patrol couple invited me to drop by their home after work. Two or three others were there, and everybody was sitting around watching TV. I took a seat on the sofa. It could have been a relaxing time of talking and getting to know each other. Instead, after fifteen minutes, too restless to stay any longer, I left.

Not surprisingly, my overemphasis on work left me frequently stressed. At home, I'd snap at Joyce without even realizing it. Fortunately, for our marriage, she didn't let me get away with it and was quick to forgive. So where was God in this frenetic and stressful scenario? Trying to get through to me. Hurriedly driving to an appointment one day, tense and exhausted after several days of more work than time, an epiphany: "Skip, if this is what it means to be a Christian, who in their right mind would want it?" The question reverberated in my mind for the next few weeks, but nothing changed. It's too bad, for I missed out on both relationships that God could have used for his own purposes as well as friendships that would have enriched my life.

There was an emotional price to pay for substituting work for relationships. Leaping from the pages of my haphazardly kept diary was the repeated entry, "depressed."

From Ambassador to Patroller

I started at Loon envisioning myself as part of a church—a team of people reaching out to the mountain's employees and guests. When the church idea fizzled, I ended up as a solo missionary—not as much fun and much more exhausting. Seven years later, my energy gone and enthusiasm drained, I needed a break. With the approval of my Board, I took a three-month sabbatical, spending the time resting and studying ski resort ministries across the country. I intended to write a "how-to" book on the subject. Beginning with phone interviews, I finished with a four-week, six thousand mile tour of resorts out west in the company of Joyce. Not only did I return refreshed, but in the example of one of them (Brad Lartigue) I realized the need to be more closely connected with Loon's employees. Looking at the options, I settled on Loon's volunteer Ambassador program. Working as an auxiliary to the ski patrol, the Ambassadors focused on skier safety. From their stations at the top of lifts, they helped those who fell, gave directions, managed crowds at accident scenes and participated in sweep at the end of the day. Already working with the patrol, this job was a natural, and I quickly formed new friendships with Ambassadors closer to my age and interests. "You're one of us now" was the surprising announcement by a patroller upon seeing me in a red Ambassador's jacket. To someone who hadn't felt part of any group for the past eight years, those words had an almost narcotic effect. Strike out "almost" and fast-forward three years to a sunny, early spring day in 2001.

"Hey, Dan!"

Rivulets of water formed shallow canyons in the melting snow on top of the mountain. Walking around in the slush and surrounded by skiers reveling in the warm spring temperatures, a thought came to me. If faith comes through relationships, and the Ambassador's red jacket made me *part* of the patrol, how much better could I share my faith with patrollers if I was actually *one of them*. That was my conscious reasoning; my real motive would remain hidden for years.

If I was going to join the patrol, I needed to talk to its director, veteran Dan Healey. Clad in a Hawaiian shirt and black ski pants, Dan relaxed at a picnic table talking to two other patrollers. When they left, I walked over. "Hey, Dan," I asked brightly, "What would you think about me joining patrol?" He paused, the question clearly catching him by surprise.

"Well, you'd have to get some medical training."

"I know—I was thinking of an Emergency Medical Technician (EMT) course."

"Oh, okay. Why don't you get the medical stuff taken care of and we can talk about it then."

Dan's hesitancy wasn't surprising. I was an intermediate skier, and the patrol only hires experts. Knowing this, after completing my medical training, I planned to work on my skiing, expecting to spend a couple of years acquiring the necessary skills.

That summer I took an EMT course sponsored by the local ambulance company. After failing three times, I finally passed the practical exam and then successfully challenged the required Outdoor Emergency Care test. All I had to do now was to improve my skiing. I never had the chance. A month into the new season and critically short of mid-week patrollers, Jeff Scholtz, the new ski patrol director, called me up. "Skip, I could really use you on patrol during mid-weeks."

As I said to Joyce, "I don't feel ready, but there's no way I'm going to turn him down."

"We'll have to check out your skiing," said Jeff when I walked into his office. He assigned the task to veteran Chuck Wyman.

Chuck instructed me to ski down Angel Street, the mountain's steepest trail while he stood at the bottom and watched. Next came "the bumps", or moguls, which I always avoided and never skied. I didn't fall, but it wasn't a pretty sight.

"Well," Chuck reported to Jeff honestly and matter-of-factly, "I've seen worse."

Jeff called me into his office the next day.

"We're going to put you on, but your skiing needs to improve."

First Day

"Skip," said the dispatcher, finishing the assignments for morning sweep and studying the sheet in front of him, "there's a race on Coolidge, so you follow Mama and head for Coolidge. Anybody have any questions? Okay, let's go." Heavy wooden chairs scraped against the floor, and people stood up, grabbing jackets, helmets, gloves and fanny packs. They bolted out the door into the frosty December air, looking forward to a pleasure that never grows old: first tracks on freshly groomed snow. The sound of a snowmobile starting up and the dispatcher's voice echoing over patroller's two-way radios broke the morning stillness. There was work to do—trails to check and signs and bamboo (colored bamboo poles warning of obstacles) to put out and the required safety checks for each chairlift, but on days like this just getting to those assignments was a pleasure. For the next hour, the mountain was theirs or, I should say, ours. It was my first day on patrol. It would also turn out to be one of the most memorable of my life, but for reasons I never expected.

Outside, I walked over to Mama, a/k/a veteran patroller Jeff Martel, and clicked into my skis. We skied off, Mama heading down the left side of the trail and me following close behind on the right. After barely a hundred yards, he angled off to the left in a gracefully sweeping arc that then became a right-hand turn, heading directly across my path. The feel of my face against the shoulder of his jacket was the last thing I remember before we both went down in a jumble of arms and legs and mercifully releasing skis. I landed a few feet above him. Well, I thought, picking myself up and brushing off the snow, this is an auspicious beginning. Mama, rising to one knee and stretching uphill to retrieve one of his skis, looked up at me.

"Skip," he said wryly, "You shouldn't be so nervous."

"I'm not nervous," I replied truthfully. "I think this is funny."

Back in skiing mode, Mama took off first. Coolidge Street was straight ahead, so I was surprised to see him continue his interrupted turn and ski down Angel Street. Oh well, he had a radio and I didn't. Maybe something changed. I shrugged my shoulders and continued to Coolidge Street.

After waiting for Mama at the top of Coolidge for about fifteen minutes, the coordinator of the upcoming race roared up on his snowmobile. Using his radio on my behalf, he called Mama, telling me that he was waiting for me at the bottom of the gondola. When I arrived, there he was, standing patiently on the snow, skis in hand. Realizing by now a misunderstanding had occurred I didn't waste any time.

"Gumby said, 'Follow Mama and go to Coolidge,' and that's just what I did. Where did you go?"

"I had Basin Street, but you're right. He owes us one."

I realized later that Gumby (a/k/a John Gutherz) had meant for me to follow Mama *down* Basin Street *for* sweep and then for both of us to go to Coolidge *after* sweep. It was a simple misunderstanding and the harbinger of many more to come.

Entering the patrol shack, Mama and I checked in with dispatch before heading out to our assignment.

"Here," said Little Bear, the rookie now on dispatch, "you're going to need a radio and a fanny pack. Take mine."

Once outside, Mama grabbed a sled in case someone needed transporting to First Aid. We arrived at the top of Coolidge Street, now populated with racers in numbered bibs and skintight racing suits, stretching and talking with friends and coaches. Gates—colored pieces of cloth about the size of a man's chest held between two upright bamboo poles—zigzagged their way down the trail marking the course. With the starting time approaching, race officials took their positions.

"Testing, one, two, three, four," crackled the loudspeakers. Racers began lining up.

"You're not checked off for sleds," said Mama, "so why don't you wait at the bottom and I'll stay up here. If you get anything, just give me a call."

I skied down below the finish line and looked uphill. As soon as the announcer declared "racer on course," I started praying—earnestly and intensely—for every racer coming out of the starting gate. "Lord, please keep him safe… don't let anything happen… please, Lord, please keep him safe." Confession time: it wasn't them I was worried about, it was me. A freshly minted EMT, this was my first assignment and even with all my training, I lacked the confidence that only experience can bring. Instead of getting to know the contents of my fanny pack in case something *did* happen, I was too busy praying that something *wouldn't* happen.

Everything was going great—God was answering my prayers and the race was almost over. Thank you, Jesus! Then I noticed a few people gathered in a group nearby, talking to each other and occasionally looking in my direction. Finally, a couple of them left the group, walking toward me.

"I hurt my finger," said one, holding up the bloody appendage. Removing the protective gloves from the top of the fanny pack, I examined the wound. Then I went looking for the gauze and tape among the pack's many other contents. That took a while.

"Sure glad we're not in a hurry," said the friend.

A patroller, going uphill on a snowmobile, stopped some distance away. "You okay?" He shouted above his sputtering engine.

"Yep—all set."

I answered Mama's radio call and told him of the injury.

"Okay, why don't you take him down to the bottom. I'll call security."

After bandaging the finger, I strapped on the fanny pack and headed toward my skis. I tried clicking into the downhill ski first, but it tilted over on its side. Another attempt produced the same results. On steep terrain to begin with, the ski sat high centered on uneven ground, the tip and tail elevated, a canyon of air underneath the footpad. Every time I tried to get into it, the ski tilted. I couldn't believe this was happening. I slammed it down onto the snow, trying to create a platform. No luck. Becoming too flustered to think straight, I then broke a cardinal rule and clicked into my *uphill* ski first. Actually, just knowing I could still get *into* a ski was reassuring, but getting into the uncooperative downhill ski was now virtually impossible.

Observing the scene from up top, Mama skied down and, quickly spotting the trouble, tried to help by bracing his boot against the rebellious downhill ski. Normally, that would have worked, but because I was standing on my uphill ski, it didn't. Following repeated attempts, Mama said disgustedly, "I'll take him down. When you get your s—t together you can meet us at First Aid." The injured snowboarder, a young man in his early twenties, retrieved his snowboard and the two set off for the bottom.

Releasing the binding on my uphill ski, I carried both skis to the side of the trail, clicked in without trouble, then skied down to my injured patient waiting at the security pickup truck. "I'm sorry," I said, flushing with embarrassment, "first day on the job."

"That's okay," he replied sympathetically, " The first day can be hard for anyone."

We climbed into the bed of the pickup for the short ride to First Aid. After examining his finger, the nurse turned to him. "You're going to need several stitches. We don't have a doctor on duty today, but there's a clinic just down the street."

"Oh that's okay," the young Canadian replied. "I'll wait until I get back home where I can get it done for free."

"How soon will that be?" asked the nurse.

"Three or four days."

"If I were you, I wouldn't wait that long. You could end up losing it."

"Naw... I'll wait."

I was listening intently, and that last remark got my attention. "Hey look," I said, beginning to worry, "the money you'd save isn't going to mean a whole lot if you lose that finger. Why not get it taken care of—the clinic's just a few minutes away."

"Oh... I don't know. I think I'd rather wait."

"You're going to wait and take a chance on losing your finger just to save a few dollars?" I asked, my voice rising. Just then, the nurse interrupted us and led the patient back into the treatment area to fill out the accident report. One of the patrollers emerged in her place, the two of us alone in the waiting room. "Hey Skip, you were really in that guy's face," he said calmly.

"Did you hear him?" I responded incredulously, "He's risking the loss of his finger just to save a few dollars!"

"I know, and you're right, but you need to back off. That's his decision, not yours. You can't make it for him."

"Yeah," I said, feeling appropriately chastened. He was right. I expected to be learning things like this and appreciated his calm correction. I grabbed my skis, boarded the gondola, and headed up to the patrol shack. When I entered, Mama was sitting in a chair, a group of red jackets huddling around him.

"Hey, spastic" one of them yelled.

I don't know what I was expecting, but it wasn't that.

Seething inside, I remained silent. My first day on the job, I was thinking, and you send me out with no orientation or preparation and when I mess up you ridicule me publicly. The thought of quitting flashed through my mind, but I wasn't going to throw away months of medical training in a moment of anger. I eventually cooled down. At the end of the day, I clocked out and headed toward my car, surrounded by the quickly darkening winter sky. Mama pulled up alongside me in his pickup.

"Can I give you a ride?" He asked solicitously,

"No, but thanks, anyway."

I appreciated his thoughtfulness and the unspoken message it conveyed, "Hey, we still like you," at a time when it felt otherwise.

While I lacked the skill to get into skis on steep and uneven terrain, I later realized I should have expected the absence of any formal training. Since I had been at the mountain for twelve years and worked with patrol the whole time, it was natural for them to assume I knew more than I did. My one regret about that day was my anger. In a replay, I'd laugh off their "hey, spastic!" with a flippant comeback of some sort. That response, however, would have necessitated a degree of love and confidence I didn't yet possess.

After Day One

In the days that followed, veteran patrollers took their turns trying to help. Denny demonstrated how to get into skis on steep terrain, Mama, how to carve a turn and "Chief," (as in fire chief) how to do the bumps. Teaching new tricks to an almost sixty-year-old dog, however, was no easy matter. Their efforts were commendable, their failure, inevitable. Then, as if things weren't already bad enough, came "the trees."

The patrol leadership knew how I looked in the bumps; they didn't know how I could ski the woods or "trees," and assigned a patroller to take me down an expert tree trail. Never having skied them before, I was a complete beginner. Shortly after we started, my examiner went around a huge tree. I got halfway around and decided to join the environmental movement, becoming—literally—a "tree hugger." With my cheek pressed against the bark and the white cross on my red jacket displayed for the whole world to see, I muttered, "I *don't* think this is looking too good."

Sled Work

In the midst of all the skills I didn't possess, I discovered one that I *could* do and thoroughly enjoyed: running the patrol's toboggans, or "sleds." With tips from Gumby and others and friends willing to be my "patient," I became somewhat proficient and unusually confident. Preparing for my first test, I asked a patroller to go out with me and give me some feedback. "You did fine, Skip," he said when we finished, "but you've got to slow down. They're more interested in control than speed." I made a mental note and thanked him.

In the back room, three patrollers talked in hushed voices. It was clear none of them wanted the job of checking me out. Finally, Denny agreed. As he climbed into my sled he announced, "We'll go down Blue Ox and turn right up the work road." I'd been at Loon for twelve years, but Blue Ox was a trail I rarely skied, and I had no idea what he meant by the "work road." Too embarrassed to ask, I figured I'd just turn right at the first opportunity. We started out, and I kept reminding myself to keep the speed down. Frankly, it was boring. Running a sled had always been fun; this was *not* fun. Then, toward the bottom, I saw what looked like a trail coming down from the right and began turning. "Where are you going?" Denny yelled. I quickly checked myself from heading up a cut-through from a neighboring trail. "Pull over," he said, and after I stopped, "Okay, let's go in. You'll have to get up a head of steam to make it over the rise onto Lower Picked." A "head of steam?" Great, I thought to myself, the exam is over, no more going slow—fun, here we come! I easily made it over the rise and set my skis straight down Lower Picked, relishing the thought of a dramatic hockey stop in a shower of snow behind First Aid. Just as I was picking up speed, however, there came a frantic call from behind me, "drop the chain!" What? There's no *reason* to drop the chain. Chains are positioned in front of the bottom of the sled to slow it down if you're going over ice or it begins to run away. To drop it, the patroller simply lets go of a rope he's holding against the handle. We weren't on ice, and it wasn't running away, so it didn't make sense. I hesitated. "Drop the chain!" He shouted again, this time, more loudly. Well, he's the boss. I dropped the chain, and we slowed to a crawl. As we drew to a stop, I turned around to face him, both of us speaking at the same time,

"Out of control?" he asked.

"Scared?" said I.

I didn't pass.

My days on patrol were numbered. As if my lack of skiing skills and misunderstandings with other patrollers wasn't enough, a third factor entered the equation.

A Matter of Balance

Soon after joining the patrol, I decided new equipment would have a helpful impact on my skiing and purchased some used skis and boots off the clearance rack of a local ski shop. I was right—the new equipment had a great impact on my skiing—not, however, the kind I was hoping for.

Skiing Angel Street was always a little intimidating, which is why I skied it. Now, however, "A-Street" was becoming more and more difficult. Once, I came close to going off the trail into the woods and on another occasion took a nasty spill. For some reason, my skiing, instead of getting better, was getting worse. For the first time in twenty years on skis, I couldn't seem to get my balance. I mentioned it to a part-time patroller/ full-time occupational therapist.

"It's not unusual for people to have balance issues when they get older," she replied.

Not exactly what I wanted to hear.

After a while, I remembered that when I put on my new boots for the first time; I couldn't get "over" my skis (weighting the front of the skis is a critical component of control). Then it dawned on me that *all* my problems with balance began *after* getting my new equipment. I went back to boots and skis similar to my "old" ones and voila!—my balance returned, my confidence skyrocketed, and my skiing improved dramatically. Knowing little about ski equipment, I had inadvertently gone from a soft boot and stiff ski to a stiff boot and soft ski. It felt great to get my balance back. It would have felt even better if the season wasn't ending.

Not Quite the 'Comeback Kid'

Jeff saved my performance review for last, calling me into his office on Easter day. "You're a real hard worker," he started, "willing to do anything and never complaining, but when you came on board, it was with the understanding that your skiing needed to improve. I'm sorry; we're going to have to let you go. It isn't up to par."

I told him of my experience with the wrong equipment and asked if he'd take another look now that I was back in the right equipment. He paused for a minute, thinking it over.

"We could do that. Let me find someone to go out with you." He sent for the two supervisors. The first showed up, explaining that the second refused with the words, "he's an intermediate skier, and he'll never be anything else." Finally, Greg, another veteran, agreed to join us.

"If I do well, can I stay on?" I asked Jeff, hopefully.

"If you do well, yes," replied Jeff, "but you're going to have to wow them."

"Wow them?"

"Wow them."

We headed to Angel Street. The skier's left was ungroomed that year, and the heavy snowfall produced unusually high four-to-six foot moguls. Excited to have someone finally looking at me, I attacked these mini-mountains with a rare aggressiveness. After regrouping at the bottom of the mogul run, we continued down the trail until it divided. Greg, an engineer in real life, asked me to pick a route, refusing to offer any suggestions. It was smooth to the left, and to the right somewhat steeper and bumped up. I chose the left, and in so doing, revealed my comfort level to one very astute examiner.

We joined Jeff in his office. "You're an advanced intermediate," said Greg. "You went down the bumps on A-Street well—attacked them aggressively—but you were using stem christies instead of skiing them parallel."

"If you're skiing improves," said Jeff, "you're welcome back. The door is open."

Expecting to pull off a dramatic comeback, I was disappointed.

"I'm sixty years old," I told Jeff, "and this is the first time in my life I've ever been fired. But it's probably for the best. I'm called to minister to the entire mountain and not just ski patrol, so this will help me keep things in balance."

I went back to an Ambassador's jacket.

Chapter 21 | AFTERMATH

Shortly before each ski season begins, Loon's ski patrol gathers for a two-day "refresher." Stations are set up, and patrollers rotate through them, brushing up on their first aid skills for the upcoming winter and fulfilling requirements for their Outdoor Emergency Care (OEC) re-certifications. In the beginning, I'd spend a few days going over the OEC manual and had a pretty good grasp of the material by refresher time. After three years, however, with no expectation of re-joining patrol, it felt like a wasted effort.

"I don't know," I said to a patroller friend riding up on a chairlift, "I'm thinking of dropping my OEC certification."

"Why? You should keep it up," he responded.

"It just seems like a waste of time if I'm not getting back on patrol."

That was only one of the reasons. Confusing their jacket with their acceptance, I felt hurt by the absence of any clamor for my return. Those feelings should have provided a hint about my real motives for getting on patrol, but that knowledge was still in the future.

Expert for a Day

It was a clear and crisp day in mid-October, three years after leaving patrol. A man and his young son were playing next to me as I practiced my serve on our condominium's tennis courts. We struck up a conversation. About six feet tall and in his forties, Clark skied at Loon and, when not working as a pharmacist, helped with his son's racing program. As the talk turned to skiing, he mentioned that he taught himself how to carve turns, an essential skill for experts and one that Mama had tried unsuccessfully to teach me.

"You did? Would you teach me?" I asked.

"Sure, be glad to. I'll give you a call after the snow flies."

Now, two months later, on an overcast winter's day in early December, the phone rang.

"Skip, this is Clark. You free this morning? I thought we could work on carving."

We exited the gondola at the top of the mountain and skied down to a gently sloping area on a beginner's trail. "Okay," he said, "feet shoulder width apart."

Check.

"Arms out in front of you."

Check.

"Okay, go." I started gliding downhill.

101

"Good, now bend both ankles to the left." My feet initially wiggled in this new and awkward position before straightening out.

"Now to the right." I bent my ankles to the right, and my skis shot forward. I straightened them out and bent them to the left, and again, they shot forward. The next thing I knew, I was flying. Because of the parabolic shape of the skis, I found that by jamming my downhill ski against the snow while turning, the built-up torque acted like an accelerator. Skiing, which was always fun, was now thrilling. Finishing the run behind First Aid, I went bursting inside. Catching sight of the current patrol director I blurted out, "Andy, I just learned to ski, I just learned to ski!"

A couple of months later, patrol friend Jason and I skied down from the top of the mountain. Arriving behind First Aid, I lingered outside while he went in. One of those inside recounted what happened next.

"Hey guys," Jason said, "I just came down with Skip. First of all, I could barely keep up with him and secondly, he was looking pretty good."

Standing outside, I was surprised when four or five patrollers burst through the back door shouting congratulations and giving me "high fives." It felt good.

I kept working on the bumps and the trees, not with any hope of returning to patrol, but because I had made them a personal challenge. Finally, in the spring of 2006, five years after leaving patrol and due in no small part to the patient tutelage of patroller Andy Novick, I finally mastered the bumps, even collecting some unexpected compliments from ski instructors.

That same spring Peter, another friend of mine, called me up to join him for a day of skiing at nearby Cannon, a steep, rugged, wind-blown mountain. Coming off the summit, we stopped at the sign for the expert tree trail paralleling the mountain's tramway. "You want to?" He asked.

We started down. Just ahead of us was a small trim man in his fifties weaving around the trees as effortlessly as if he was walking. "How are you doing that so easily?" I asked.

"Plant your pole downhill in front of you and then ski around it," he replied. I did, and it made all the difference. When we reached the bottom, I had negotiated the entire trail with no falls (and no tree hugging).

My Plan—Not God's

I could now ski the bumps and the trees, but enjoyed neither. That was my goal. I finally attained it, and I never skied them again. For some people they're fun, but for me the joy of skiing was in going fast, and that wasn't going to happen in moguls and trees. If I had maintained the required OEC certification, I would have qualified to rejoin patrol, but by then I knew something I didn't know five years before: God never intended me to be on patrol in the first place. That was my idea, not his. It made so much sense at the time that I never ran it by my board of directors or anyone else. If I had, I'm sure things would have turned out differently. "In the multitude of counselors, there is safety," the Bible tells us (Proverbs 11:14). How did I know it wasn't God's plan? While the Bible clearly reveals God's will in moral decisions, in *amoral* decisions such as where to live, what job to pursue and in this case whether to join patrol, it's been my experience that God uses people and circumstances to guide us. Looking back, God tried, but I wasn't listening. Consider: from the time I first decided to join patrol, not one person ever told me they thought it was a good idea. On the other hand, two people—relative strangers—questioned both my decision and my motives. Besides people, God tried to reach me through circumstances. I failed the EMT practical test three times before finally passing, my first day on patrol was a disaster, there were frequent misunderstandings with the other patrollers, I purchased the wrong skis and boots, making my skiing worse instead of better, and I failed the sled test. Just in case I still didn't get the message, I was fired. The delayed enlightenment didn't end there. My motives, which at the time I thought were so spiritual and other-centered, turned out to be just the opposite.

Epiphany

Seven years after leaving patrol, Joyce and I had Jason over for dinner. He was sitting on the couch, and the two of us were reminiscing about my time on patrol when out of my mouth came the words, "I joined patrol because I wanted to be one of them."

I was stunned. Where did *that* come from? I had never even thought such a thing and more disturbingly, the words were true—an unearthed nugget mined from deep within my subconscious.

A minister friend of mine, who habitually goes into bars, buys a beer and engages his bar mates in conversation, once said of the practice, "I'll never be 'one of the guys.'" In the months to come, I couldn't figure out why those words kept coming back to me. Now it made sense. I would never be 'one of the guys' either, and consciously I knew it, but unconsciously, entering that stage of life when relationships become much more important, I was trying to do just that. For the most part, I was accepted in my roles as chaplain and ambassador. As the chaplain, I visited the seriously injured and kept patrollers informed of their condition. "I don't know," said one veteran patroller in mock disgust, "we call up the hospital to check on a patient, and they don't tell us anything, then Skip goes in, and they tell him everything." I went to their parties and occasionally joined them in the bar after work. I had found my niche. Now, however, that wasn't enough, and I ignored a cardinal rule of relationships: acceptance and role go together. A person who is acceptable as a colleague may be unacceptable as a boss. The person you've come to accept as a skilled mechanic would produce far different feelings if you went to your dentist's office and saw him bending over you with a drill. In the role of a chaplain and ambassador, I was accepted. Expecting that same acceptance to follow me as a patroller was simply unrealistic. God was using these guys to try to get through to me. Unfortunately, I wasn't listening.

I continued to help with sweep, following up on injured skiers and joining patrollers in the bar from time to time, but in my last few years, as leaders changed and e-mail lists were updated, with no OEC certification, a natural distancing occurred. I no longer received notices of their social functions and attended very few of their parties.

Looking back on my tenure with ski patrol leaves me with feelings of gratitude, amazement and regret. I'm grateful that in the three months I wore their red jacket, while my experiences may have been humiliating and hilarious, they were never harmful. Nobody got hurt because of a well-intentioned but misguided foray into a place I didn't belong. My worst mistake was arguing with a patient who risked losing his finger to save a few dollars (and who later changed his mind and had it stitched up). I could easily have made a medical error with far more serious consequences.

I'm amazed at the power of my unconscious needs to affect my conscious decisions. Here I am thinking I'm joining patrol for the spiritual welfare of the patrollers when I was really joining to meet my own need to belong. What I thought was about *them* was really about *me*.

I'm also amazed at how easily I can confuse my will with God's will. With all the time I spend in prayer and reading the Bible, you'd think I'd do a better job of discerning between the two. Apparently, however, as soon as my emotional needs enter the picture—vis-à-vis my first two marriages—I completely blow it. Fortunately, when God's in the picture, our mistakes aren't the end of the story. He would shortly redeem this one, too.

My one regret is dropping my OEC certification and the inevitable distancing that occurred with the patrollers. By seeing it only as a means of returning to patrol, I completely missed the unspoken message of the patroller on the chairlift who encouraged me to keep it.

Chapter 22 | "You're Not Going to Believe This"

Besides ministering to Loon's employees and guests, I was involved in a third outreach involving both of them: visiting injured skiers.

As soon as I arrived at Loon, I began visiting hospitalized guests, but the practice took a major leap forward one afternoon about eleven years later. After letting me go from Loon's patrol the previous season, Jeff Scholtz stopped me in the hallway outside his office.

"We need someone to follow-up on those we send to the hospital and let us know how they're doing. Would you be interested?"

Twist my arm. At the time, I was following up on only the most seriously injured. Now Jeff wanted me to include *everyone* sent to the hospital—serious or not—and inform patrol of their condition. To head off any HIPAA (Health Insurance Portability and Accountability Act) privacy concerns, Loon put me on their payroll for eight hours a month. For the next ten years, I followed up on everyone sent to the hospital. If their injuries were minor, they'd receive a call, if serious, a visit. Either way, I emailed my findings to the patrollers, first aid personnel and later to the ambulance crew. With the most seriously injured, Loon's General Manager and Director of Ski Operations also received emails. "That was huge," Jeff later commented on the follow-ups.

Helpful on several fronts, my visits to hospitalized skiers provided them with emotional and spiritual support, especially appreciated when the injuries were serious. In communicating a concern for the injured, the visits also helped Loon's public relations, and possibly resulted in less litigation. Lastly, my reports helped patrollers measure the efficacy of their treatment, provide closure for them and served as a conduit for messages of gratitude. I often had the pleasure of conveying those messages myself, but at other times the patient would ask, "Who was that who took care of me?" before their note of thanks appeared on the First Aid bulletin board.

Open Mouth, Insert Foot

It was the most bizarre injury ever to occur at Loon. According to the teenaged victim, he was bending over, lapping snow in the Snowboard Park, when a runaway ski sliced through his mouth, almost completely severing his tongue.

"It was the bloodiest accident scene I've ever witnessed," commented one patroller.

The owner of the runaway ski retrieved it, alerted ski patrol and then took off. Nobody saw him again.

I traveled the hour-and-a-half to Dartmouth-Hitchcock Medical Center about two or three times a week to visit with the boy's family and monitor his progress. They stitched the tongue together, and to ensure an adequate blood supply, kept their patient unconscious while employing a centuries-old treatment: leeches. Called "medicinal leeches" today, they draw the blood from the healthy part of the tongue into the reattached portion. It worked, producing a 90% recovery and leaving only the very tip not functioning properly.

Leaving Loon for Dartmouth-Hitchcock one day, a gondola attendant mentioned that because of the accident, they were checking people's skis to make sure the brakes weren't disabled. Skis have brakes that automatically deploy when the ski comes off the boot to prevent it from running away. Some Snowboard Park users deliberately disable their brakes to prevent them from interfering with tricks. The news that our gondola attendants were now checking for this left me impressed at their diligence, and shortly after entering the hospital room, I proudly announced what they were doing. No sooner had the words left my mouth, however, than a chill shot up my spine. I had just made Loon potentially liable for the boy's injuries ("It's Loon's fault for not checking the brakes on that runaway ski."). Driving home, I drew some comfort in the knowledge that they may well not sue, a hope that evaporated within days.

"The family is suing us," announced Ralph Lewis, Loon's Director of Ski Operations, at the next staff meeting.

I knew I had to tell Ralph and Rick Kelley, Loon's General Manager, about my slip-up. I entered Ralph's office that afternoon and broke the news. About 5'10" tall, of trim, athletic build, with an easy smile and short gray/white hair, Ralph's gift for listening, calm demeanor and concern for employees made him a popular member of Loon's senior management. I probably visited him more frequently than anyone else and always emerged from his office feeling better than when I entered. I told him what I had said.

"I wouldn't worry about it," Ralph said dismissively, "people are always trying to sue us."

Relieved, I walked out of Ralph's office and headed for Rick's. His door was ajar and I was about to enter when I thought, "wait a minute. Ralph said there was no need to worry. Why run the risk of getting Rick upset about something that's not going to happen?" Retracing my steps, I left the building.

Two Years Later

"Skip," said Mama, "when you look at the accident reports, don't put your initials at the bottom. Lawyers who look at them want to know what they mean, and it might cause problems." That was just the beginning. I started receiving other requests relating to my follow-ups. The family was suing us. Unable to find any other reason to justify their suit, they recalled a Loon employee telling them about Loon's practice of checking bindings. At $150 an hour, Loon's lawyers had already run up a bill close to $20,000 in the discovery process. The news sickened me.

With more important things on his plate than a worried chaplain, Ralph had long since forgotten our conversation. At the time, management was thinking someone from Lift Operations had said the incriminating words. Heading for the administration building, I approached Rick as he was leaving.

"Do you have a minute?" I asked

"Sure," he replied pleasantly. Of medium height, trim build and balding head garlanded by short, gray-white hair, we had been friends for years. Even when disagreeing with some of his decisions, I've always admired Rick. You can't help but be impressed with a man who, without a college education, started as a lift attendant and worked his way up to be the longest serving General Manager in Loon's history. His relaxed and unflappable temperament is well suited to an industry where uncontrollable weather patterns can wreak havoc on carefully crafted budgets. At those times when rain was driving away thousands of potential skiers, his "let's make the best of this" attitude protected employee morale. "We can't do anything about the weather," he'd say, "but we can provide the best possible product so that our guests want to return."

Standing side by side with him on the steps of the Admin building, I started. "I'm the one responsible for telling the family we were checking the brakes on people's skis. I've been visiting people for twenty years. I know what to say and what not to say. I just blew it."

Quiet by nature, he didn't respond with any derogatory remark or reprimand as I repeated my confession. He didn't need to say anything. His grimace and tightened lips said it for him. "Well, okay," he replied as we parted.

There proceeded a series of orders effectively pulling the rug out from underneath my follow-ups, the most damaging prohibiting my e-mails in order to reduce the written records vulnerable to subpoena. I could phone the patrollers and others, but with the number of follow-ups, the time required to reach everyone by phone made it impractical. Rick's reasoning was understandable. Since the senders and receivers of e-mails could both be deposed, at $150 an hour they'd attract lawyer's fees like bees to honey. Rick was a "bottom line" person whose goal was to make certain that Loon was profitable. Committed to eliminating any unnecessary expense, I could hardly blame him for protecting the mountain against the potentially enormous legal costs of my e-mails.

One of my reasons for the follow-ups was to discourage lawsuits. The news that I was now responsible for one left me devastated. The patrollers, first aid personnel and ambulance crew who received my updates were generous with their thanks, confirming my contribution to the Loon community when my real reason for being there—to share the Gospel—was considered of little importance. With the rug pulled out from underneath the follow-ups, feelings of uselessness now accompanied my guilt. Thoughts of resigning flitted through my mind. My successor, however, was preparing to move to Loon to work with me on a nine-month transition of leadership. There'd be no resigning.

There was one thing I could do, however. If my actions were costing Loon money, then I could reimburse them. They shouldn't have to pay for my mistake. We'd be selling our home and were going to put the proceeds toward my retirement, but I could put those monies towards Loon's legal fees. I told Joyce, and she appeared to take it well, but a friend later confided that the news put her in tears for fear of what it would do to our retirement plans. I sat down with her, and we worked out a compromise. Instead of the entire proceeds from the house going to Loon, we'd limit it to $30,000. Retirement would be tight, but we could live with it. My Board of Trustees didn't agree with me, but I was adamant. It was the least I could do. Loon's management wouldn't know about it until they got the check.

Guilt kept me away from Loon's administration building for the next month. Finally realizing that mistake or no mistake I was still the chaplain and had a job to do, I walked into Admin and found Ralph in his office. We started talking, and I asked how things were going with the suit.

"You wouldn't believe what just happened," he replied. "Our snowboard park crew was out at Park City, Utah for their annual competition. As the grooming machines were constructing the jumps, one of our guys happened to mention to a bystander, 'We've got to be pretty careful in building parks these days ever since that accident a couple of years ago.'

"'You mean the one where the ski went through the guy's mouth?' replied the bystander.

"'You know about that?' said our park guy.

"'I was there.'

"'You were?'

"'Yep.'

"'Well,' continued the employee, 'apparently the kid was lapping up snow when a runaway ski went through his mouth, almost completely severing his tongue.'

"'Oh, no' replied the stranger, 'that's not what happened at all.'

"'It isn't?'

"'Nope. The kid who was injured was lying on his back at the bottom of the jump while his friends jumped over him. His friend on the snowboard made it over fine, but when his skiing buddy hit the lip of the jump, one of the skis pre-released and ended up going through his mouth.'

"'Would you be willing to sign a statement to that effect for our lawyers?'

"'Of course.'"

The mountain now had the basis for a countersuit to recover their legal expenses.

I was talking with Rick Kelley shortly afterward. "What are the chances of something like that happening?" I asked.

"Sometimes you just get lucky," he replied.

Yes, I thought, and sometimes God works miracles.

Chapter 23 | MARCUS

Earle Morse, one-half of the clergy couple succeeding me at Sugarloaf, called me one afternoon. "Skip, there's a part of me who doesn't want to give you this guy's name because we'd like him to take over for us when we retire, but you're closer to that than we are, so here goes. I'm talking about Marcus Corey. He has a condominium up here at Sugarloaf and recently sponsored a Christian snowboard video that packed one-hundred-and-fifty teenagers into the chapel. He's working full-time for Moose River Outpost, a Christian camp in Jackman, Maine, and career-wise has reached a dead-end. I think he might be interested in Loon."

Shortly before Earle called, with retirement two years away and having no one to take my place, I announced in our quarterly newsletter that the ministry might fold upon my retirement. Within two weeks, I received the names of three potential successors.

Marcus and I became acquainted through emails and phone calls. I discovered he started skiing as a toddler and had recently taken up snowboarding. He loved the outdoors, was captain of his high school football team, graduated from Bible school, grew up in a Christian family with a dad who's a part-time lay minister, and was blessed with a supportive wife and three small children. At Moose River Outpost, he directed their Conference and Retreat program, expanding it from a hundred to over two thousand yearly guests. It wasn't long before I was exclaiming, "Marcus, you're a better fit for this place than I am!"

My impression of Marcus only improved after we met. At 6'3" tall, 250 pounds and with a ruddy complexion, he looked every bit the outdoorsman, his round face, shortly cropped beard, quick smile and exuberant voice offsetting his rugged appearance. "Hey buddy, how're you doing?" he'd almost shout with joy upon seeing you. A real "people magnet," his greeting alone made you feel like the most important person in the world. Pointing to his dynamic personality and vibrant faith in Christ, a staff member of the high school he attended remarked, "He influenced the whole school when he was there."

That summer, I invited Marcus and Heidi to visit Loon over a weekend, providing them with a hotel room for at least some personal time away from the kids, if not the precursor to a permanent move. "When we were driving to Loon," Marcus told me afterward, "Heidi and I were talking, and my attitude was, 'I'm willing to take a look, but I've got no interest in pastoring a church that just happens to be in a resort.' Then, when we attended your service and saw what you were doing, well, it was a pretty quiet ride home."

I was excited at the possibility of Marcus succeeding me, and we continued communicating. While things seemed to be falling into place, I had yet to receive a commitment from him. Finally, at the end of November, I called. After exchanging pleasantries and details on his upcoming winter visit, I put the question to him.

"Marcus, we've talked a lot about you coming to Loon, but you've not said anything definite. Are you interested?"

"Yep," came the subdued reply.

"So you agree to be my successor?"

"Yep," he said in a matter-of-fact tone without the enthusiasm that's typically Marcus. It wasn't until several weeks after he moved to Lincoln that I found out why.

The Hiker

In early September, boxes of belongings littered the wrap-around porch of Marcus' rented home just blocks from Lincoln's busy Main Street. The late afternoon sun was setting, and shadows were appearing when he took a break from moving to sit on the porch and chat with one of his new neighbors. On the sidewalk about fifty feet away, a young man walked in the approaching darkness, plastic bags of groceries dangling from his hands. "Hey," he shouted up at them, "do you know where the AT [Appalachian Trail] hostel is?"

"Don't ask me," replied Marcus, "I just moved here from Maine."

There was a brief silence. Then, in words punctuated by disbelief, "Is that you, Marcus?"

The last time the two had seen each other was at a church camp fifteen years earlier when both were high school students. A few years later, the young man entered Bible school, only to be expelled after refusing to recant a paper advocating the legalization of marijuana. Turning his back on God, a process that likely began before his dismissal, he was now re-examining that relationship.

As they talked and caught up on each other's lives, the young man posed a question.

"What do you think about marijuana?"

"Well," said Marcus, "We've all got pacifiers. Mine is buffalo wild wings and the NFL. I don't think it makes any difference what you're pacifier is, nothing satisfies like God."

The hiker paused. "I've got some friends back at the hostel. Is it all right if I bring them over?"

"Sure," said Marcus beaming, "Why don't you join us for dinner?"

Several hikers joined the Corey family that evening. Marcus and Heidi talked one of them, a girl who was ill, into staying a few days until she was feeling better.

For those who might question his response to the question about marijuana, Marcus wasn't about to give a discourse on the evils of drugs to a young man whose greatest need at the time was simply for his acceptance.

Transition

Our ministry could provide Marcus' housing for a nine-month transition period, but he would need a full-time job for his other expenses.

After talking with Loon's ski patrol director, Marcus took an OEC course in preparation for a promised full-time position on patrol. Then came an unexpected budget cut, and the typically high return of former patrollers, and the promised job disappeared. No sooner had Marcus told me the news than I received an email. Loon was looking for a manager for their Mountain Host program. For a people-lover like Marcus this would be ideal, I thought, and excitedly forwarded the email to him. Blazing through the required interviews, Marcus secured the position, providing close connections with not only Loon's employees, but also its management and guests.

A few weeks after he arrived, Marcus and I were talking in his living room when the reason for his initial reluctance to commit himself to the ministry surfaced.

"What if I fail?" He asked, genuinely concerned.

"It's not your ministry to begin with," I replied. From inception to growth, I viewed the ministries at Sugarloaf and now Loon as God's doing and not mine. They belonged to Him, and not me. The response seemed to satisfy him.

Our nine-month transition period was supposed to be a time for me to train Marcus, but one afternoon those roles were reversed. Deep in conversation, Marcus and I were walking from the parking lot toward the gondola building when we passed a man coming toward us balancing four pairs of skis on his shoulders. In mid-sentence, I suddenly realized I was alone. Turning around, I saw Marcus a few feet away, lifting a couple of pairs of skis from the man's shoulders. Uh, Skip... maybe you should help? I caught up with them before they had gone too far and took the guest's third pair of skis. By the time we reached the man's car, Marcus' thoughtfulness and our animated conversation led to an unexpected announcement: "I'll see you Sunday morning," said our new friend.

Marcus' energetic personality, spiritual maturity, and love for people, soon made it clear that he was as called to take over the Loon ministry as I was called to start it. Interestingly, his popularity also created a problem with the local police. So many people were coming and going from his house for après ski gatherings, parties, open houses, Bible studies and Sunday afternoon football that they had to remind him of the town's ban on street parking.

After I left Loon and Marcus took over, the ministry exploded, reflecting the energy and passion of its new leader. Attendance at both winter and summer services increased significantly. He also attracted a growing number of locals. Drawn by both his love of God and his love for them, so many townspeople began showing up at the mountaintop services that Marcus was compelled to start holding services just for them. The community center became their meeting place, providing room for both worship services and a church school program led by his wife, Heidi.

Marcus' ministry continued to expand. With attendance at local services growing, they sponsored a successful Vacation Bible School program during the summer of 2015. An outreach on the following Halloween raised Sunday school attendance from thirty-five to fifty. The appearance of full-time volunteers and interns added significantly to Loon Mountain Ministry (LMM) programming, enabling them to offer an action-packed youth ministry in the summer and expanded opportunities in the winter. Through the generosity of church members Scott and Sharon Bartlett, Marcus and Heidi acquired a home large enough for both their family's needs and the needs of the ministry. Complete with a large room for group activities and apartment-like housing for interns; this unexpected provision left Marcus exclaiming, "It feels like I'm riding on the 'God-Coaster,' yelling at the top of my lungs with arms in the air wondering what's next."

Just recently, Marcus took up ski tuning as a way of developing relationships with snowboarders and skiers. "I love it," he says, "With ADD [Attention Deficit Disorder] I'm not a good listener. Tuning their skis takes care of my restlessness so I *can* listen to them—it's great!"

In the summer of 2015, LMM successfully sponsored their first evening of mountaintop music and worship. Called "Wondermount," Marcus wrote later in a newsletter, "Who wouldn't want to praise the maker of heaven and earth as the large orange ball in the sky sinks behind a hillside curtain of deep blues and greens?"

LMM continues to expand, and as I write these words, Marcus just received the go-ahead from the Board of Directors to hire a full-time associate starting in the summer of 2016.

From ? To !

In my last years at Loon, I didn't feel I was accomplishing much. There were no conversions that I knew of and, with one exception, nobody's faith was coming alive. The question wasn't burdensome. I knew I was supposed to be there, enjoyed the people I was working with, and the job was never boring. It wasn't until Marcus appeared that I viewed those years of "holding down the fort," to be important.

When Marcus and I were working together, it wasn't unusual to be standing next to him when someone would come up and rave about his ministry. Uncomfortable with their adulation in my presence, Marcus anxiously deflected the attention my way, pointing out what *I* had done. I'd grin and think to myself, "not necessary, Marcus, not necessary," and it wasn't. In those beginning months, he didn't realize it, but the better he did, the better I felt. Every one of his successes increased the value of my contribution in maintaining a healthy ministry for him to take over.

Some might wonder if Marcus' unbridled popularity kindled any feelings of jealousy. Not... one... bit, and for two reasons. First, as already mentioned I viewed Loon as God's ministry and not mine. Beginning with Phil Gravink's unprecedented welcome, it was obvious Someone was preparing the way for me. Yes, my role was important and necessary, but that didn't make it "my ministry" any more than a commercial pilot at the controls of his plane can claim to own the airline that employs him.

Secondly, until Marcus appeared, it looked like the ministry would fold upon my retirement. His appearance reversed that picture. Without knowing it, Marcus replaced the potential sadness of a funeral with the joy of a birth.

Chapter 24 | # LOOKING BACK AND GOING FORWARD

At a thoughtful and generous retirement party hosted by Loon Mountain in the spring of 2013, Joyce and I received ski passes, a framed trail map and a couple of cards with my picture on the front. The trail map, its matting liberally decorated with signatures, along with the cards containing notes and more signatures, hangs today on the wall of my home office, the names conjuring up familiar faces and kindling a host of warm memories.

Leaving Loon brought feelings of both joy and sorrow. The excitement of the solo missionary gig had long since given way to a spiritual isolation gradually moving my extrovert/introvert dial from a slight extrovert to a definite introvert. After twenty-two years of fringe relationships, the thought of again belonging to a church family, surrounded by people who unabashedly loved Jesus, was taking on the aura of a homecoming. Those feelings weren't hidden. In the patrol shack at the end of the winter, a seasoned patroller commented, "This is the first time I've seen you laugh."

The downside of retiring was that I'd be leaving a large group of friends—the kind of people who cause you to light up inside when you see them. I'll never forget the startling announcement by one of them.

"Thank-you for helping me find my faith again. I've gone back to church," said the mid-manager I had known for years. Her words came as a complete surprise. We had never talked about anything spiritual.

Most employees didn't share my faith, but they did share my life, and I thoroughly enjoyed working with them. They were a great bunch of people who made Loon a fun place to work, and I came to love them. Because of this, however, the finality of this good-bye lengthened the feelings of depression normally accompanying the end of a ski season.

A Glance in the Rearview Mirror

Looking back over my life from youth to retirement, I'm grateful. While I didn't grow up in a close family, ours was a stable one, no small blessing in these days of fifty percent divorce rates. I grew up wanting to please my dad, and when encountering youthful temptations, it made all the difference. "What if I go ahead, and the church finds out? There's no way I'd ever want to hurt him like that." Reflecting on those experiences, I'm grateful for such a father, and a bit more understanding of those who aren't so blessed. Dad and I weren't close, and his lack of attention in my younger years led to an embarrassingly stubborn resentment later on, but whenever a crisis arose, I didn't have to ask twice for his help.

I'm also grateful for my spiritual upbringing. My faith has grown and changed considerably since those early years, but it's hard to imagine a childhood absent the knowledge of God's love and certainty that he had a purpose for my life. Before "do-it-yourself" value systems became so popular, the Judeo-Christian faith was the commonly accepted norm. Its "dos and don'ts" established internal boundaries and promoted external behavior that left me both happy and secure. While our nation back then had its sins, racism being the most easily fingered, it's interesting to note that the very moral environment in which this aberration survived was also responsible for its demise. Preceding the name Martin Luther King is the title "Reverend," pointing to a Judeo-Christian heritage that ultimately overturned racism in the public arena and to the One who does the same in our personal lives.

Professionally, I'm grateful for God launching me into an exciting, freelance evangelistic ministry with youth. It was both a barrel of fun and spiritually fruitful. He then led me into a decade of being a "regular minister" where churches grew as the faith of their members came alive. After my impulsiveness resulted in the humiliating embarrassment of two divorces, he turned my career in a direction I would never have envisioned that first Easter on top of Sugarloaf. Then, following eight years at the "Loaf," he led me to Loon Mountain, where I spent the next twenty-three.

In-between Sugarloaf and Loon, God introduced me to a woman and to my first experience of a marriage where conflicts are rare, and harmony reigns. For example, in the beginning years of our marriage, Monday was "our day." If other responsibilities interfered one week, Joyce and I would take *two* days the next week, often at a friend's cabin an hour away. Being alone for seven years, I still had a need for solitude and about once a month would take a day or two for myself—at least in the beginning. Then one day, several months into our marriage, I was in a bad mood. Without realizing it, I snapped at Joyce for what must have been the umpteenth time. A few minutes later, she came up to me.

"Do you need some time by yourself?"

She didn't yell, and there was no reprimand for the way I was talking to her, both of which would have been justified. It was just a simple question, and it stopped me in my tracks.

"You know," I said after a moment, "I think I do."

"'Okay,' she continued, 'Monday and Tuesday are supposed to be for us, but you need them more than I do, so why don't you go to the cabin and have some 'alone time'"?

Because of Joyce, I had the emotional strength to dive into starting a ministry in a new community, our marriage enabling me to meet new people and launch new ideas without getting too upset when encountering the occasional rejection and failure. Besides being a beautiful woman and a great cook, she's one of the most emotionally mature, gentle, compassionate, and steady-as-a-rock people I've ever met. Calling her a "blessing" is an understatement.

Past Failures in a New Light

I'm also grateful for my failures while in New Hampshire, for reasons hidden from me at the time. In the early years, a couple approached me at the end of one of our summer services. "We're from Waterville Valley, What are the chances of holding services there?"

We started that winter, meeting at the top of the Valley Run trail. The setting provided breathtaking views of the valley and its distant mountains. Good-sized crowds appeared in the first five years. Then the mountain shortened the chairlift so that it no longer went all the way to the top. Instead of being at the top of the run, we now stood on the side of the trail a third of the way down. Instead of the beautiful view of the valley below, we were looking at a chairlift about a hundred feet away. Not the "aesthetically rewarding experience" people are seeking. Attendance nose-dived. The numbers took another hit the next year when the mountain replaced my large red and white sandwich board sign in the base area with one much smaller, affixed to a pole so tall that no one noticed it. Following three more seasons of declining numbers, I finally called a halt.

My experience at Waterville Valley was a lesson learned. Developing the relationships necessary to establish a ministry requires two things: availability and accessibility. Neither is possible for a person commuting from a half-hour away.

While the ministry at Waterville Valley ultimately failed, the employees and residents I met there provided several rewarding memories. Realtor Bill Gorwood comes to mind, one of three people I had the privilege of supporting during their battles with cancer.

"Bill's going down to Massachusetts General in Boston for treatments," announced Debbie, the Realty's secretary. Knowing Bill from earlier visits, I gave him a call.

"'Hello Bill, Skip Schwarz here. Look, I heard you're heading down to Boston for treatments and will be there for a few days. Would it be okay if I skipped down to visit you? Oh, okay, good. I'll check with you beforehand to make sure I'm coming down at a good time.'" I had occasion to visit Bill several times during his stays in Boston. Having known him for some time, I felt comfortable in sharing the Gospel with him during one of my early visits. He wasn't ready, so I left it in God's hands and continued to pray.

Some months and a few visits later, his battle was ending. He was still alert when Debbie, the Realty's secretary and a committed Christian herself, called me up. "He could go any day now. If you want to see him, it should be soon. I'll be praying." As I drove down to Boston, I recalled past visits and their lack of privacy. Someone was always in his room, if not friends, then the medical staff. That would pose problems with my anticipated conversation. I arrived in the early evening to a darkened room, brightened only by the fluorescent light over the head of his bed. A few people were present when I entered. Within minutes, however, everyone, even the nurses, left.

"Bill, some time ago I shared with you how you can receive God's gift of eternal life. Do you have any questions about that?" He shook his head. "Is that a decision you're ready to make?" "Yes," he whispered.

We prayed together.

He passed away the next day.

Besides the demise of the ministry at Waterville Valley, there were other disappointments. The idea of training interns for Loon seemed like a natural. Besides providing extra help, they might even catch the vision and start ministries of their own. After sending out publicity to New England seminaries and even paying for an ad in a national religious magazine, I sat back and waited for responses to pour in. They never came.

Very few Loon employees could attend our regular Sunday morning services because of their work schedules, so we started a service just for them, held after the mountain closed on Sunday afternoons and providing pizza as an extra inducement. It lasted four weeks.

It was only later that I realized God's "no" was to protect his "yes." When I landed at Loon, I was pushing fifty. In those beginning years, my energy kept up with my enthusiasm, yet as the fifties turned into the sixties, the inevitable happened. My physical energy decreased, while my mind sailed blissfully on, formulating ideas more appropriate for someone twenty and thirty years younger. Simply put, God prevented new responsibilities from sapping the energy needed to sustain those he had already given me.

Only after Waterville Valley ended did a new ministry appear, and it wasn't even my idea. Following a Christmas Eve candlelight service, several workers from South Africa asked me to start a weekly Bible study for them. We held it in one of their rooms, and it was a great time, with every study preceded by a simple meal provided by Joyce. We'd sing a few songs, share our lives with each other and discuss a Bible passage together. Joyce and I remained in touch with some of them for years to come.

Taking a Handoff for a Touchdown

I thank God for my successors at both Sugarloaf and Loon. Following me at Sugarloaf were Earle and Pam Morse, a clergy couple who moved from nearby Farmington to turn the winter ministry at Sugarloaf into a full-time year-round church; something I could never have done. It was a winning move for the entire family. Earl branched out into his own successful interior decorating business and Pam became known as a gifted preacher and speaker. I've never heard a sermon of hers that didn't leave me enlightened. Their sons Ben and Sam grew up to be prodigious skiers as well as strong men of faith, sharing the Gospel with other students through Christian Athlete Training, a popular outreach started for their classmates at Carrabassett Valley Academy.

With Earle and Pam following me at Sugarloaf, and Marcus at Loon, what I have frequently said about Sugarloaf I can now say about both mountains: the two best things I did were to come and to go.

Going Forward

Preaching is something I enjoyed for over a half-century. Mining the nuggets of God's word to strengthen people's faith was thrilling. Within a year of retiring, however, I lost all interest, declining opportunities to preach that I would have normally jumped at. I never saw it coming. Nor did I ever envision that an interest in writing would take its place. Most of us have known couples who started out hating each other only to fall in love. That's writing and me. It started with my guilt-motivated (for taking three months off work) 1997 sabbatical plans to write a "how-to" book on ski ministries. Discovering that the Southern Baptists were already experts at it, I shelved the idea. Or rather, I *tried* to. My wife wouldn't let me. While not nagging, she continued to ask about "the book." From time to time, others would, too. The dike broke one evening at a conference of resort ministers in Lake Tahoe, California. "I wish somebody would write a book about ski ministries," declared a young minister about to embark on one, "I could really use it." It was all my lovely wife could do to keep from burying her elbow in my side. "Okay," I thought, "I got the message. I'll do it, but I don't want to."

I didn't know the first thing about writing, so I took some online courses and attended some workshops. In the process, the strangest thing happened:

I fell in love. Reluctance gave way to acceptance and then to pleasure and now passion. The book that began as a "how to," transformed itself into a memoir. Then, quickly becoming bored with my own story, I remembered my wife's words in '97 as I was making phone calls to resort ministers around the country: "I've never seen you this excited about ministry since we first came to Loon." If those stories inspired me, I thought, they might do the same for others.

In the following pages, you'll meet a man who was excelling in seminary and on track to enter a Ph.D. program when his marriage fell apart. Another man worked as a farmhand because "the advantage of working on a farm is that the cows don't care if you're stoned." A third almost drowned on two separate occasions before excelling so much as a swimmer that he now teaches lifeguards. Besides ministering at ski resorts, all of us share other similarities: we've all received Christ's forgiveness, transferred ownership of our lives to him, and rejoice when others do the same. We're all ordinary men, but as these pages reveal, we're following an extraordinary God. I believe his greatest miracles are the lives he's changed. Mine is one of them, and you're about to meet many more.

The was the Sugarloaf chapel as it looked in the 80's. Named after Richard Bell, a beloved member of the early Sugarloaf community, the chapel hosted both our services and Catholic masses.

Photographs

Joseph Pojmanski—God used his forgiveness to turn my life around. We reconnected in 2014 and have been friends ever since.

Dating Days—with Joyce in the summer of 1989.

Bar Harbor Summer Evangelism Project with host pastor Rev. Mark Williams and family. David Hall, who came to Christ after we met him on the streets, is to the right of me. Others are a mix of project members and friends.

Daughters in 1985. Leanne was 11 and Lori, 15.

Picture taken of me in 1996 for the British Broadcasting Corporation. Made into a large poster, it hung in the Summit Café at Loon Mountain for several years.

Parents and Sisters, 1984. Oldest sister Christie, in the middle, is the public defender, and Lynette, on the right, the counselor.

Doctor of Ministry Group. Dr. Norman Thomas, the faculty member from Boston University, is to the right of me. Getting me off to a good start in resort ministris was Jack Grenfell, seated at the far right. He was the one who suggested I tour the country to visit and study the ministries already operating.

The 1984 Inter-Varsity Christian Fellowship summer evangelism project on Martha's Vineyard. It was my first evangelism project. Many of our project members came from Eastern Mennonite College. They so impressed me that to this day my heart smiles whenever I meet a Mennonnite.

The amphitheater at Loon Mountain, site of our summer services.

Group picture at the end of one of our Downhill Worship services at Loon Mountain.

DANN MASTERS

Chapter 1 | "The Poorest Family in Town"

It wasn't from a sense of entitlement. I requested a three-month sabbatical in the spring of 1997 out of desperation. I knew the symptoms: lack of energy, no enthusiasm, going through the motions while counting the Sundays until the season ends. Burned out after seven years at New Hampshire's largest ski resort, I needed a break. With a friend filling in on Columbus Day weekend, I chose the time between mid-September and mid-December, Loon Mountain's off-season. Feeling guilty over such a long break from work, I decided on a project: I'd write a handbook on starting ski ministries. Interviewing ministers at other ski resorts would be the natural beginning point, so I compiled a list of eighteen. The plan? I'd interview them over the phone and then visit several during a four-week tour out west.

While my body remained in the woods of New Hampshire, my telephone (old-fashioned landline in those days) took me all around the country. One moment I'd be in Lake Tahoe, then Alaska, and then Colorado. Armed with a list of questions, I asked my subjects about their ministries—how they started—what worked and didn't work—what were the challenges they faced? I wanted to know their stories—to connect with them—ostensibly to write a book, but there soon emerged a deeper motivation. Out of touch with my feelings—a malady common to my gender—the light dawned when an interviewee mentioned a frequent problem in resort ministry.

"Because we deal with a transient population and the lack of permanent relationships," he began, "emotional isolation is a big problem among resort ministers." It was a big problem with me. In my interviews, however, camaraderie replaced isolation, and inspiration removed exhaustion.

Six weeks later, and after hours of telephone conversations, Joyce and I boarded a plane for our month-long tour out west.

Arrival

The afternoon sky was blue; the November air teasingly crisp when the thump of the plane's tires hit the runway of Las Vegas International Airport. I stared out the window at an endless row of distant hangars rushing by the plane's wingtips.

"I'm sorry," said the clerk at the rental car counter, "we don't have any compacts available. Would a free upgrade to a Dodge Stratus be okay?" I tried not to act too disappointed as I leapt for joy inside. It was exactly my hope. With six thousand miles ahead of us, we *needed* the larger car we couldn't afford to reserve.

Weaving along the remote mountain highway from Taos to Angel Fire, New Mexico, I kept a respectful distance from the guardrail and steep drop-off on my right. Like most destination resorts, Angel Fire sits like an island of civilization in the middle of nowhere, its inhabitants drawn to a barren mountainside transformed into a skiing mecca in the winter and a golfer's paradise in the summer. Abutting the mountain is a close-knit community of residents and second-home owners, joined in 1986 by Rev. Dann Masters and his family. Having just served as the interim Senior Pastor of a large multi-staffed church in Dallas, Texas, Dann accepted a call to Angel Fire Baptist Church, a new church with a much smaller (six-member) congregation. However, by the time Joyce and I visited—almost twelve years later—the church had grown to over two hundred.

We arrived for our meeting at the white-stucco church on a Saturday morning. Walking through the open door into his office, Dann rose from behind his desk and came around to greet us, offering a friendly smile and a soft "welcome." Dressed in a light brown suit and tie, his casual and relaxed demeanor quickly created an atmosphere of friendly informality. Tall and slim, he looked like the stereotypical basketball player or long-distance runner. As we took our seats, I felt so much at home that I was briefly tempted to put my feet on his desk. Instead of my feet, I placed the tape recorder on his desk, and we settled into our seats.

I began by asking Dann to describe his childhood. His calm demeanor gave little indication of the traumatic story awaiting me. Beginning with this interview, I was to hear of the poverty of his childhood, of a family broken by alcoholism and death, of his own unwanted divorce and subsequent rejection, and his struggle with a life-long illness. From these hardships, however, there emerged a creative personality, a childhood encounter with God, a gifted musician, a wife and daughter sent from heaven, an unexpected healing and a ministry introducing scores of people to a life-giving relationship with Christ.

The Shotgun House

Little Dann's feelings of relief began as soon as his uncle's bronze and white fifty-seven Chevy pulled into the driveway of their home in Sulphur, Oklahoma. His mother fetched the family's one suitcase along with the paper grocery bags carrying the children's clothing and personal belongings and stuffed them into the trunk. She then joined her brother in the front seat while Dann, along with his two brothers and sister, climbed into the back. Their father, of course, would not be joining them—he never did. Years before, he would visit them occasionally, but after the drinking took over—well, it was just better this way. These days, his contribution to family vacations was to make them necessary. Summers with their grandparents—seventy miles away—protected the children from their father's Jekyll-Hyde transformations—the too common story of alcohol turning a good man, bad.

While some alcoholics mellow as the alcohol enters their brain, others, like Dann's father, become violent. Their mother tried her best to shield the children, with mixed results. It wasn't always like that. Both of Dann's parents had excelled in school (a success later shared by their children), and the marriage of the popular athlete to the girl with the beautiful voice held all the promises of a fairy tale. Then came the Korean War, and the man who went over was not the man who came back.

There is an emotional protection afforded those who fight wars from a distance that's not available to the common infantryman. Those whose nightmares include the faces of the men they've killed know the difference, and the fact that thousands of them share the same horrific trauma doesn't make it easier on any of them. For Dann's father, those memories would continue to ravage the lives of his innocent wife and children. This year, however, there was another reason he wouldn't be joining them: he was serving a three-year sentence in the state prison.

"I don't know the whole story," said Dann, "but he got into a fight with some policemen and hurt some of them. He didn't kill anybody or anything, but he hurt several of them."

Dann's uncle turned off the main highway in Bennington, Oklahoma. Two miles of a dusty gravel road lay ahead, broken only by the sound of pebbles hitting the car's undercarriage. Dann's eight-year-old heart raced at the thought of another summer with his grandparents and caregiver aunt, an annual respite from the tensions at home. "At the end of the summer, I never wanted to leave," he recalls.

Their car turned into the dirt driveway of Bryan County's oldest "shotgun house," so named for the unobstructed view provided from the front door to the back door through a single hallway. Rooms sprang off to either side, bedrooms and bathroom walls providing shape and form to the hallway while the living room and more public areas opened directly into it. A door leading from the kitchen/dining room onto a farmer's porch at the rear of the house stood like a sentinel at the back wall. Once in the driveway, the car's inhabitants gazed on a house sided with slab wood—the most economical building material of its time, its bottom edges resembling a series of black, rolling waves. The same slab lumber was inside the home, sharing wall space with the popular floral-printed wallpaper of the day.

"We're here," announced Dann's uncle, pulling on the emergency brake. His words were barely past his lips when the car's back doors opened in an explosion of children running up onto the porch and into the waiting arms of their aunt.

It was a wild, joy-filled melee of hugs and kisses.

"Oh, look how big you've grown" she exclaimed.

The children's grandfather, an aging Choctaw Indian, was of much calmer temperament, responding to his grandchildren's hugs with a tolerant smile and an indulgent pat on the back.

After bringing in their things, the new arrivals, in what had become almost a ritual, quietly walked into their grandmother's room. She spent most of her time in bed these days, the victim of a series of strokes that left her physically immobile and mentally impaired. After the last stroke, Dann's aunt moved in to help with her care.

Following their mother's lead, the children greeted their grandmother, held her hand and bent over to kiss her cheek. Occasionally a smile would cross her wrinkled face, hinting at memories still deep within her clouded mind.

The Contest

A few days after Dann and his family arrived, the kids were clearing the table after dinner when Dann's aunt took him aside. "Danny, I got news for you," she said, the hint of a smile on her lips. "I've seen your stuff. You gotta gift—just like your mama. That large furniture store in Durant? Well, they're having an art contest for you kids! You get to do a picture. Gotta be crayons or water colors and there's gonna be prizes! Well, I know how much you like drawin', so I signed you up!"

Dann's eyes brightened, and his mouth dropped.

"I knew immediately what I wanted to paint," he recalls. "In our classroom at school was a poster-sized picture of Mt. Fujiyama—it was the most beautiful picture of a mountain I had ever seen. After finishing my assignments, I'd often sit in my seat just looking across the room at it.

"The next morning I asked my grandfather if I could use the discarded cardboard refrigerator box that was in the shed out back. He agreed, so I took a pocketknife and cut out a two-by-four-foot piece to use as my canvas.

"We were the poorest family in town," Dann explained. "It didn't bother us because we didn't know any better, but without any money we had to be creative. I did most of my artwork at home on the back of the butcher paper used to wrap our meat. It was actually pretty good paper—it was thick, and the wax coating on the inside kept the colors from bleeding through."

His grandparent's kitchen/dining room soon became Dann's studio and the family's large oak dining room table, his easel. Standing over his cardboard canvas, Dann went to work. Then, as pencil outlines gave way to colors, a problem arose.

"I was using my brother's watercolor set, and soon ran out of paint. I found I could squeeze some more paint out of the little wooden trays by putting water in them and letting them set for a while. But this was a big picture, and there still wasn't enough paint. So I began experimenting. I discovered that you could get colors from flowers, plants, and even tree bark, so I would go outside and traipse through the fields, collecting flowers and plants. Then I'd press and squeeze my collection and add water. It took a while, but I was finally able to make the colors I needed."

With the time-consuming task of making his own paints, it took Dann almost three weeks to finish the picture. Dann's aunt drove them to nearby Durant, where she carried the picture into the furniture store. They walked into a surprise. Pictures of every conceivable size and shape were hanging on all the walls and supporting pillars of the store. Whole families crowded its aisles, and every now and then one of them, usually a child, would point to a picture. If the owner was hoping to increase customer traffic, more than five hundred entries guaranteed his success. "I was proud of what I had done," said Dann, "it really turned out well, but up against so many, I wasn't holding my breath."

While Dann's family spent most of the summer in Bennington, it wasn't unusual for them to return to Sulphur for brief visits. On one such visit, the phone rang.

Dann's mother answered, spoke for a while, and then called to Dann. "It's your aunt," she said, handing him the phone.

"Danny" came the happy voice at the other end, "Guess what? You won the Grand Prize!"

Danny's quiet nature prevented him from shouting for joy, but a satisfied warmth filled him inside and a smile spread across his face.

Returning to their grandparent's home, Dann, accompanied by all his extended family (except grandpa who stayed home with their grandmother) drove to the furniture store to claim the prize. The owner presented him with a set of gold cufflinks in the shape of small easels, together with a check for $10. A photographer from the local paper posed the young artist next to the grandfatherly storeowner. The picture, to the delight of both the storeowner and Dann's family, appeared in that week's edition of the Sulphur *Times-Democrat*.

Chapter 2 | REV. RITZINGER

God listens to a mother's prayers—a fact that many a child gratefully acknowledges in later years. "My mother prayed for us often," Dann remembers. "As she tucked us into bed at night, she would pray for each of us. It was the traditional 'now I lay me down to sleep…,' but even though it was the same prayer and repeated nightly, those words gave us a sense of security that God was watching over us."

Falls Creek

The summer day was bright and clear at the end of August and temperatures hovered in the mid-eighties. Eleven-year-old Dann and his classmate Mark rode their bikes into Mark's driveway as Mark's father was opening the door of his blue and white Ford pickup.

"I'm going to Falls Creek to drop off some supplies," he said, motioning toward the boxes in the back, "Would you two like to come?"

Would they like to? Throwing their bikes down on the lawn, they rushed toward the pickup's open door. With everybody seated, Ray Cleveland backed out of the driveway and drove down the street, stopping a minute later in front of Dann's house. Dann ran inside and almost as quickly raced back.

"It's okay," he said between breaths, "she said I could go."

For a boy with an absentee father, Ray Cleveland was a godsend. In the years that followed, he became the father Dann never knew.

"It broke my heart when he moved away a few years later," Dann recalls.

They called him "Coach Cleveland" at the high school. Living just down the street, his son Mark and Dann became friends and playmates. Sensing the need in Dann's life, Ray would often include him when running errands and in family outings and celebrations. The two families had known each other for several years, and Ray always liked Dann, so it wasn't a sacrifice. There was something else about Ray, and it would affect Dann for the rest of his life. Ray loved Jesus, a love that Dann would experience himself in a few days. Today, however, they were off to Falls Creek.

Founded in 1917, the Southern Baptist Conference Center at Falls Creek lies nestled in the Arbuckle Mountains of Oklahoma. By 2006 more than 1.8 million people had visited, 45,000 in that year alone. With more than 200,000 decisions for Christ made on its grounds, the 160-acre site has been the setting for thousands of transformed lives. Besides the conversions, there were "the calls." As proudly stated on the center's website, "More missionaries have experienced their call at Falls Creek than any other place on the face of the earth."[4]

The sight of so many kids running, laughing and playing made a deep impression on Dann. He felt drawn to this new and wonderful place with its many cabins and large open-sided tabernacle. That attraction remains to this day. As of this writing, Dann has been to Falls Creek every year for over fifty years, with people from his church joining him every fall for weekend Bible Conferences or retreats.

Taking the scenic route to the camp kitchen to show Dann as much of the grounds as possible, Ray dropped off the supplies. Finishing the twelve-mile drive back to Sulphur, he stopped in front of Dann's house. Dann was reaching for the door handle when Ray turned to him,

"I'll be singing at Calvary Church for the evening service Sunday night. Would you like to come?"

He didn't have to ask twice. The smile on Dann's face said it all.

"I've gotta ask my mother."

"Of course," Ray replied, "You go ahead. We'll wait here for you."

As quickly as the first time, Dann was in and out of the house.

"I can go," he said excitedly.

"That's great," Ray responded. "The service is at 7. I'll be by around 6:30."

That Sunday night, several cars were already in the parking lot when the Cleveland family-plus-one arrived at Calvary Baptist Church. Dann found himself looking at the largest church in town, a white spired cream-colored brick edifice that could seat close to five hundred. Although Ray had asked Dann and his family to join him several times in the past, this was Dann's first visit.

As they entered the church, Dann hesitated. The Cleveland family went up front to their regular seats, but this was new territory for Dann. He hung back, taking a seat by himself in one of the back pews. Mark, leaving his family, came back to sit with him. The singing was lively and spirited and while the hymns were new to him, Dann, who loved music, was beginning to enjoy himself. Ray's booming bass voice filled the sanctuary with song, and as the congregation sat down following yet another rousing chorus, Dr. Tom Ritzinger stood to deliver the sermon. He was dressed in a dark suit, with dark-rimmed glasses and thinning hair combed back flat against his head.

"I remember it like it was yesterday," says Dann. "There was Brother Tom, standing at the front, hands clasped, turning slightly from side to side to look at everyone as he spoke."

Although Dann no longer remembers the sermon, he has no trouble recalling the end of the service. The organist was softly playing "I Surrender

All" as Brother Tom gave the invitation.

"The Lord wants to do business here tonight. There are some of you who have not yet said 'yes' to Jesus Christ, who have not said 'yes' to his forgiveness, who have not said 'yes' to his love. There are some here tonight who have not yet said 'yes' to his gift of eternal life. For you, tonight could be the night when all that changes—the night you become part of God's family. If you'd like to say 'yes' to Jesus tonight, then I'm going to lead you in a prayer. I'll pray aloud, and you can repeat it to yourself, right where you're sitting. It's as easy as that." He continued with his prayer, pausing for people to repeat the words silently: "Lord, I thank you for sending Jesus to die on the cross… I thank-you that he died for my sins… I thank-you that when I accept Him, my sins are forgiven, and I am born again into his kingdom… and so Lord, I accept Jesus Christ as my Savior tonight… I accept Jesus as my Lord tonight… thank-you that your Holy Spirit is born in me this night… thank-you for what you can do with my life… and thank-you that I am now your child and you are my Father… through Jesus Christ our Lord, Amen."

"Now," Brother Tom continued, "I want all of you who prayed that prayer for the first time to stand where you are… good, thank-you. Now I'd like you to move out of your pews and come down front. Jesus says that those who deny him, he will deny, but those who confess him before men he will confess before his Father in heaven. If you've done business with God here tonight, God wants to bless you by giving you the chance to confess Him before men, right here and right now."

Rev. Ritzinger's words hit a responsive chord deep within Dann.

"It's hard to explain it, but I can remember that moment to this very day. It was the one thing in my life that made sense. The rest of my life was confused and dark, but the salvation message really made sense. The Lord cared about my life and what I wanted to do."

Oblivious to anything or anyone else, Dann stood, made his way out of the pew and walked to the front. "I don't remember a lot about that service, but as I was going down front, I still remember thinking 'This is the right thing to do—this is what I was meant for.'"

Dann and some others stood at the front of the sanctuary facing Rev. Ritzinger, who spoke with each privately as the organist continued playing in the background.

"What's your name, boy?" asked the preacher.

"Dann Masters," came the reply.

"Dann, did you pray the prayer I just prayed?"

"Yes, sir."

"And did you mean what you prayed?"

"Yes, sir, I did."

"Well congratulations, son," the preacher replied, putting one hand on Dann's shoulder and shaking his hand with the other, "and welcome to God's family."

For Dann, even at the age of eleven, it was a life-changing event. In his words, "Of all the things in my life that I've gone through, the certainty that God loves me and cares about my life is the one thing I've held onto. As a teenager, I didn't always live out my faith. I'd stray and do things I shouldn't have done. They weren't big things; I didn't break any laws or get into drinking, drugging, or womanizing. I was still well behaved and respectable on the outside, but on the inside, I was angry. I had been angry from my youth, probably because of my dad leaving. From that evening, however, the Lord has been the one thing I could hold onto. He has been the one thing that kept my life steady. My faith in Him was the one thing that kept me going in difficult times because His love for me was the one thing I knew to be true."

In the course of that year, two other events would leave a permanent mark on Dann's life. The first occurred shortly before the above experience.

Dann and his family visited their father regularly while he was in prison.

"Once a month we'd all catch a bus for the two-hour trip to McAlister. Mother packed a picnic lunch, and we'd meet Dad out in the yard. We'd have a little picnic for an hour or two, and then we'd go back home. He wasn't drinking, of course, so the visits went well."

After serving two years of his three-year sentence, news came that their father would be released. "We hoped that when he got out, all the bad stuff would change, and we could live a somewhat normal life." Unfortunately, that's not what happened.

"He went back to work as a painter and back to his old drinking friends. I don't remember the particulars, but one day he and my mother told us that he was going to leave, that he felt like he could make a better living out in California. He was a lumberjack, and he was going to work in California and the Northwest. It wasn't a terrible experience when they told us. It was explained that we would be better off since we'd be away from the drinking and everything and maybe we could get some money from social security."

His father's return to the bottle was the family's return to the nightmares of the past, so Dann understood something of what his parents were saying. Still, the news saddened him.

"You know as you're growing up, no matter what your father does, you love him." The announcement, however, left him confused. This wasn't what they were expecting when he came home.

"I remember sitting around thinking that it didn't make sense, but I was just a kid. It also meant they were getting a divorce, but we didn't know that at the time."

The worst was yet to come.

"Heading to the Northwest, my father first went to California. His mother, brothers, and sister lived there. From there he traveled north, and that's when it happened. He was in Oregon, on his way up to Washington, when he died in a house fire.

"Sometimes, people suggest that my father's death led to my conversion. I know what they're thinking, that his loss made me especially open to the Gospel, but the truth of the matter is that I came to Christ before he died; not after.

"Another life-changing event that year was the guitar my mother gave me for Christmas. As guitars go, it wasn't an expensive one, but it was for her. We were poor, and it was no small sacrifice on her part. From the moment I started playing, I knew God wanted me to be a musician."

Chapter 3 | THE CALL

"There are times in your spiritual life when there is confusion. It is not a matter of right and wrong, but a matter of God taking you through a way that you temporarily do not understand. Only by going through the spiritual confusion will you come to the understanding of what God wants for you."
—OSWALD CHAMBERS, *My Utmost for His Highest*, September 12, edited

Within months of receiving his Christmas guitar, Dann joined three other budding eleven-year-old rock stars to form their own four-piece band. Dann played lead guitar and the others bass guitar, drums and electric organ (the less versatile predecessor of today's keyboard). Asked if his musical talents made him a celebrity at school, he responded:

"We were celebrities all right. In the beginning, we were celebrities because we were so bad. We played so poorly that people would laugh and make fun of us. They effectively chased us out of town. We got better, and when we did, we started playing in town again. After a while, we cut a record, which became a local hit. Most of our playing was at school dances [they called them 'mixers' back then], the local Elk's club and the armory. School proms and an occasional wedding rounded out our more common gigs." Dann was hoping for a career in music, and dreamed of making it to the "big time." There was little question that he had the talent. God, however, had other plans.

It happened the summer before his junior year in high school. As he had every summer for the past several years, Dann was spending a week at Falls Creek's youth camp. One day, having just returned from supper, he was sitting on the bunk in his cabin waiting for the evening service. Usually, he'd ask a girl to accompany him—the services were a popular dating activity among campers, but tonight the person he asked couldn't make it, so he was by himself. The solitude lent itself to a time of reflection. He glanced at his watch. It was 6:30. The service was at 7 p.m. and only a few minutes' walk, so he had some time.

Like many seventeen-year-olds, Dann was dealing with a couple of unanswered questions: what should he do with his life and with whom would he share it? The second question could wait awhile, but approaching the last two years of high school, the first had him wondering.

For the past six years, music had been God's elixir for this quiet and shy young man, giving him not only a means of self-expression but also the acceptance and admiration of his peers. He could easily envision his band duplicating—at least to some degree—the success of groups such as the Beatles and the Rolling Stones. There would be concerts, increasingly larger ones, perhaps even a top ten hit if they were lucky. That was his dream plan. But Dann was too practical to count on dreams, so he had a "plan B."

Dann's "plan B" was to go to college, then law school and from law school into politics. His interest in law was to bring a measure of justice and fairness into people's lives, especially those who didn't have anyone to stand up for them. He looked toward politics for the same reason. He readily admits that it was the idealism of youth, yet untainted by his experiences in college.

Dann's faith in Christ continued to provide a source of inner security during this time of uncertainty. Ever since that evening six years ago when he slipped out of his pew at Rev Ritzinger's invitation, he lived with the certainty that God cared about him. In the midst of the confusion and anger of a fatherless childhood, Dann found a source of calm. He didn't know what God had in store for him, but he knew God cared about him, and that's all that mattered. For the past couple of years, he had even given some thought to being a preacher. It began following his eighth-grade summer at Falls Creek. Upon returning, he shared his experiences with the congregation, and when he did, something quite unexpected happened.

"The people were impressed by what I said. I think the thing that impressed them the most was that this shy kid was talking. I also sensed that God was in the words I was speaking. The way they came out and the way people reacted told me that something was happening. I didn't know what it was, and I didn't understand it at the time, but I had the definite feeling that God was behind it. "

While Dann may not have known what to make of it, others did. Following his presentation, the pastor's wife came up to him.

"Dann, you need to give up that band of yours and be a preacher."

Others felt the same way, and every time he gave one of those reports they would tell him the same thing. "So, of course, becoming a preacher was something I was thinking about."

Still lying on his bunk, Dann checked his watch—it was 6:45—time to get going. The screen door banged behind him as he walked onto the gravel road leading up to the tabernacle. The evening was calm, and a gentle breeze brushed his face, carrying with it the fragrance of pine. Lengthening shadows appeared on the road ahead of him as the sun sank below the horizon. The road crossed over a bridge and up a hill. Perched at its top was the tabernacle—a large imposing structure standing guard over the grounds below.

As he approached, Dann heard a medley of familiar Gospel choruses coming from deep within the building's cavernous interior. A piano and organ, together with an orchestra of over thirty campers provided a musical prelude as people streamed in from all sides of the open-sided building. By the time everyone had found a seat, the tabernacle roof covered a crowd of close to five thousand, including a three-hundred-voice choir. Dann slid into a wooden pew on the left, close to the front. The speaker's platform was just in front of him with the choir seated on risers at the back. He recognized the Camp Director sitting behind the pulpit. In the chair next to him sat the speaker for the evening. He was short—very short, and Dann noticed two wooden Dr. Pepper boxes positioned side by side behind the pulpit for the height-challenged speaker. Following the customary congregational singing, special numbers by the choir and evening announcements, Rev. Charles Warren, visiting from England, stood to speak.

"Again, I don't remember what the sermon was about, but toward the end of it, I had the unmistakable feeling that God was calling me to be a preacher. A dialogue started in my mind. No sooner would I raise objections and questions than other thoughts would enter my mind to silence the objections and answer the questions. The whole process didn't take more than a few minutes, but when it was over, and people were asked to come to the front, I didn't hesitate. Most went forward to commit or recommit their lives to Christ. I went forward to accept God's call into the ministry."

Dann returned to his seat and sat motionless, deep in thought. The people around him stood to leave. After a while, someone turned out the lights, but still Dann sat, unable to move. Finally, a half-hour later, he made his way outside, walking around the conference grounds for another hour, immersed in thought. "I was trying to figure out what I was supposed to do. I was willing to be a preacher, but I didn't know how it would fit in with everything else in my life."

If one imagines Dann's life as a partially completed jigsaw puzzle, he was now holding in his hand the piece shaped like a preacher, not knowing where it belonged. "My greatest handicap all through life has been my ignorance. I just didn't know what to do. Nobody tells you after you get 'the call' what you're supposed to do with it, they just assume you'll know, but I didn't know. What does God want me to do? I didn't have a clue." The problem? Dann couldn't see himself as a preacher, at least not in the style of those he knew. "I just couldn't see myself following in their footsteps. They were fine men, and they were doing God's work, but I couldn't see myself doing what they were doing."

It was Dann's other love.

"Music was always a big part of my life. It was where I found my identity. It was how I expressed myself. I couldn't see God giving me such a gift if he didn't want me to use it, and I couldn't see how he wanted me to use it if I was to be a preacher."

In today's world of contemporary Christian music and churches filled with praise bands and electric guitars, Dann's confusion is hard to understand. Today's world, however, wasn't Dann's world as a teenager. In those years, a church service consisted of organs and pianos accompanying people singing decades-old hymns. Under no circumstances would the popular music of his time, with a beat that permeated one's soul and melodies that one hummed all day, find its way through the thick doors of those churches. Then, something happened that changed the sound of church music forever.

In 1969, the Christian musical "Tell it Like it Is" swept the country. Its toe-tapping songs lifted people's spirits and tugged at their hearts. Slowly, painfully, church doors started creaking open. The biblical message and emotionally appealing melodies written by composers Ralph Carmichael and Kurt Kaiser found a passageway into people's hearts, inspiring a new genre of music. The new minister of music at Dann's home church asked Dann and his drummer to join them in performing the musical, supplemented by church musicians and a youth chorus of twenty voices. Following a series of rehearsals, the performance was a smash hit. Word spread, and invitations poured in from other churches.

"That was an important experience," Dann recalls. "For the first time in my life, I began to think that maybe my love of music and my call to preach *could* go together." Soon afterwards, a performance in a very large tradition-bound church in western Oklahoma came close to destroying Dann's hopes.

"We moved in all of our sound equipment and staging and presented the musical with our typical joy and enthusiasm. After we finished, the host pastor took our leader aside. 'You will never again be welcome to return to this church and play such music.' When our leader told us this, we were stunned. What had we done wrong? Only later, did we realize that it wasn't us; it was the pastor. That church—or at least the leadership—wasn't ready for anything new. Still, it discouraged me at the time and made me wonder if I could ever fit into a church ministry."

Graduation from high school brought with it a long-anticipated trip to Los Angeles. By that time, Dann's band had been together for eight years, had a recording under their belts, and was yearning to move into the big time. Using their single recording as a calling card, they successfully negotiated their first hurdle.

"The Buck Owens organization offered us a combination managing/recording contract. It was designed to develop the band on the West Coast over a two-and-a-half-year period and then release us nationally." It was an exciting moment, followed by a crushing realization.

"I was the only one ready to make that sort of commitment," recalls

Dann. "One of our band members was only a junior in high school, and another was looking forward to getting married, so they weren't in a position to sign a two-and-a-half year contract. We returned home, and everyone went their separate ways. It was a great disappointment."

Discouraged, Dann turned his attention to "plan B." That meant college. In those days, any Oklahoman thinking of the ministry would have headed to Oklahoma Baptist University. The only problem for Dann was their tuition: $3000 a year. With state schools charging only $12 a credit hour ($384 a year), the choice was obvious.

Dann entered Oklahoma University (OU) still nursing the wounds of a shattered dream and the loss of his band. Emotionally exhausted, what he found at OU didn't help. "I was shocked at the liberal values and immoral lifestyle on campus. Class instructors were clearly anti-Christian. My school friends began to change. Some became involved with drugs, others with sex, and most dropped out. Viet Nam and the civil rights movement turned the campus into a flash point for anti-war rallies and race riots. It was an entirely different world than I was used to."

Lesser men would have folded under the pressure. Many of Dann's friends had already discarded their faith, replacing it with the values of the world around them. For Dann, however, the thundering wave of cultural pressure broke against the steel hull of his convictions. He stayed the course. "I didn't fall into the many problems that my friends struggled with, but I had my own issues to deal with: loneliness, temptations, a sense of insignificance, and whether or not my faith, which I had held onto for so long, was really relevant."

Home became an oasis during those college years. Dann would return to Sulphur on weekends, playing in bands and attending services at Calvary Baptist. "The only problem with the church was that they had no clue as to what was happening in the outside world," he explains. Still, his faith, along with those weekends, sustained him. "God never let me down; although I am sure I failed Him many times. He kept me safe during those years, and I'm sure that's the only reason I survived."

During the summers, Dann would habitually travel the few miles to Falls Creek for a week of camping, supplemented by nightly visits to the tabernacle. "I'd come home from work, get cleaned up, and head up to the campground."

It was the summer before his sophomore year in college that he met her. She was intelligent, pretty, had an attractive personality and, since she regularly attended church, was obviously a Christian. There was an immediate and mutual attraction. The tall and shy guitar-playing singer had just met someone who turned out to be everything he was looking for in a wife. She was a sophomore in high school when they met, an age difference that encouraged the relaxed and casual relationship they shared. Over the next four years, they would see each other often: at Falls Creek, at a multitude of church and youth functions and occasionally for a date.

As his four years of college ended, uncertainty clouded Dann's plans for the future. His musical dreams lay shattered, and he really didn't fit in with the other prelaw students. The college administration, noticing that most prelaw and premed students didn't end up in those professions, encouraged those students to select a second major. Dann chose Social Studies. He didn't want to go into teaching but saw no practical alternative.

Having received a call to the ministry, why didn't Dann head to seminary?

"Creativity was the driving force in my life," he explained. "I feel closer to God when I'm creating something than at any other time, and I saw no opportunity to use my creativity as a preacher. The musical 'Tell It Like It Is' gave me some hope, but not much more than that."

It wasn't just the church's music that was an obstacle; it was the church's resistance to *anything* new. "In those days ministry was pretty dry. Other than for someone like Billy Graham, a minister was a preacher who became the guardian of tradition. The music person might be good, but he was doing the same thing they had been doing for a hundred years. I couldn't see myself in that position."

Following graduation, Dann made a return trip to California to see if he could break into the music industry on his own. He hired an agent and succeeded in landing a contract as a backup musician in a recording studio. His story, however, was not that of a John Denver rising from backup musician to celebrity. To begin with, he felt disconnected from those in the music industry. They'd good-naturedly call him their "preacher" because Dann didn't drink anything stronger than a coke when he joined them in the bars. "They were good people, and I liked them, but we didn't have a whole lot in common."

Then a few things came together that sent Dann packing. First, his sister contacted him to tell him about an opening at the school where she was teaching. Then, a stunning discovery:

"My roommate and one of my closest friends, a guy I played music with and shared a lot of time with, told me he was gay. I didn't know what to do. In those days, this was not a common revelation, and this guy was like a brother to me. I just didn't know what to do, but I felt I couldn't stay there." Two more unnerving events sealed his decision to move. "I was in a restaurant, and there was a shooting next door. Then, the next day a friend and I were across the street during the robbery of a jewelry store. I thought, 'this isn't a safe place to be, are you sure you want to be here?' I finally said 'no.' We didn't have a phone, so I ran down to the Roosevelt Hotel and called home. I told my mother I was catching an overnight flight and asked if she'd have my brother James pick me up at the airport. I had no idea what I was going to do after returning home, but the music door had closed, and closed hard."

Once home, Dann got into his car one evening and drove to the evening service at Falls Creek. The tabernacle hadn't changed much since that night seven years ago when he received his call to preach. The gray weathered barn board and steel structure looked just the same. Yet the young man who entered the building that night had changed considerably. He had tested the waters of a music career and found them wanting. He had given up on a career in law and was considering teaching, but his heart wasn't in it. With the death of his musical career, there seemed to be no opportunity to express the creativity God had given him.

The preacher for the evening was Dr. John Bisagno, a well-known author, and pastor of one of the flagships of the Southern Baptist Convention, the First Baptist Church of Dallas, Texas. His words changed everything. As Dann remembers it, Rev. Bisagno began his message by telling of his own call to the ministry. "He told how he played the horn and used to be a jazz musician. When he received God's call into the ministry, he didn't know exactly what he should be doing, so he just started doing what he could to help out in the church. As he did, God started using him." Like Dr. Bisagno, Dann wanted to be a musician and wanted to be a preacher, but saw no way the two could ever come together. Now, standing before him was a highly successful man who was doing both. Suddenly, Dann knew where to put that piece of the puzzle that he had been holding for the past seven years. Already following Jesus in his personal life, Dr. Bisagno's example showed Dann how he could do the same in his professional life. "If he can do it, I can too," Dann thought to himself.

Seminary would normally be the next step, but Dann had already applied for the teaching position at his sister's school, and an interview was coming up. He *wanted* to go to seminary but was uncertain about the timing. In need of some reassurance, he imitated Gideon's method of discerning God's will in the Old Testament by "putting out a fleece" (Judges 6:36-40).

"Lord," he said, "if I'm accepted for the teaching job, then I'll take it and consider it to be your will for the present, but if not, then I'll know you want me to go to seminary."

Dann knew there was little chance he'd land the teaching job. "It was a pretty conservative school district, and I was a long-haired rock musician." The superintendent, however, looking beyond the length of Dann's hair, liked what he saw. "Congratulations," he said to a surprised Dann, "the job is yours."

Chapter 4 | An Uncertain Future

There comes a time when the excitement of new experiences and new surroundings gives way to the desire for stability and permanence. The nesting instinct now welled up within Dann. With a full time job and heading toward the ministry, Dann now turned his attention to the second question confronting him since his teen years: with whom will I share my life? He didn't have to think long. "Judy was everything I was looking for in a wife," he remembers. "I was convinced that she was the one God wanted me to marry." They had been seeing each other for four years—on dates, at youth rallies and church conferences and summers at Falls Creek. She was an attractive girl with a pleasing personality and a strong Christian background.

"I proposed over the phone. I told her that of all the people I've ever met; I felt she was the one God wanted me to be with. I went on to say, 'I don't want you to give me an answer now. Wait until you've had a chance to do what you want to do.' She was planning on being a flight attendant and moving to Dallas to receive her training. I told her to give me a call when she was ready. Well, I didn't hear from her and then about a month later, she called. 'If that's what you want to do, then I'm ready.'" Within the year, they were married—where they met—at Falls Creek.

Although Dann enjoyed teaching and loved the kids, it was time to prepare for the ministry. In the summer following his second year of teaching at Ft. Cobb High School, he sent in his resignation. He and Judy began packing for their move to Ft. Worth, Texas, home to the nation's largest theological seminary.

Seminary

Just as Falls Creek Conference Center boasts of sending more people into the mission field than any other place in the country, Southwestern Baptist Theological Seminary claims the same distinction for training clergy. Since its founding in 1908, the sprawling nine-hundred-acre campus of large Greek-pillared buildings and acres of tree-dotted lawns, has sent over forty thousand graduates into ministries throughout the world.

Following their arrival at Southwestern, Dann and Judy moved into their home for the next three years—a small one-bedroom apartment comprising half of a ranch-styled duplex. Dann busied himself with registration and buying the required books and supplies, while Judy went job hunting, landing a clerical position with General Dynamics Corporation.

As Dann picked up his books and headed out the door for his first day of classes, mixed feelings of eagerness and nervousness accompanied him.

"I'll never forget my first preaching class. The instructor gave us a passage from Scripture and told us to exegete it. When he said "exegete," I had no idea what he was talking about. Most of the other students were Bible school graduates. I came from the University of Oklahoma—and that was no Bible school. I thought to myself, 'I'm a dead man.' After class, I approached the instructor.

"'You said you wanted us to exegete this passage, and I don't know what you're talking about.' The professor laughed, then explained,

"'To exegete a passage is to find out what it meant at the time it was written. Don't worry; you'll do fine.'"

The instructor's response was not only encouraging, it was prophetic—Dann ended up at the top of the class. As for the rest of his studies, the academic motivation that had served him so well in high school, only to desert him during his college years, now reasserted itself. Seminary both stimulated him intellectually and strengthened him personally. This was where he belonged, a feeling due in large part to the seminary's music program.

Southwestern's music department of eleven professors guided hundreds of students through classes and performances. Even in that large of a pool, however, Dann stood out. Popular for his friendly and easygoing personality and admired for his intellect, Dann was frequently called upon to share his musical talents at private gatherings as well as campus and public events.

As graduation neared, Dann began looking at the seminary's doctoral program. He enjoyed the atmosphere at Southwestern, and a Ph.D. would provide him with the credentials needed to teach on both the university and seminary levels. His plans got a boost when a professor offered him a teaching fellowship to help with the expenses.

Life was good for Dann, and his future looked bright. That future, however, was about to change.

The Letter

It was a late October afternoon, and a chill was in the air as Dann opened the door to their duplex. Having just taken the Graduate Record Examination in preparation for entrance into the Ph.D. program, he was exhausted but elated, confident that he had done well. Plans for his future were on track. Walking past their bedroom door, he saw his wife sleeping. Must be resting up for the party we're attending tonight, he thought to himself. Picking up the day's newspaper, he plopped his tall, lanky frame into the easy chair, rising a few minutes later to raid the refrigerator. It was then that he noticed it. On the dining room table, protruding flag-like from his wife's purse was an envelope. Seeing her name written on the outside in a hand he didn't recognize, curiosity took over. Holding the envelope in his hand and noticing it wasn't sealed, he was soon reading its contents. His pulse quickened, even as his breath almost stopped, the words striking him with the force of an electric shock. Physically stunned and mentally reeling, he returned the letter to her purse.

As they dressed for the party, Dann tried hard to pretend that nothing was wrong. Being a quiet person can sometimes have its benefits. Asked to provide entertainment for the party, he grabbed his guitar on the way out.

Judy's sister decorated her home for the Halloween party with carved pumpkins, bowls of candy corn and black and orange streamers looping from the chandelier hanging from the high dining room ceiling. The large room easily held the forty-plus guests at rectangular banquet-style tables. Dann and Judy found two empty seats and joined four other couples. Little talk passed between them as they ate. If Judy noticed something was wrong, she didn't say anything. Following the meal, Dann took his guitar out of its case and went to the microphone. He had planned a 30-minute set, but after the fourth song things changed. A man he didn't recognize, a little older and with dark, wavy hair, claimed Dann's seat at the table. Alarm bells went off, but Dann continued singing. Finally, as the conversation between his wife and the stranger appeared to become more intense, Dann couldn't take it any longer. Wrapping up the set, he put the guitar back in its case and looked up just in time to see the stranger leaving. Sitting down next to his wife, Dann looked at her for a minute before speaking.

"I don't know about everything," he said quietly, "but I know something's going on."

She looked startled. "We'd better leave," she replied quickly.

Once home, there wasn't the free-flowing conversation to resolve the problem that Dann had expected. Instead, there were tears, and then silence, and over the next few days, more silence. Judy finally agreed to join him for counseling, but admitting to her lack of commitment to the marriage, the counseling went nowhere. For the next several weeks, a sense of the surreal permeated Dann's world. Occasionally she would revert to her "old self," but more and more her countenance steeled into a hardness he found as baffling as it was impenetrable. His own emotions ran the gamut from hope to hurt to anger to despair. The unexpected excitement that initially accompanied this personal challenge gave way to resignation. All of his attempts at reconciliation proved futile. A few days after New Year's, Dann received a call. The marriage that started with a phone call was about to end with one.

"I've packed my things," Judy said, "I need to leave and think things through."

She never came back.

Southwestern had a standing policy. Any student going through a divorce while in school would be required to take a leave of absence for two years to "reconsider your calling" before applying for re-admission which, of course, would be denied. With only eight credit hours remaining before graduation, Dann winced at the thought. He prayed and thought, and thought and prayed.

Several days later Dann walked up the steps of Southwestern's administration building, down the hallway and through a door marked "Russell H. Dilday, President."

"You can go in," said the secretary, "Dr. Dilday is expecting you."

Rising to greet his visitor, Dr. Dilday extended his hand and motioned Dann to one of the two mahogany leather armchairs facing his desk. Dr. Dilday took the other.

"What can I do for you, Dann?" He asked, concern in his voice.

Dann related his story.

"I've tried everything I can think of to stop this from happening," Dann said, "and nothing has worked. If you have any suggestions, I'd be glad to try them, but at this point I'm heading for a divorce, and there isn't anything I can do to stop it."

Dann paused before continuing.

"I like being at Southwestern and have studied hard. I'm only eight credit hours away from graduating, and now it looks like everything I've worked for is going down the drain. Is there anything I can do?"

Dr. Dilday looked down for a moment, pondering the question. After a short while, he leaned forward, his eyes fixed on Dann.

"Here's what I suggest," he said, his voice radiating a thoughtful confidence. "You continue attending your classes and doing your course work. I'll meet with the trustees and talk with them."

Dann breathed a sigh of relief. Southwestern's president had a reputation for compassion, and he had just given Dann reason for hope. Rising to leave, Dann extended his hand, the firmness of his grip communicating the gratitude in his heart.

"Thank-you, sir," he said, "thank-you very much."

Eight months later, clad in a robe with the rest of his class, Dann Masters walked across the graduation stage. With a nod of recognition and a look of satisfaction, Dr. Dilday handed Dann the first diploma ever given to a divorced student.

Following his graduation, supporters advised Dann to put his doctoral work on hold for a couple of years and allow the emotional dust to settle.

"They said I needed a break," Dann remembers, "and they were right."

Having successfully graduated, Dann thought that the worst consequences of his divorce were over. He was wrong.

Slammed Doors
Jesus' fierce denunciations of the Pharisees show how seriously He viewed the toxic threat of legalism [a strict adherence to the letter of the law rather than the spirit, affecting an attitude of judgmental self-righteousness]. Its dangers are elusive, slippery, and hard to pin down. I believe these dangers remain a great threat today.
—PHILIP YANCEY as quoted in *Our Daily Bread*, September 21, 2009
(bracketed definition by author)

In search of a church, Dann sent out resumes. Churches, seeing his name among Southwestern's top graduates, began contacting him. Yet both resumes and letters of interest ended up in the trash. Some were polite; others rude and dismissive as soon as they read the word "divorced." Dann's world, once filled with approval and acclaim, now exploded in a hailstorm of rejection, and occasionally contempt, from people he regarded as family. For many, the gifted musician and proven scholar had just become a leper.

The rejection left Dann shaken and confused. "I didn't know whether God could use me," he remembers thinking. Yet in the midst of everything, he never felt abandoned by God. While confusion reigned, his Sunday evening experience as an eleven-year-old remained a bastion of comfort.

Dann also received support among those who knew him. From church members to pastors to school officials and denominational leaders, those who looked under the label "divorced" saw in Dann not its perpetrator, but rather its victim. Both visibly and behind the scenes, these people pled Dann's case and supported him.

"I received a letter from Professor Jack Gray at the seminary. He was a mission's professor and a real man of prayer. He wrote to point out that 'the gifts and calling of God are without repentance.'" (Romans 11:29, King James Version. The New International Version reads, 'God's gifts and his call are irrevocable.'").

"I thought to myself, 'well, that's true.' Those words became a source of strength and I've never forgotten them. So I said to the Lord: 'God, I don't know what you've got in store, but I trust you.'"

With churches closing their doors ("A large church would contact me and I'd get my hopes up only to have my heart broken when they found out about the divorce"), Dann looked for work. He tried to join the Navy but lacked the experience to enter as an officer. He applied to Wal-Mart as a management trainee, but they turned him down. Finally, he found an evening job going into high-rise office buildings and rearranging their modular cubicles.

Two years passed. It was springtime when Dann received a call from his sister. Oklahoma Baptist University was searching for a counselor to add to their staff in the fall. Dann interviewed. "You've got the position," said the department head. While it wasn't a pastorate ("Dann was pretty much ready to get out of the ministry at the time," recalls his future pastor, Eddie Malphrus) it appeared that Dann's life was finally going somewhere.

With a prospective job awaiting him, a still broken and confused Dann went back home to Sulphur to put his life back together. In doing so, he was about to meet two people who would forever change his life: the man who would become his mentor, and the woman who would become his wife.

Krista

Arriving in Sulphur, Dann encountered a familiar face in the grocery store. It was his best friend's uncle. "I heard Krista's back in town," he said. "She has a little girl…went through a really tough divorce."

Dann remembered Krista Woodruff as a young grade school girl, seven years his junior. As his best friend's cousin, she was frequently at their family gatherings. He heard of her winning the Miss Texas talent contest with her singing—the whole town was abuzz with that news, and later on, someone mentioned that she had married and given birth to a daughter. Three years before, Dann saw her briefly at a funeral, but the last time they talked was at a family gathering when she was a fourth grader and he was a high school senior.

Krista moved back to Sulphur for three reasons. First, both her ex-husband's family and her own were prominent members of their small—in this case too small—Texas community. Some understood the reasons behind the divorce, others didn't, but there were enough people who took sides to make it awkward and uncomfortable. Secondly, she needed to put the pieces of her life back together. Thirdly, her grandfather had recently passed away. While her grandmother was a strong and capable woman, she could use some company and was delighted at Krista's willingness to bring her daughter Natalie and move in for a while. Dann called on her that afternoon.

As Krista remembers, "I had been through a lot of hurts, heartaches, and disappointments. I tried fixing things on my own, but nothing worked. I finally realized I couldn't do it on my own—I had come to the end of myself. About this time, Danny came to visit. He knew the family well, so it wasn't unusual for him to come over. In talking with him and looking at Scriptures in the coming weeks, I came to realize what was missing. I had a lot of 'head knowledge' about God. Growing up in a religious family, I knew a lot about those things, but I had no 'heart knowledge.' I lacked a personal relationship with Christ and a daily walk with him. Through my meetings with Danny, and through his example, I found the answers I was looking for."

Since both Dann and Krista were divorced and meeting on a regular basis, one might assume they were attracted to each other. However, as Krista explains,

"I never thought about Dann in those terms. To begin with, after what I had been through, I wasn't even looking for another relationship. Then there was the age difference—seven years between us. Also, from the time I first met him as a five-year-old, I never particularly liked him. He was a long-haired hippy type rock musician—a far cry from the kids I ran around with."

From Dann's perspective, although he found Krista's personality pleasant and her appearance attractive (the divorce had not affected either his judgment or his eyesight), it wasn't "love at first sight." The lingering pain of a three-year-old divorce and the fear of a rebound effectively inoculated him against romantic pursuits. Had it not been for God's intervention, he may well have succumbed to his fears and missed the best years of his life.

About the same time Dann met Krista, he also met Rev. Eddie Malphrus. From the coach who invited him to church, to the pastor's wife who told him he should be a preacher, to Dr. Dilday who saw to it that he graduated from seminary, there are a number of people who have played significant roles in Dann's life, but none more important than Rev. Eddie Malphrus.

Chapter 5 | EDDIE MALPHRUS

The mooing of cows, the cackling of chickens, and chug-chug of the rusty farm tractor were familiar sounds to young Eddie Malphrus. "We were essentially sharecroppers," he explains of his childhood years on a farm in South Carolina. To this day, the smell of wet hay, the musty odor of livestock and the sight of a freshly harrowed field still triggers feelings of nostalgia. Farming, however, was not in his future.

Eddie was only nine years old when he went forward at the end of a church service and accepted Christ's forgiveness and new life. Awhile later, on a summer's evening at a mission-centered church camp, he yielded to God's call into full time ministry. In 1964, his heart set on becoming a missionary and accompanied by his new bride, Eddie entered Southwestern Theological Seminary. Then, two years later, he and God had a difference of opinion.

It was the last day of the missions' conference. The speaker asked everyone wanting to commit to full-time mission work to come forward. For years, this was Eddie's desire. It was why he came to Southwestern and his plan upon graduation, which is why what happened next completely stunned him.

"I couldn't move. I did everything—I bargained with God, but I could not get out of my seat and go forward. I had taken all of the mission courses, but I just couldn't do it."

The words weren't written on any wall, but Eddie got the message: being a pastor was still in, but missions was out.

In his third and fourth year of seminary, Eddie served as a student pastor in a small Baptist church in Mill Creek, Oklahoma, a hundred fifty miles away. While his wife taught school, he drove about 400 miles every weekend. The traveling continued as he entered Southwestern's doctoral program. In 1969, with only a semester and a dissertation standing between him and a Doctor of Theology degree, he accepted his first full-time pastorate at the Baptist Church in Hico, Texas, a small not-so-prosperous community located seventy-five miles from campus.

One year later Eddie's wife gave birth to their first child, a boy. Congratulations came from all directions as Eddie phoned their families and close friends with the good news. Following the delivery, mother and son played for a couple of hours until, having a hard time keeping her eyes open, she handed her baby to a nurse and went to sleep. She never woke up.

With today's medical knowledge, the story would probably have had a different ending, but at the time, they didn't know as much about brain aneurysms as they do today.

Eddie was devastated. They had waited seven years to have children, and now this? When the shock and disorientation subsided, a gut-wrenching pain, depression, and anger blew violently, yet briefly, through his normally confident and peaceful spirit. Did he ever question his faith in God?

"The responsibilities of work and parenthood did not leave a lot of time for reflection or emotions. There was a deep sense of aloneness, but God filled that void with himself, a demanding schedule, and a host of people who gathered around to help. I don't remember ever being angry at God, maybe because I needed Him so desperately. There were the usual questions and the inability to understand it all, but there was also a peace; I knew God would work it out. Over the next months, that peace turned into an expectation that God would do something special. Perhaps it helped that I became a Christian at age nine and grew up on a farm, the son of a sharecropper. I had seen hard and difficult times and had always seen the hand of God revealed in the end. God enabled me to see the death of my wife as one of those hard and difficult times. I knew that he would show himself faithful. Looking back, I saw him at work bringing me through those days. He is a good God!"

And he's faithful.

"I soon realized that God was providing for me and my child even before the death of my wife. The people I needed to help care for my son were already in place, and I couldn't have belonged to a more supportive and understanding church."

And how did Eddie's loss affect his ministry? He answered the question before I could ask it. "What God did in my own life has been a tremendous help in offering hope and reassurance to others."

In January of 1972, a year after Eddie's wife passed away, "God blessed me by introducing me to my present wife, Cynthia, the crowning point of my awareness that God still had a wonderful plan for my life. In looking back, I can see God preparing us for each other even before I met my first wife." Eddie and Cynthia were married later that year and shortly after that, Eddie accepted a call to the First Baptist Church of Sulphur, Oklahoma. He would stay there for the next thirty-two years. As it turned out, Eddie *did* become a missionary. Not the medical missionary he first envisioned, or even a pastoral missionary in foreign lands, but rather a missionary of mercy, impacting the lives of hundreds of people, including many who went on to become successful pastors and church leaders, among them Dann Masters.

First Baptist, Sulphur

No sooner had Dann arrived in Sulphur than he began looking for a job to tide him over until the fall. With the idea of starting a Christian counseling center, he visited pastors in the area to gain their support. Dann had heard about Eddie over the years—his reputation as a Bible scholar and man of compassion was well known, yet as he walked into Eddie's office in the spring of 1982, a nervous tension accompanied him. He had received too much rejection from Southern Baptist ministers to feel relaxed when meeting another one. Stepping into Eddie's study, Dann's eyes took in the cream-colored cement block walls and rows of books reaching almost to the ceiling. Eddie came out from behind his desk, the warmth of his smile and the firmness of his grip both unexpected and reassuring. At Eddie's invitation, Dann folded his lanky frame into a cushioned chair and began talking about the counseling center. Intrigued by the young man before him, Eddie began asking questions, not about the center, but about Dann. The dam broke. Encouraged by Eddie's response—a welcome change from the icy stares of past interviews—Dann peeled back the layers of his story. Contributing to the seeds of their friendship was the deep and common loss they shared: Eddie of his wife twelve years before, and Dann of his, three years earlier. The circumstances were different, but the pain was the same, and it provided an understanding shared only by those who have experienced such heartbreaks. Further attracting Dann to his new friend was Eddie's two loves in ministry: studying the Bible, and mercy. Dann's intellect responded to the first and his brokenness to the second.

What did Eddie think of Dann's divorce?

"Dann and I spent a lot of hours talking and working through it. I just encouraged him to know that there was no limit to what God could do," recalls Eddie.

For those who take the Bible seriously, the most problematic passage on divorce for someone in Dann's position is the one in St. Paul's letter to Timothy:

"Now the bishop must be above reproach, the husband of but one wife… A deacon must be the husband of but one wife…" (I Timothy 3:2, 12)

Eddie's thoughts on the subject were enlightening.

"You should know that I am probably a greater stickler on strict Biblical interpretation than most people you will run into. I am adamant that if you can't prove it by Scripture, you have no business using the Bible to tell people what to do. Now the other side is that if I'm going to do that, I need to know what the Scripture says. That has led me to a pilgrimage in several areas, divorce being one of them."

Eddie then shed some light on the above passage—insights that would escape the casual reader.

"First of all, this scripture does not use the word 'divorce,' even though Paul [who wrote the letter to Timothy] had access to it. In doing the research and looking at the origin of the word, I discovered it literally means a 'one-woman man.' In those days, that applied to the practice of polygamy. That was a sore spot for the early church, a socially acceptable thing going on around them and the church needed to make a stand, so that's what 1 Timothy 3 does. I completely agree that a preacher shouldn't be married to two or more people at the same time," Eddie says, laughing. "If you're going to be true to the Bible, that's where you have to go with that.

"My view of 1 Timothy 3 allowed me to encourage Dann to examine himself to see if he was a 'one-woman man' or was he hopping from one woman to another without ever making a lifetime commitment. He did not initiate his divorce. Obviously, all of us have a part in what goes on, but the divorce was something that happened *to* him; it wasn't something he wanted. Therefore, I had absolutely no problem in encouraging him to stay open. I told him that God could do whatever he wanted to do, and the divorce wasn't going to negate God's plan for his life. The most important thing, I told him, was to do what was right."

Eddie then makes a compelling argument in addressing the issue from another angle.

"Secondly, I don't believe that any sin is unpardonable except the rejection of the Holy Spirit. The Scriptures are very clear about labeling *that* as the unpardonable sin and nothing else. Therefore, if you have a pardonable offense, and the individual has gone to God and dealt with it correctly, he has received God's forgiveness. That being the case, if we hold that person guilty for the rest of his life, then we have usurped God's role, and that's not a position I'd ever want to be in."

Healing

"Love is not premeditated—it is spontaneous;
that is, it bursts forth in extraordinary ways."
—OSWALD CHAMBERS, *My Utmost for His Highest*, April 30

Dann's relationship with the people of First Baptist Church of Sulphur restored his crushed spirit. "They just loved on me," Dann recalls. Still reeling from the rejection of so many in his denomination, the people of First Baptist were a healing balm.

"By the time Dann arrived, our church had become known throughout the area as a church where people cared for each other," comments Eddie. "In fact, we had become a model for Southern Baptist churches in that part of the country."

Eddie's pastoral success sprang from two loves: his love for the Bible and his love of mercy. Mercy became a priority for Eddie in the 1980's after he went through Nexus—a program for identifying one's spiritual gifts.

Eddie explains: "The gift of mercy is divided into 'healing' [1 Corinthians 12:9, 28] and 'ministry' [Romans 12:8]. I view healing as directed toward those within the church and ministry to those outside. By 'healing,' we mean meeting physical needs, healing damaged emotions, soothing bruised spirits and repairing the broken lives of those in the church. 'Ministry' is providing relief to the poor, helping the sick and aiding the needy outside the church. The inner gift of mercy is the Holy Spirit-given ability to see the genuine needs of people and respond in compassion. As the 1980's progressed, our church became known for both its emphasis on the Bible and for the gift of mercy."

Having experienced the power of mercy in his own life, and witnessed its effects in the lives of others, Dann reached a conclusion: "this is the kind of church I want to lead."

Chapter 6 | WHEN ONE DOOR CLOSES

As the school year approached, Dann's life changed course yet again. Following the resignation of the president of Oklahoma Baptist University, the institution undertook a major reorganization. Instead of adding one counseling position, they eliminated two. Dann no longer had a job. The timing, however, couldn't have been better.

"We just expanded the church staff to add a minister of music," said Eddie Malphrus. "Before we could begin searching for someone, Dann told me what had happened. After discussing it with the leadership, we offered him the position of Interim Minister of Music."

Still focused on the pastorate, it wasn't the kind of job Dann was looking for, but the opportunity to work with Eddie and serve the people who helped put his life back together was irresistible.

The Commercial

Invitations to play his guitar and sing followed Dann wherever he went, and Sulphur was no exception. A particularly rewarding invitation came through the vice president of the local bank, Krista's grandmother. Her chain of Oklahoma banks was looking for singers to record a jingle for a commercial, and besides her granddaughter, she knew just who to ask. Dann rounded up a third musician from the church and they headed to the recording studio. Filled with laughing and joking, the hours spent in taping the commercial marked a turning point in Dann and Krista's relationship. Their conversations had brought them closer, but now, her beautiful voice and the laughter they shared created an attraction that Dann could no longer ignore. He had been looking for a female vocalist to join him in forming a duet. He now realized he had found her and, perhaps, much more. Following the taping of the commercial (which aired locally), Krista began attending First Baptist Church. A short time later, Eddie Malphrus was wrapping up the Sunday morning worship service with his traditional invitation when Krista slipped out of her pew and walked forward. Her talks with Dann about issues of faith had provided answers, and now it was time. While not the emotional experience of some, after realizing what was missing in her life, accepting Christ was the natural next step. Having already sensed her readiness, Dann wasn't surprised, but watching her walk forward gave him a feeling of warm satisfaction—as much for the future as for the present.

While Dann and Krista's friendship blossomed into romance, theirs was a far different path than most. Prompted by a concern not often considered by divorced people these days, they reigned in their feelings, deliberately and purposefully. The reason? God's greatest desire for any broken marriage is reconciliation. Committed to doing things God's way, the implications for their relationship were clear. They were also difficult, especially for Krista.

In their first meetings, Dann described his many attempts at reconciliation with his former wife, and Krista was amazed.

"I couldn't believe what he was saying," she recalls. "I remember the intense rage I felt when I told Dann: 'I'd rather be dead than reconciled' and I meant it."

Krista, however, was now a Christian, and her life was changing. If she clung to the anger toward her ex-husband, it would be at the cost of her newfound faith—a price she wasn't willing to pay. "Brother Eddie" (as his congregation knew him) helped her to understand: it's one thing if a person *can't* be reconciled; it's quite another if they *won't* be reconciled. The former is acceptable in the life of a Christian; the latter isn't. With Brother Eddie's counseling and Dann's support, she came to the point of earnestly desiring the previously unthinkable: reconciliation.

Feelings of love for her ex-husband were still absent, but God did a work in Krista's heart. "God showed me *how* to love him," she said. "I knew that if reconciliation occurred, I *could* fall in love with him again." Decades later, she describes this time in her life as "truly miraculous and life-changing."

"You should have been a part of that process," Eddie said to me in an email. "It was unbelievable. Determined to exhaust every possibility, Dann and Krista went right up to their marriage day trying to repair fences and offer reconciliation and forgiveness to their ex-spouses."

After a meeting with Eddie, in which Krista's former husband made it clear he was *not* interested in reconciliation, Dann and Krista took their relationship out of neutral and put it into gear. They began singing together at churches, civic groups, and in concerts of their own. As their musical lives intertwined, so did their personal lives, the two so closely connected that neither of them can tell you when they had their "first date."

"More likely than not," says Dann, "it was probably a dinner before or after one of our concerts."

Pastor in Training

Under the tutelage of Eddie Malphrus, Dann became intimately acquainted with a style of ministry not unique to First Baptist, but certainly perfected by them. As explained by Eddie, "It didn't make any difference what was going on in your own life, if you were on our staff and someone went to the hospital, you went, too." Under Eddie's guidance, the care of their fellow members moved from lip service to action and soon became the focus of Eddie's church. "Our church became known as the church that cared for people," recalls Eddie.

When Dann returned to Sulphur, he initially distanced himself from close relationships—an understandable response from the pain he had experienced. Soon, however, things changed, and Dann moved from an emotionally distant intellectual to an involved and caring pastor.

Recalls Eddie, "as God brought healing into his life, Dann grew tremendously over the years. You could see the growth in his sermons. They became people-oriented. He identified with his listeners and communicated a genuine love." Eddie gives an amusing example of other changes: "When Dann first came to Sulphur he couldn't visit in a hospital—he'd turn white at just the thought of blood. I would go into his office and start talking to him about a surgery, and he'd say to me, 'now buddy, you're going to have to stop right there, I'm losing it.' I've seen him go from turning white at just the thought of an operation to holding the hands of people who were dying and ministering to them in unbelievable situations."

Besides caring for their own members, First Baptist Church of Sulphur served their community. Eddie set the example by visiting those in the hospital regardless of their connection with his church. The results of that approach were evident when it came time for him to move.

"The last day I was at Sulphur, I went to the hospital, and several nurses came and hugged me and told me they would miss me. I got to looking at them and realized that only two belonged to our church."

Dann's experience under Eddie prepared him well for his next church, which would take everything he had to give and test everything he had learned.

Moving On

First Baptist Church of Sulphur occasionally sponsored revival services—special services intended to lead people to Christ and renew the faith of those who already believed. Invited to lead a series of revival services was a former pastor of the church, Dr. Loren White. After becoming Senior Pastor of a large church in Dallas, Texas, Dr. White looked forward to his returns to Sulphur and reconnecting with many long-time friends, Eddie Malphrus among them. In one of their conversations, Eddie brought up Dann.

"Loren, I'd like to talk with you about Danny, our Minister of Music," Eddie began. He then proceeded to tell Dann's story. After discussing Dann's divorce, musical gifts, pastoral gifts and calling to the ministry, Eddie then concluded with a question: "Do you know of any ministry opportunity in your area that he could take on?"

News of Dann's divorce piqued Dr. White's interest. He had just stood by his own daughter through an unwanted divorce, and the memories tore at his heart. Seeing her agony caused a soul-searching re-examination of his views on the subject.

"Let me see what I can do when I get home," he responded.

A short while later, Dann received a call,

"How'd you like to be our Minister to Singles and Young Adults?" asked Dr. White. "There are over a half-million singles in the Greater Dallas area, and we'd like to have a ministry to them."

"Dann was excited about the possibility," recalls Eddie, "but before he could serve at East Grand Baptist Church, he had to be ordained [the process by which a denomination confers the recognition and authority of a minister]. In the Southern Baptist denomination, a local congregation ordains a person.

"When Dann and I first began talking about his divorce and his call to ministry it was in the early eighties. At that time, it was almost unheard of for a divorced person to be ordained as a Southern Baptist minister. Our church had to deal with this issue if we wanted to ordain him, so I took our people on a pilgrimage. In sermons on Sunday evenings and Bible studies during the week, we studied what the Bible said about the subject. By the time we finished, it was clear that ordaining Dann was the right thing to do, and his ordination was one of the most beautiful services I've ever been a part of."

Wedding Bells

It had been three years since Dann's divorce, but the scars remained. In spite of the healing, and in spite of his feelings for Krista, marriage frightened him. His fear resulted in a rather unusual proposal. While presently the source of smiles and laughter, at the time it was the best he could manage. Scratch the romantic candlelit dinner with an engagement ring springing unexpectedly from its concealed hiding place. He sprang the question in his car in the church parking lot following a Sunday service. It was a crisp November morning, and the two were talking about the future when Dann, sounding more like a discouraged door-to-door vacuum cleaner salesman than a love-smitten suitor, turned to Krista: "You wouldn't want to get married, would you?"

While hardly sweeping Krista off her feet, Dann's proposal was a relief. She realized that Dann was so frightened by the idea of marriage that she might have to bring it up herself. Unsure about Dann's seriousness, that was a doubtful possibility. "He's not a person who easily shows his feelings," she recalls. "I thought that if he didn't ask me to marry him soon, we would probably part ways, and I'd remain in Sulphur."

With the wedding planned for March, Dann moved to Dallas in January, living with his brother and fixing up the church-owned house that would be their first home. As soon as he arrived in Dallas however, he knew something was missing.

"It wasn't until I moved that I realized how much I missed Krista," recalls Dann. "I didn't want to be there without her." They moved up the wedding date.

Replacing the church's Sunday evening service, and surrounded by members of neighboring churches who cancelled their own evening services for the event, Dann and Krista were married on February 20, 1983. To the unease of several, Eddie's message was not your normal marital fare. From their vantage point at the rear of the church, Dann and Krista observed people squirming in their seats. Opting for scriptural truth over sentimentality, Brother Eddie launched into a sermon on divorce and remarriage. He mentioned how God hates divorce, how God's will is for people to be married to one person for life, and what happens when one marriage partner decides to break their vows. He discussed the freedom God gives us to follow Him or to go in another direction. He pointed to the responsibility of the believer to do all that they could to effect a reconciliation, and how first Dann, and then Krista, had done just that. He talked about how God's love is extended to the victims of divorce and how He seeks to redeem their sufferings and sometimes unites them with a partner who is also following Christ, as was happening that evening. From this thought provoking and for some a disturbing message, Eddie then transitioned from preacher to officiant and presided over Dann and Krista's marriage.

Following an abbreviated three-day honeymoon in San Antonio, the newlyweds packed their belongings into a rented U-Haul and, with little Natalie in her car seat, drove the two-and-a-half hours to Dallas. Unknown to Dann at the time, what awaited him at East Grand Baptist would underscore Krista's presence as a gift from God.

Chapter 7 | AN UNFINISHED WORK

Initially excited about his first pastoral assignment, Dann's arrival at East Grand Baptist portended anything but a pleasant experience. The church had just completed a million-dollar building campaign at a time when it was losing members. They were now in a financial crisis. Among the members who remained was an influential group that wanted the senior pastor fired. Thinking Dann came to spy on them, they employed criticism and personal attacks to undermine him, even questioning the legitimacy of his marriage and the validity of his ordination. Dann's response?

"Some of them wouldn't even talk to me, but I'd just go up and be friendly and ask them how they were doing and pretend nothing was wrong. I prayed for them, and I prayed for me, and I just kept on going."

If there was a safe harbor from the storm engulfing Dann and Krista at East Grand, it was Tony and Ann Whitten. Following a career with the Dallas, Texas police department, Tony retired, becoming the part-time bodyguard for the president of a bank holding company. Other than missing their three grown children, now spread around the country, Tony and his wife enjoyed their retirement years, especially their involvement at East Grand. Tony served as chairman of their Board of Deacons and Ann devoted herself to a ministry of prayer. Their respective roles brought them into close and frequent contact with Dann and Krista. Spurred by the discovery that both husbands grew up in fatherless homes, the two couples soon became good friends. Dann felt comfortable with this tough but gentle and big-hearted ex-cop, a man who enjoyed providing for his own children the father he never knew himself. Now retired, their children gone, but with parenting instincts still very much alive, Tony and his wife were ready to "adopt."

"We felt drawn to Dann and Krista from the beginning," says Tony. "They were a sweet, loving and mature couple. Dann is one of the kindest men I've ever known. It didn't take long before they were family."

"They just reached out and took us under their wings," Dann recalls.

Following the Senior Pastor's resignation, the church began the search for his replacement, appointing Dann as the interim. Finally possessing the needed authority, Dann was eager to implement changes to reverse the church's decline. The first change, however, didn't originate with him. The Personnel Board directed him to fire a key employee whose hostile attitude was poisoning the church community. Dann agreed with the Board's reasoning, but this wasn't the way he did things. Nevertheless, he complied, and after witnessing the results, was glad he did.

"Things began to change after that," he remembers. "Maybe it was that employee's influence, or that people realized we wouldn't tolerate such hostility, but the people who had been against me treated me differently following the firing."

As Dann sees it, there was yet another reason for the turnaround: a group of women he calls the "three plus fourteen."

"This small group consisted of Krista, her two close friends, Ann Whitten and LaDonna Thurman, plus fourteen shut-ins recruited for the sole purpose of praying for the church.

"I'm not trying to be overly-spiritual about this," says Dann, "but I'm convinced it was their prayers that made the difference. After those fourteen women joined the original three, things started to change."

Dann went to work on the church's finances, cutting the budget and changing fiscal policies. For the first time in years, the church now had a healthy balance sheet. Within a few months, the turnaround was complete, and an atmosphere of hope and encouragement replaced the former acrimony. Then the church located a new Senior Pastor, and Dann had a problem: a large number of people wanted him to continue in that position.

"I didn't know what to do. The man they had called was a good man. I didn't want to create problems for him, which meant I had to leave, but I didn't know where to go. Most doors were still closed to me." Wrestling with uncertainty, Dann and Krista welcomed the invitation for a getaway with their good friends Tony and Ann.

Residents of Dallas usually chose either the mountains of Colorado or New Mexico for their vacation destinations. Tony and Ann favored New Mexico, encouraged by the availability of a condominium at Angel Fire, a ski area transforming itself into a four-season resort. Ready for a change of scenery, the Whittens made plans to rent the condominium over Labor Day weekend and invited Dann and Krista to join them.

"The pastorate can be tough on folks," Tony explains. "Church people can be quite critical, and the pastor's job can be pretty lonely. We thought they'd enjoy the chance to get away, and I knew we'd enjoy having them along. As it turned out, I was glad I asked. I came down with a flu bug that pretty much incapacitated me. If Dann hadn't been along to do the driving, we couldn't have gone. We just purchased a new Ford minivan—it was the first year they came out with them—and I spent most of the trip asleep on the back seat."

Following their all day drive from Dallas, it was near dusk when the party reached Angel Fire. Driving by a new building with a sign on the lawn reading "First Baptist Church," Tony exclaimed,

"That wasn't here last time we came. Why don't we come here for church?"

That Sunday morning, two couples from Dallas walked into an unfinished sanctuary and took their seats on folding chairs resting on a plywood sub-floor. The visitors easily outnumbered the handful of regulars that holiday weekend and the congregation of 70-80 almost outnumbered the available chairs. During the announcements, the visiting preacher apologized. He had another commitment that evening, so there wouldn't be a Sunday evening service.

As people were munching cookies and sipping coffee after the service, Tony went into action. Meeting new people was something he enjoyed, but this time, he had a mission. Going from one regular to another, he'd shake their hands and talk about his friends Dann ("he's a preacher") and Krista ("boy can she sing!"). Working his way over to the guest speaker, he repeated his mantra. Finally...

"Do you think he'd be willing to preach for us tonight?" said the speaker.

"I've never known a preacher who didn't want to preach," laughed Tony. Dann had one foot out the door when he felt a tap on his shoulder.

Back at the condominium, Dann reached into his briefcase. He typically carried a couple of sermons with him for this very contingency. Recalling the condition of the new sanctuary, one of the titles leaped off the page: "God's Unfinished Work."

Question: If you're God, and you've got a preacher in need of a church who doesn't like snow, can't ski and has an aversion to the cold, what do you do? Right! You give him a wife who also doesn't like the cold, can't ski, and send them both of them to a ski resort.

Following the evening service, the people of the church knew it, and so did Dann and Krista. "Are you thinking what I'm thinking?" He asked her as they walked back to the van. Two months later Angel Fire Baptist Church invited Dann to be their first pastor.

After making the necessary arrangements and submitting his resignation, Dann was in for a surprise. East Grand Baptist Church sponsored a "Dann Masters Day," a well-planned and exuberant celebration of his brief two-and-a-half-year tenure. Among the organizers? The same people who made life so difficult for him when he first arrived.

Chapter 8 | ANGEL FIRE

It's a breathtaking sight seen by very few. The Ute Indians, according to legend, named the phenomenon "fire of the Gods," only to have it renamed "fire of the angels" by Christian missionaries and then (as legend has it) shortened to "Angel Fire" by none other than Kit Carson of Wild West fame.[5] It occurs about once or twice a year. The rays of the setting sun, ricocheting off a low layer of clouds hovering over Aqua Fria Peak, coat the top of the peak in bright yellows, neon oranges, and flaming reds, prompting gasps of awe from privileged observers.

Angel Fire is a destination resort—a bustling island of recreational activity springing like an oasis in the middle of a state populated with more sagebrush than residents. Visitors hail from New Mexico (the state capital is only three hours away), Oklahoma, Texas, and Kansas. In the winter, snow guns and grooming machines transform the mountain into a skiing mecca. Like other destination resorts, underneath the seasonal population explosion of thousands lie a much smaller number of year-round residents. When Dann and Krista arrived, Angel Fire numbered three-hundred-and-fifty residents, forming a close-knit community with all the advantages and drawbacks of a small town.

The lack of healthcare and educational facilities were the two most notable inconveniences for Angel Fire residents. The closest hospital was in Taos, thirty minutes away, and children had to be bussed out of town for school. The end of the bussing began in 2000 when a small group of highly motivated citizens, tired of sending their children to faraway communities, looked at alternatives. On September 4, 2001, a crowd of teenagers burst through the newly opened doors of Moreno Valley High School—New Mexico's newest charter school. In spite of its small size (less than a hundred students) the school provided a first class education and became the epicenter of town pride when the 2008 *Newsweek/Washington Post Challenge Index* ranked it as the forty-first best high school in the country.

Not only was Angel Fire without a school in its beginning years, it also lacked a church. Those desiring worship services drove out of town. Seeing the need and opportunity, the gargantuan First Baptist Church of Dallas, Texas, with twenty-five thousand members, took an interest. Working with their denominational counterparts in New Mexico, First Baptist provided the funding to put up a building and start a ministry. In the summer of 1985, less than a year later, the not-quite-finished church hosted their first Labor Day weekend service. Among the visitors that day were Tony and Ann Whitten and their friends Dann and Krista Masters.

Behind the scenes, Dann's road to the pulpit of Angel Fire Baptist Church wasn't a smooth one. Objections came from both within the church and among the local association of Southern Baptist churches. Their reasons were, by this time, all too familiar. While Dann and Krista were unaware of the controversy, God wasn't. When the church voted on calling him as their pastor, one woman got her whole family together to vote against him. Then, inexplicably, she did just the opposite. As she told Dann several years later, "When I entered the church I felt God was telling me to vote *for* you." With a stunned family looking on, she did just that.

Two families left in protest following the church's vote to call Dann. Several years later one of them returned for a visit. After the service, the husband caught up with Dann outside the back of the church.

"I was wrong," he said looking down at the ground. "I'm sorry, I just didn't understand."

Soon after the church's vote to call Dann, the local association of Southern Baptist churches, assuming an authority they didn't have, voted on Dann's calling to Angel Fire. A denominational executive told him, "The vote is split down the middle," he said, "I don't think you should go."

"First of all," Dann replied, "the church has already called me, and secondly, the association doesn't have any authority in the matter." The executive nodded in agreement.

"Years later he came up to me after a service at Angel Fire and said 'Dann, having you come was the best thing that ever happened to this place.'"

Stuck Out in the Middle of Nowhere

From Dallas, Texas, population 1.2 million with 3605 people per square mile, Dann and Krista moved to Angel Fire, New Mexico, population 350, whose thirteen residents per square mile— if evenly distributed — would be invisible to each other. There would be many adjustments to this new setting, including Dann's attitude. Given his later success, his original thoughts are amusing.

"Well, this is God giving me a chance to preach," Dann remembers thinking, "I'll probably be stuck out here in the middle of nowhere hidden away from humanity and lost forever."

Sparking Dann's brief foray into self-pity was an intense desire to succeed. Anyone questioning his gifts or abilities would find proof of both at his former pastorate. In many denominations, East Grand would have been the first of a string of ever-larger churches, his past successes rewarded with greater responsibilities. But Dann was divorced, and the fact that his first wife chose to break her vows became an impenetrable barrier to advancement in Southern Baptist churches. For the people of Angel Fire, however, it was to be a fortunate injustice.

Arrival Day

"We arrived at Angel Fire on January 2, 1986, and for a very godly reason," says Dann, smiling. "The University of Oklahoma was playing in the Orange Bowl on New Year's Day, so, of course, the Lord wouldn't want me on the road when I could be at home rooting for them." Dann's support apparently helped. The Sooners trounced Penn State that year 26 to 10.

Dann's four-vehicle convoy pulled into the snow-blanketed resort on a cold and sunny winter's day. Dann led the way with the U-Haul followed by Krista and now seven-year-old Natalie in the family car. Two loaded pickup trucks brought up the rear, driven by volunteers from East Grand. Afternoon shadows were lengthening as they pulled into the parking lot of the new church and, for the Masters, their new home. Lacking the resources to provide their pastor with a house, the church converted the upper floor of their building into a two-bedroom apartment.

Following a brief tour, the group made their way to the local general store/pizza parlor for dinner. A light snow was falling when they emerged. Stepping out into a pitch-black landscape, Dann sensed that something was out of place. Then it struck him: "The darkness—we were from Dallas, a city that was awash in lights even in the middle of the night and we had just moved to a town that didn't even have a street light. That night, there wasn't even any moonlight. We couldn't believe how dark it was."

Kindled by the darkness and isolation of their new surroundings, a mantel of despair fell on Dann. "We were the only ones in the condominium complex. The whole building was empty. As far as you looked, the only things you could see were the scattered lights of a few houses." The emptiness felt like the rod of God's judgment. Wrapped in discouragement, he thought to himself, "My life will never make a difference." Unknown to him at the time, in that remote, out-of-the-way place, Dann would end up preaching to thousands, his words bringing hope and new life to many times the number who would ever have heard him in a non-resort church.

Dann and Krista moved into their new home the next day with different feelings. For Dann, a growing sense of excitement quickly replaced his despair of the night before. The homemaker of the family, however, wasn't all that enthusiastic. Recalls Krista, "Our home was nice, and we were grateful for it, but it was very small and had a kitchen the size of a closet." The

850 square foot two-bedroom apartment, complete with its closet kitchen, would be their home for the next four-and-a-half years.

As the family settled into their new surroundings, Dann's perceptions of Angel Fire began to change. What he initially viewed as God's punishment now took on the aura of a divinely ordained gift. "I felt like God had finally given us a place where we could minister openly, freely and creatively."

Krista's adjustment to her new surroundings took a bit longer. Like Dann, she didn't like the cold, a word defined in Dallas by evenings that dropped into the 50's. Neither she nor Dann were outdoor folks who eagerly waited to click into their skis and fly down the slopes. Moreover, for Krista there was an added adjustment: she had never lived away from her family and missed them intensely. For the first several months, she would pile Natalie into the car and drive off to visit her grandmother back in Sulphur or her family back in Texas. Her feelings on the way home from those trips were the same as she experienced at East Grand: "it felt like a gray cloud hanging over us."

Tragedy in Paradise

After the previous night's snowfall, five to six inches of new powder greeted the day's skiers. The night's accumulation allowed the resort to open more of its wooded areas and tree trails. Depending as they did on natural snow, those trails were always the last to open at the resort, and that morning some were still closed for lack of cover. Skiing closed terrain is an illegal but common practice at many resorts. For those who love skiing, nothing is more enjoyable than first tracks on new snow. To some, a sign reading "closed" after a fresh snowfall is more of an invitation than a warning. On his last run of the day, an eighteen-year-old ski patroller turned off the groomed trail. Ducking under a rope onto a closed trail, he shot into the woods. The new snow under his feet was pure joy. He darted around trees, stumps and small boulders, his skill, experience and muscular thighs enabling him to turn ever more quickly. The more quickly he turned, the faster he skied. We'll never know if it was a moment's distraction or catching the metal edge of one of his skis on an unseen root or rock, but one minute the young patroller was enjoying life in all its fullness, and the next moment his lifeless body lay crumpled at the base of a tree.

Dann was in his office when the call came from the Legends Hotel telling him of the young man's death.

"Would you go over and meet with the family?" the voice inquired.

It was a local family. Approaching their home, Dann saw several cars already parked out front. Word travels fast in small towns. A friend of the family opened the door. Dann introduced himself.

"Come on in, Reverend," said the woman and then over her shoulder, "it's the Reverend." Dann followed her into the living room. Seated on the couch were the boy's parents. The husband's arm was around his wife, who was dabbing at her eyes with a handkerchief. He stood up as Dann entered, extending his hand.

"Thank-you for coming," he said nervously, "here, have a seat."

Dann pulled up a chair across from them as the husband introduced his wife.

"I'm so sorry," Dann said to her softly, his eyes repeating the message.

Dann took the hand she extended, pressing it warmly between both of his.

"This whole thing has…" she stopped short, retrieving her hand and choking back a sob while covering her face.

"I understand," said Dann, touching her shoulder, and he did. He had never lost a child, but he was well acquainted with a broken heart.

"Uh… we haven't had much time to think about it," said the father uncomfortably.

Dann knew what was coming next.

"I don't want to impose…but… if you're not busy… would you be able to…"

"Of course," said Dann, mercifully interrupting.

"I wonder… the funeral home…[the nearest was a half-hour away in Taos] maybe the school?"

"You're welcome to use the church."

"Really?" the father replied, surprised. "We're not churchgoers."

"No difference. We'd be honored."

"Oh… well…that's very kind of you." He paused for a moment. Then, turning to his wife, "Honey?" She looked up and nodded.

"Well, I guess that's what we'll do."

Dann, reaching for his wallet: "here's my card. Just give me a call. We'll get together to plan the service. Would you like me to offer a prayer before I leave?"

At times like this, most people are open to such a request, but you never know, so Dann was pleased to hear the husband respond, "Please."

"Let's join hands," said Dan. A simple act adding comfort in times of shared grief, Dann was no stranger to the practice.

Dann bowed his head and began, "Lord, at times like this, words are so inadequate. We're still in a state of shock and disbelief. Someone we dearly love is now gone. That's hard to accept. We ask 'why?' But there is no answer, and even if there were, it wouldn't make any difference; it wouldn't bring him back. Yet in the midst of our pain and loss, we thank-you. We thank you that you love us. We thank you that you care for us. We thank-you for the life and hope you offer to us through Jesus Christ. We pray that you would pour out your comfort on this family and these friends; that you would be very close and very real to them during this time of grief. In Jesus' name, Amen."

Most of the town turned out for the service a few days later and heard words of comfort and hope. Many liked what they saw and heard from the newest member of their community.

"He's the type of man who will go the second mile for you," said one acquaintance.

"He doesn't judge people," said another.

"The first couple of weeks after I arrived we were running about thirty people in church," recalls Dann, "but after the funeral, the attendance shot up to 80. I think the locals realized that we were sincere, wanted to help, and weren't interested in shoving anything down anyone's throat."

In looking back over Dann's ministry, one soon realizes that the funeral service simply sped up the inevitable. If not at that service, then at some other venue or from repeated personal contacts, the people of Angel Fire would come to know Dann as a man who cared deeply about them, for both this life and for the next. With his slow, Oklahoma drawl, Dann communicated a compelling compassion. People got the message, and many embraced the Jesus he shared. As the town grew (its size tripled during Dann's stay), attendance at Angel Fire Baptist mushroomed.

Chapter 9 | WE'RE NOT IN DALLAS ANYMORE

The epiphany happened on Dann and Krista's wedding anniversary. They were on their way to the theater when Dann—the incurable romantic—turned to Krista and said, "Let's do a few house visits on our way." As Dann remembers, "it just seemed like the logical thing to do [fortunately for Krista, Dann's concept of logic has changed since those days]. We were called to Angel Fire to bring growth to a new church. When we started, we did what we were trained to do in Dallas—we went out knocking on doors. There were three places I wanted to visit. Nobody was home at the first two, but I clearly remember the third one. We were all dressed up—me in a suit with shoes shined and Krista wearing high heels, and here we were walking through the snow and trying to make our way up this icy driveway. I was slipping, and Krista was trying to steady me, then she was slipping, and I was trying to steady her. At one point, we just looked at each other and broke out laughing. I thought to myself, 'we're not in Dallas anymore.'

"Our experience that night was a microcosm of the difficulties of sharing Christ in that setting. Not only was it difficult to get to people physically, but it was also difficult spiritually. In doing what we did—knocking on doors—we were simply trying to be obedient to what we thought God wanted, but in trying to be obedient, we were stupid. Even worse, we were laughable."

In the Beginning…

Dann and Krista had adjustments to make when they arrived in Angel Fire, and so did their church. In those days, when Southern Baptists started ministries they chose from one of two models: a "preaching station" or a "church start." A preaching station might occur at motorcycle rallies and racetracks where the preacher has a one-time opportunity to address a crowd—a common scenario in resort areas. A church start, however, focuses on building a group of people into a permanent church.

When Dann arrived, Angel Fire Baptist regarded itself as a preaching station. They viewed Dann's job as simply to "preach the Gospel," and not worry about the community. In reality, the ministry at Angel Fire resort was both a preaching station *and* a church start. Unlike a normal church, during ski season Dann would look out over a congregation filled with exponentially more visitors than local residents. He soon concluded, "If we're to fulfill the ministry that God had given us, we need to teach our people how to minister to the tourists." Dann helped his flock understand that God was not only calling *him* to such a ministry, he was also calling *them*—they were in this together. Over the next two years, the church joined Dann in his vision of serving both visitors and community members.

Eddie Malphrus comments: "If you're going into an area like Dann did where you have three or four families, you go into it with the idea that 'I'm going to go and love these people and care about them and see if they can be molded into a group that will reach out and minister to the resort population.' That was Dann's contribution, and God used him to build a nucleus of people that grew." As with many other protégés of Eddie Malphrus, Dann was simply passing on the powerful example he experienced in Sulphur.

Getting to Know You

In reaching out to his new neighbors, Dann found a culture far different from the friendly and outgoing people of Oklahoma where chance meetings on the street would turn into lengthy conversations.

"It wasn't that the people were unfriendly—when you got to know them they were great—it's just that they were more guarded than the people Krista and I had grown up with. I felt I just *had* to get to know them."

Dann's first stop? The local coffee shop and drug store with its old-fashioned lunch counter. If someone were sitting alone at a table, he'd soon hear a friendly voice with an Oklahoman drawl, "Hi, mind if I join you?"

Because Angel Fire is a small community, it wasn't long before Dann would be sitting down at tables with two and three people, most of whom he had met before.

In addition to their guests, like most ski resort communities, Angel Fire consists of several groups of people: corporate management, employees, small business owners, second homeowners and retirees. One of Dann's first and more pleasant discoveries was that the same people who didn't want you knocking on their doors greeted you warmly when you showed up at their place of work.

"I'd visit with the merchants and get to know them, saying that the church was there to serve them and inviting them to call on me if we could help." That attitude was the secret of Dann's success: he and his church members saw themselves as servants. More than any one of the church's many programs, it was this approach that contributed to the church's growth. To love people is to serve them—something that Jesus himself sought to drive home to his disciples—and it's that kind of love, as Dann and his people would experience, that draws people.

Grateful business owners didn't hesitate to take up Dann on his offer of help, and he soon found himself counseling with their employees and providing other forms of assistance. After Dann and Krista's first Christmas, business owners invited Angel Fire Baptist to sing at their annual Community Christmas tree lighting program. Following the singing, Dann would take his choir caroling at nearby establishments.

Not all groups in Angel Fire were easy to reach. One of the hardest was the affluent, who showed little interest in the church or its programs—a response not unique to Angel Fire. Wealth has a way of luring its possessors into a false sense of security, drowning out their spiritual needs and leaving them with feelings bordering on omnipotence.

There was another group that was difficult for Angel Fire Baptist Church to reach, ironically not because of their affluence, but because of their poverty. This was the predominantly Catholic and Hispanic population, which, since they couldn't afford to live in town, resided some distance away. A group populated by the clerks and housekeepers and janitors on the mountain, Dann and his church opened their arms to them. "Their priest would come around only about once a month, so when there was a funeral we'd open our church to them and let them use our fellowship hall. They didn't switch and become Baptists, but they'd often visit our services."

Soon after arriving in Angel Fire, Dann found himself with mixed feelings of excitement and uncertainty. As people got to know him, experiencing his pastor's heart and counselor's ear, it was a short trip to Angel Fire Baptist on Sunday mornings. But what about the tourists who descended upon the area? He was excited about reaching out to the tens of thousands of visitors, yet uncertain how to go about it. It seemed incongruous to him that a church in a resort such as Angel Fire didn't have a strategy for ministering to the crowds who skied in the winter and golfed in the summer. There must be a way to reach them, but how? The answer wasn't long in coming.

Chapter 10 | SHOW TIME

While Dann and Krista had little interest in the sports that drew thousands to their resort community, their presence in Angel Fire was still a match made in heaven: Angel Fire was not only skiing in the winter and golf and tennis in the summer, it was music all year 'round. Shortly before Dann and Krista arrived, there began a series of concerts known as "Music from Angel Fire." Violinists and cellists went out from the resort into surrounding townships, bringing the beauty of chamber music to the remote villages of New Mexico. Dann and Krista were in a community that loved music.

With the approach of summer, the Angel Fire Repertory Theater announced tryouts for the 1959 off-Broadway musical "Little Mary Sunshine." For Dann and Krista, it was a natural. Expressing interest in participating, they received an invitation to an organizing meeting the night before the auditions.

"The opportunity was attractive," explains Dann, "because the community didn't offer anything for families in the evenings and the Repertory Theater provided a wholesome, family-oriented program." While Angel Fire drew people who loved music and were good at it, the town's small population reduced the likelihood of possessing the best talent. Enter Krista and Dann. Word of their talents quickly spread, and the leader of the organizing meeting astonished Dann and Krista with an invitation:

"We'd like you to take the two leading roles."

"We were pretty surprised to be asked," remembers Dann. "They were a close group, and would normally give the important roles to friends who had already proven themselves. A lot of their members were younger people with theatrical degrees."

The seasonally empty base lodge hosted the auditions the next afternoon. Dann and Krista shared the lead roles as the Royal Canadian Mountie and Little Mary Sunshine in a musical their friend Carolyn Granger labeled "kind of corny but a whole lot of fun." The new pastor and his wife were a smash hit and the arts community immediately embraced their new stars, a blessing for not only Dann and Krista, but also for their church.

Musical Christmas

As fall wore on and Christmas neared, Dann and Krista pondered what to do for the church's yuletide celebration. The two of them could certainly present a musical program, but that idea didn't excite them. It felt more like an "if all else fails" alternative. Their church had a small choir by then, but it was too small for anything serious. Then it hit them.

"What would you think of putting on a Christmas musical and inviting the Repertory Theater to join us?" Dann said to Krista one day.

"You know," she said reflectively, "I was thinking the same thing."

"We'll put together our own cantata," added Dann, a note of excitement in his voice. "We'll include both church and secular music so the unchurched will feel at home. It'll be fun!

"We quickly discovered," said Dann, "that our involvement with the community theater eliminated any sense of competition with them. At our first cantata, the guy who headed up the arts group even came and played the piano for one of the songs."

Not only did Dann and Krista's participation in the Repertory Theater eliminate a sense of competition, it also led to the church's growth.

"We had several people show up for services because of our involvement with the community theater. In fact, one of the ladies who started coming, Carolyn Granger, turned into one of our most faithful members. Although a nurse by training, she was very active in the arts program. We've remained friends ever since."

"I was president of the Repertory Theater at the time," Carolyn reflects, "and got to know Dann and Krista through 'Little Mary Sunshine.' I started going to church after that and then joined their adult Sunday school. A couple of years later in 1988, even though I wasn't raised Baptist, I became a member."

"What was it that kept you coming back to Dann's services?" I asked.

"I began going to the church because of my relationship with Dann and Krista. After attending for a year or two, I joined primarily because of Danny's messages. He didn't preach at us, he taught us, and that's what was missing all of my life. I would go to a church and listen to somebody preach *at* me, but Danny wasn't like that. He is a fantastic teacher, and Krista is a good music teacher, so I learned from both of them. In the first year I was attending, they started doing Christmas Cantatas and I love to sing, so I was in all of them. I learned a lot about music from Krista, and because of my background in the theater I could help them with their own productions."

Cowboy Christmas

Dann strolls out in front of the audience in the church's auditorium, guitar in hand. What catches one's attention is not the guitar, however, but his clothing: white buckskins topped with a white cowboy hat and the outline of a white mask. He's dressed as the angel Gabriel for the church's annual Christmas pageant. This year it's Robert Sterling's comic Christmas musical *For Unto Y'all—a Cowboy Christmas*. One-hundred-and-fifty people pack the small auditorium for the first of four holiday performances. Dann's introduction is warm and friendly, inviting children to join him on stage and talking to them as if he was in his own living room. Then, to the amusement of the audience, Dann's four-year-old son Adam wanders down the aisle and up onto the stage. First-time visitors hold their breath, wondering if the boy's in for a scolding, but Dann greets his son as if this was the most natural thing in the world, resting his hand on the boy's shoulder and speaking a few words to him. With Adam at his side, Dann turns his attention back to the audience, lifts his guitar and leads both audience and children in a medley of Christmas music: "Jingle Bells," "Rudolph," and "I'm Dreaming of a White Christmas." It's not your normal church fare, but then one remembers: "this isn't Dallas anymore."

Explains Dann, "'Jingle Bells' in a church auditorium says to a person who doesn't usually attend church: 'you're welcome here—just as you are.'" It was a compelling message.

The "Cowboy Christmas" pageant was one of the more unique musicals presented by Angel Fire Baptist Church. Re-casting the Christmas story in a small New Mexico town in the late 1800's complete with sound effects and choirs of angels (dressed in cowboy outfits, of course), the script has Mary responding to the announcement by the angel Gabriel of her impeding motherhood with an incredulous, "Yes, but how . . I mean… I'm still a… well, you know."

As the last chords drift away, the audience springs to their feet in enthusiastic applause. Wrapping up the program, Dann comes out to thank them for their attendance, recognize those who made the production possible, and fend off any potential critics with the statement that he's fully aware that Jesus wasn't born in New Mexico in the 1800's. He concludes by encouraging those who would like to talk more about their own relationships with Christ to approach him after the program.

From their first Christmas pageant in 1986, the popularity of these musical offerings continued to grow, attended by both residents and the large influx of resort guests vacationing over the Christmas holidays. The growth wasn't an accident.

"We concluded that if we were going to reach the visitors, we'd have to do something they'd want to include in their schedules. So we thought about a Christmas musical. But we had a problem that first year because we didn't have a full-time accompanist. We did have a fellow who worked at the mountain who said he could get away to accompany us for one song. That was a start. We used accompaniment tapes for a couple of songs; did some of them without accompaniment, and I played my guitar for others. We had costumes made—some people sewed their own—and we advertised it. It went over well, so we decided we would do it again next year, and do it better. The people from the first year came back, and the second year was ten times better. We had costumes, sets, and everything. Every year after that, we were [I was] driven to do better."

Dann and Krista's musicals didn't have much in common with old-fashioned church Christmas programs complete with robed choir members on risers. Instead, with the staging, lighting, acting and singing, they were closer to a Broadway production.

"We didn't have great voices ourselves," says Dann, a bit too modestly, "but we had people visiting from all over the world who wanted to be a part of it, and they did have good voices. Our budget was limited, so we made many things ourselves. I told one fellow what we needed for lighting, and he went out and made it. We had a couple of ladies who worked on scenery—I'd do the research, tell them what we needed, and they'd paint it."

The pageants grew in popularity. One family from Israel told Dann that because of them, they decided to make Angel Fire their permanent destination for Christmas vacations. A Bible school a few states away sent a film team to bring back to their school a demonstration of what a small church can do to reach their community.

"If you had friends visiting for the holidays," says Ruth Bush, founder of Angel Fire's largest real estate agency, "you wouldn't think twice about inviting them to the pageants—they were just that popular and well done." A local hotel even requested a special performance for their guests. Carolyn Granger goes on to explain one of the reasons for their popularity: "Dann is a perfectionist. He wanted things done right. He was a performer striving for the best possible performance. He made us realize that we should do our very best because we were doing it for God. So you did your very best, and you understood why he was such a perfectionist, as was Krista."

After Angel Fire Baptist Church's first Christmas pageant, there followed a host of other musical offerings during the rest of the year—both religious and secular. Dann and Krista developed a symbiotic relationship with the performing arts community. The two of them would help with the repertory theater's Broadway musicals in the summer months, and the performing arts people would join the church's musical offerings in both summer and winter. In the beginning, the church would borrow lighting and stage equipment from the theater, but as the church's musicals grew, the theater ended up borrowing from them. Concerts and musical performances became one of the church's most effective forms of outreach.

"Music attracts people," says Dann. "We did Christmas programs and Easter programs and programs on the Fourth of July. In the summer, we would do Broadway musicals and western musicals—"Sons of the Pioneers" and the like—and those performances drew many people. Even if it's music about something they're not sure they agree with, they'll come because they like music, so it can be a powerful medium for sharing the Gospel."

Dann and Krista's musical programs, both religious and secular, produced a steady stream of visitors to their church. Drawn by the talented and soft-spoken young pastor and his attractive wife with the beautiful voice, some of those who visited on a Sunday morning continued attending. Bunny Jankowski was one of them.

"My husband and I moved to Angel Fire in 1992. When we arrived, I discovered that the only church that had an active congregation was the Baptist church. I'm not Baptist, but I went one Sunday, and I was overwhelmed with the charisma of Dann Masters, with the congregation, and with the music program. I felt so uplifted that I continued going."

Services Designed for the Guests, not the Regulars

Angel Fire Baptist geared not only their musical productions but also their worship services to the tourists and vacationers who flocked to the area. This meant two things: they had to "do church" differently, and they had to adjust their expectations.

"On Sundays we'd have fifty to a hundred attending our services from all around the world," reports Dann. "Most of them would never be back, but it was good to know that the message we were giving them would be spread to the ends of the earth. It kept us from thinking of ourselves as just a little hole in the wall someplace."

During the winter months, Angel Fire Baptist even had services on top of the mountain. On Sunday afternoons, Dann carried his guitar up the lift and eight to twelve skiers joined him around a small cross stuck into the snow. "Many of those who attended services on top of the mountain later found their way to the church in town," Dann reports.

"Doing church differently" required some changes. "When people come to resort areas they come to get away from the ordinary. As a church, we need to offer people something that's both familiar—so they'll feel comfortable, but also different—so they can walk away thinking 'that was a part of our vacation.'

"On any given month, we know where our visitors will come from. Then we try to be creative but not so different that they feel they've been slapped instead of hugged. For instance, there are things you can do with a congregation from California that you couldn't do with a congregation from Texas. You couldn't do an interpretive dance in the church if your crowd was from Texas because they don't do that in Texas, but the Californians would love it."

Evidence mounted that the church was hitting the mark. "One lady just wrote to say that we had helped her see that God cared for her and that her life was now back on track, and she was doing great. We'll probably never see her again this side of heaven, and she'll never contribute to our church financially, but that's not important. We're here to reach people when they come by our door, and our door happens to be next to a ski mountain in the winter and a golf course and tennis courts in the summer."

The focus on ministering to visitors and tourists required an adjustment not only in the church's methods of outreach but also in their expectations.

For most churches, when people come to faith in Christ it automatically translates into increased attendance and financial support. When those people are resort guests, however, neither occurs. This makes resort ministry "the purest form of ministry" says Dann, "because it requires you to minister without thought of return." He shares an example: "On one occasion, the police brought me someone who was threatening to shoot himself. The police took his gun and brought him over to the church, and we talked for a couple of hours. During our conversation, he began to see things differently and felt that he could go back and start over. He later wrote and thanked me for talking with him. About half of our ministry was to people like that. They would never become part of our church, but God used us to reach them, and that's what's important."

With a growing acceptance by the community and an enthusiastic response from visitors and guests, it would seem Dann had covered all the bases at Angel Fire, but there's one we've not yet mentioned. In comparing a resort to the human body, the mountain corporation is the heart.

Shortly after arriving, Dann introduced himself to Angel Fire Corporation's management team; it was the beginning of a lengthy friendship. "We remained friends all the time I was there," he reports, "even when we opposed them in the state legislature."

Chapter 11 | ANGEL FIRE CORPORATION

As Dann explained, "The Corporation needed a chaplain. Sometimes things would happen to their many visitors, not to mention the employees, and we'd be there for them."

After earning their trust, Angel Fire Corporation management and employees turned to Dann with increasing frequency. "Employees would come to me over the years—and sometimes transients—who would get themselves into trouble and be depressed or have marital problems and the corporation would call on me. I've counseled a lot of employees. They know they can come here—they don't have to be members of the church—and I'll talk to them, or they can call, and I'll go see them. They know I'm available."

Dann cites one example: "We had a baby one night who died in his sleep and the father wouldn't give him up until a minister came. So I went, and after I arrived, he gave the baby to the coroner. It was a great loss, and the parents needed someone to bridge the gap between God and the void they were feeling. That's what we do. We don't feel we're very good at it at times, but people see us as a bridge between themselves and God, and we're glad to be of help in that way."

In his relationship with the corporation, Dann strove for two things: helpfulness and availability. "I'd do services on the mountain when they asked—Easter sunrise services and occasionally others. I might not always agree with what they asked me to do, but I saw it as a means of breaking the ice and making contact with them and would do it if at all possible."

Like any community, there were marriages and funerals. Since the town didn't have its own cemetery, those who felt an attachment to the resort would occasionally request a memorial service and to have their ashes scattered on the mountain. "I might not agree with them theologically, but they thought a minister should be involved so they'd ask me, and I'd do it. I never compromised what I believed and used those opportunities to preach the good news of Jesus Christ—to tell what I believed to be the truth between life and death."

When it came to weddings, some of the requests were a bit unusual.

"People would want to be married on skis halfway up the mountain. I would agree to do it as long as they brought proof of pre-marital counseling or allowed me to do it. In the beginning, I used to require them to be Christians and had other expectations that ended up driving them away. Then it dawned on me that they were going to get married whether I did it or not, and I could be a part of their lives and try to influence them for the Gospel, or I could drive them away. I decided on the former."

Like most ministers, Dann required pre-marital counseling, but his policy regarding the customary wedding fee was unique. "At the end of our counseling sessions I'd make an offer: 'If you let me share the Gospel with you, I'll waive the fee.' No one ever turned me down, and I ended up marrying a lot of people other preachers turned away."

Taking A Stand

With a desire to help the corporation, one wouldn't expect that Dann would take a public stand against them, but that's exactly what he did—not once, but twice. On two separate occasions and under two separate owners, Angel Fire Corporation petitioned the state of New Mexico to allow casino gambling at the resort, viewing it as a revenue panacea. Dann and others saw it differently.

"The people who work at the mountain are struggling on their low pay. If you brought gambling into the picture they'd take the money they're spending on groceries and rent, and put it into the slot machines. Besides that, Angel Fire is a family resort, and that would no longer be the case if gambling was introduced."

Others felt the same way, and Dann organized them into a committee to fight the corporation's plans. "We were doing what we were supposed to be doing with this issue," he said. During the hearings at the state capital, the Corporation presented its case to the legislators and Dann and others rose to testify against them. Amazingly, it didn't change his relationship with the corporation. "We'd still talk with each other and remained friends through both of their attempts," recalls Dann. How did things turn out?

"We won," he said, "both times."

From another perspective, the community won...both times.

Outreach to Employees

Ski resorts are typically the playgrounds of the rich served by the sweat of the poor. With some exceptions, skiing is still a rich man's sport. Besides lift tickets, which at this writing can run up to $100 at major resorts, there is the equipment (a new set of skis, bindings, boots, and poles can easily cost over $1000), lodging and meals, not to mention transportation. Other than those in management positions, the ski industry normally pays close to the minimum wage.

Underscoring the industry's low pay, one popular ski instructor I know worked a season at McDonald's as an experiment. What he thought would happen, did happen: he made more money at McDonald's than he did teaching skiing. Low wages forces many seasonal employees to hold down two jobs. Lift attendants and ski instructors during the day serve as bar tenders and wait staff at night.

In their late teens and early twenties, most seasonal workers bring with them a variety of needs ranging from financial to social and emotional. For Dann and his church, these needs were opportunities. A special fund was set up to provide financially strapped employees with temporary housing and clothing as well as the occasional tank of gas. The church provided Continental-style breakfasts free of charge. The Wednesday night suppers were the most popular. Church members and area merchants donated food; tables were set up in the fellowship hall, members took turns preparing and serving, and the church flung open its doors to anyone wanting a free meal. Of course, as at all of the church's programs, Dann would invite people to drop by and talk.

"We had some of our people who worked at the mountain driving shuttle buses who loved inviting people to the church's programs, and we'd take out newspaper ads and put brochures in hotels and condominiums. Following the free meal was an elaborate musical show—it was a full-scale production. Those who came to the suppers didn't have to stay, but many of them did." Moreover, many of those who stayed were glad they did.

"There was a fellow from New Hampshire or Vermont," says Dann. "He had been a pretty rough character with a rough past. After going to several ski areas, he came to Angel Fire and one of our people invited him to a dinner and show. He came to every one of them, and they're all the same—they don't change every week. Noticing that, some of our people sought him out and began to talk with him. He was lonely and searching. In his forties, he admitted to his life being empty and we were gradually able to lead him to the Lord. This guy changed so much that his family members told us, 'he's a different man!'"

Not only did the church grow by reaching out to others; it also became a healing community similar to First Baptist in Sulphur. "A mountain employee started coming to the seeker's class at our church, invited by some of our people. At one time, he was heading into the ministry but became discouraged and dropped out. While in our class, he concluded that God *had* called him and after leaving us, re-enrolled at Baylor University.

"We've had other situations. A young lady came to the church. She was pregnant and came to escape from her small town and from her family's rejection. Our people opened their arms to her. Now she's had the baby and is back in Texas. I received a call from her the other day, and she's doing great."

Chapter 12 | COMMUNITY IMPACT

Dann's approach to the community was simple: "We would do anything, by any means possible within our conscience, to get a foot in the door." Angel Fire Baptist sponsored musical and dramatic programs, opened their building for community activities, loaned out their sound equipment, provided free counseling and gave economic assistance to those in need. The church's influence soon permeated the small community.

Until the late nineties, Angel Fire Baptist served as the town's community center. Before the town had its own school, yellow buses, belching diesel fumes, would pull into the church parking lot, picking up and discharging students from schools many miles away. After school, the multi-purpose room at the church echoed with the laughter of children playing while awaiting rides home. On Wednesday nights, a big dinner always ensured a large turnout for the children's choir practice and for Teen Kids. When the town built their own community center in the late nineties, in order to maintain their connection with the community, the church moved many of its own activities to the new building.

It was important to Dann to meet the needs of the town, but his first priority was elsewhere. "We were there for the sake of the Gospel, and everyone knew that right up front. Even though it wasn't the most popular thing in the area, we never tried to hide it or pretend we were something else."

Dann's openness to people of other religious persuasions turned Angel Fire Baptist into a place of worship for everyone, not just Southern Baptists. With arms embracing the whole community and a message uncompromising in its faithfulness to the Gospel, the church had an impact rarely seen today. "A lot of people told us that we 'tamed' the area for the Gospel," said Dann. "From what I understand, before we came, Angel Fire was an ungodly place with strong drug problems, both in town and in the surrounding areas. But after we went in, the real estate people would tell us all the time that the reason they sold homes and people were buying in the area was because we were there."

Besides real estate agents, merchants also profited from the church's presence. As word of Angel Fire Baptist spread to outlying areas, Dann received calls from other churches wanting to visit the resort. "Most were Baptist, but it didn't make any difference to us—we treated them all the same." Dann referred visiting church groups to local businesses such as ski rental shops, restaurants, and grocery stores. Business owners loved him.

A few years into Dann's tenure, he experienced an unexpected setback common in resort areas. "The first time it happened, it scared us to death.

After three years, we finally had a youth group numbering in the twenties. Then the resort went through a major downsizing and close to a hundred residents of our small town left within a week. Our youth group shrank to four people. It was like starting all over again. Individuals were always leaving, especially in management, but fortunately never again such a large group. The experience reminded us that ministry can't be something you're storing up for yourself."

Day Care Center

Seven years after it began, the church was in a position to respond to one of the community's greatest needs. "The workers of the community begged us to open a day care center," explains Krista, "a big need after the resort closed their own."

Krista and a group of women studied the state requirements. "At the time, our church was building an addition for Sunday school space, so we built it to comply with state requirements for a daycare facility. We also discovered that a certified teacher was required to lead the program." Enter Bunny Jankowski.

"Although I was never involved with young children," says Bunny, "my background was in children's theater, so I did have the right educational credentials and agreed to help. I didn't put it together—Krista and her group of ladies did a marvelous work organizing it—but I said 'okay, I'll do this for a couple of years, but I have to be honest with you when I say that this is not my gift.'"

From Church to Churches

Given the fractured nature of the Christian church in America, it was only a matter of time before it happened. In the late nineties, as Angel Fire grew (2008 census counted 982), other churches began appearing. Within a few years, there were four: a Lutheran church, the "United Church of Angel Fire"—a cooperative effort by the Presbyterians, Methodists, United Church of Christ and Christian Church (Disciples of Christ), a Pentecostal church, and Catholic masses held monthly by a visiting priest. How did Dann and his people respond to the newcomers?

"We'd help them. We invited every one of those churches on different Sundays to come and tell us what their vision was, and how we could be of help. Of course, they had some ideas that our people didn't hold with, but their presentations were interesting, nonetheless. We hoped those invitations would be a two-way street, but they never reciprocated." Not only did Dann welcome the new churches to the community, he encouraged those of his own flock who felt more at home among the newcomers to join them, something as common as a manager of McDonald's sending people to Burger King.

"Some of our people missed the liturgical worship services they were used to. When we talked, I said, 'well if that's something you feel you need then we'll do what we can to help you,' and we did. Most wanted a more formal service than we provided. Some wanted a more emotional experience, and they attended the Pentecostal church. That church didn't grow very well, and the others were pretty small at the time. These churches had their problems. We'd lose some of our people to them and then they'd come back."

Dann was hoping the new churches would join him in ministering to the community, but that didn't happen. Worse yet, instead of unity, the new churches brought division. "The appearance of other churches split the community," explained a disappointed Dann. "People's loyalties would be to different churches, and some saw themselves in competition with us, which effectively turned community members against each other. Also, the other churches were a little bit jealous because we were the biggest. I'm sorry to say that having those other churches come into town was bad for the community."

One could view Dann's words as the sour grapes response of someone who saw his own influence wane in the midst of unwelcome competition, but such a view would be wrong for two reasons. First, Dann had long ago replaced the desire of building a large congregation with the goal of serving the community and its visitors. Secondly, he reached out to these new churches because he viewed them as opportunities to *increase* the Christian influence in the community; he never viewed them as competitors.

Angel's Attic

In the fall of 1993, Dann joined one-hundred-and-fifty other Southern Baptist ministers from around the country for the National Resort Ministries Conference in Lake of the Ozarks, Missouri. The five-day conference covered almost every aspect of resort ministries, including starting thrift stores as a means of both funding and outreach. Rev. Tom Moore of Boone, North Carolina, presented a workshop using his RAM's Rack Thrift store (RAM an acronym for Resort Area Ministries) as an example. Tom described the financial benefits for both the ministry and the community. Dann attended, took notes and went away convinced.

"From that moment, I knew it was something we could do."

Back home, Dann soon realized "the church wasn't ready for it and the area wasn't ready for it."

Instead of feeling discouraged, he simply adjusted his sights.

"I began by just planting the idea. I learned this from someone a long time ago—I don't remember who, but when you want to do something new, you need to give people a chance to get used to it and provide time for the idea to percolate. So I planted the idea and then let it drop. About a year later, I brought it up again. This time, we talked about it a bit, and then I set it aside. The third time you present an idea you ask, 'what can we do with it?' With the thrift store, I realized we had enough interested people and access to enough donations of clothing and household goods that we *could* do it, and we did."

While RAM's Rack began as a source of funding *and* ministry, Dann started Angel's Attic solely as a ministry to the community. Its ultimate goal—like his entire ministry—would be spiritual, not material. Unfortunately, it was a goal never fully embraced by all the thrift store employees. After opening, the thrift store took on a life of its own; some of its workers sharing Dann's vision while others viewing it as an outreach with no spiritual implications. Carolyn Granger represents the first group.

"Sometimes people will come and just need someone to talk to. There's one guy who comes, and if there's any food, he'll help himself and then he has a book, and he'll just sit there. People will walk by and greet him with a 'Hi, Jack.' It's something he needs—he doesn't need the food or coffee, he just needs the company. We've had several people like that. They'll come by just to have someone to talk to or a friendly face to say 'hi, how's your day?' To me, that's more important than being able to sell them a T-shirt for a dollar, even though I'm glad we can. Many of those we minister to end up in church."

Chapter 13 | DANN THE MAN

People were attracted to Dann, both as a person and as a pastor. Why? Dann loved people as they were. His faith was strong and uncompromising, but he accepted people regardless of their beliefs (or lack thereof). For example, if you were among the many who believe that heaven is a reward for good behavior, Dann would nod and listen to you, and you'd soon feel that you were talking to a friend. Then, you might hear something like, "would you be interested in what the Bible says about that?" In words calm and reassuring, he would point out how eternal life is an inheritance given to members of God's family, and how you could belong to that family. Whether you did or not, however, he was still your friend.

As Bunny Jankowski explains, "I think the reason the church boomed was because Dann has always been so open to people of other faiths. He accepts others with open arms, regardless of their beliefs. In this way, he brings them to a better understanding of Christ. There were many from other denominations who came to our church. Another thing that helped was his experience as a professional musician. Because of it, he had a very natural way of approaching people instead of thumping them on the head with the Bible," she says with a laugh.

Tony Whitten, the retired street-wise Dallas police officer, remembers Dann and Krista as "very mature, sweet and loving people. Dann is the perfect gentleman, kind to everybody, very articulate, knows his limits and knows what to say to people."

"I think people responded to Dann and Krista," says Carolyn Granger, "because they weren't the strict 'holier than thou' type of people. They welcomed others into the church and made people feel that they were an important part of the church's mission. After Dann and Krista appeared, the community started to view church people in a different light, and felt comfortable in coming to church. If they came once, I don't know why they wouldn't come back. Dann teaches and preaches the message in a way that is special."

Her last words piquing my curiosity, I asked her to elaborate.

"Well, he would always connect his points to everyday living. For me, having sat in a lot of college classes, I could understand and relate to what he was saying more than at any other church I ever attended."

In the small and isolated community of Angel Fire, there was another reason for Dann's popularity: his counseling. "Stop in and talk," he'd say, and many did. A gifted counselor, he didn't charge for his services, and those who turned to him quickly felt they had a friend as well as a counselor. When their lives were spinning out of control, many turned to him. Sometimes they'd come to the church office and other times he'd go to their homes.

"He is a gifted and caring man," says Krista in explaining why so many sought his counsel. "People saw both his sincerity and his heart."

When I asked real estate owner Ruth Bush to reflect on Dann, she replied, "Dann was a very interesting person. He was strong and quiet, not loud, boisterous or arrogant. He was made of steel and didn't waver in his beliefs. He taught what he believed and lived what he taught. He was a terrific example for the community. When he first arrived, our community was like part of the Wild West. If you wanted to do something and had guts enough to do it, you did it. But he was different. He was true and didn't vacillate. What you saw today, was what you saw tomorrow, and the same the week after. I have a tremendous amount of admiration for his integrity."

A Protective Congregation

My first contact with Dann was over the phone in the fall of '97. Receiving no answer after calling his office, I finally reached him at home. He spoke with the slow and soft Oklahoma drawl that was to become so familiar in the years to come. After introducing myself, and explaining the purpose of the call, he replied, "It's good you didn't reach me at the church."

"Why's that?"

His answer took me by surprise: "I've been going through a depression. My people are trying to protect me from any outside sources of stress, so they wouldn't have let you through."

I mistakenly dismissed his depression as the result of some recent loss, but the reaction of his congregation impressed me. Their response bore witness to a relationship rarely seen between a flock and their pastor. Not only did they throw a protective mantle over him when he was depressed, a year later they responded with unprecedented generosity to his resignation and a few years later when he finally moved, there came an equally unheard-of response by several families in his church.

Not many congregations would respond to Dann's depression like Angel Fire Baptist. For a few, there would be a cold, "we hired you to do a job, and if you can't do it, then we'll have to find someone who can." For most, however, there would be a much more caring and compassionate, "we'll do what we can to help you lick this," along with an automatic "we'll be praying for you," while at the same time maintaining a respectable distance. "We don't want to be too intrusive," would be the explanation. Accompanying people's fears of intrusiveness would be feelings of helplessness, "I'm not a counselor, I wouldn't know what to say." In Dann's case, however, there were no such fears and no such helplessness. Amazed by such a compassionate and generous response, I began asking questions.

The bond between Dann and his people wasn't an accident. His explanation of the phenomenon was succinct and to the point. "If you love people, they'll love you back." That love, however, had a history, and for Dann, it was a very personal history.

"When Dann came to us," says mentor Eddie Malphrus, "he was a broken person. The church rallied around him, and we ended up giving him an interim staff position as Minister of Music. While serving in that position, Dann came to realize that if you take care of the people in the church and if you love them, eventually that love will become a two-way relationship."

Ruth Bush recounted an example of this kind of caring from Dann— one that still leaves her choked with emotion over a decade later. "I was scheduled to have a hip and femur replacement in Albuquerque [three hours away]. I had gone down for my preliminary work, and everything turned out fine. In preparation for the next day's surgery, I checked into the hospital late one evening. They prepped me and then I wrapped myself in my nice warm blanket. When I looked up, there was Dann. It was amazing. I was flabbergasted! I mean .. just .. um ... that he did it," she said, pausing to regain her composure. "So .. I have a very soft spot in my heart for Dann."

Bunny Jankowski worked closely with Dann as the head of the church's daycare program. Her office was across the hall from his, turning her into his de facto secretary. "How would you explain the closeness between Dann and his congregation?" I asked her.

"The corny answer is that he was so genuinely supportive of people and their needs that a bonding occurred. In reality, during my time at the daycare center, I saw him deal with people who not only *had* problems but people who *caused* problems. Because Dann doesn't play favorites, even *they* would end up feeling he was their friend. He tries to bring people together and solve the problem without taking sides, and that really brings him close to people. In watching him from my office across the hall, I would say that everybody he talked to left feeling they were family."

One thing became clear: Dann would extend so much support that people had a natural desire to reciprocate. Apparently, the Biblical, "We love because he first loved us" (1 John 4:19) can be as true a dynamic in human relationships as in our relationship with God. But there's more to the picture.

First, there's the *kind* of love Dann shared—an accepting, nurturing, non-judgmental, almost maternal love—the same kind prompting calls of "mother!" from dying soldiers on a battlefield.

Next, there's Dann's transparency. Close relationships require both the desire to reciprocate *and* the opportunity. Dann created opportunities by openly sharing his needs and struggles. When I suggested this might be one of the reasons for their bonding, Dann agreed. "I think that's true. We've always tried to be as honest with people as possible, and in doing so, they feel a sense of ownership."

In addition to Dann's love for people and his vulnerability, to be a part of Dann's church is to belong to something bigger than yourself— a group of people with a divinely-ordained purpose. It's a view that Dann actively encourages. He once said of his church, "We have a common feeling that God is up to something with us."

The sharing of a common purpose gave people a feeling of significance. "I believe," Dann once said to me in a conspiratorial tone, "that God had called our people and us to Angel Fire for a reason." The reason, of course, is to win the community to Christ, and Dann kept reminding his people that each one of them played an irreplaceable role in that quest.

"Was there a sense that you were participating in God's special purpose for your church?" I asked Carolyn Granger.

"Oh yes," she replied, "that was the reason I was there. Dann helped many people to realize their purpose and calling not only in the church but also in the community. He said we were not only a church family, but we also were part of the community, and it was our responsibility to care for them, too."

Besides Dann's love for people, his vulnerability and transparency, and helping people see they were part of God's greater plan, there was another reason for the close friendships Dann built: he *wanted* them. Considering his father's absence during the war, followed by his alcoholism, imprisonment, and finally death, I wondered if Dann's desire for close relationships wasn't to compensate for a youth when, in his words, he felt "out of place" even in his own home. His mother did her best. She deeply loved all her children and protected them as well as she could, but the shattering of her hopes and dreams for their marriage and family took its toll. Her husband's love and support left when he went off to war, remained frustratingly unavailable when he returned, left again when he was in prison, and then forever disappeared with his death. Sustained by her faith in God, Dann's mother succeeded in the arduous challenge of raising a family and providing for them at the same time, but those were not happy years for any of them.

After a youth void of close connections, the most intimate relationship in his young adult years ended in a heart-wrenching divorce. Two years later, he went back home to Sulphur to await his counseling job, but he was, as Eddie Malphrus puts it, "a broken man." Then, everything changed. Accepted, loved and embraced first by Eddie, then his church, then Krista, Dann not only went through an emotional healing; he entered a new life. It wasn't just a mended Dann who left Sulphur for East Grand Baptist; it was a new Dann.

We *could* view Dann's close relationships as simply compensating for past deprivations, but there's much more to it than that. Feeling that I was missing something in my conclusions about Dann, I turned to my youngest sister. With thirty years of experience in counselling, she would have a perspective I lacked and insights beyond my own limitations. I described the close relationships Dann has today, talked about his father and his childhood and mentioned the divorce. I neglected to mention the renewal that took place in Sulphur, but I didn't need to. She alluded to it without even knowing about it.

"Dann sounds like someone who wanted more intimacy than he got," my sister began. "He became aware somewhere along the line that what was important and satisfying in life was a deep connection with another person: a truly intimate and honest connection when you're seeing and valuing another person and they're seeing and valuing you back. He became vulnerable, and let others know him, so he found a way to get the intimacy he values through these other people, and it has worked. Somewhere along the line, he discovered that what was most valuable and meaningful to him was close connections: genuine, honest, close connections with other people who were mutually supportive. So that's what he went after, and that's what he's doing, and it's working beautifully."

There's another contributing factor perhaps more important than any yet mentioned: Dann is a Jesus-follower. The connection should be obvious. Who or what we're following determines how we behave. It's no coincidence that in Dann, people found a non-judgmental acceptance—the same kind that Jesus exhibited so often to the common people of his day. It was that acceptance that made Dann's close relationships possible, and perhaps even inevitable.

By now, it's obvious that "Dann the man" attracted people to both Angel Fire Baptist and to the Lord he served. At this point in his life, he seems to have put behind him the struggles of the past: the poverty he grew up in, the emotional abandonment and physical loss of his father, the pain of his divorce and the resulting rejection by those in his denomination. Both his success at Angel Fire and his many close relationships would certainly suggest this. However, there yet remains a missing piece of the puzzle of "Dann the man," and it's a big one. Suffering from it his whole life, it wasn't until his mid-forties that Dann finally knew what he was dealing with. Then, it took another two years to overcome the stigma and finally accept it. During our initial interview in 1997, I dismissed Dann's depression as coming from some kind of personal loss. I was wrong. The cause wasn't external, it was internal, and he'd been dealing with it his whole life.

Chapter 14 | ACCEPTING THE UNACCEPTABLE

From the very beginning, Dann and Krista's musical productions were of a professional quality rarely seen in most churches. Dann was a perfectionist. "If it's worth doing, it's worth doing well, especially if it's for the Lord," was his mantra. Unfortunately, there's a downside to feeling that every year has to be better than the one before. The Christmas program had been going on for ten years to great acclaim from expanding audiences at four and five performances when the quest for perfection took its toll.

"I had times of intense anger. The volunteers would sometimes goof around and be lazy. We had a small group who were the workhorses, but others just fooled around.

"We once had this lady who was playing an angel. She got it into her mind that she wanted feathers on her costume. Well, we looked into it and talked about it among ourselves, and we decided "no" because they wouldn't look good in that scene. We had one guy, a big football player, who was an angel in a costume with feathers and it looked real good. The two women angels who accompanied him were dressed in golden robes and they all looked nice together. We considered putting feathers on them, but it wouldn't look good, especially compared to his. Well, this woman kept after us and kept after us to have feathers on her costume, and finally, we had to come right out and tell her, 'No!' Well, wouldn't you know it, on the opening night of the program, she showed up in feathers. She had sewn them onto her costume. She looked like something out of *Lost in Space*. 'What are you *doing*?' I asked incredulously. We laugh about now, but at the time I was pretty mad."

While the lady with the feathers was one of the more memorable, she wasn't the only one triggering Dann's anger in those days. This wasn't the Dann who treated people with such love and grace that they couldn't wait to reciprocate. One morning during his prayer time, Dann took a hard look at himself and didn't like what he saw: angry, short-tempered, feeling he had to be the bad guy in order to get things done. It had to end.

"I told Krista, 'I'm through. I'm never again going to give in to an ungodly attitude to produce a godly result. I'm not going to stoop to yelling at people about their hearts not being right or getting angry with them in order to put on a program like this. If I can't do this in a godly manner, I won't do it at all.'"

The musical productions weren't the only source of stress. The church had grown considerably in the past eleven years, and more people meant more work. For eleven years Dann had been telling people to "drop by, and we'll talk" and a growing number took him up on his offer. Counseling was now taking up a major part of his time, putting pressure on his ministry and his family life.

Dann agonized over what to do. Finally, he decided he wasn't going to sacrifice his health or his family. He needed a break, but he didn't know for how long. Unwilling to put the church into an indefinite holding pattern, he saw only one answer.

The Meeting

Seven men—leaders of the church who had been involved from its beginning, walked into the church's parlor in response to Dann's call. With paintings on the wall, carpeting on the floor and couches and easy chairs for furniture, the parlor had all the warmth and ambiance of a living room. Dann began with prayer.

"Lord, you're a great God. You've done great things through this church and the men in this room. Thank-you for the many people we've been able to introduce to you over the years and for the privilege of pastoring this church. We don't know what the future holds for any of us, but we trust you. We pray for your guidance during this meeting, that what we do will be in keeping with your will, in Jesus name, Amen."

When Dann looked up, looks of concern and confusion met his eyes. Leaning forward in his chair and clasping his hands in front of him, he looked down at the floor before beginning.

"My stress levels have got to where I can't control them anymore. As some of you know, I've found myself losing my temper and not being very receptive to people in my own family as well as in the church. I just feel I'm not going to do the church or anyone else any good until I take some time off to sort this out. I don't know how long that will take, so I think I should just tender my resignation."

Silence filled the room. Desperately searching for another answer, the men processed Dann's words.

"Why don't you just take some time off?" asked one.

"Well, I thought about that," replied Dann, "but the problem is that I don't know how long this thing will take, or what the outcome will be, so it just wouldn't be fair to the church."

Other ideas emerged—hiring someone to help him, going part-time for a while, taking a long vacation, but nothing fit. Finally, looking at the others, one of the older men spoke. "There's got to be a solution that's not so drastic." Turning to Dann, he continued, "Before we bring this to the entire church body for their consideration, why don't we pray on it for a while and get back to you."

Several days later three men entered Dann's office and stood before him.

"We've got a proposal," said their spokesman. "First of all, we'd like you to take a year off with pay. You can consider it a sabbatical. You're free to do whatever you want—take a vacation, enroll in a course of study or just rest—whatever you need to do to get out from under the stress. Secondly, to help you figure out what's going on, we're setting aside $5000 for you to spend two weeks with Dr. Louis McBurney, the Christian psychiatrist who specializes in treating pastors. There's got to be an answer to what you're going through, and we figure if anyone can find it, he can."

This wasn't what Dann was expecting, and their words caught him by surprise. "Okay," he responded, both stunned and humbled. Dann later told other pastors what his people had done. "We've never heard of *any* church doing such a thing," they exclaimed.

After hours of interviews and an extensive battery of tests, Louis McBurney arrived at his diagnosis. "You've got bipolar disorder," he said, "and you're fortunate because there are some very effective medications that can stabilize your emotions." Dann's reaction was a mixture of relief and uneasiness. It's something he'd heard before and rejected, unable to accept the diagnosis of a mental illness.

"Back then it was called manic-depression. It took me a long time to admit it. Others probably knew it since someone was sending me the monthly Manic-Depressive Newsletter. Back when we were trying to figure it out, I remember reading a notebook I kept in high school. Along the margins, I had written, 'Lord, just get me through this day,' and I must have written 'help me' a million times. I didn't know what it was. I just figured that everybody went through it. At one time, it got so bad I thought I was going to die, but God was good to me."

In fact, it took yet another doctor—the third—to confirm McBurney's findings before Dann took the medications. As soon as he did, however, he regretted the delay. Eliminating the drastic mood swings, they worked wonders.

"Now I've got it under control, and I'm in the best place I've ever been. As soon as I started taking them, I felt alive for the first time in my life. When your stress cup is completely filled," explains Dann, "it doesn't take much to cause it to overflow. The meds emptied the cup halfway so that things didn't overwhelm me like they used to."

After the magic wrought by the medications and six months off, Dann shared his story with his congregation, reassuring them that he was okay. "There was no hesitancy among the people to have me return," Dann recalls. "Looking back, I can't believe how supportive they were."

Chapter 15 | FAMILY MATTERS

Dann and Krista arrived in Angel Fire in '86 accompanied by seven-year-old Natalie. A year later, Krista gave birth to Rachel, followed by Hannah in '91, and Adam in '93. There's more than one way to grow a church.

With Dann's demanding workload and limited time, Krista did for Dann what Ruth Graham did for her famous and often absent husband Billy: she ran the home. Fortunately, Angel Fire Baptist wasn't East Grand Baptist. At East Grand, they were newlyweds, while at Angel Fire they had three years of married life behind them. Furthermore, where East Grand presented serious problems, Angel Fire held great promise. In Angel Fire, there were no resentments to overcome, suspicions to allay or budgets to cut. Instead, Dann was free to do what he did best: create. Like an artist set loose in a room filled with paints and empty canvases, Dann eagerly went to work, collecting along the way the Southern Baptist's equivalent of three Grammy Awards: Mission Church of the Year, Mission Pastor of the Year and Small Church Pastor of the Year.

Krista had few responsibilities at East Grand, but she played a significant role in the ministry at Angel Fire. Besides helping Dann when he counseled with women, she directed the church's music program, selected the musicals they performed and oversaw the rehearsals. In musical terms, East Grande was a solo performance by Dann with Krista providing critically needed backup. Angel Fire, however, was a duet. "It's hard to think of Dann without thinking of Krista," said Bunny, "they were a team. In addition, all four of their children have chosen very different paths. Dann and Krista's ability to let them grow without restricting the direction they took served as an example and inspiration to many other families in the community."

I asked three of Dann and Krista's children—Rachel, Hannah, and Adam—what they recalled about their years in Angel Fire.

"I remember Christmas," said Rachel. "It was a magical time. Not only because of the pageant our church put on, but the town itself. Everybody came to Angel Fire to see the decorations—a very homey and inviting atmosphere."

For Adam, it was something else. "Before they built the community center the church would host a traveling children's community theater from Missoula, Montana. They'd travel around the country, putting on a show in a week, bringing their own costumes and casting local kids. It was a fun experience."

"What challenges did you experience?" I asked the three of them.

"There was nothing for the kids to do," said Adam. "I didn't experience it, but there was a lot of partying going on with kids of high school age and younger. They'd ski during the day and party at night."

The isolated setting that enhanced the magic of Christmas could be anything but magical the rest of the year. "We drove an hour each way to school," said Rachel. "It was a forty-five-minute drive to Taos to play sports," added Hannah, "an hour to Wal-Mart for groceries, and a good mall was three hours away."

Then there was the third challenge, and it caught me completely by surprise.

"Tell him how often you were able to play outside," prompted Krista. Rachel responded: "We had a designated period to play outside because of the bears and mountain lions."

"The what?" I asked.

"The bear problem—it was man-made," explained Krista. "People fed them. There were about 150 bears in a community of 750 people, so they were a pretty common sight."

So common in fact that the children of the community rehearsed "bear drills." "It was a big joke when we moved to Missouri," said Rachel. "They couldn't believe that we never had tornado drills—which they have all the time, and were surprised when we told them we had bear drills which, of course, they never have."

One of the few Anglos in the small high school in Cimarron, Natalie became a target for prejudice. The students in Cimarron were primarily Hispanic while those from Angel Fire and Eagle Nest were Anglo. But, as Natalie insightfully pointed out, "The prejudice wasn't racial or ethnic, it was economic."

A look at Cimarron's demographics reveals a picture that hasn't changed much over the years. In 2012, Angel Fire's median income was $50,617.[6] For Cimarron? Almost a third less at $36,667.[7] To make matters worse, "Cimarron was dependent upon the tuition students from Angel Fire and Eagle's Nest for a large part of their school budget," says Krista, further explaining their resentment.

What did Natalie experience? Along with more passive forms of rejection, if one of the boys found her attractive, she'd soon be jumped and physically assaulted by Cimarron girls.

"Not only were the students prejudiced, so was the faculty," adds her mother. "Either you were from Cimarron, or you were one of the kids from 'the Valley.' Natalie was an accomplished athlete, but when it came to playing her, the Cimarron teacher/coaches saw to it that she was often the last person called and had the least amount of playing time."

Natalie didn't just defend herself in that situation; she went on the offensive. An outstanding soccer player during grade school and basketball player in middle school, she now added volleyball and track to her athletic repertoire. She also excelled academically, graduating second in her class of thirty-eight. As of this writing, she is a graduate of Texas A&M, married, the mother of two and working as a teacher and coach.

Attending her fifteenth class reunion, Natalie found many of the students who gave her a hard time repentant and apologetic. "I can't believe we treated you like that," said one of them. For one of the teachers, however, it was a different story. "After all these years she still treated me rudely. I couldn't believe it," said Natalie.

I had forgotten about Dann and Krista's aversion to the cold and lack of interest in winter sports but was about to receive a reminder.

"Do you ski?" I asked the three teenagers.

"I skied under a girl's legs once, and that did it for me," said Rachel, laughing. She was into drama, not sports. In 2009, she graduated as a drama major from the University of Missouri. Her student teaching so impressed her host school's leadership that she's now in charge of their drama department.

Hannah was into music. In a school of three thousand students known for its performing arts program, upon her graduation in 2009, she received the female vocalist of the year award.

Adam's spent his last two years in Angel Fire playing T-ball ("we'd drive over to Cimarron once a week"), but his first love was also music, specifically percussion, and he placed first in a statewide competition in 2009.

In addition to their personal accomplishments, there's another reason for Dann and Krista's pride in their children: their spiritual lives, something you rarely hear mentioned by parents these days.

"They're big into reaching people for Christ and aren't afraid of sharing their faith," says Dann. "The other day I caught Adam on the computer giving a non-believer a tremendous apologetic [explanation and defense] of the Christian faith. I know God's going to use our children for some great things. When I say 'great things,' I mean things that nobody may know about until we get to heaven. All of them are creative, love the Lord, and are firm in their faith. We're real proud of them."

Moving On

In a 2005 study, Southern Baptist ministers averaged between seven and eight years in the same church. Dann and Krista were in Angel Fire for fifteen. They would have stayed longer if a growing problem in the church hadn't prompted a move.

With strong lay leadership and the help of an associate pastor, Angel Fire Baptist continued to function almost normally during Dann's sabbatical. New people became members, including several from Texas, who had held positions of leadership in their former churches.

"They came to our church because it was different and they liked it," says Dann, "but then they tried to make us like the churches they came from."

Initially, the appearance of the newcomers wasn't a problem. About three years later, however, another transplanted Texan, whom Dann had always considered a close friend, became a member.

"He was from the Dallas area and very wealthy and had visited for years. Then he joined the church and the next thing I knew he was inviting all these folks over for dinner. He was a very outgoing fellow, so I didn't think much of it until some of the people came to me and said, 'there's something you need to know.' They went on to say he was telling people it was time for me to leave and that I had too much power. That was the thing that kept coming up, that I had too much power. I really didn't have any more power than the people gave me. After all those years I knew the ideas they'd be open to and those I'd have to wait on, so they agreed with most of the things I suggested, but for him, that was "power," and I had too much of it."

"Then along came some other people," continued Dann, "and they were from Texas and they loved our church too, but they also wanted to remake it into the churches they came from."

"What was it they wanted to change?" I asked, curiously.

"Well, they didn't like our deacons [those who helped govern the church]. That was the main issue. They wanted an official Board of Deacons. Some of them had served on deacon's boards in the churches they left, and they wanted to get back on. They wanted only men deacons, and they wanted them organized into a separate board. Then, instead of the cooperative leadership we practiced, they wanted the pastor to be accountable to *them*. Many of these men are highly successful in their fields and they're used to running things," Dann explained. Think "Type A" personalities—the kind of people who get things done and don't tolerate excuses. As Dann was about to discover, a lack of concern for the wants and feelings of others also accompanied this group.

"We had a young lady in our church," explains Dann, "she was an interior decorator, and she had painted the nursery a certain color. It wasn't my favorite color, but it seemed fine. Then some people from this group came in and repainted that room. Without asking anyone, they repainted the room.

I had to go to them and say, 'you can't do that.' Their response was 'what's the big deal?' I said, 'the big deal is that you're assuming that what you want is more important than what others want.' They wanted to paint the sanctuary a different color too, and there's nothing wrong with that, but you don't move into someone else's house, even if you're adopted, and say 'we're going to change this house.'"

Adds Bunny Jankowski, "They were uniformly strong-willed, united, and unwilling to bend; their attitude was 'my way or the highway.'"

Dann tried his best to work with the group, but repeated attempts got nowhere.

"These were men who had been successful financially and had powerful positions in other places. They felt they weren't being consulted, but we always left the floor open for anyone to speak at church meetings and invited them to come and speak on any issue. Instead, they went behind people's backs and were causing division in the church."

The thrift store's success brought things to a head. Having outgrown their building, they needed to expand and approached their landlord about purchasing the property.

"We couldn't get a clear title, so I asked the church to pray about it and said we'd wait. Well, in this group of people was a man who said, 'we don't have to wait, we can go forward, we can get this place, it'll all work out.' I finally called them together—a group of fourteen men—and I sat down, and I told them, 'I've been hearing what you're saying, and there's some disagreement about moving forward. I'm concerned because it's creating division in the body. I thought we might talk about this.' So we began to discuss the issue and finally this one fellow who was a friend of mine said 'we asked you in that meeting what your desire was, and you didn't give us any leadership, you weren't leading us.' And I called him by name, and I said, 'that's not true. You asked me what I thought we should do as your pastor, and I said I thought we should wait and pull ourselves together in prayer until we were of one heart. But you chose not to hear me.' I looked around the group, and I said, 'and all of you heard me say that.' And I looked at him, and I could see he was angry, as were half the others. They were angry because they knew I was right, and I told them so. I said I still wanted the thrift store to expand, but there was a time and a place, and for the health of the church we shouldn't let ourselves become divided over the issue."

After the confrontation, a reflective and discouraged Dann realized he had two options: first, he could confront this group head-on and bring their issues to a vote of the membership. He knew he would win such a vote, but because of the group's growing influence, he also knew it would split the church—an unacceptable solution. His second option was to leave. Quitting wasn't in his nature, but he saw it as the lesser of two evils.

Our major decisions in life often hinge on several factors, and this was now true for Dann. While considering his alternatives, he received an invitation to pastor Fruitland Road Church in Springfield, Missouri. The more Dann and Krista looked at the opportunity, the more they heard God calling. In addition, they had their children to consider. Natalie had successfully negotiated the rough waters of high school, but Dann and Krista were less inclined to launch their other children, with temperaments less steeled than hers, into such difficult waters. Since Rachel was getting ready to enter high school, if they were going to move, now was the time. Fruitland Road said Dann and Krista could live anywhere, which opened up some exciting opportunities for their three remaining and musically gifted offspring. Providing a peak into their family life, Dann and Krista let their children decide what school system to attend (which meant where the family would live). The children chose the schools in nearby Willard. With 926 students, Willard High School had such a good reputation—especially for their music program—that many of their students commuted from surrounding towns.

A series of good-bye events climaxed in a large farewell celebration attended by Angel Fire residents as well as those from surrounding communities. When all the festivities finally ended, Dann and Krista piled the family into the car and left their ski resort ministry for a small church on the outskirts of Springfield, Missouri.

Like many pastors serving churches near ski resorts, Dann's primary calling wasn't to be a resort minister. Rather, he was a pastor who happened to land at a resort, and his creativity and compassion for people made it a perfect match. Spurning tradition when it proved ineffective, he found new ways of sharing God's love with both the residents and visitors of Angel Fire, meeting people's needs in hopes of sharing the answer to their greatest need. Other pastors employ the same principles with similar results, but the deep attachments Dann formed with his congregation marked him as unique. So unique in fact, that something unheard of happened when Dann and his family left Angel Fire. Shortly thereafter, four other families, later joined by two more, also moved from Angel Fire. Their destination? Springfield, Missouri. Their new church home? Fruitland Road.

Photographs

Eddie Malphrus, the pastor at First Baptist Church, Sulphur, when Dann arrived back home to await his counseling job. Eddie's church became a place of healing and inspiration, mending lives and sending scores into the ministry, including Dann.

Dann and Krista on their wedding day with flower girl and daughter Natalie

Artist's portrait of First Baptist Church of Sulphur. The congregation has since moved to a new building and embraced a new name, Crossway First Baptist Church.

Dann and Krista performing together shortly after their marriage.

The cast of one of the numerous Christmas musicals presented by Angel Fire Baptist. Carolyn Granger, a real estate owner and close friend of the Masters, is the blond in the middle of the second row. Two to the left is Krista. Dann is front row; far right.

After a few years of Dann's leadership, Angel Fire Baptist Church had to expand.

Dann plays the angel Gabriel and Krista the virgin Mary in the comic Christmas pageant *Cowboy Christmas*. Performed in the late 90's, it was one of the most popular of the church's Christmas pageants.

A growing family. Behind Dann to the left is Adam, and the right is Hannah. Front row far left is Rachel and far right is Natalie. Dann and Krista proudly hold two of a growing number of grandchildren.

Dann and Krista in costume for another Christmas musical. The church presented a variety of other musicals during the course of the year.

Steve Hoekstra

Chapter 1 | "The Cows Didn't Care If I Was Stoned."

He never saw it coming.

"Oh s--t!"

For twenty-four-year-old farmhand Steve Hoekstra on a cold spring morning in 1974, the expletive described more than just his feelings.

The rising sun illuminated patches of melting snow as Steve mechanically stepped outside for his morning chores. This wasn't as much fun as it used to be. He took a deep breath of the frosty air, laden with the familiar barnyard odors. Clothed in jeans and a Levi jacket, he pushed his empty wheelbarrow toward the pens, each of which housed a prize Charolais show bull. It was a thoughtfully designed building: several pens, each fifty feet long, jutted out from the opened side of the metal barn, allowing the bulls the option of basking in the sun on pleasant days, or retreating under the roof in foul weather.

Shovel in hand, Steve went to work mucking out the pens. It was hard, backbreaking work—work that Steve used to enjoy, but the joy was disappearing. The wheelbarrow now filled, he grabbed its handles and began the short trip to the growing pile at the far end of the barn.

Then it happened. His right foot, coming down on a patch of ice, shot skyward, hurling him sideways. His left arm, pushing down on the handle, hit the muddy ground, spilling the wheelbarrow's contents over his arm and side. Disgusted, he slowly picked himself up. "I don't mind working on a farm," he thought, "but I don't want to be slipping and falling in cow crap for the rest of my life."

Actually, at that point, Steve *did* mind working on a farm. His life was going nowhere, and over the past few weeks, it was beginning to bother him. The marijuana didn't help, a habit he picked up while partying in college. He dropped out of college and later got married, changes which decreased his party life, but not the relationship with his seven-leafed friend. The results were predictable, and frequent job changes became a way of life. The past couple of years, he was working on farms. "Farming was attractive," he recalls, "because the cows didn't care if I was stoned."

Gradually, there emerged within Steve a long dormant desire and accompanying restlessness. He wasn't looking for money—both he and his wife shared a mutual disdain for material possessions. Instead, he wanted something that money couldn't buy—a calling in life—a meaning and purpose that he could pour his heart into—something that he enjoyed and something with a future. "I didn't know what kind of a future that was," says Steve, "I just knew it wasn't working as a farmhand for the rest of my life."

In the weeks before his fall, Steve gave some thought to what he'd *like* to do. Remembering the camping trips he took as a boy—the refreshing scent of pine—the feelings of pleasure and freedom as he traipsed through the woods— he mused to himself, "I wouldn't mind working in the woods." In the weeks following, the thought took root.

Financial problems frequently accompany the abuse of alcohol and drugs, and they showed up in Steve's life. In a prelude to the industriousness characterizing much of his later life, Steve addressed his need for money by becoming a producer as well as a consumer and selling to his friends. On the morning he slipped and fell, a large stash of containers was filled and ready for distribution. They were never sold.

After the morning's accident, the rest of that day went no better than its beginning. In Steve's words, "If anything could go wrong, it did." By day's end, he was not only exhausted, he was depressed.

Steve pulled back the quilted bedspread and climbed into bed. His wife Janice was already asleep. The clock on the nightstand read nine o'clock; its alarm set for four-thirty. His mind was just leaving the world of consciousness when a ringing telephone rudely brought him back. Quickly, but carefully so as not to wake Janice, he made his way to the kitchen, hoping to get there before the ringing woke her up. "Hello?" It was his friend Kathy. Meeting at a church camp in their pre-teen years, they became "camp sweethearts," and even dated sporadically through high school. The casual dating continued into college until once, while home on break, Steve called to ask her out. She declined, saying she had met someone else (the man whom she would later marry) and fixed Steve up with her girlfriend. Kathy's matchmaking succeeded, and the two married couples remain close friends to this day. A few months earlier, Kathy and her husband Mike had applied for a teacher exchange program in Australia, and when Steve answered the phone, her excited voice jumped through the receiver. "Mike and I have been approved. We're going to Australia! We just got the letter in the mail today. We'll be flying over the end of August—it's a dream come true."

"Uh, that's great, Kathy," Steve responded, the tone of his voice betraying the words of his mouth. Yet he *was* glad for them. She and her husband were both great people, and they deserved it. On this particular night, however, their success only served to heighten Steve's growing restlessness and sense of failure. "Look what they're doing," he thought to himself, "and look what I'm doing." Feelings of envy and jealousy erupted within him, mercifully masked from the other end by Kathy's own excitement. After a few minutes, he congratulated her once again before hanging up.

Numbly, Steve retraced his steps and crawled back into bed. Sleep, however, was evasive. After such a discouraging day, the emotions set loose by Kathy's call made rest impossible.

"It really bothered me that they got to do that," he recalls. "I always wanted to be successful like them, but I never really worked at it. They were going to Australia on a teacher exchange program and here I was stuck on a farm in the mountains shoveling cow manure. I was pretty torn up about it."

Reality intruded. This won't do, Steve thought. If I'm going to be getting up at four-thirty in the morning, I need some sleep. Slowly pulling the covers back, he went out to the living room in search of a literary sedative. There were two books that would do the trick—his art history book and the Bible. He came upon the Bible first. Turning on a lamp, he sat down in an overstuffed chair. To this day, he doesn't remember what he read, but it wasn't important. It wasn't the words as much as the book itself—a book he had grown up with—an unconscious connection with a life filled with safety, security, and hope for the future. In spite of all the changes that had taken place in recent years, he still read it daily—a habit he began as a boy. As he was about to discover, it's a book that leaves its mark on a reader even when its words don't sink in at the time. Now, like the seedling splitting the boulder, its long-buried influence was about to burst into the light of day. Overwhelmed by feelings of failure exploding against the backdrop of a promise-filled childhood, Steve dropped to his knees. The prayer that came from his lips revealed a man whose life had run out of options. "I said to God: 'either take my life and kill me or take my life and do something with it.'" The answer wasn't long in coming.

"Immediately there flashed into my mind the image of a theater marquee and, in bright lights, the word 'ministry…'"

Freeze frame.

Anybody who has heard a number of stories of people's conversions can finish Steve's story. Having "seen the light," in this instance dramatically displayed on a theater marquee, Steve turns his life around. He leaves the drugs and the farm, finishes college at a Bible school, goes on to seminary, and spends the rest of his life preaching and ministering in ever-larger churches. He even writes a book about his spiritual journey that serves as a beacon of hope for those who caught up in drugs and separated from God. Not quite.

"… the word 'ministry,' which I immediately changed to 'forestry.'"

It was Steve's "other love." For Dann Masters, it was music, for Steve, forestry. To Steve, the ministry meant indoors, not outdoors. It meant a shirt and tie—standing behind a pulpit and sitting behind a desk—not an appealing thought to a man who found his greatest pleasure in traipsing through the woods. As Steve explains, "Sometimes God gives us a direction, and we say, 'well that's okay, but I'd rather go another way.'"

Steve is careful to describe his experience that night as "not overly-spiritual." There was no vision of heaven, no choir of angels, no feelings of warmth, no light surrounding him. "Instead," he says, "it was simply a sense of direction that I never had before. I was going to go into forestry. My dream was to secure a job on a fire tower. There, with my family, I'd spend the rest of my life."

Chapter 2 | THE EARLY YEARS

Arriving on August 30, 1949, in Denver, Colorado, Steve was the first of three children born to U.S. Air Force radar technician John Hoekstra and his wife Barbara. After a year's assignment in South Dakota, Steve was three when the family returned to Denver, moving into a new white clapboard bungalow across the street from the local junior high school. Its 700 square feet were barely large enough for the three of them when a fourth announced its impending arrival. An accomplished carpenter, Steve's father finished a two-bedroom addition just in time for the birth of the family's first daughter followed four years later by a second son.

Besides Steve's family, a swarm of relatives called Denver "home." Frequent visits to aunts, uncles and cousins cemented a close family bond, creating a safe, secure and loving environment for Steve.

"I joined the 'Jet Cadets'—a boys program at the church we attended.[8] I was always outside doing something, my only indoor activity being the junior high school bowling league. I kind of liked school, but sure didn't like the work that went along with it," says Steve, grimacing at the memory.

Two life-long loves sprouted during Steve's boyhood years: individual sports and the outdoors.

Individual sports have always been a large part of Steve's life. "The elementary school was less than a block from my house and across the street was the junior high school, where we'd frequently gather for softball games. Except for softball and a junior high bowling league, I didn't do a lot of team sports," he recalls. "I was a loner I guess, even then. Gymnastics was my primary interest. We had a horizontal bar in my backyard. Being across the street from the junior high, kids would come over after school. Also, since my dad was in the Air Force Reserves, we could go to Fitzsimmons Army Medical Center [now part of the Denver campus of the University of Colorado], where I took swimming lessons in their pool."

Steve fell in love with the outdoors through scouting, a major interest in his early life. Pack meetings during the week, softball games on the weekends and camping trips in the company of his Scout leader father filled his childhood. "Active" is the word Steve repeatedly uses in describing those years.

And Steve had a third love in his early years. "I was raised in a church home. We attended Ashgrove Sunday school in Denver, now known as Holly Hills Community Church. My dad served as a deacon and ran the Sunday school for many years.

Just as a church camp was instrumental in Dann Master's life, so it was in Steve Hoekstra's.

"When I was nine years old I attended church camp for the first time. It was Camp Id-Ra-Ha-Je, from the phrase, 'I'd rather have Jesus,' and it's still around. I remember lying in my bunk one night and praying to accept Christ."

"What changes occurred after that?" I asked, wondering how a nine-year-old would experience conversion.

"I was already going to church and Sunday school. After accepting Christ, I was more inclined to invite friends to church, but I don't remember any other changes." While Steve's acceptance of Christ as a nine-year-old wasn't a dramatic experience, when a child of that age is "more inclined" to invite their friends to church, you know that something's happened.

Steve's conversion to Christ at a church camp isn't unusual. Surrounded by other Christians, the natural world of trees and lakes and the sight of glowing campfire embers, many young people make a similar decision. With anecdotal as well as statistical evidence abounding, the church camp has long exerted a powerful influence on young lives. Many have shared Steve's closeness with God in such a setting and responded with a similar commitment. "Camp had a tremendous effect on me," recalls Steve. "It was probably the spiritual highlight of the year." Four years later, attending Camp Id-Ra-Ha-Je as a thirteen-year-old junior counselor, Steve made another important life-altering decision. "I don't remember exactly how it occurred, but it was probably following a challenge from the camp preacher at the evening service. When I got back to my cabin, I made a vow to God to read the Bible daily." With brief lapses, Steve has kept that vow to this day, and that left me puzzled. How could he be so faithful to reading the Bible while at the same time becoming wrapped up in drugs and pulling away from the church?

Curious, I asked him. "When you were reading the Bible, was it just out of habit or..."

"Are you asking me if it made a difference? Did I read it to study it? No, study would be too strong a word. Did I read it to get something out of it? Yes. Did I read it sometimes just out of habit? Yes. I'd start at Genesis and then read through to the end, and then go back and start all over again."

A thought entered my mind. "Could it be," I asked, "that the Bible kept you in touch with God so that at the age of twenty-four when you *did* make him Lord of your life, you knew what he expected of you?"

"Yes, absolutely, that's exactly right," Steve responded, "It was pretty much the only contact I had with God during that time."

"Any other memories of camp?"

"Just sitting in the chapel one night singing 'I'd Rather Have Jesus' and seriously contemplating what that meant."

While Camp Id-Ra-Ha-Je was instrumental in Steve's spiritual life, it was by no means the only reason he kept going back. His next words sent us both back to our camp years.

"It was fun."

"What did you enjoy the most?"

"I liked the mountains and the camp itself and, later on, the privileges that came from being a junior counselor. As a junior counselor you could hang out in the kitchen when the campers were elsewhere and then," he said with a chuckle, "sneak back after lights out and raid the refrigerator."

"What other memories do you have?"

"Pillow fights, but not like in a dorm. We actually had a pillow-fight pole. You'd arm yourself with a pillow and walk out onto the pole and try to knock the other guy off into a sawdust-filled pit."

The time Steve spent at Camp Id-Ra-Ha-Je was to pay lasting dividends in his domestic life as well. "When you get up to junior high age the boys and girls start pairing off. You have a camp girlfriend and that kind of thing. My camp girlfriend was Kathy, who later introduced me to my wife, Janice. Paul Eiselstein, the Camp Director, performed our ceremony. He has since passed away, but was a spiritual mentor of sorts and a man I always admired."

With numerous friends and a large extended family, Steve experienced an active and enjoyable childhood. Besides Camp Id-Ra-Ha-Je, there was scouting, Jet Cadets, softball, camping, bowling and gymnastics. Surrounding him in these activities were people he had known for years and in whose company he felt both safe and valued. His childhood was almost idyllic in its simplicity, happiness and security, and all that was about to end.

Chapter 3 | LOVELAND AND BEYOND

Two-thirds of the way through the eighth grade, Steve went through the most traumatic event of his young life. His father was transferred. The Hoekstras moved from Denver—with its half-million people, scores of relatives and many close friends—to the community of Loveland, Colorado, population five thousand—no relatives and no friends. Torn from long-established relationships and a familiar environment at one of the most vulnerable times in a young person's life, Steve was devastated. As he recalls, "It was horrible—not knowing anybody. I grew up in one church all my life with one group of friends all my life and we moved at the end of the school year to a new city and a new school. By the time I started school everyone had their own friends and I was the outsider."

A poignant scene on his first day of school remains etched in his memory. "I had just gone through the lunch line and was standing with a tray full of food." Rows of cafeteria tables filled with a sea of strange faces confronted him, their voices loud in conversation and laughter. Some looked at him quizzically—new kids stand out in a small school—but most ignored him. No friendly voice called out his name; no hand beckoned him over. Feeling awkward and out of place, he finally walked over to a nearby table, choosing a seat far enough away to avoid having to talk, but close enough to dampen his overwhelming feelings of loneliness.

Eventually, isolation gave way to new relationships. Steve became friends with two classmates who lived across the street. Friends, however, weren't the only thing that changed with Steve's move. Scouts and church in Denver were replaced by partying and motorcycles in Loveland. His interest in gymnastics continued, but there were no classmates joining him after school in his backyard. "In Denver our house was right across the street from the junior high and gymnastics was popular. Our home in Loveland—an agricultural community—was three miles from the school, and gymnastics *wasn't* popular," he explained.

At the start of his junior year, Steve and his fellow students thronged through the doors of a brand new high school. One of its prized features was a swimming pool, and its magnetic appeal soon had Steve dividing his time between the gymnastics team and the swim team.

Spiritual changes also took place with the move to Loveland. Back in Denver, his family was part of a close religious community, their lives intertwined with the life of the church. In Loveland, however, there were no such friends and no such community. "When we moved to Loveland we never got back into the church. We tried a few times, but it never worked."

Steve's return to Camp Id-Ra-Ha-Je the summer following his move was a welcome reunion. After being the "new kid," it felt good to be among so many long-time friends. Those feelings, however, didn't last. By the following year, these same old friends evoked quite a different reaction. Steve had a new set of friends in Loveland, and the word "church" wasn't in their vocabulary. Yes, it was nice to see the familiar faces, but the longer he was with them, the more separated he felt. His camp friends hadn't changed, but he had. It was the last summer he attended.

To the casual observer, there was nothing in Steve's high school years that would have marked him as a Christian. Neither he nor his family attended church. When not occupied with sports, Steve devoted himself to partying and motorcycles. He kept reading his Bible, but there was a growing disconnect between Steve and its author. He contends that he still loved God, but stopped serving Him. By "love," Steve is referring to the feelings of affection that often define the word today, and not the Biblical definition equating love with obedience ("If you love me, keep my commandments." John 14:15).

Steve found many new interests in Loveland, but schoolwork wasn't one of them. "I just didn't like going to school. I was more interested in playing and partying, doing sports and riding motorcycles—anything besides school. It just wasn't that important to me, and I didn't put any effort into it." The truthfulness of these words was evident upon graduation. "Out of a graduating class of 272, I graduated around 270."

As Steve looked ahead, college was a given. He received a swimming scholarship to Colorado State University, but injuries sustained in gymnastics prohibited him from using it. Without a scholarship, a four-year college was out of reach financially, so he and some friends enrolled at Mesa Junior College in Grand Junction, Colorado.

In Steve's sophomore year at Mesa, world events threatened to disrupt his studies. To meet the requirements in Viet Nam, the draft was plucking young men from civilian life and depositing them halfway around the world on jungle hilltops and in towns with names they couldn't even pronounce. Fortunately for Steve, a lottery system determined who was drafted, and his number 333 out of a possible 366 effectively shielded him from military service.

Spurred by his grandfather's offer to match his summer earnings toward college expenses, Steve began his summers working in a large commercial laundry before heading to the mountains to cut firewood for campers. He liked the firewood job—it was outdoors—with his friends—and they could continue their partying ("a big part of my life at that time" reports Steve).

Steve majored in art at Mesa, and while he was interested in it, there were other factors contributing to that decision. "I was doing some drugs by then and unlike other areas of study, you can do drugs and art and get away with it."

"What led you into the drug scene to begin with?" I asked.

"Probably just friends—the social aspects of it."

Introduced to marijuana his first year at Mesa, he would experiment with other drugs in the years to come, but "grass" was a constant.

Two years after entering Mesa, and one semester away from graduating, Steve dropped out of college to teach skiing at Powderhorn Ski Area in Colorado. His introduction to the sport occurred several years earlier while attending winter camp at Camp Id-Ra-Ha-Je. "My folks rented some equipment for me, and we went to Geneva Basin, which doesn't exist anymore." It was his first experience on skis, and he was hooked. "Some high school friends joined me and we skied together at Hidden Valley, located just north of Loveland—it's since closed, too."

"How would you describe your time as a ski instructor?" I asked, expecting him to tell me how much fun it was to teach others to ski.

"Party hearty. I just partied all winter long."

The partying was soon to end. It didn't end because he "saw the light." It didn't end because he got hurt or got into trouble. It didn't end because of anything bad. Instead, it ended because of something good.

Steve's attraction to girls started long before he was twenty, but it was to take a life-changing turn at that time in his life. Following his tour as a ski instructor, he worked in the mountains of Estes Park operating a jackhammer on a blasting crew. Returning home for a visit one day, he looked forward to seeing his "camp girlfriend" Kathy—it had been awhile. They dated casually through high school and during Steve's two years at Mesa. A feeling of pleasant anticipation accompanied his call.

"Oh, hi!" She said, surprise in her voice.

"It's been awhile," Steve said, "how you'd like to go out?" There was a pause at the other end.

"I'm sorry, Steve" she replied, "I can't. I'm seeing someone else [her future husband]. But I've got a girlfriend I think you might be interested in," she continued, relief and eagerness in her voice. She could so easily picture the two of them hitting it off. "Her name is Janice… "

Steve called her up, introduced himself, and asked her out.

"Sure," she replied.

It was a two-hour drive from Estes Park to Janice's home in Lakewood and a two-hour drive back to Estes Park. "There were dances and things like that going on," he explains. He didn't gain too many points with her father when he brought her home late, but Kathy was right—they hit it off from the beginning. "She was cute and a lot of fun—a back-to-nature kind of gal. She liked to hike, knew a lot about flowers and outdoorsy kind of stuff. She grew up in the mountains of Evergreen, Colorado, so she knew a lot about plants and different things like that. She sewed her own clothes and did her own embroidery, which I thought was really cool—in the late sixties and early seventies that stuff was pretty popular."

The attraction was mutual. When I asked Janice when she knew their relationship was heading for the altar, she replied, "I knew the first time we met. As we were walking and talking, I thought: 'we're going to be getting married.'"

In Janice, Steve found a soul mate: a creative woman with an entrepreneurial spirit. When they first met, she was making decorator pillows in her father's factory. As their relationship deepened, she moved to an apartment in Ft. Collins, closer to where Steve lived and opened a clothing store featuring her own handmade clothing. She specialized in the granny dresses that were popular in that hippy era, and her clothing line appeared briefly in The Denver Dry Goods, a popular Denver department store.

Shortly after their first date in the spring of 1970, Steve left his job in the mountains ("I didn't keep jobs long back then") and ended up at Colorado State University (CSU) in Ft. Collins, working first on grounds maintenance and then as a trainee for operating heavy equipment. It was while he was at CSU in May of 1971 that he and Janice were married. Steve recalls the day, with a memory for clothing details the envy of any society column editor.

"It was supposed to be an outdoor wedding, but it was going to rain that day, so we used our backup plan and got married in a church. Janice made all the wedding clothes: the men's pants and shirts and bridesmaid dresses as well as her own dress. The men wore black pants, and I had an embroidered blue satin drop-shoulder hippie shirt. All the guys wore white muslin shirts with embroidery on them, and Janice and the gals had on white muslin dresses."

Janice's father offered Steve a job working in his pillow factory, where he stayed until his father-in-law's death two years later. Then it was off to Grand Junction, Colorado, and a groundskeeper's job at the local golf course. Their home was an old rented farmhouse forty-five minutes away in Unaweep Canyon. "It was cool because it was out there all by itself. It was an old farmhouse with a barn and a lot of trees and just a neat place. We loved it."

Steve's employment at the golf course gave way to working for a farmer down the road. After a few months of doing everything from running a bulldozer to guarding the farm during hunting season, it became clear that the farmer couldn't afford to pay Steve a living wage, so Steve went to work caring for a herd of prize bulls kept by their landlord on the farm where they lived.

With his use of marijuana increasing, it was easy to see where Steve's life was headed. Fortunately, it never got there.

One of the most popular stories in the Bible is Jesus' parable of the prodigal son (Luke 15:11-32). It's the story about a young man who asked his father for his inheritance and upon receiving it, left the family farm for a distant country where he spent his fortune in "riotous living." After a while, his money gone and reduced to feeding pigs to support himself, he realized that he would be better off working as a servant on the family farm. Turning from the mud and muck of a pigsty, he set his face toward home.

The prodigal son's father was out in his fields when he saw a familiar-looking silhouette in the distance. The sight had betrayed him often in preceding months, so with the skepticism born of shattered hopes he continued to gaze. This time, however, the longer he looked, the shorter his breaths. Finally, he recognized the familiar gait. Like an arrow, the father shot across the fields as fast as his aging legs would carry him , sweeping up his son in a suffocating embrace. The son's prepared speech of contrition and offer to work as a servant quickly became irrelevant. With a lavish banquet to celebrate his son's return, his father welcomed him back into the family.

Late one evening, kneeling on the cold wooden floor of a farmhouse, Steve experienced the same welcome.

Chapter 4 | THE NEXT MORNING

The Steve who climbed out of bed the next morning was not the same one who picked up the phone the night before. "I woke up knowing that I was alive and that God had blessed me with something. I had the desire to live a different life and go in a different direction."

"What changed after that night?" I asked.

"Everything. One of the reasons I was on the farm was because I couldn't hold a job and I didn't want to go back to school. When I went back to school, I found that God had restored my mind and the next job I had, I kept. Everything changed."

When I first heard Steve tell the above story I referred to it as the story of his conversion, but it wasn't, and he quickly corrected me, "You misunderstood. I came to Christ when I was nine years old. This was when I made him Lord."

"Oh, okay," I said, but I was confused. How can you come to Christ without making him Lord? They're two sides of the same coin. My respect for Steve's knowledge of the Bible and his intelligence meant I had a problem. After several weeks, I finally thought I knew what happened, and called him. "Steve," I asked, recalling our earlier conversation. "When you came to Christ as a nine-year-old did you also make him Lord of your life at that time?"

"I guess you could say that," he replied, "at least as much as it's possible for a nine-year-old." That's what I thought. Steve was returning to a relationship with God he had known fifteen years before. What happened to Steve on that farmhouse floor was similar to the prodigal son in the Bible: he came home. Making Christ Lord of one's life will have different implications for a twenty-four-year-old than a nine-year-old, but regardless of age, a changed heart is a changed heart. Steve was close to the Lord as a child, distanced himself after moving to Loveland, and then returned when he was twenty-four. The first signs of his new life occurred the very next morning.

"When I climbed out of bed that day, I said that if I am going to be a Christian and act like a Christian, then I had to get rid of all my drugs. I had about 30-40 quart mason jars full of pot. I took it all out to the trash can and burned it."

A mischievous smile crossed my lips. "You didn't suffer from smoke inhalation did you?" I asked.

"No," he said, grinning, "but when I want to get a laugh out of people, I make sure to tell them that I was standing downwind."

Steve's spiritual homecoming didn't consist of just rejecting drugs; it also involved returning to something that hadn't been a part of his life for a long time. "Sunday was coming, and I thought we needed to go to church. That's not something we had done before—my wife and I had gone maybe three times in our whole marriage. But we decided that we were going. We looked in the yellow pages for the church closest to us. At that time, without our own car, we'd have to don our backpacks and hitchhike into town for groceries. There was a farm pickup, but it wasn't registered for on-road use, so we weren't supposed to use it—especially since we were supposed to be working that day. To minimize the chance of being caught, we were going to attend whatever church was closest. It happened to be a Southern Baptist church, which I hated because I didn't like Southerners back then. We had chores to do that day, so we walked in late. We must have been quite a sight. My long hair ended at my jean jacket pockets; I had a full beard and wore jeans and a western shirt with boots that smelled of cow poop. Janice had on a granny dress with hair down over her shoulders. We must have looked like hippies from the mountains, and here we were in a blue-collar church. The music director was leading the congregation in singing when we walked in. When he caught sight of the two of us, his arms froze in midair."

The church Steve and Janice attended that morning could have responded to them in one of three ways. First, they could have ignored them. I remember that kind of reception in a small fundamentalist church I once attended. It was a "fortress church"—a church that functions to provide a place of safety and security against the threatening world outside, and if they didn't know you, you were immediately considered part of that world.

A second response to Steve and Janice would have been more likely. They would be welcomed. People would talk to them; they'd receive a visitors' card to sign, and the pastor might send a nice letter and perhaps even visit. But like peeling back the layers of an onion, that welcome would eventually give way to an unspoken message: you don't belong here. People would be polite of course, but making Steve and Janice feel like part of the family? No way. Tolerated? Yes—after all, we're Christians and we're nice, but embraced? Not here.

A third possible response was the response Dann Masters received—an arms-wide-open, "we-love-you-how-can-we-help?"-type of response, which took a broken, discouraged and confused young man, put his life back together, then launched him into a powerful ministry. Fortunately, just as Eddie Malphrus and his people embraced Dann, so Rev. "Dub" Chambers and the people of Trinity Baptist Church welcomed Steve and Janice. Using Steve's fear of getting caught driving the farm pickup, God led him to exactly the right church, a conclusion confirmed as soon as the service ended. "That whole church loved us in a way that I had never before experienced. The pastor visited us that week, and I'm still in touch with him. They brought 'food for the hippies in the mountains,' and even had the youth up to our house for activities such as camping out in our orchard and things like that."

While Steve Hoekstra wasn't coming out of a broken marriage and shattered career as was Dann Masters, he had just turned his back on a lifestyle that the church opposed. He wasn't experiencing the same emotional trauma as Dann, but in his decision to return to Christ, he was just as vulnerable. Steve and Janice were in need of the same love and acceptance extended to Dann, and from Dub and his people, that's exactly what they received.

Pastors set the tone for a church, but it's the people who ultimately determine the church's character. Propelling them into ministries that have brought life to thousands of people, the unsung heroes in the lives of Dann and Steve are the members of two small churches who, as Steve puts it, "loved" on them. It's one thing to be loved by a single individual; it's an entirely different and infinitely more powerful thing to be loved by a whole group. Steve would eventually enter the ministry and—as of this writing—has been in it for over forty years. It wasn't a position he ever anticipated while growing up or one that anyone (with one exception) would have thought possible. He simply didn't fit the mold at the time. Farmer? Yes. Forester or outdoor guide? Yes. Preacher? Not on your life. However, propelled by the reception he received from Dub and the members of Trinity Church, that's exactly what he became.

Chapter 5 | THE CALL(S)

His heart set on forestry, Steve headed back to school. With Mesa Junior College's open enrollment policy guaranteeing his acceptance, he and Janice moved to Grand Junction, Colorado. Fully aware that prolonged drug use affects one's cognitive abilities and memory, returning to school brought an anxiety to Steve unknown to most other students. "I carried a load of sixteen credit hours, including an hour lab in biology and chemistry and a higher math course. I was just trusting God to find out whether I still had a brain or not."

"How did you do? I asked.

"I came out with straight A's and I'd never done that before—never," he recalls, his voice still registering surprise.

As a pre-forestry major, Steve had to take all the classes he made it a point of avoiding his first time around: core classes like biology, chemistry, and mathematics. Encouraged by his first semester's performance, he increased his academic load to a full eighteen credit hours. How did he do? "I think I got one 'B,' the rest were 'As.'"

"The grades must have been pretty encouraging," I suggested.

"They were, and I loved doing it."

"I loved doing it," is an interesting statement coming from a man who never liked school and graduated at the bottom of his high school class.

If God is anything, he's persistent, and while attending Trinity Baptist Church, God spoke to Steve a second time. To help people discover their spiritual gifts, Rev. Chambers was leading his flock through a series of Sunday evening services on the spiritual gifts mentioned in the Bible. "Dub walked us through almost every gift, but God never spoke to me about any that I might have. I was getting pretty discouraged. Then one night he was talking about the gift of pastor/teacher and by the time he finished, I just *knew* that's what I was supposed to be doing." Dub extended an invitation for those with the gift of teaching and preaching to come forward and commit those gifts to the building of God's kingdom. Steve's response, after his epiphany in the pew, wasn't what you'd expect. "Instead of going forward I grabbed onto the pew so hard I must have left my fingerprints in it." There was no way he was going forward. God might be calling him to be a pastor/teacher, but forestry was still his first love, and there was no room for anything else.

This wasn't the first time God called Steve into the ministry. Following the vision of the lighted marquee, it wasn't even the second. Steve's first prompting came quite early in life. "I was seven or eight years old. We were over at the home of some friends, and the adults were playing cards. As I was leaving the living room to rejoin the kids outside, one lady said to me, 'Steve, one of these days you're going to be a preacher.'

"I turned around and laughed and said, 'yes, sure,' and went out to play. I never gave it another thought.

"The next time was years later when I was working at the golf course in Grand Junction. I was just riding a lawnmower. I don't remember what was on my mind or why I said it, but I found myself saying, 'God if you need me to be a preacher or anything like that, it's okay with me.' We weren't even going to church at the time, and I have no clue where that came from."

Fortunately, God didn't give up, although after the fourth time one might think he was tempted. Many years after the woman's comment, two years after the episode on the golf course, months after the vision of the marquee and weeks after digging his fingers into the pew, "I was studying for final exams at Mesa in the little windowed-in front porch of the house we were renting. I studied late at night, going to bed around 1:30-2 a.m., and always finished by getting down on my knees and praying. This night I got down on my knees with my back to the window. My mind was tired. I started rambling, and my mind started wandering. Then it was as if someone yelled at me from the window. It wasn't audible to anyone else, but it scared the crap out of me. I jumped up and turned around thinking one of my friends might be trying to frighten me—it was just that loud. I looked around, and nobody was there. I thought I knew what had happened. I got down on my knees, and I said to God, 'Okay, you've got my attention, and I'm awake. Now, what is it?' And he said to me just as plain as can be: 'I want you to teach, and I want you to preach, and I don't want you ever to be ashamed of anything you have to say, and I'll be with you always.'"

Steve paused, reliving the moment.

"Pretty powerful," I finally commented.

"It was to me—probably the only thing that would have moved me from where I was at the time. Anyway, I said, 'OK.' I got up the next morning and told my wife: 'God's called me to preach,' and she said, 'Oh no! I hate it; I hate it!'" Janice didn't mention this response when I interviewed her, and for an understandable reason: when I asked her the role she played in Steve's ministry, she responded without hesitation, "to be a support." When Steve made his announcement that morning, he was making it to a wife who had not yet come to faith in Christ. For Steve, the changes that were taking place in him constituted a return to the faith of his youth. For Janice however, with no religious background, what was happening to the man she loved was pushing her into an entirely new world—an unfamiliar world filled with unsettling surprises. As Steve puts it, "I wasn't who I was, and I wasn't who she married.

She tolerated it, perhaps thinking my return to Christ would straighten me out to where I *could* hold a job." That it did, and quite a bit more.

After making the announcement to Janice, Steve hopped on his bike and rode over to the church to break the news to Rev. Chambers. The response he received was not what he expected. "'Hey Steve,' said Dub, 'you can't do that; you're into forestry. Look at yourself; you're not really preacher material.' He did just about everything he could do to talk me out of it."

"Was this a deliberate attempt to determine how committed you were?" I asked.

"That's what he says now," Steve says, smiling.

Rev. Chambers' doubts are understandable. Nothing had prepared him for someone like Steve. Fortunately, sensing Steve's seriousness and commitment, he recovered quickly and began a mentoring relationship. Twice weekly, in the early hours of the morning before they went to work, Dub would meet with Steve and a young student pastor who was attending Bible school. They'd read the Bible together, discuss it, and pray.

Shortly after Rev. Chambers began his mentoring program, his two students and their wives attended a revival meeting at church. Of course, it included an invitation to come forward and accept Christ. Steve sensed a movement next to him and looked up. Janice was making her way out of the pew. It wasn't an impulsive decision on her part. While not thrilled with the changes in Steve's life, she had learned to roll with the punches. In her own words, "I thought, 'Okay, well life goes on, and now I'll go to church with you.' I didn't have a personal relationship with the Lord at the time, but I thought I was okay because I was a nice person."

Then things started to change.

"Dub Chambers was doing a series of sermons and at the end of them, he had a simple illustration. 'Listening to God is like this paper,' he said. 'You say to yourself: yes, you're making sense to me Lord, but I'm not going to give my life to you because it's too embarrassing and it's too hard, and it's too…whatever.' Then he took the sheet of paper and tore it in half. He repeated the illustration. 'Every time the Lord speaks to you, and you say 'no' to him, like this paper that's torn in half, again and again, his voice gets smaller and smaller.' The first time he tore that paper in half, I'm thinking I don't know this God he's talking about, but it *is* too embarrassing. We're in this church, and I'm teaching Sunday school. I can't get up and admit I don't know the Lord after teaching these kids. To make a long story short, I just went home and said to the Lord, 'I can't do this,' and then 'yes, I'd better do this,' then 'no, I can't do this, it's just too scary.' At the end of all that, he spoke to me and said, 'Janice, I love you.' And then I said, 'Oh good, then I'm okay like I am because he wouldn't be saying this to me if I wasn't.' Then I said 'Lord, I love you, too.' And he said, 'then why haven't you ever come to me?' And by that time I said, 'well, okay, here I come,'" she laughed. "So I came to the Lord when I was ready to do it *his* way and accept that Jesus came to die for my sins."

"What happened after that?" I asked.

"I went and talked to Dub and came forward at the end of next week's service."

Steve wasn't the only husband pleasantly surprised that night. Another person passed in front of him on her way to the front: the wife of the Bible school student and pastor.

"They had two preacher's wives saved that night," Steve recalls proudly.

Buoyed by academic success and his newfound love for studying, Steve received his Associate of Arts degree in Art Education and enrolled at Grand Canyon College in Phoenix, Arizona, a private Christian college. He majored in the Bible and, at the recommendation of the registrar in case he ended up as a part-time pastor, Art Education.

In Steve's last year at Grand Canyon College, his well-known love for the outdoors led to an invitation. "They had a program called 'Outdoor Ministry' or something like that. I took a group of college students, and we went up on the Mogollon Rim, [elevation 8000 feet] and spent a week up in the Superstition Mountains just east of Phoenix." While an experienced outdoorsman, it was the first time he led such a trip. It wouldn't be the last.

Chapter 6 | LATE ONE EVENING

Steve was planning to enter Golden Gate Seminary following his graduation. Then, late one evening, those plans changed. "I had finished studying. It was two in the morning, I was praying for direction, and that's when it happened. It wasn't an audible voice, but one that was so clear and pronounced that I knew where it was coming from. 'You're to move back to Colorado. I've got a church for you there.'"

Cancelling plans to attend Golden Gate, Steve and Janice took their infant son Jake (their second child Holly would arrive two years later) and moved back to Colorado, renting a home near friends in the small town of Paonia. Upon arriving, Steve discovered that indeed there *was* a church in town looking for a pastor: North Fork Baptist. He applied for the position. Everything was coming together, he thought to himself. This was his reward for his faithfulness in responding to God's call that night—it almost put a swagger in his step.

North Fork Baptist Church turned him down. He wasn't what they were looking for. Steve's confidence gave way to confusion, his certainty, to doubt. Was it really God's voice he had heard? He tossed the question over in his mind, but the more he thought about it, the more certain he became. Still, if it *was* God's voice, where was his church?

Two months later, a letter, covered with crossed-out addresses from Grand Junction and Phoenix, finally caught up with him. A church in New Castle, Colorado, was looking for a pastor. Someone had given them Steve's name.

New Castle was hardly an attractive opportunity. With the recent completion of I-70, the hundreds of cars and trucks that daily made their way through the town were now taking a different route. In a scene duplicated in hundreds of small towns along the path of the nation's new interstate highway system, Main Street businesses folded. By the time the Hoekstra family arrived, the once-bustling little community of several hundred was beginning to look like a ghost town. Steve's flock barely broke into double digits: eleven adults plus a few children. The church building itself? "It was an old miner's cabin about twenty-five feet wide and fifty feet long. They'd taken out the walls and put in pews. Next door was a trailer for Sunday school and next to that was a trailer they called the parsonage." After four weeks of leading worship services, the church voted unanimously to call Steve as their pastor. The pay?

"A hundred dollars a month plus the trailer to live in."

Shortly after settling in, Grand Canyon College called. His hikers from the previous year had been talking. Would he be willing to lead another outdoor adventure group, this one in the winter?

"They sent a group to Colorado, and I took them cross-country skiing for a week. We backpacked, built snow caves and lived outside the whole time."

The people at Grand Canyon College weren't the only ones thinking of Steve. Before pastoring Trinity Baptist in Grand Junction, Colorado, Rev. Dub Chambers led the First Baptist Church in Westcliffe, located two-hundred-and-fifty miles away on the western border of Colorado. While there, he took fifteen boys from the church's Royal Ambassador (RA) program (a Southern Baptist program to introduce grade-school boys to missions) on backpacking trips into the Sangre de Cristo mountain range. "Those trips were spurred by my love for the outdoors and the desire to use that passion to reach people for the Lord," Dub explains.

Dub's trips were so popular that he widened the umbrella and invited kids from RA programs in Denver and Colorado Springs. It didn't take long to realize the program's potential. After leaving Grand Junction to take a church in Aurora, Colorado, Dub talked with the Royal Ambassador's state leader, Jim Rich, and the two hatched the idea of including a backpacking trip as part of the state's RA camping program. Unfortunately, most boys lacked the necessary equipment, and only a small group responded. Jim and Dub took the problem to Glen Braswell, the state Director of Missions ("D-O-M's" as they were called, had the primary responsibility for starting new churches and ministries) who lent his support and $5000 in funding to provide the needed equipment. Now all they needed was someone to lead the program. As Dub recalls, "Knowing how much he loved the outdoors, I recommended Steve Hoekstra."

Steve explains what happened next. "We started a backpacking ministry, later calling it 'Royal Ambassadors Adventure Trips' or 'RAAT Patrol' [pronounced "Rat Patrol" after a popular 60's TV program]. Chuck Clayton, a good friend, was a big help in getting us started. He had this thing called Christian High Adventures[9] and took us to the National Outdoor Leadership School for training." While Steve led the program, all three men shared in the work. Steve was in charge of assembling the equipment and supplies, Jim took charge of publicity and fundraising, and Dub was the idea man and promoter.

Word of the backpacking trips soon spread. Three years later, they opened the doors to include Southern Baptist Acteens, a program similar to RA for girls in grades 7-12. The trips would continue for the next twenty years.

Steve arrived in New Castle with the same goal as Dann Masters in Angel Fire: to build a church. The setting was different, but the challenge the same. Just as Dann experienced an epiphany on how to reach his community, so did Steve. "We had about twenty to thirty people coming when I arrived," says Steve, "and most were women. There were some men, but not many. I'd ask the women where their husbands were, and they said they were out hunting, fishing, cutting wood, or working on their cars. After six or seven months I decided that the only way I was going to get a chance to visit with those guys was to go out and do things with them. I was a fisherman and had done a lot of fishing, so I'd talk with them about fishing when visiting in their homes. I would never make an appointment for a visit, but just drop by on a Saturday afternoon when I thought they'd be out working on their cars, etc. I also spent a lot of time hanging out at the local bar and restaurant, at that time one and the same. I'd hang around the grocery store and talk fishing with the grocery store owner. I'd tell them that I'd like to go fishing, but I didn't know where to go, or that I was having trouble with this or that particular fly, which was all true. They'd see themselves in a position to help the preacher, and as they did, we got to know each other pretty well."

And Steve utilized another approach. "I thought it was important for me to be out there helping folks. If a guy was having a hard time getting his wood in, I'd go over and lend him a hand; if someone had to get his cows in, I'd go over and help. I worked on a lot of people's cars and homes because I had some carpentry skills and car skills. It takes a long time to get a coal miner into church. Sometimes when we'd go fishing or cutting wood, it'd be an hour's drive out and back and that gave you time to talk to them and get to know them. It was through those times together—fishing, hunting, hiking or cutting wood—that I won a lot of those guys to Christ."

Steve's approach followed Jesus' example of serving others in washing his disciple's feet and was as effective as it was old. "Many people outside the church view the church as taking from the community, but when the church sees itself as a servant—as giving—then things start to click." "Click," they did, and the pews began to fill. Steve's approach stood in sharp contrast to another local pastor.

"The town had an annual festival called the 'Burning Mountain Days.' One minister, viewing it as nothing more than an excuse for a lot of excessive drinking, left town in protest and encouraged others to do the same. I found it much more effective to stay and exert a Christian influence. We did it by having a float in the parade and a booth in town. One of our members even sold a car and hired a contemporary Christian band to come and play—they were more rock and roll style. The community loved it!"

Things were going well in New Castle. With the church's growth came a salary increase enabling Steve and family to move out of the trailer into a more comfortable home in plenty of time for the birth of their daughter Holly. A community that had never before seen such a combination of preacher and servant revered him, and what began as a job with a goal quickly became a home surrounded by friends. They would have liked to stay longer, but word of their success spread, and with it came a call.

Chapter 7 | VAIL

Founded in 1962 by two WWII veterans from the 10th Mountain Division who had trained on its slopes, Vail, Colorado, consistently ranks as the nation's number one ski resort, both in guest reviews and the number of skier visits (1.62 million in 2014-2015). Charles D. Vail, its namesake, was the former chief engineer of the Colorado Highway Department in the late 30's, responsible for choosing a plan for the old Route 50 (now I-70) that made Vail's future possible. Vail opened in 1962 with a single gondola, two chairlifts, eight ski instructors, nine trails and a $5 lift ticket. By 2014, the mountain had thirty-one lifts, one hundred and ninety-three trails, a thousand instructors and a $145 lift ticket.

The phone rang in Steve and Janice's home in New Castle.

"Steve, this is Glen," announced the voice at the other end. Dr. Glen Braswell served as the Southern Baptist's Executive Director for Colorado, overseeing all Southern Baptist churches in the state. After opening pleasantries, he got to the point, "Steve, we'd like you to go to Vail."

Steve's response wasn't what Dr. Braswell was expecting, but then Vail had a well-deserved reputation for catering to the rich, not to mention a housing market priced three times higher than the state average. Steve, happy in New Castle, was put off by Vail's affluence. "'No thanks,' I told him. 'I don't want to raise my kids with all those rich people.' Dr. Braswell only half listened—as Executive Directors can do—and asked me to pray about it."

Two weeks later, Dr. Braswell called back. "I've talked to the Home Mission Board [HMB, the agency overseeing the church's missionary outreach in the United States and renamed the North American Mission Board in 1997] and they want you to do it."

"When he said that," Steve responded, "I wasn't worried. I knew I didn't qualify to be a home missionary since I hadn't been to seminary. I pointed that out to Dr. Braswell, saying once again I wasn't interested in going."

"Well... continue to pray about it, will you?" he asked.

"We were just heading out of town to visit my parents in Denver when he called a third time. He went through the same spiel again. This time, he said he had talked to the HMB about my lack of seminary education and they said they still wanted me to apply for the position and would waive the seminary requirement."

To their credit, the HMB was willing to think outside the box. Given Steve's leadership gifts, their decision was simply common sense. Just as the purpose of voice lessons is to train a person to sing, the purpose of a seminary education is to train people to be pastors. And just as some people are gifted and can sing beautifully without lessons, others can provide skilled pastoral leadership without formal training.

"Well... okay Glen," Steve responded.

Leading the ministry at Vail at the time were John and Diane Haeger, members of the Southern Baptist's two-year stateside volunteer program (abbreviated "US-2").

"I'll drop by and visit with John and Diane. We'll talk to them, then think and pray about it."

"And we did just that. After leaving John and Diane's house, we were halfway up the Vail Pass when my wife looked over at me and said, 'We're going to be moving, aren't we?'

"'Yeah... I think so.'"

Steve's assignment was a twofold job: he would serve as the Christian Social Ministries consultant for Colorado Baptists as well as the Resort Ministries consultant to Vail. Interviewed by the man in charge of Christian Social Ministries, Steve received a less-than-enthusiastic response. "Well, you wouldn't be my first choice to be here, but Glen Braswell really wants you, so that's what we'll do."

In July, the Vail church voted unanimously to call Steve as their pastor. The Hoekstras packed up and left New Castle. With a congregation of between eighty and ninety people, the church they left was in far better shape than when they arrived. As a result, "They were able to call a full-time pastor and not a kid like me," says Steve.

The ministry at Vail met in the Vail Interfaith Chapel, a white stucco and brown-trimmed building serving as home to several churches. In a town of prohibitively expensive real estate, Rev. Donald Simonton, Vail's pioneer clergyman, had the idea of a single building serving many groups. The logic was irrefutable. As of this writing, the chapel is home to six congregations: Roman Catholic, Episcopalian, Southern Baptist, Presbyterian, Lutheran, and Jewish. While the concept made sense, that very openness would, years later, set the stage for the most violent attack ever leveled at Steve.

John and Diane Haeger were the third team of US-2'ers at Vail. They did their job well. By the time Steve arrived, an on-mountain service was in place and a small group of twenty attended services in the chapel.

As at New Castle, new insights accompanied the beginning of Steve's ministry at Vail. In making the rounds of local business owners and introducing himself, Steve received some puzzling responses.

"I kept getting the brush-off," he recalls. Bewildered, he looked for help. "The mayor had been around for years and was a neat Christian guy, so I sought his advice." It was an enlightening meeting.

"You're from a coal-mining town," the mayor began, "and you know, flannel shirts and blue jeans are just not the attire up here. Let me introduce you to my cousin who runs a clothing store in town."

After visiting the clothing store, Steve noticed a definite change. "As soon as I started dressing differently, doors began opening."

Steve is quick to point out that what was true of Vail isn't necessarily true of other resorts.

"Aspen is not that way—blue jeans or slacks make no difference, but at Vail in the nineteen-eighties there were some well-defined expectations."

Steve's move to an affluent resort community from a poor coal-mining town was unsettling. He sums up his early memories in two words: "real scary." The affluence and wealth—so far removed from his experiences and values—were unnerving. Then, a conversation with God changed his whole outlook. "I remember walking across the street one day and looking up at the hill and seeing all those multi-million dollar homes. One particular house made of stone was just huge, with its own indoor swimming pool. I remember walking across the parking lot and seeing all the BMW's and Mercedes and Cadillacs. I was driving a rebuilt Scout that I'd fixed up. Its body was in rough shape, and blue smoke poured from the tailpipe. I remember saying to God, 'you know God, I believe you know what you're doing, and I believe in your sovereignty, but I believe in this case you blew it, you really blew it. I don't know why you've got me here, but I don't fit.' Then something came over me and with it a message that sunk home: 'all these cars and all these houses are parked and built on your Daddy's land, so you don't have anything to be ashamed of.' I counted on that realization a lot when I would visit people in log cabins with dirt floors—where some of the students and poor families were living—and then that same day would drive up to Beaver Creek and visit someone in a ten thousand square foot, five million dollar home. If I didn't remember those words I would have been blown out of the saddle, for there's no way that a minister like me could fit in with those people. Those words gave me a shot of confidence—it wasn't that I never felt intimidated again, but I had a confidence I didn't have before."

Fitting into a new community is important for almost everyone, but for someone in Steve's position it was critical; the effectiveness of his ministry depended on it. Fortunately, doors began opening. The people of Vail appreciated and admired those who excelled, and Steve was a gifted runner. "I was entering a lot of races in those days—10K's and half-marathons—and my name would often end up in the papers, giving me some helpful recognition and opening doors with a lot of people."

While running is an individual sport, it was a love he shared with others. One fall morning at the end of a run, his running buddy started talking about some of the projects he was involved in as part of the local Rotary group, then stopped himself in mid-sentence. "Say, Steve, have you ever thought of joining Rotary?"

"Well, no, not really. We didn't have one in New Castle. Why?"

"I think it'd be great to have you as a member. We're involved in projects that help the community and you've said that's one of the things you're all about, so I think it'd be a great fit. You interested?"

It was the most rewarding invitation Steve ever received. "Rotary was the greatest thing, providing me with a lot of personal contacts and an important role in the community. It was my key to the town. I became the secretary and vice president and by joining them in activities such as the World Cup ski races and Fourth of July parade—when I dressed up as Uncle Sam a couple of years in a row—I was seen as a contributing member of the community."

Coinciding with Steve's move to Vail was his appointment by Colorado Baptists as their consultant for resort ministries. While new to this himself, so was everybody else, this form of outreach being in its infancy. Steve's skill at growing churches, however, and his love for the outdoors, made him the natural choice.

Chapter 8 | RAAT PATROL

"By the time I moved to Vail," explained Steve, "Dub had moved out of the state, and Jim Rich was also leaving, so I just took over the direction of our backpacking ministry and changed the name to Recreational Alpine Adventure Trips, shortened to 'RAAT Patrol.'

"We would do between four to six trips a year, each a week long. Groups would arrive on Monday and leave on Saturday. They came from all over the United States—entire youth groups as well as individuals. I led an Adult Leadership Trip in the spring for those guiding the trips."

Visitor at 13,000 Feet

It was during one of the Adult Leadership Trips that Steve and his group experienced something so unexpected it bordered on the mystical, leaving many baffled and awestruck. As recounted by Joe Chambers, a RAAT Patrol leader at the time and the 38-year-old son of Steve's former pastor, Dub Chambers, "One of us said, 'What is that moving this way?' Someone reached for their binoculars and described what they saw. At thirteen thousand feet and walking toward us a half a mile away was a man with no backpack, rain gear, or anything you might normally consider important while climbing the alpine ridges of the Sangre de Cristo mountain range in Colorado. Yet, there he came as quick as you please.

"He was wearing a floppy straw hat with a red bandanna wrapped around the sweatband secured by a cord tied under his chin. He wore a plain white Fruit-of-the-Loom undershirt and sky-blue, polyester dress slacks cut off at mid-thigh. Left unhemmed, the stray strands blew in the breeze. On his feet was a pair of cheap suede hiking shoes and underneath, cotton athletic socks. Dangling from his leather belt was his water container—an almost empty gallon milk jug.

"As we heard this description our mood moved from disbelief to confusion to incredulity. We had seventy-pound packs, three hundred dollar backpacking boots, and to protect against hypothermia, wore not a stitch of cotton. We had rain gear, rope, and food for six days, water purification tablets, sleeping bags, emergency gear, and a first aid kit. We were totally prepared for these rugged mountains, but not this guy.

"When he approached our resting and astounded group, he smiled. ' Howdy,' he said. His thick glasses fogged up as he looked at us. He had been walking quickly at an altitude of over thirteen thousand feet, yet was barely breathing hard. He scratched his right forearm, then his neck and then his thigh. Someone asked where he was camped. He shrugged, tossed his head to his left down a line of ridges heading south and said, 'Back thatta way.'

"'Where you headed?' We asked. With the same vagueness, he jutted out his chin northward and said, 'Thatta way.'

"We sat on a 13,200-foot pass where there was no trail. Any viable campsite was hours away. Where had this guy come from? Where was he going?

"He untwisted the lid of his jug, took a swallow from the little water it contained, wiped his mouth and grinned. We were dumbstruck. He was dressed more like a beach bum from Southern California than a hiker on the alpine ridges of Colorado. An awkward silence hung between us. Finally, someone asked if he needed anything.

"'I'm all right' he said. 'Bugs are really bad aren't they? I could use some insect repellent if you could spare any.' Pink bumps completely covered him, some scabbed over, and some looked infected. Smallpox or a hornet's nest were the first things that came to my mind as he stood there scratching.

"My friend Jim jumped up and said, 'I have a second bottle of Jungle Juice I'll give you.'

"'No. Just squirt me a little in this sandwich bag.' He reached into his pocket and pulled out a crumpled up baggie, turned it inside out dumping some crumbs, and held it open for Jim. 'About six or seven good squirts is enough,' he said. He twisted a knot in the top, put it in his pocket, and rubbed the spillage over his arms, legs, neck and face.

"'Don't get any of that juice on your glasses, it'll dissolve your lenses,' someone offered. Nervous laughter rippled around our group.

"'Well,' he said. 'I'd better get going. Thanks for the bug juice.' He grinned, looked northward and off he went. We watched him drop down over the edge of the ridge, and never saw him again. Looking around at each other, checking for some clue of understanding at what we had witnessed someone asked, 'What just happened? Was that even real?'

"If you look at Crestone quadrangle topographical map there is an unnamed ridge between Cleveland Peak and Tijeras Peak. That's where we saw him."

The Hoekstra Way

Steve continued his description of the RAAT program. "I would do two trips a year, the leader's trip in the spring and one of the student trips. We supplied all of the equipment, the food, and guide service for the weeklong hikes. I'd send the students a list of the clothing and boots to bring and we provided everything else."

When it came to the preparations, Steve was strict. As Joe Chambers recalls, "Steve is very particular about backpacking, very particular. You have to wear a certain kind of clothing; you have to wear a certain kind of boot; you have to pack your pack a certain way. He was drill-sergeant strict when it came to that. There was a right way—the RAAT way—and it was Hoekstra's way. You could inform it, and you could make suggestions, but if I were to put him on a flexibility scale, it would be 80% his way, 10% your way and 10% negotiable. That was good because he knew what he was doing, but it was irritating as all get out to strong-willed folks like me."

"That sounds like quite a program," I said to Steve. "I expect the experience dramatically changed kids' lives—any memories that stand out?"

"Many, with both adults and students. For a couple of years, we worked with the Arkansas Juvenile Detention Facility and took out ten convicted felons a year. They came to us through Benny McCracken, now pastoring in West Yellowstone, who was the youth chaplain for the Arkansas Department of Corrections."

Benny

Rev. Benny McCracken picked up his breakfast tray in the dining room of the hotel hosting a conference he was attending and looked around for a place to sit. Catching his eye was a man clad completely in buckskins and sitting at a table by himself. "He's got to be one of us," Benny thought as he made his way over to the strangely attired figure at the table. They began talking, and Steve quickly invited Benny to join him. As they ate, they shared their stories with one another in what turned out to be the start of a long and rewarding friendship. Hearing Steve talk about his RAAT Patrols fascinated Benny both personally and professionally.

"I always wanted to go hiking and backpacking, but could never find anyone to go with me. Now here comes Steve, who loves both hiking *and* backpacking and he said he'd be glad to take me." Then, thinking about Steve's RAAT Patrols, "I thought, wouldn't it be great if we could take the boys from Juvie on that kind of experience? I bounced it off Steve, who was all for it. Both of us, however, thought it doubtful that a state agency would ever give us permission for such a thing."

Before Benny was going to present the idea, he needed to experience it for himself. Steve invited him to join the leader's trip in the spring. "I run and bike and was in pretty good shape," said Benny, "but I'll have to tell you, hiking at 12,000 feet with a sixty-pound pack, Steve just about killed me! Still, I loved it and drew up a plan for a group of ten boys on a weeklong trip.

I walked into the superintendent's office and let him read my proposal. His next words surprised me. "'Chap, I like this, but I'm going to have to run it up through the system.' He took it and ran it through the state system and to my total amazement they approved it. They agreed to provide us with a van and two staff to accompany us, but we had to pay for everything else. So I took time off and raised the money and developed a program to select the kids."

Knowing the strength and endurance needed for the weeklong event, Benny drew up a physical training program for the thirty to forty boys who signed up, a program he participated in himself. By the time the surviving ten were ready to leave, they were spending two hours a day running and exercising, excused from work details and classes in order to train.

Steve led the first year's hike and Benny the second. Unfortunately, two years after they began, the unexpected closing of the facility ended any future trips.

As Steve recalls his time with Benny, "Many things happened on those trips. We'd have kids who'd try to run away and others who would find cigarette butts and pick them up to smoke or hide for later. We had to collect their hiking staffs in the evening so they wouldn't beat each other with them. They couldn't have knives, of course, only forks and spoons. We had some tough gang members, but when we'd be climbing a peak and get up to 12,000-13,000 feet, some of them would just start crying. They were so far out of their element and so scared they'd just start weeping, and you'd hear things like, 'I can't go any farther.' We'd take a break, sit down and maybe do team-building games or role-playing. In the end, though, we saw to it that every one of them summited, and when they did—accomplishing something they never thought possible—their whole attitude changed."

Benny discovered that most of the kids had never been more than fifty miles from home and had little knowledge of the world beyond their poverty-filled surroundings. "I took pictures of the area we'd be hiking," said Bennie, "and showed them the snow, which they had never seen, and all the mountains and peaks and valleys." During a training run, Benny remembers running alongside one little boy who was having a rough time keeping up. "This little guy and I were running along and just talking, and he looked over at some of the tall pine trees we were passing and said, 'Mr. Chaplain, are the mountains in Colorado as big as those pine trees?' I've never forgotten it. It said so much about their limited understanding of nature and the outdoors. When we drove to Colorado and went through the Eisenhower tunnel and dropped down into the Vail Valley, they were just beside themselves with what they were seeing."

"O God, Lord Jesus, save me!"

In talking about the backpacking trips, one boy stands out in Benny's memory, a story he's told "about a hundred times."

"On the trip I led, we went to the ski resort at Beaver Creek and took a chairlift to the top—a completely new experience for them. There was quite a difference in altitude between home and Beaver Creek. Two days before, we were in Arkansas with its 700-foot elevation, and now we're starting our hike at 10,000 feet. We quickly hit snow—serious snow about waist deep. It was miserable, and we realized we weren't going to get to our objective that night. We were out of daylight and out of energy so we decided to do the only thing we could do: camp on the snow. Then the altitude hit us, and all the boys were throwing up. They were just a mess. The guide and other leader and I were the only ones who didn't have altitude sickness, so the three of us set up the boy's tents and got them inside and into their sleeping bags. Then we made hot Jell-O and all kinds of stuff to get them hydrated.

"The next morning we got up. We canceled our plans for the day. The objective now was just to get them down and get them out of there and out of that snow. We started down and came upon a steep boulder field, I mean *really* steep, with big boulders sticking out of the snow. The kids looked down, and they were scared, 'We can't do that, we can't do that!' I said, 'Oh yes you can. You don't have a choice; we're camping down there tonight—just head for the bottom.' So they took off, and they were down on all fours, crawling. It was kind of comical to watch them.

"There was this one young feller. He was a gang member and a gang leader. We figured he'd probably killed a few people. That wasn't why he was in Juvie, but he was just that kind of a young man. We got going and were perhaps a third of the way down when this guy stopped. He froze and wouldn't move. We tried to help him and encourage him, but he wouldn't budge. We worked on him for maybe forty-five minutes, but he refused to go anywhere. Finally, I said, 'Okay, guys, you head down; I'll stay and deal with him.' The two of us sat and talked for maybe another fifteen minutes, and when he still wouldn't move I said, 'You know what? I'm not going to stay up here with you. If you die, we'll give you a good funeral, but you're on your own, I'm out of here. Good luck, I hope you make it, and I'll see you in camp if you do.' So I took off, and he didn't know it, but I went down about twenty to thirty yards and then crawled into a bunch of boulders to watch him. I wasn't going to leave him up there. He was standing there bawling like a baby. Then there came the most sincere prayer I've ever heard prayed in all my life. Still crying and with tears streaming down his face, he said,

"O dear God... Lord Jesus, save me!" I nearly rolled down the mountain laughing, but you know, God answered his prayer. He finally started down and began to see that he really *could* do it. I stayed out of sight and worked my way down, keeping my eye on him the whole time. When it was clear he was going to make it, I went on down myself. When he came into camp that afternoon, he had the biggest smile on his face that I've ever seen in all my life. He had accomplished something—something big. All the others were congratulating him and slapping him on the back. It was incredible. It was the first time in his life that he had to face himself and confront his own helplessness. He dug down deep and came up with what it took to get him off that mountain. That accomplishment stayed with him for the rest of the trip; you could see it in his smile. Back at the Training Center, he was still smiling. He was released a few days later and, because of confidentiality, we weren't allowed to contact the boys after they got out. My daughters live in his city, however, and whenever I visit, I always think about him."

All the positive responses from these wilderness trips intrigued me. Why did these trips leave such a mark on people's lives? On a mission of discovery, I put the question to Steve and others leading similar programs. From their responses came two contributing factors, to which I added a third of my own.

The Wilderness
"Nature is the theater of God's glory."
—JOHN CALVIN, 16th-century theologian, and pastor

All of the life-changing experiences coming out of RAAT Patrols, Christian High Adventures, and similar ministries share one thing: they all took place in a wilderness setting. For many of us, wilderness and outdoor experiences have etched upon our spirits a new perspective on life. I remember the breathtaking view upon hiking to the top of Mt. Katahdin in Maine. My personal concerns shrunk into insignificance as I gazed upon the expanse of mountains and valleys stretching below me.

Distractions, however, can easily neutralize the power of the wilderness. These days, give a kid an iPod or cell phone and a couple of ear buds, and he might as well be home. More than one study has reported that for the wilderness to leave its life-changing impact, it must be free of such distractions. On RAAT Patrols, Steve prohibited kids from taking along *any* electronic devices. In those days, it was transistor radios and Sony Walkman tape players. At the beginning of each trip, participants left those devices and even their watches, at the trailhead. "To this day," Benny reports, "I don't carry a watch in the backcountry. I carry a phone just in case of an emergency, but I never turn it on. I appreciate it now, but it took some getting used to. In the beginning, I'd frequently check my bare wrist for the time until I realized I didn't need to know."

"Spending an extended amount of time in the wilderness free of the distractions of civilization leaves people all the more receptive to the love of our Creator," says Joe Chambers. "You're in the present, separated from the past you left behind and the future which lies before you, and it's in the present that God meets us."

A Significant Accomplishment

In talking about the kids from the Arkansas Department of Corrections, Steve says with well-deserved satisfaction, "Everyone summited." Steve and his staff saw to it. One can only imagine the impact of such an achievement on those whose prior bragging rights came from the length of time they were stoned, the amount of alcohol they drank, the number of women they bedded, or the haul they reaped from their robberies. By summiting, every camper succeeded in a challenge as physically demanding as it was experientially new. Their accomplishment started with a learning experience. In fact, the whole week was a learning experience. They learned how to pack a backpack, the equipment needed and the skills required to set up camp, start a fire, cook a meal, and survive in this new environment. "A lot of them didn't know anything," recalls Steve. "We started out with how to tie your shoes correctly, and why we wear wool instead of cotton, and how you set up a rainfly. We didn't set up tents; we set up rain flies, and why do we have rain flies instead of tents."

"Why *do* you have drain flies instead of tents?" I asked, feeling a bit foolish. His answer provided a glimpse into the world that's home to him and unknown to many of us.

"For several reasons," Steve answered. "First, they're lighter. Back in the seventies and eighties, the lightest backpacking tent weighed six to six-and-a-half pounds. A ten-by-twelve-foot rainfly is not even a pound. Secondly, they're more versatile. You can set it up high and let the breeze blow through it if the mosquitos are bothering you, or you can bring both sides down to the ground, giving you more protection if it's raining or snowing outside. With ski poles at either end, which is what we use for hiking staffs, you can set them up in a forest or a rock field. Thirdly, if a rainstorm is coming, you can set them up very quickly. We'd get a half-dozen people underneath them in no time. If it was cold, we'd boil some water for a hot Jell-O mix providing both warmth and quick energy."

The "learning mode" required for backpacking, hiking and camping also carried over into the participant's spiritual lives and, according to Steve, paved the way for many conversions.

Besides a wilderness setting free of distractions and the joy of achieving a difficult goal, I would suggest a third contributor to changed lives, perhaps too close to those I interviewed for them to mention.

A Faith-filled Staff

The staff of any wilderness trip provides both the emotional atmosphere and the spiritual framework for that experience. On Christian trips, this normally translates into an atmosphere of mutual caring among members of the group and a Biblical reference point for their discussions. The caring atmosphere provides emotional security, and the Biblical framework enables people to connect God the Creator with Christ the Redeemer. The message is simple: the God who has created all of this *for* you is the same God who is offering his love *to* you. Benny provides an example of a caring atmosphere.

"That second year got cut short when I broke my ankle," said Benny. "We were at 13,000 feet on a peak. It was a clear, sunny and beautiful day. We looked over at a peak away from us and saw a cloud forming up. That thing developed like crazy and caught us. We quickly picked up our packs and hurried to get away from the danger of lightning. I'm legally blind, and I don't see really well. We were running down that boulder field with packs when I turned my ankle. I thought it was okay, so I kept on going. We reached the tundra and walked about a half-mile when it happened: my ankle just popped. I can still remember the sound. The neat part was that they couldn't get a helicopter in for me until the next morning, so I got to spend the night on the mountain. The storm rolled in and, fortunately, we had tents that year. But what was so neat and surprising was watching those rough, tough kids discover in themselves a caring and tenderness *they* didn't even know they had.

"'Mr. Chap, can we get you anything? You want to use my sleeping bag for a pillow? Can I cook something for you? Here, let me help you.'

"I was just amazed at their care, their tenderness and their concern for me. It was so special to watch that come out of them."

Benny wouldn't say this, but I suspect his kids were simply returning the same care and concern he had shown them.

Besides encouraging participants to care for each other, a faith-filled staff freely shares their own relationship with Christ. For those already Christians, such talk is strengthening, and for those who aren't, it may well be an introduction to a God whose name they've only known before as a curse word. Steve's mixture of a serious faith, a fun life, the courage to "tell it like it is," together with the grace that accepts people where they are, drew kids to Christ. As reported by Joe Chambers, "Steve takes Jesus very seriously. As much laughter as the two of us have shared together—and we've shared a lot—that's one subject he's quite serious about.

"The thing that's compelling about Steve is that no matter what you've done in your life, he always believes in you. No matter how much of a sinner you've been, he's big on giving you grace. By nature, he's a truth-teller: he'll tell you what you don't want to hear about yourself, no matter what. He's told me things I didn't want to hear—been wrong about some, but right about most. He's also a big grace-giver. You may have made the biggest mistake of your life, but he'll still be your friend and stand by you.

"There was this guy in one of his churches who came to Christ and Steve invested a lot of time in discipling him and training him to be a follower of Jesus. By all appearances, his student was on the right track, even taking a leadership role in the church. Then, out of nowhere, he gets involved in an affair and leaves his wife and the church, too. He moved in with this gal, but after a few months, it didn't work out and she left. After they had split up, Steve went over to visit. The guy was pretty surprised to open the door and find Steve standing there, but invited him in, and the two of them started talking. A few weeks later, he dropped in on one of Steve's services. It took courage because he expected rejection, but the people, taking their cue from Steve, welcomed him like a long-lost friend. He started coming regularly and after a while re-committed his life to Christ. His repentance came too late to save his marriage, but he's back on the right track and has been ever since, and that was several years ago. A couple of years after he returned to church, he remarried, and they now have a family. The story would have had a far different ending if Steve hadn't extended God's grace.

"In my experience, those who are big on grace soft-pedal the truth, and those who are big on truth, don't have much grace, but Steve strikes a healthy balance between the two."

"Okay," I said, "the kids are in a relaxed and loving atmosphere, doing things they've never done before and in a learning mode, and that opens them up spiritually, too?"

"Yep," replied Joe, "especially in the evenings—they're exhausted, they're tired, they've had a good hike, and you're sitting around the campfire or stove, drinking some hot chocolate. Youth will really open up and listen in that setting. I'll never forget the story I heard from a staffer on one of Bennie's trips.

"It was their second night out, and everybody was sitting around the campfire. The kids were exhausted. Actually, everybody was tired because they were still getting used to the altitude. Desiring to know them better, the staffer asked the boys to describe the apartment or home they lived in. They really got into it as they told stories about rats and roaches and tried to outdo each other for the most far-fetched tale.

"'We got ourselves a rat that's so big when ma put food on the table she thought he was one of us,' said one.

"'That's nuthin',' said another, 'We got a pair of rats, and they're so quick the food is half gone before it even hits the table.'

"'So, all of you have mothers at home?" the staffer asked. Loosened by the joking, they readily responded. Six were living with their mothers, two with relatives, and the other two came out of group homes. The staffer continued, 'Do any of you have fathers living with you?' Silence. He feared he might have gone too far when one kid finally said,

"Hell, I don't even know who my father is.'

"'Me neither,' piped up another.

"'We used to visit my dad in prison,'

"'My mom's got a picture of mine,' said yet another. ' When I was four, he left, and we've never seen him since. My mother hides the picture, but I seen it, so I know what he looks like.'

"I'm wondering," the staffer continued—an idea flashing into his mind, "If you could order up a dad for yourselves and he came to live with you after you got out of Juvie, what would he be like?"

'That's easy,' piped up the kid whose father left when he was four, 'he'd do things with me. We'd play hoops, throw a football around, and practice baseball. Maybe he'd even be a coach if I went out for Little League. I expect he'd be a lot harder on me than my mom, and I wouldn't like that, but that'd be okay if he came to my games and stuff.' A couple of heads nodded in agreement.

"'You know, I would have wanted that too,' the staffer continued. ' My dad died when I was eight—killed in a car accident, and I grew up wanting the same things you just mentioned and a whole lot more.' All movement stopped—the restless carving in the ground with a stick and playing with a branch in the fire—the kid's eyes were riveted on him. He continued, 'I don't think anything can take the place of a real dad who does things with you, but when I think about the dad I don't have, I remember the dad I do have, and that helps.' Puzzled looks appeared on the boys faces, and he went on. 'My mother would always take us to church on Sundays. When I was your age I didn't want to go, but she said, 'Your dad would want you to go,' and since he always went, I'd go.'

"'I'll never forget this one Sunday,' continued the staffer. ' The preacher was talking about people having bad fathers and some not even having fathers, and that sure got my attention. Then the preacher went on to say that God wants to be our father and wants to love us; that when we open our hearts to Jesus, are really sorry about the bad things we've done, and accept his forgiveness, we become part of God's family, and he becomes our father. The preacher invited anyone who wanted God to be their father to show it by coming down front as they sang the last hymn. When people stood to sing, I was the first one down front. Something happened to me that day. I can't explain it, but ever since then I've always known I've got a father in heaven who loves me and is watching over me. I've had some rough times, but God's helped me through them, and without him, I don't know where I'd be. You know,' he said, wrapping up, 'you don't have to be in church to make God your father. You can ask him anytime, and anywhere, even here and even now.'"

"Many people accepted Christ on our RAAT Patrol trips," said Steve. "I'd also hear stories about changed lives and God coming into their lives after they got home." Such experiences are common to participants in many Christian wilderness programs, including those of Solid Rock Outdoor Ministry. The following testimonies appeared on their website in 2014:

"Spiritually, there is nothing like a trip to the wilderness, away from routine, to bring you back to the face of the Creator." *Scott Edinger, 16*

"This trip has changed my life. It has opened my eyes and my heart. Never before has God ever talked to me so much." *Janna Bennet, 17*

"I found Him. It is no wonder that so many of the prominent men in the Bible took a similar reprieve in the wilderness." *Peter Barker, 19*

A participant's parent wrote the following letter to Andrew Arnold, Executive Director of Solid Rock Outdoor Ministry.

"I've waited a few weeks before writing to you regarding Tim's participation in the 40/40 trip (40 days and forty nights) because I wanted to see what kind of lasting affect it would have on him. In one word, it's been *positive*. Tim has taken a real and substantial step forward toward adulthood because of this experience. He is clearly more confident in himself and has a more relaxed demeanor. He has accomplished a task worthy of respect, and the fruit is showing. I want to thank you sincerely for blessing Tim with this life-changing experience. His whole family and I have benefited from the growth that has taken place in him, and he has benefited from this experience in ways that he has not yet realized."

People like Steve and Joe and Bennie and other leaders can provide the wilderness setting, the caring atmosphere, and the Biblical framework, but the ultimate effect on a participant's life is outside their control. The Gospel still comes as an invitation requiring an open heart and the awareness of one's need. For those who accept that invitation, as did Steve, there lies a future as rewarding as it is surprising.

Chapter 9 | A LIFE-CHANGING FRIENDSHIP

In the summer of 1967, Rev. Donald Simonton and his family unpacked their moving van in front of their new home on the outskirts of Vail, Colorado. Called by the Lutherans to develop a ministry at the newly created resort sharing the town's name, he soon became a respected and valued member of the community. Besides pastoring the local Lutheran congregation, Don was also a mountain employee, working part-time as a ski school supervisor and instructor. The esteem accorded him rubbed off on the clergy who followed, Steve among them.

"He was one of the old timers," Steve recalls, "so much a part of the mountain that his credibility remained intact through several changes of ownership, three of which occurred in just the nine years I was there. Don made a lot of inroads into the community, and I owe him a lot for helping me get established." As evidence of Don's influence, pastors who moved into the area automatically received complimentary ski and golf passes.[10]

Sundays kept Steve busy. Starting with a 9 a.m. home Bible study replaced a few years later with an 8:30 service at Copper Mountain, he also led a 6:30 p.m. Sunday school at Vail followed by a 7:30 service. It was his 12:30 p.m. service, however, that marked his ministry as different from most others. Designed for skiers, it took place outdoors, on the snow.

The idea originated with Don Simonton, who held on-mountain services at the top of the former gondola in an area called "mid-Vail." Don introduced the unique setting to Tim Kendricks, one of the US-2'ers preceding Steve. Upon arriving at Vail, Steve took over these services outside the mountain's Far East restaurant (now called "Two Elk").

Steve would begin the service at Far East by climbing on top of a picnic table inside the restaurant.

"Can I have your attention please?" He yelled above the din.

Conversations stopped, and heads turned.

"It's a tradition at Vail," he continued, "to hold worship services at each of four on-mountain locations and the service today will be held on the east side of the building at 12:30. The services are non-denominational, and we'd love to have you come out."

He repeated the announcement at 12:15. As 12:30 approached, Steve went outside, grabbed a large cross out of a closet off the back deck and stuck it into the snow. Skiers emerged from the restaurant in ones, twos, and occasionally entire families. Steve, and his children Jake and Holly, welcomed them, handing them a single page song sheet.

"Sometimes I'd ask where people were from, but with fifteen people that gets old fast, so I didn't do it all the time. After some singing and a reading, I'd do a fifteen-minute devotional, have a closing song, perhaps another reading and then dismiss them with a prayer. I'd invite them to stay behind if they'd like prayer for anything, or wanted to join me for some skiing. Sometimes they'd respond and sometimes they wouldn't, but I always offered it.

"On a nice day the services lasted about a half-hour, but the length depended on the weather—you had to be flexible. Also, if a church group showed up with their own song leader, thirty minutes could easily turn into forty-five. In town, we drew mostly residents and employees, but the on-mountain services catered primarily to the resort guests." On at least one occasion, those on-mountain services resulted in a life-changing friendship.

Mike Storace

A thirty-eight-year-old patent attorney and hard-driving businessman, Mike Storace was looking for some solace the day he and his wife attended Steve's outdoor service. He was in good health at the time, and no one in his family had died, but a large business deal entailing a significant investment had just blown up in his face. Like any businessman, Mike entered the deal with the hope of making a profit. Unlike most, however, he had another agenda.

"I had gone into this thing partly to lead this guy into the light of God," Mike remembers.

It was not to be. In a move catching Mike completely off guard, his business partner and supporters turned against him, replacing the hope of financial profits with a costly loss. Now, instead of bringing enlightenment to his business partners, he was wrestling with spiritual doubts of his own.

"I was really down in the dumps," recalls Mike. "I was wondering if I had failed God and if He was angry with me."

He turned to Steve.

"Steve befriended me and showed me Jesus' love in a way I had never before experienced. He reassured me that God wasn't angry with me, and I hadn't failed Him, making it one of the most remarkable periods of my life. Steve made a profound difference."

The changes Mike experienced didn't happen in Steve's office; they occurred as the two of them were riding chairlifts and racing down the slopes together.

"We'd go out some days and beat ourselves up on the slopes, and then we'd go down to his office and be so exhausted that all we could do was sit in our chairs and laugh, which was great, just great."

Skiing wasn't the only activity they shared.

"He taught me to hunt. He's a great outdoorsman and we shared a lot of adventures together."

"What happened during those times?" I asked.

"We talked. He's a guy I could really talk to about intellectual as well as heartfelt questions. We didn't always agree on everything, but we could always discuss the issues, look at all sides, and come away still very secure in our friendship."

"Any specific memories?" I inquired.

"There are two that stand out. One was when we were skiing with his daughter Holly. We were trying to get into some powder, and we saw some wind-blown stuff and thought we could make it over. Steve and I were always pushing each other, but this time, we found ourselves in a very slick spot. Holly fell and broke her leg. Steve felt terrible about it. He just started..." choking with emotion, Mike stopped in mid-sentence and changed the topic. He returned to it later in defense of his friend.

"The appearance of that slick spot was deceptive—one of those places that looks soft but when you get into it, discover that it's bone hard. There was no way you could tell. It was the one time I was able to..." He paused again before continuing. "I saw the softer, vulnerable side of Steve. He needed God's church—other believers, too. I think it deepened our friendship a lot—at least it did for me."

Mike shifted to less intense memories.

"We'd also go hunting, and I swear there were times I thought he was trying to kill me. One time I remember we hiked up very high on the east side of Vail. He put me in one place, and then went over to another, and we sat there waiting for the elk. I saw this storm front coming in from the west. I could see it coming down the valley along I-70. It rose as it came up the mountain toward us, and caught us, eventually dumping two feet of snow. Steve came over and found me. Ever the woodsman, he moved us under a big pine tree. Then he got out his flint and some kindling and started a fire to keep us warm. It was a real survival thing. That experience was a great memory. You know how quiet it can get when it snows, and we were just talking, reflecting, and praying. I remember climbing up and down those mountains and forcing Steve to wait for me. I'm a flat-lander, and he was raised in the mountains. We'd be carrying our rifles and 60-70 pounds of elk on our back. It was great. In a physical sense, it was far more than I thought I could do. In later years, it resulted in an increased confidence whenever things got hard."

Chapter 10 | MAKING A DIFFERENCE

The rich urbanites and poor college kids at Vail were a different breed than the coal miners of New Castle, yet Steve used the same two principles for both places: getting out among the people and building friendships.

Rubbing Shoulders

Resort communities have a high population turnover. Jeff Wagner, former head of resort ministries for Southern Baptist's North American Mission Board (NAMB), draws an accurate picture when he says, "In a resort community you are ministering to a parade of constantly moving people."

Steve recalls his introduction to one couple:

"'This is Steve Hoekstra,' the man said, 'our new pastor in town.' Then, turning to Steve: 'We'll see how long *you* last.'

"In Vail you weren't even considered a resident until you had been there three or four years," Steve continues. "Essentially you also build a new congregation every three to four years. In a church of a hundred, you need thirty-five new members a year to maintain your numbers, and fifty a year to grow. To get these numbers, you have to meet and visit with one-hundred-and-fifty people a year. The only way you can do that is to be involved in the community."

Fortunately, for Steve, the chapel itself was a drawing card. Strategically located in the middle of town, visitors would see it, pick out a service, and show up. With his office in the building, Steve would frequently give tours or, seeing someone praying in the sanctuary, offer to pray with them.

Like any other pastor, Steve made himself available for counseling, but his setting was far different. "Ski resort employees weren't about to come into my office, so most of my employee counseling took place on the chairlift or in a restaurant because that's where they felt comfortable."

With his love for the outdoors and desire to meet people, Steve mingled easily. In addition to visiting the shops and businesses of Vail, he talked with guests on the chairlifts and employees on the job. When he declares, "I love people," he means it. In a nation populated mostly by extroverts, Steve fits right in, which is strange. He's not an extrovert; he's an introvert. Puzzled when he described himself that way, I asked the obvious question: "Why does an introvert like you hang around with people so much?"

"Necessity, I think. It'd be real easy for me to sit behind my computer or ski by myself. In reality, the introvert is not one who avoids people; he's one who recharges his batteries by being alone. There are people who recharge their batteries by being around others, and they're extroverts. Those who do it alone are introverts, and that's what I am. After my third year at Vail, I had to go skiing somewhere else to do that. I did the Myers-Briggs [Personality Inventory], and it was enlightening because I discovered that introverts are not necessarily shy and retiring. Instead, they just need to be alone to recharge. It isn't that I don't enjoy being with people, most often I do. I enjoy crowds and events, but then I need to get off alone, or I become tense, irritable or cranky. My wife will say, 'you need to go fishing, Steve.' I'd take her up on it and come back feeling much better."

Friendships Matter

In Newcastle, Steve's ministry grew through friendships. It grew the same way at Vail, but there was a difference. "In Newcastle, I built friendships by helping people get their wood in, fixing their car or pounding nails. At Vail, it was different. I discovered that relationships are built through play, so I skied with them. People at Vail aren't concerned so much with where you come from or what you do; their first question is often, 'where did you ski today?' Later on might come the questions 'what do you do?' and 'where are you from?' This was a real revelation for me. Yes, people still want to talk about themselves, but they want to begin with where and how they've been playing: 'Have you tried these new skis or taken that new trail?'"

Mike Storace wasn't the only person whose life was changed through their friendship with Steve. New York native and mountain employee Kevin Erickson was another.

Kevin Erickson

A freshly minted junior college graduate from New York, Kevin's introduction to Vail came after he joined some friends on a trip to Colorado and ended up with a dishwasher/cashier's job at one of Vail's on-mountain restaurants. "They asked me if I knew how to ski, because back then if you worked at one of their on-mountain restaurants, you had to ski down after work. I really didn't know how, but I wanted the job. My uncle had taken me a couple of times, so I told them I did." Fortunately, nearby Copper Mountain came to Kevin's rescue, opening two weeks before Vail—just enough time to learn how to ski. After several employees were fired for pilfering from the tip jar, and the new manager injured himself in a snowmobile accident, Kevin received a request. Vail's food and beverage director, who had come to know

Kevin, asked if he'd run both the Far East and Wildwood, another small on-mountain restaurant a mile away. Although barely twenty-one years old, Kevin agreed, beginning his career in food service management. While at the Far East restaurant, he met Steve.

"What was it that drew you to him?" I asked

"Steve understood the importance of building relationships. The thing I liked best about him was that of all the people I met who were Christians, Steve was the first one I met who was a regular person—he skied, laughed, and was fun and you could hang out with him. I never met anybody like that before who also loved the Lord. We both liked to hunt, and fish, and play racquetball and ski. All the things I really enjoyed doing in life—and rarely found in other Christians—I found in Steve. He could do all those things, but was still an upstanding guy—he wasn't immoral, never said anything off-color, and I can never remember seeing him angry."

"Any memories that stand out?"

"It was my birthday and to celebrate it, Steve took me out fishing in Meeker, Colorado. I'll never forget it. We saw a golden eagle, were catching dozens of white fish and had so much fun that day. I really looked up to him and the fact that he made time for me made me feel very special."

And of course, they skied. Kevin could barely stand up on skis when he arrived at Vail, but with a growing love for the sport, that soon changed. "I remember skiing with Steve and he'd scream and holler and whoop it up just like a little kid. He was a lot of fun and had a great sense of humor."

Kevin was living with his girlfriend, and the two of them began attending church. "I think Steve was planting seeds when he talked with us, but he never judged us and never talked to us about our living arrangements." Until, that is, early one evening the following June.

The phone rang in Kevin's apartment. "You don't mind if I come over, do you?" asked Steve, "I'd just like to share with you a bit."

"That was almost thirty years ago," says Kevin, "But I remember it as if it were yesterday.

"We had a first-floor apartment in a cute little Swiss chalet. It was located in a residential area of Vail and had a deck that extended out from the dining room. We sat around the table outside. I had been brought up in the Methodist church and knew a little bit about being born again, but didn't understand it until that night. Steve brought his Bible and shared some scriptures on how we could be born again and how Christ died for us. He took us through the steps to become a Christian and by the end of the night, my girlfriend and I both accepted Christ as our Lord and savior. Steve was honest about things, so he talked to us about our living together. I took our decision for Christ seriously, but my girlfriend was *really* serious. We weren't ready to get married, so we split up, and she left and moved back to Washington. We never saw each other again."

Steve began several discipleship groups for those he led to Christ. "There were quite a few of us," Kevin recalls. "Steve had this very simple program for new Christians. We met weekly and immersed ourselves in the fundamentals of the Christian faith—how to "walk the walk" and not just "talk the talk." We also had Bible verses to memorize—Steve placed a lot of importance on Bible memorization, and I can still recite several of those scriptures thirty years later. He was very good at encouraging new believers. I went to so many of those meetings that Steve began letting me teach them—my first experience in teaching, and now I'm an elementary school principal. Once a month he'd invite all his discipleship groups over for a barbecue at his home in East Vail—it was a beautiful home, and he had a great family. Those barbecues were a lot of fun."

Steve's love for people, his involvement in their lives and his desire to see them come to Christ had its predictable effect. "The church at Vail grew from nearly nothing into a very vibrant church. We were a really tight unit for a while," recalls Kevin.

Steve not only introduced people to faith in Christ, he also strengthened the faith of those who already believed.

Marc Wentworth

As of this writing, Marc Wentworth is the dispatch supervisor for Vail, Colorado's police department, which handles all of Eagle County. He and Steve met in the fall of '84, when Marc and his wife moved to Vail following their purchase of the local horse and outfitting concession. Seeking a church to attend and with only Sunday evenings free, they showed up at Steve's service, and liked what they heard.

Elk hunting brought Steve and Marc together. Marc wanted to hunt but didn't know the area. Steve wanted to hunt but didn't have any horses. It was a mutually beneficial arrangement that resulted in much more than just some enjoyable hunting. "He changed my life," says Marc.

"In what way?"

"Before Steve came along, I wasn't interested in knowing any pastors or ministers. After I got to know Steve, I found myself thinking that it wasn't that bad of a thing to know a pastor. I was a casual Christian before meeting Steve. Through our hunting trips and hikes, however, my personal relationship with Christ changed dramatically. I remember the first time we went out hunting, he brought his Bible with him and when we pitched camp, he took it out and started reading it aloud. Then we'd start talking about what he read—a lot different than the church setting I was used to. Just lying around camp talking about Paul's adventures and other things in the Bible was a huge life changer for me."

"In what ways?"

"Well, my faith became personal after that. My Christian walk before meeting Steve was more structured and formal—going to church on Sunday and things like that. I accepted Christ in 1974 when I was fourteen years old, but the pastor left shortly after so I didn't learn much about being a Christian. It wasn't until Steve came along that I realized Christ is not stuffy, and you don't have to be in church to meet with him."

The picture of Steve reading and discussing the Bible around a campfire captivated me.

"When you went hunting, would you both bring your Bibles?" I asked.

"Steve always did, but the first time we went, I didn't," he laughed. "Then I was annoyed at not being able to read along so after that we both did. It was amazing. For Steve, Christ was always right there. We'd be out horseback riding. He'd be up ahead, and you'd hear him break into a chorus of 'How Great Thou Art.' Then you'd ride up beside him and see this awesome view. The first thing on his mind was not the view, but the greatness of God. That always amazed me."

"Anything else about Steve that drew you to him?"

"Steve was the first pastor I'd been around who would say what he felt, and not because it was something the Bible said, or that the curriculum taught. It was one of those things that convinced me he wasn't jerking me around just to use my horses. I don't want to say bad things about other pastors, but when Steve said something, you knew he believed it. He wasn't just mouthing what he had been taught or what the Bible said or what others believed. Whether he was talking about the Bible or how he liked dinner, he was just very real and transparent. I was 23 years old when I bought the outfitting business, had worked for other ranchers and spent time on some big ranches. I believed that when you worked for someone, you rode for his brand and were completely committed to him. In the same way, Steve was completely committed to Christ. If he was convinced of the truthfulness of something he would tell you, and not soft-pedal it for fear of offending you."

Unfortunately, there would soon come the time when Steve's outspokenness and honesty earned him enemies instead of friends.

Chapter 11 | COMMUNITY SERVANT . . . AND TARGET

In addition to getting out among the people and building friendships, Steve was looking for ways to serve the community. "Even in a wealthy area like Vail, the community runs on volunteers," he points out.

Just as Dann and Krista Masters volunteered their time through the local performing arts group, Steve gave his through Rotary, plus two annual ski races: the World Cup and the Legends.

"For years, I was in charge of the banner committee for the races," he recalls, "and after putting up the banners, I'd visit the racers and workers in the race tent. I got to know a lot of them that way."

To strengthen area families, Steve's church hosted the highly popular video series "Focus on the Family," which catapulted its author, Dr. James Dobson, to national fame. Steve recalls the event. "We'd have 80-100 people a night show up, and a lot of first-time visitors."

Providing an alternative to the bar scene after skiing, Steve held an "après ski" at the chapel. From 4-7 p.m. three or four nights a week, the church provided refreshments and the opportunity for people to hang out together. "I had some cards printed up that read: 'are you tired of the bar scene?' We'd put out coffee and donuts and people had a good time."

The ski resort itself later adopted two ideas started by Steve. "For three or four years we sponsored a 'Christian Roommate Service' and we'd have a computer set up to help people find roommates. That worked well for a while and then Vail Associates set up a similar service of their own and the need for ours disappeared." The same thing happened with a day camping program in the summer that drew 20-30 kids. Following Steve's departure in 1990, Vail Associates started their own on a much larger scale, negating the need for the church's program.

Steve served as chaplain to the local Search and Rescue team and directed the hospital's chaplaincy program, both positions providing opportunities to help those going through physical and emotional trauma. Steve relates one particularly tragic and reoccurring phenomenon. "Over a period of nine years, there were five baby deaths. I don't know what caused them—perhaps the altitude had something to do with it." Steve's 'perhaps' was more accurate than he knew. A 1998 scientific study in Austria discovered a positive correlation between high altitude and Sudden Infant Death Syndrome.[11] "People would go out skiing and come home to find their babies dead. I worked with the families to help them deal with the shock and pain and sometimes guilt."

While the mountaintop worship services drew visitors, the residents and employees of Vail attended Steve's services in the chapel. The younger crowd came for several reasons, none of which were religious. By the time they left, however, many of them were different people. "Working with the young group involved hard work and heartaches," recalls Steve. "The joys came from helping them find their way in life. At that age, a lot of them were searching. My approach was to get them to ask the question 'what does God want to do with my life?' I helped a lot of them answer that question, which was really cool for me." Then there were the heartaches. "You'd lead someone to Christ, and they'd start growing in their faith, and then they'd ruin their lives with alcohol or pregnancies and such, and I wondered, 'did I really do any good?' It was a real downer. Then you'd hear back from some of them years later. They'd say their time with us very helpful even though they messed up, and that God has since restored them."

"Yes," I responded sympathetically, "It's hard when you invest yourself, and they take everything you've given and throw it away."

"Yeah," replied Steve, "but you know, you and I do that to God all the time. If we're really truthful about it, we do."

"Make Sure It Fits"

Don Simonton's Interfaith Chapel—housing many worshipping communities under one roof—was a model just waiting to be copied. Not surprisingly, ten miles away at Vail's sister resort of Beaver Creek, several people came together for that very purpose. They turned to Steve and Don for help. As the two of them pondered the chapel's design, Steve drew on the principle he used for his outreaches: make it fit the people you're serving. This time, however, it wasn't a program he was working on, it was a building. "Take Crested Butte for example," said Steve. "It's a wonderful resort with a 1960-70's flavor. To fit that community, you'd need a ski-lodge-type building built with logs and looking like a chalet."

"We did some serious research," said Steve, "and modeled the chapel after a European church since the community had a European flavor to it. We were going to make it out of wood and stucco because stucco is cheaper. Thanks, however, to former President Gerald Ford, whose retirement home was in Beaver Creek, it ended up as a very attractive rock building. 'No stucco,' Ford said after learning of our plans, 'we're going to do it all in rock.'"

"Contextualization" is the official label Steve places on the process of designing programs that meet the needs of a community. He cites Collette O'Connell's 1990's ministry in Winter Park, Colorado, as an example.

"Collette [wife of Rev. Pat O'Connell] discovered that the kids showing up to work at the resort didn't even have enough money to do their laundry. She arranged to rent the local laundromat one night a month and do everyone's clothes for free. In the beginning, she expected kids to drop off their laundry and leave. Instead, they hung around and relationships developed. The results? Employees came to Christ, joined Bible studies, and sent quarters to her from all over the country to support the program. It turned into a fantastic ministry. Collette simply saw a need and met it."

Attacked

The Vail Religious Foundation oversees the Vail Interfaith Chapel. Each leader of a church using the chapel is a Board member, and anyone wanting space in the chapel must first secure the Board's approval. A local group of Mormons submitted their request. Marc Wentworth tells what happened next.

"Every other pastor on the Board voted against it, but afraid to say why they gave reasons such as 'we don't have the storage space' and 'we don't have a time slot.' It was Steve who stood up and said that he didn't want them because the chapel didn't allow religious groups that proselytized, which is a basic practice of the Mormon Church. He didn't beat around the bush and took a lot of heat from it. People even watched his house. There were death threats and horrible articles in the *Denver Post* about the bigot that pastors the Vail Baptist Mission. Steve was severely persecuted but didn't back down. Unfortunately, it may have eventually contributed to his leaving, but he established the foundation for a church that is still very much alive.

Steve's memories of the experience remain vivid, even after all these years. He begins on a positive note. "The congregation supported me in my stand, and it was a good experience for our church. For the next three years, I preached a series on the doctrines of the Christian faith and by the time I was through, they knew what they believed. They also discovered what the Mormons, the Jehovah Witnesses and the Baha'i's believe, as well as the beliefs that define Christianity. Personally, it made me dig deeper into the Scriptures to solidify my own beliefs, and I found out what the Mormons believed, so it was good for me."

Unfortunately, there were also negative consequences. In a culture that places tolerance at the top of its pinnacle of values—*especially* religious tolerance, many people regarded Steve's response as nothing less than hate-filled bigotry. "I got death threats in the email and over the phone. It caused some problems in our family because they lambasted my kids. They would go to school, and the other kids would give them a hard time, and they had no idea what was going on."

"If you were to do it over again, would you do the same thing?"

"Yes, but I would have been a little gentler and more tactful. I've grown more diplomatic over the years. I'd hope the results would be the same, but the way I handled it would probably change."

Moving On

Steve's success at Vail and his value to other resort ministries didn't go unnoticed. Eight years after arriving at Vail, he received a call from John Allen, the Southern Baptist's D-O-M for Western Colorado. After exchanging pleasantries, John popped the question: "Would you be interested," he began, "in moving from Vail and working throughout the state as our resort consultant?"

"I'd be interested in praying about it," Steve responded (he was learning).

"That'd be fine, let me know what you decide."

So Steve and Janice prayed. "I really didn't want to leave Vail. I skied, I hiked, I loved the people, and I loved the area. We were successful and had just expanded into the Beaver Creek Chapel. Attendance had increased. It was now between 100-170 at both chapels and 200-250 in the winter with the on-mountain services. I was at the height of my career and loved what I was doing. Then I started thinking. I was already doing what John wanted me to do. Whenever anybody asked for help at another resort, I'd go and take time away from the church. In trying to handle both Vail and those requests, I was burning out. After a while, we got a word from God that it was the thing to do."

It was not easy on his congregation at Vail. "I've been in Colorado all my life," Steve recalls. "If you're around long enough you fall in love with the churches and their people. You get close to them, and when you leave, it tears people apart. When I made my announcement at Vail, three people walked out of the sanctuary. I found out later they went outside and cried."

Marc Wentworth recalls his feelings upon hearing Steve's announcement, "We were dumbfounded. We didn't know what it meant because for many of us he was the first pastor we ever had." Steve took no pleasure in the grief expressed by his people, but it bore witness to having built something far deeper than the church's attendance.

Chapter 12 | DIRECTOR OF SPECIAL MINISTRIES

After fourteen years of leading churches, Steve and family moved to Aspen, Colorado, where he exchanged his pulpit for a steering wheel. His official title, "Team Leader for Resort and Leisure Ministries," sent him crisscrossing the state promoting "Special Ministries" that included everything from parades and four hundred mile bike rides, to outreaches at ski resorts. To assess their ministry potential, Steve and his family embarked on a two-year goal of skiing every one of Colorado's major ski resorts (such are the sacrifices one has to make in the Lord's work). Now that he was in charge of developing resort ministries across the state, the time had come for Steve to implement two long-nurtured ideas.

"The first was to unite resort ministries under a common logo so that people could go from one to another and have some idea of what to expect." Something like a religious franchise, the goal was to provide resort guests with a predictably rewarding experience. Steve got the idea from Dan Holzer and Debbie Wohler in Lake Tahoe, California, who had several ministries operating under the banner of "Tahoe Resort Ministries." Steve recalls thinking: "Why couldn't we do that? There could be Alpine Resort Ministries Winter Park, and Alpine Resort Ministries Aspen, etc. We could have training events to teach people the basics and a special track for those new to resort ministries."

Excited about the possibilities, Steve knocked on the doors of pastors serving churches near Colorado's major ski areas, offering to help them reach out to their neighboring ski resorts. The responses he received weren't what he expected. "There was a total lack of interest."

It wasn't the idea they objected to—many agreed that it *was* a good one—it's just that they weren't interested in pursuing it. Discouraged, Steve backed off, uncertain about the next step.

He didn't have to wait long.

"It just so happened there was a mass exodus of Southern Baptist pastors in resort areas and most all of them left between 1990 and 1992." Steve visited one of the first replacements who, much to his surprise, readily agreed to start a ski ministry. That set Steve thinking, why did this one respond while the others didn't? Then it hit him: the former pastors were already so committed that they had no time to invest in anything new. Steve now knew what to do. "Whenever a new pastor arrived, I was on his doorstep the next day, inviting him to do a mountain ministry. Because their plates weren't filled, they were interested, so I gave them some training and that's how we've been going for seven years.

"I love starting new things; it's what I'm good at. I'm not good for the long haul, staying twenty-five years in the same church. That's why I like resort ministries—you're always doing something new. The seasons change, people change, and the resort changes, and that's something I enjoy. I love preaching and teaching, but I'm not really a good caregiver."

Janice objects to that last statement, and for good reason. At first glance, it's as if Steve's saying he doesn't care about people, but anyone who knows him knows that isn't true. Just ask their widowed next-door neighbor, whose garden Steve weeds in the summer and whose driveway he plows in the winter. When Steve says "caregiver," he really means "long-term hand-holder." Steve's good at short-term and crisis intervention counseling, but long-term counseling? No interest. He's a builder, not a maintainer. Any church content with the status quo drives him crazy, but if they're interested in growing, that's a different story.

The man now emerging as a skilled and gifted leader is a man of contrasts. In personal matters, he keeps things close to his chest, but in matters of ministry, he's outspoken and honest to the point of bluntness. To those who don't know him, he can appear detached and indifferent, even intimidating, but to those in his flock, he's outgoing, caring and longs to be of help. The quiet and serious man observed by acquaintances is, to close friends and family, the fun-loving tease who whoops it up while tearing down the slopes. Among Steve's close friends, Jeff Wagner's experience is common: "I might not talk with him for months, but when I pick up the phone there's an immediate connection, and we're soon laughing and joking."

While there may be contradictions in the way people experience Steve, there are no contradictions in what drives him, what's important to him, and what he expects. As colleague Debbie Wohler observes, "He expects excellence, and high-quality results that honor Jesus. I for one appreciate this."

Five years after moving to Estes Park, Steve received official responsibility for something he was already doing: planting churches in resort communities. A year later, Rev. Veryl Henderson moved from Hawaii back to his home state of Colorado, becoming the state's D-O-M. On the charts, he was Steve's superior, but as Veryl reports, it was a relationship between equals. "Steve was a peer-level worker, and we had a great time. He taught me the importance of connecting a resort ministry with a sponsoring church. If it's an individual ministry, it leaves when the individual leaves, but if a local church sponsors it, it'll continue. I wish I had known that when I was back in Hawaii."

In Veryl, a creative thinker who loved resort outreaches, Steve found a kindred spirit. With Steve focusing on establishing resort outreaches and

Veryl handling everything else, over two hundred new churches and resort ministries sprang up in Colorado between 1995 and 2003. This was due in large part to their innovative approach. "We just gave people permission to do whatever God wanted them to do," says Veryl. "They started churches for snowboarders and people recently released from jail and Native Americans and cowboys. Bikers liked to worship on Fridays, so we had a Harley Davidson Biker Church with about a hundred people. If people sensed God leading them, we gave them permission to do it. Let them design a church that fits their context; not ours."

It was during this time that Steve started winter programs at thirteen of Colorado's twenty-three major ski areas and summer services at more than forty campgrounds, all under the banner of Alpine Resort Ministries.

Having developed close relationships with those he left at Vail, Steve kept in touch with several, including Marc Wentworth. "If you were to describe Steve to someone who didn't know him," I asked Marc, "what words would you choose?" It was a question I put to all those I interviewed, but Marc Wentworth's response left me stunned.

A Prayer and a Miracle

"Let me answer that with a pretty personal story," Marc begins. "In January of 1992, my wife Glenda had a stroke. She was 32 years old and working at the Vail Chapel as the pre-school director. We later discovered a major artery in her brain was 98% blocked and the arteries in her neck were 50% blocked. Steve wasn't around, having moved to Estes Park a couple of years before. The ambulance took her to the local hospital, and I was right behind it. Dr. Petrie, our general practitioner and friend, met us there. The emergency room staff didn't need him, but he was there, in the corner of the room, down on his knees with a nurse beside him, and they were praying. This was my first sign that..." Marc paused to regain his composure. "At the time I thought his praying was overdoing it—that her stroke wasn't that big of a deal, but in looking back, it was the best thing he could have done.

"Glenda was flown to Denver. There wasn't any room for me in the helicopter, so Mike Ricks, our interim pastor, drove me to Swedish Hospital, the neurological trauma center for Western Colorado.

"Now the miracles start piling up. Dr. Miller, the best neurosurgeon in Colorado, happened to be in the hospital when Glenda arrived. The radiologist said he and another neurosurgeon had just returned from a conference where they had attended a workshop on a new procedure for dissolving blood clots in the brain. Of course, they had never done it before, but they thought this new procedure might save Glenda. They asked me to sign a consent form. I asked what would happen if we didn't do anything.

"'In that case,' Dr. Miller replied, 'you can go in now and be with her because she's not going to make it.'

"So, of course, I signed the paper, and Mike Ricks and I started praying. A woman serving as the hospital chaplain came in and showed us to a private room where we prayed and talked for about an hour. Mike Ricks was making phone calls all the time, and one of them was to Steve Hoekstra. After a while, Dr. Miller came down to tell us they finished the surgery, and there was no hemorrhaging. That was their biggest concern. Pulling up a chair, he continued, 'She has a 5% chance of living through this and a 0% chance of living without major disabilities. You can see her if you'd like, but she doesn't look good.'

"I said I'd like to, so we walked down the hallway. The doors to the procedure room opened, and she was on a gurney. I was walking up to her when at that very moment Steve appeared. He pushed me out of the way along with Dr. Miller and an attending nurse at the head of the gurney. I can't say this without breaking down." Marc paused. "Steve put his hands on her head, and he prayed for her healing right there, invoking Christ and in his name. It wasn't a long, loud, or dramatic prayer, and if you heard him, you'd think he was just talking to Glenda. As Steve was praying I felt the Holy Spirit—physically—sending shivers down my spine, causing the hairs on the back of my neck to stand up, but leaving me with a feeling of hope. When Steve was through, they wheeled her to ICU and were very brusque about it. They didn't want us to see her or interfere anymore because she was basically dying. Steve drove back to Estes Park, but I stayed the night. They said I could see her at eight the next morning. I was there at seven.

"I went in to see my wife, and there she was sitting up in bed eating a breakfast of eggs. Her eyes weren't coordinated—one of them was pointing away—but she knew who I was, and she wanted to go home. After a week, she did go home, and ten years later, she ran the Chicago marathon. She has to wear glasses now, but her bad eye corrected itself. She has the tiniest bit of dyslexia, but she's learned to deal with it and runs five miles a day.

"I know Dr. Miller did a great job and had been prepared for that, but I also know that Steve Hoekstra's faith in Christ is why I have my wife today. There's no question in my mind. I've told some people who look at me with a smirk and make fun of the idea of God healing people and that kind of thing. All I know is that Steve brought Christ into that hallway and his faith and the purity of his belief saved my wife's life."

Steve's memory of the event is striking for what he *didn't* know at the time. "It was a pretty intense time," he recalls. "When I got the call, I was in Estes Park and remember driving down the canyon praying for Glenda. It wasn't until later that I realized how serious things were. When I prayed for her at the hospital, I had no idea she was at death's door."

Chapter 13 | THE INSTITUTE

Steve enjoys mentoring. He enjoys coming alongside someone, contributing his knowledge and encouragement, and helping them succeed.

"He works well with pastors in small mountain communities, and he's a great encourager," says Rev. Veryl Henderson. "He would walk alongside new resort ministers until they learned how to do it and I think many would have left without his support."

Wrapped up in starting resort ministries across the state, Steve soon encountered a threat to many of them; one that he couldn't handle alone.

In our secular culture, a sense of isolation is common among clergy. In 2002, the Lilly Endowment funded a program within the American Baptist denomination to address this very need by organizing pastors into collegial study groups. By 2009, over 2300 pastoral leaders were participating in 225 such groups. While regular church pastors can easily find colleagues to provide needed support and encouragement, this isn't true among resort ministers—a ministry so different that we can easily feel isolated in a room filled with other clergy. In the winter, the world of a ski minister naturally revolves around skiing—the furthest thing from the minds of most church pastors. Also, most pastors work with a consistent group of people from week to week, while the congregations in resort settings can change completely from one Sunday to the next. While most clergy belong to a stable community, resort ministers spend their time among transients. Even those with established congregations are not immune. People who are there one day could well be gone the next. In the mass exodus following the mountain's layoff in Angel Fire, New Mexico, Dann Masters lost a third of his congregation overnight.

For the new ski resort minister, ignorance of the transient nature of a resort community can produce bewilderment, confusion, and discouragement. Steve experienced all three after his first Easter at Vail.

"On Easter, we had four to five hundred in the chapel, twelve hundred for the sunrise service at the top of the mountain, one hundred at the regular mountain top worship service and four hundred at the evening service in the chapel. I was pumped!

"Then, next Sunday, I don't think we had three people show up for all the services. There was no one in town—I mean no one. I was stunned. My first thought was that I had done something wrong. I felt like a big failure. Then I discovered that following seven months of winter, everyone in Vail leaves for warmer climates after Easter Sunday. The whole town goes through a major shutdown. The weekly paper goes to a biweekly. People do return for the summer, but between seasons, everything pretty much dies. When you don't understand this dynamic it really throws you."

Steve was now hearing his new resort ministers echoing the same bewilderment and discouragement. A few were even thinking of quitting. They needed encouragement, support, and spiritual renewal, but Steve was only one person and couldn't do it himself, so in 1991, Rocky Mountain Resort Ministry Institute (RMRMI) was born.

When I interviewed Steve in 1997, he reported that RMRMI usually had 55-65 people in attendance at their annual three-day event, and the numbers were growing by 10-20% a year. The daily schedule started with Bible studies and seminars in the morning, a break from 10-3 for skiing followed by seminars until 6:30. The seminars were how-tos on ski ministries, summer campground ministries, and outreaches to retailers. The evening would conclude with an inspirational speaker and a time of worship, which Steve reported, "could last two to three hours."

With little time for skiing since leaving Vail, Steve especially appreciated the opportunity provided by the Institute. Joining Steve for skiing, however, could be dangerous. Debbie Wohler, of Tahoe Resort Ministries, recalls one particularly harrowing experience. "Steve was leading a group of us down the slopes, and we were going ninety-to-nothing. I was following and suddenly the next thing I knew I was airborne. We were jumping off a cliff—at least it was a cliff to me. It might have been only five feet, but I had no idea it was coming. I made it down and feeling glad just to be alive, went up to him, 'Steve, what in the world were you thinking?'"

Fortunately, the Institute involved more than just the joys (and occasional terrors) of skiing.

"It was a time of real refreshment," recalls Steve, and provided the needed antidote to a common malady among resort ministers: burnout. "Resort folks burn out three times faster than those in other ministries," says Steve. "There are a number of contributing factors—the intensity of the season and lack of a stable population base being two of them. In addition, the affluence of the ski area means you're going to have to rent a house since you probably can't afford to buy one.

"The Institute also aimed to help pastors develop customized programs to fit their resort. And lastly," he concludes, "it's a time for training. Although I've led mountain top worship services, no one ever trained me how to do it, so I wrote up some materials to share with the others.

"The most important thing is to encourage those already on the field. I know three people who wouldn't be here today if it weren't for what they found at the Institute."

The above information came from my first interview with Steve in 1997. It was a slightly different picture when I talked to him thirteen years later.

"RMRMI is no longer going?" I asked disbelievingly.

"We hold it occasionally, but not every year because it's no longer necessary. Most of the people who have been attending have been in resort ministries long enough that they could teach the classes. It became a bunch of us older guys who were just coming together to ski, and we thought we didn't need to be spending $500-600 just to do that."

Chapter 14 | ASPEN

On a crisp November day in 1997, the bare branches of the town's aspen trees stood silhouetted against a blue sky. Aspen Mountain towered Gulliver-like above the Lilliputian community at its base. Following my phone interview from New Hampshire, this would be our first face-to-face meeting. I pulled our rented car into a parking space on the street in front of a small office building nestled among the quaint European-like shops of the town's older district. Steve's sign was on the small lawn out front. Once my wife and I stepped inside, I inquired of the young cashier in the gift shop just inside the front door.

"Who?" he replied.

"Steve Hoekstra. He has an office here."

"I'm sorry, I don't know him, but there are some offices upstairs."

Knowing the importance Steve places upon getting out into the community, the clerk's response surprised me. Upon hearing of it, Steve winced. "That really bothers me," he replied. "I make it a point to know the people in this building. I've even brought them cookies." He paused. "I'll take care of that," he said, determination in his voice. Lucky clerk, I thought to myself, he's about to be cookie-bombed. Interestingly, Steve had already introduced himself to the clerk behind that cash register, perhaps just a few weeks or couple of months before. Due to the high turnover in resort areas, however, I had talked to his replacement, and possibly even his replacement's replacement.

Steve's presence in Aspen fascinated me. The community's reputation as a haven for the rich and famous was well known. Local homeowners such as Jack Nicholson, John Denver, Goldie Hawn, Martina Navratilova and Lance Armstrong guaranteed frequent mention of the community in the nation's tabloids and newspapers. Not surprisingly, as the area became the playground for the rich and famous, property values soared, making home ownership impossible for all but the wealthiest. Only the town's foresight in creating a price-protected sub-division of affordable housing spared the middle-class workers of the community from distant commutes.

A town of six thousand wealthy residents didn't seem like the most inviting environment for a man like Steve. One of the most skilled and knowledgeable ski resort ministers in the country taking on the haven of the rich and famous? "This should be interesting," I thought to myself.

Steve's presence in Aspen came from the merging of two streams: his past success at starting churches in resort communities and the desire of denominational leaders to plant a church in this affluent town. "The decision took a lot of time in prayer, seven months to be exact. I was excited about moving back into a ski area and also starting a new ministry, but I wanted to make sure it was God's leading and not just mine." This time, distinguishing between the two wasn't easy.

"I had a very difficult time discerning whether this was my will or God's. In decisions like this, I don't do anything without a direct word from God, so I waited. All the research pointed toward going, but I hadn't received a word from God, which only comes during my prayer time. Then one day when I was in Arlington, Texas, and my wife in Estes Park, the word came to me. Interestingly, and without my knowledge, it came to her too, and at exactly the same time.

"It took us a year to sell the house in Estes Park, something we had to do since Aspen wasn't a cheap place to live. While we waited, I spent a year traveling back and forth. I researched the kinds of people, the number of people, the number and kinds of churches, the number of beds, what had been tried before, on and on—everything I could find out about Aspen. We did our homework."

When Steve arrived, an evangelical church already existed in Aspen. The First Baptist Church, founded in 1963, had a winter attendance of 150, with 250 in the summer, a figure that would grow to 500 in 2011. Steve visited the church and liked what he saw. "They had a pretty good ministry. I liked the people there and enjoyed getting to know them. They had a good worship program and good music. Of those who attended, most weren't Baptist, which is probably why they later changed their name to Crossroads."

Steve's approach at Aspen would be completely new and untried in two areas: the people comprising his core group, and the church's meeting place. "Instead of jumping right in and holding services, I wanted to start a church that would be ministry-based, one that would emerge from people wanting to meet the needs of the community. There is a ton of opportunities in town and beginning a church that way would be more of a grass-roots approach.

"About three to four years ago, Benny Clark [Steve's successor at Vail] and Pete Owen [another veteran resort minister] did some research in Aspen. Nobody there saw a need for another church. Demographics point to a need, as does the growth, but people didn't see it because they view the church as taking from the community rather than giving to it." Unfortunately, as events would later reveal, there was more substance to Benny and Pete's study than was apparent at the time.

Looking forward to leading a church again, confident in his ability to succeed where others had failed, and eager to try some new approaches, Steve moved to the Aspen area with a clear vision and high hopes. There was, however, a personal cost to their move. Steve and Janice would eventually develop friendships in the area, but when Joyce and I visited him in his office on that November day a few months after the move, he left us with a candid admission. "It's very lonely here right now. Both my wife and I are introverts, and I'm traveling a lot." The traveling was necessary because of his continuing work as the state's Director of Resort Church Planting. He then said something more significant than he realized at the time. "Starting this ministry in Aspen is only a part-time responsibility."

Unable to afford a home in Aspen (where a thousand square foot home was then selling for one-and-a-half million) the Hoekstras settled in Snowmass (or "Old Snowmass" as the locals call it) fourteen miles away. Their home in Old Snowmass still cost $250K in 1997 dollars, or about $375K today. The day that Joyce and I visited him, Steve mentioned he was meeting with denominational executives in the afternoon to show them some houses in the area. He was hoping to impress upon them the need for purchasing a home in Aspen. Prompting this desire was more than wanting to live in the community he was serving. Besides starting a church with people wanting to serve their community, Steve had another new idea: his church would be meeting in people's homes. Steve wanted to start a series of house churches, a movement just gaining traction at the time. "I would start winning people to Christ and build up one house church after another. It would be a process of multiplication and in 5-10 years we would have 20-25 house churches going."

As reported eight years later by Lorin Smith in *The House Church Movement*, "A largely hidden, yet growing phenomenon is changing the face of Christianity in the West and profoundly affecting the way in which Christians are choosing to practice their faith. Disillusioned by the lack of New Testament realities, abusive authority and the spreading apostasy within large segments of institutionalized Christianity, thousands of Christians across America, Australia, Canada, New Zealand and the United Kingdom are gathering in homes to study the Scriptures together, pray, share the Lord's Supper and experience the fellowship and simplicity of first-century Christianity."[12]

A January 2011 survey by Barna Research revealed, "5% of Americans, about 11.5 million American adults, say that at least monthly, they attend a house church or similar church, which is not associated in any way with a local congregation." That's up from 4%, about 8.8 million adults, in 2006. It's clearly "more than a passing fancy. It has staying power."[13]

When not driving around the state as the Special Ministries consultant and as a resort church planter, Steve continued his research on Aspen.

"I gathered information from the chamber of commerce and mountain publications as well as newspapers and church bulletins to find out what they were already doing. I also attended as many town events as possible to become a familiar face, to hear what people are talking about, and to get to know them. I asked a lot of questions and gathered a lot of information." It was a carefully thought out plan.

"About two to three months from now I'll interview the main people in town—the town planners, police chief, and mayor, to see what they perceive as the needs of the community. Then I'll put together a strategy to meet those needs."

Steve knew this new ministry would be different than Vail. "In coming to Aspen, I had to remind myself not to simply copy what I did at Vail. For instance, I thought about a thrift store ministry like Vail has, but Aspen already has two in town, so that wouldn't work. We need to look in other directions to find the needs and where we fit in."

Steve's studies produced some interesting observations.

"Here at Aspen, it's important that you be a good skier. At resorts that were towns before they became ski areas, it's not as important and people are more accepting. At Aspen, however, competition is everything, and you're either good at what you do, or nobody wants you around. Most residents have been successful, and that's why they're here. Everything in Aspen is 'to see and be seen.' That's the reason I'm trying to lose thirty pounds. In Aspen, it's important to be in good shape."

Steve also had an interesting take on the "us-them" dynamic common in resort areas.

"In Aspen, the 'us-them' dichotomy is not between the locals and visitors; rather it's between those who are affluent and can afford to be here and those who can't afford to be here but are trying to play the role. The latter are the kind of people who end up angry, demanding, unhappy, and uptight. They're the ones who blow up at restaurants and on the mountain because they've put themselves in such a stressful position."

Regarding the area's wealth, Steve's greatest obstacle left him with more questions than answers.

"We evangelicals are really good at ministering to the poor but don't know much about ministering to the affluent. We have no idea where to begin. My desire is to find a way to reach them in Aspen. What are their needs? Where are they hurting? How can we reach them?"

Steve had obviously come a long way since his first intimidating days at Vail. Like Dann Masters, he quickly realized that the tried-and-true methods of spreading one's faith that worked so well in other places weren't going to work in Aspen. "If you try traditional evangelism techniques such as going door-to-door, they'll probably call the cops on you. They would view that as intruding, not ministering. The only way to 'get in' is to be invited in as part of the golf club or some other group. How do we reach out to them? I don't have an answer yet, but I know we're not going to do it by knocking on doors."

Steve then described an encounter with the very kind of person he was trying to reach. "Yesterday I was having lunch at a restaurant, and I started talking to this guy who is very wealthy. He owns homes here and at Steamboat Springs and in Texas. At the end of lunch, he asked me if I had read a certain New Age spiritual book. I hadn't, but I told him that I would get that book and read it. If I do, it'll give me a way of reaching out to him. Eating at the same restaurant provided an opportunity for interaction. The problem is that lunch there is much more expensive than at McDonalds. We're talking a $15-20 lunch rather than one that's $5-7, but if I'm going to reach these people, I've got to be there. I'll get that book he mentioned and read it and contact him with an invitation to go skiing or something. Then I'll bring up the book and see if it can open some doors.

"I'm not in the same league with these people, and that makes it hard. For instance, to join a country club is out of reach for most pastors. The Aspen Club [fitness center and spa] is where we want to reach people, but I can't afford to join that club [the 2011 initiation fee was $3000 plus $185 a month], so I've got to raise enough money to join because that's where our target group is located."

Steve's approach was logical and consistent with everything he learned about meeting people on their own turf and developing relationships. Unfortunately, it was also impossible. Steve was seeking to participate in a lifestyle he was in no position to enter. He would never raise the money for the Aspen Club, and he would never become part of the community. Even if his denomination *had* the money, they'd find it hard to justify purchasing such an expensive home. While he couldn't afford to live in Aspen, he could still find ways to serve the community.

Notified that he was receiving eighty high school students and their chaperones for a week of work, Steve queried Aspen's mayor about ways they could be of help. At her suggestion, the group redeemed the town's wetlands by planting them and then cleaned up the city's alleyways, earning them a citation of appreciation, a complimentary article in the local newspaper and the town's profound gratitude.

Chapter 15 | THE REST OF THE STORY

In a phone call to Steve in 2010, I was eager to find out what happened in Aspen. When leaving his office in '97, I thought, "If anyone can start something here, it's Steve." However, in the conversation that followed thirteen years later, Steve convinced me I was wrong.

"When I visited you in '97," I began, "you were going to start a series of house churches made up of people wanting to meet the needs of the community. How did that work out, and what happened after you left?

"In answer to the first question," he began, "poorly, and in answer to the second question, not much. I made many mistakes there. House churches were a new movement in '97, and I thought it would be remarkable to get them started in resort communities. I think that would work in many resorts, but it didn't work in Aspen."[13]

The failure gnawed at Steve. He wasn't used to setting his heart on something and failing. After a considerable amount of reflection in the years following, he concluded that the cause of the failure was, in his words, "my low-key approach. In Aspen, if you're not somebody, you're nobody. So it would have been much better for me to have gone in with a big splash: 'Steve Hoekstra is here, and he's going to start house churches!'"

"Would you have felt comfortable with that?" I asked. It wasn't an image that fit the Steve Hoekstra I knew. "You're the one who objects to people promoting themselves."

"I wouldn't have felt comfortable, but if I was convinced it was the thing to do, I would have done it." Then, as if acknowledging the unlikelihood of such a scenario, he quickly continued. "I just think I wasn't the right person for that community. We lived fourteen miles outside of town. If I had been a different person and living in a rented condominium in Aspen, I would have done much better."

"What kind of person do you think *would* have been right for Aspen?" I asked.

"If I could paint a picture he'd be around forty-five, very active, and have a background in coaching or something similar. Aspen is a very sports-intensive town. Either he or his wife would be very successful in business. It would be better if they were Democrats rather than Republicans. They would be social entertainers, loving to have people over to their house. Their home would always be open, not just in a friendship way, but for entertaining. In Aspen, you don't just go over to somebody's house and knock on their door. You're invited, and it's an affair. You always take a gift like a bottle of wine or some hors d'oeuvres. Even fourteen miles away where I was living in Snowmass, you didn't just drop in at a neighbor's. You had to be invited, and you'd write thank-you notes when you got home. With all of that, I just didn't fit in. We're a much more relaxed family."

The more I think about Steve's hypothetical "right person," the more I agree with him, to a point. Such a couple would be an ideal match for the community. Finding them would be difficult, but an aggressive search by the Southern Baptists would probably succeed. Only after these "missionaries to the millionaires" began their ministry, however, would they recognize the insurmountable problems they faced.

Simply put, Steve took too much credit for a failure that was inevitable and over which he had little control. His concluding assessment pointed to only one of the stab wounds in the body of his dream, and it wasn't the fatal one. Three factors doomed the ministry at Aspen from the beginning: nonexistent needs, inadequate resources, and unattainable goals.

Aspen didn't need Steve's ministry, something that the previous Southern Baptist survey concluded, and Steve dismissed. He reasoned that those surveyed saw the church as taking from the community instead of giving to it. While that may be true, it's also irrelevant. People in the original survey were asked about their desire for another place of worship. There was none. In Aspen's First Baptist Church, there already existed a healthy, growing evangelical community with a compelling program.[14]

Steve's research of Aspen's population growth contributed to a premature optimism. From 1990 to 1997, the town *did* grow by 17%, and if that continued, the increased numbers might well spawn the need for another evangelical ministry. That growth stopped, however, the very year Steve arrived.

It wasn't just the lack of need that doomed Steve's ministry; inadequate resources guaranteed that the idea would never get out of the starting gate. Steve didn't have the time, and the denomination didn't have the money to make Aspen work. Steve was no longer the preacher showing up in New Castle or Vail with no other mission than to grow those churches. Instead, he was now on the state staff with responsibility for helping start resort churches and ministries across all of Colorado. After meeting those responsibilities, his available time for Aspen would never be sufficient to feed such a hungry challenge. Timewise, Aspen beckoned like an inviting harbor to a ship caught by overpowering currents carrying it out to sea. There were never enough hours to build the necessary relationships. "He wasn't around a whole lot," commented one pastor. No amount of knowledge, skill or wisdom, all three of which Steve possesses in abundance, could compensate for a lack of time. To make matters worse, Steve was facing a challenge far more demanding than at New Castle or Vail. In Aspen, he wasn't just growing an already-existing church, he was attempting to start one from scratch.

Unable to purchase a home in Aspen with its seven-fiure price tag, Steve and his family settled in Old Snowmass, fourteen miles away. Because accessibility is critical to fostering the relationships required for a new church, Steve's fourteen-mile commute constituted a permanent barrier.

Lastly, while Steve's goals were laudable, they were also unattainable. Starting a church populated with people desiring to serve their community certainly makes sense. A group like this would have a powerful impact on those around them, but such people would be very difficult to find. Most individuals pick a church to meet their needs; not the needs of others. The people Steve was looking for were other-centered pioneers—not a well-populated group. Steve's idea was a commendable idea, a noble idea and most certainly a Biblical idea, but it stood no chance in Aspen. Interestingly, it *has* worked elsewhere. Matthew Barnett serves as Senior Pastor for both Los Angeles' historic Angelus Temple and the Dream Center—a ministry founded to address people's physical, material, and spiritual needs. The concept is the same as Steve's and implemented by the same kind of people that Steve had in mind for Aspen. While Matthew found his people, Steve didn't. Why? Matthew was looking in a city of ten million while Steve was searching for his in a town of five thousand.

It wasn't only the ministry-centered people who were unattainable, so was his target group. For Steve, the wealthy residents of Aspen were out of range economically, a mismatch socially and unreachable spiritually. The Biblical encounter between Jesus and the rich young ruler in Matthew 19:16-22 illustrates the latter.

"Now a man came up to Jesus and asked, 'Teacher, what good thing must I do to get eternal life?' 'Why do you ask me about what is good?' Jesus replied. 'There is only One who is good. If you want to enter life, obey the commandments.' 'Which ones?' The man inquired. Jesus replied, 'Do not murder, do not commit adultery, do not steal, do not give false testimony, honor your father and mother,' and 'love your neighbor as yourself.' [It's interesting to note the commandments Jesus omitted which include, "Thou shalt have no other gods before me," and "Thou shalt not covet."] 'All these I have kept,' the young man said. 'What do I still lack?' Jesus answered, 'If you want to be perfect, go, sell your possessions and give to the poor, and you will have treasure in heaven. Then come, follow me.' When the young man heard this, he went away sad, because he had great wealth. Then Jesus said to his disciples, 'I tell you the truth, it is hard for a rich man to enter the kingdom of heaven. Again I tell you, it is easier for a camel to go through the eye of a needle than for a rich man to enter the kingdom of God.'" (Matthew 19:16-24 NIV)

Another way of looking at the young ruler's "great wealth," is that he didn't possess it; it possessed him. Jesus' words about the rich are as much an observation as a judgment. By fostering an illusion of self-sufficiency, wealth obscures people's need for God. The rich young ruler's rejection of Jesus' invitation wasn't a reflection on Jesus; it was a reflection on him. In the same way, the rejection of faith by the rich says something about them, not God. First Baptist (now Crossroads) Church in Aspen has a thriving ministry with a weekly attendance of a few hundred in a town of six thousand residents. The vast majority of their worshippers, however, are the middle-class inhabitants of the town's affordable, cost-protected housing. Tellingly, only a handful come from Aspen's wealthy majority. There's little reason to expect that Steve's target group would have been more responsive to him than to the evangelical presence already in their midst.

While the points above are true, they may also be irrelevant. It's possible that instead of failing, Steve unknowingly succeeded in doing exactly what God wanted him to do. Consider: where God leads, he provides. He provides the needed contacts, opportunities, relationships, financial support—whatever his servant(s) need. If that's true, what might one conclude when contacts are *not* forthcoming, opportunities are *non*-existent, relationships *don't* develop, and financial support is inadequate? How about, "Right area, wrong town"?

Snowmass

Pioneers such as Veryl Henderson, Chuck Clayton, Bill Lee, Joel Land and Roy Owen led the way into the uncharted territory of resort ministries, casting the vision and establishing its guiding principles. They were the first, but certainly not the last. Virtually every new resort ministry needs its pioneer—someone willing to step out into the unknown, hopefully as part of a nearby church, but sometimes with nothing more than a trust in God's leading, as Steve did at Snowmass.

Located only five miles from Aspen Mountain, Snowmass is the largest of Aspen's sister resorts. Steve was itching to get back on skis again and from Snowmass's opening day, spent hours flying down its slopes, getting to know its employees, and scouting out the possibilities for an on-mountain service. After meeting an executive of Aspen Ski Company at Rotary, Steve asked permission to start a ministry at one of Aspen's resorts. He was referred to Doug MacKenzie, General Manager of Snowmass. Aided by the discovery that they were almost neighbors, Steve and Doug hit it off immediately. Steve received the go-ahead for his ministry.

"I didn't even ask him for a ski pass," recalls Steve, "because I didn't want him to think we were in this for ourselves. After two years they provided me one in appreciation for all that we were doing for their guests and employees." One of Steve's ideas—as tasty as it was creative—became so popular that since then it's been copied at resorts across the country. Every Sunday, Steve walked and skied around the resort, delivering bags of cookies to lift attendants, maintenance personnel, and as many ski patrollers as he could find. "I'd start out Sunday morning and on my way to the lockers, drop off three to four bags of cookies at the rental shop. Then I'd change into ski gear and grab my skis. If they weren't really busy in the base area, I'd stop, give the ticket sellers a bag of cookies, and then go up to the lift shack. At the top of the lift, I'd give a bag to the 'catcher' and the guy in the top shack. Snowmass had twenty-two lifts back then, and I'd get to every lift every Sunday. In the beginning, we baked the cookies at home, but we were handing out between eighty-five to ninety bags a Sunday and with three cookies to a bag, it got to be too much, so we started buying them."

And the results?

"It provided me with opportunities to do a lot of counseling and to ski with guys I wouldn't have skied with otherwise."

The ministry on the mountain grew to include a second service, this one led by Dave Hurd, a seminary graduate and RMRMI participant. Along with a successful ministry at the mountain, Steve also started a house church in his home, doing in Old Snowmass what he couldn't do in Aspen. When Steve left the area in 2005 to assume expanded state responsibilities, he could look back upon Snowmass as a job well done. Right area, right town.

Chapter 16 | THE "C" WORD

There was no answer when I called Steve for our scheduled interview in the spring of 2011, so I left a message and called back.

"How are you doing?" We asked each other in unison. I yielded.

"Oh… well, one of the reasons I didn't call you right back—I was on the phone yesterday." He paused briefly. "I've got some problems."

In all the years I had known Steve, this was a first.

"What's up?" I asked.

"I've got prostate cancer," he said.

There was no sense of alarm, no "I could die" tone of seriousness in his voice. Instead, he registered a degree of disappointment and annoyance that you'd expect from somebody who had just had a flat tire. My own reaction wasn't quite so calm.

"Oh, no!" I said, almost yelling into the phone.

"Yep, so I was making some phone calls. It's operable. Looks like everything will turn out all right."

"Oh, that's good," I said, feeling relieved.

"I just found out about it yesterday, and so I had to let some people know. I called my executive director and a friend of mine who has gone through this. So, sorry I wasn't there when you called, but I had to deal with stuff."

"That kind of news would shake you up a bit," I offered. Then, perhaps more for my own reassurance than his, "I understand those who have the surgery end up pretty well off."

"Well yes, for the most part. I told the doctor that there are really no good options, but surgery for me will probably be the best."

"That news must have thrown you for a loop," I said, fishing.

"Yes, it did. We knew it was a possibility for about a month. I did a health fair kind of blood test, and the PSA count came back high enough to cause concern. I was due for a physical anyway—it had been five years—so I went in, and the doctor said he felt something. He sent me to a urologist, and the urologist felt something, so I had to go back for a biopsy. Anyway, got all that done and Janice and I went in yesterday and talked about what we were going to do."

"It appears you've caught it pretty early."

"I think so. I thought, 'well let's just get it out. I don't want to mess with it and worry about it.' So that's where we're at."

"So the prognosis is good?"

"Yep, I think so."

Having dealt with the unsettling news of his cancer, I looked at the questions I had prepared, and heard the sound of metal against metal in the background. "How much time do you have to talk right now?" I asked.

"I'm working on a tractor right now, so however much time you need."

Our conversation ended about an hour later. I felt I had his undivided attention and not having heard any more metallic sounds, expected a "no" to my next question. "You've been fixing a tractor all the time we've been talking?" Again, I was wrong.

"Yes, it's hard for me to sit and talk on the telephone, so whenever I do, I'll walk around the office or sit and sort books. I borrowed a tractor from this guy, and while I was using it, a part broke. He said he'd come over to fix it, but he's just gone through a bout with kidney cancer, so I thought if I could take it apart so all he had to do was put the new part in, it'd be great. It's turning out to be a lot more work than I thought."

That Steve would do such a thing didn't surprise me—he has a reputation for such thoughtfulness. What surprised me was his ability to multi-task—a rare skill among men. Sensing I was impressed and not offended, he continued. "Every time I've talked with you I've been doing something else."

I called the following month after his scheduled date for surgery. Everything had gone well, and he was already back to work, frustrated by an energy level not keeping pace with his self-imposed schedule.

A question monopolized my thoughts as Loon's busy summer season forced a break from writing. Fed by his surprising openness and in spite of his apparent aplomb, I couldn't help but think the "C" word had shaken him. When Loon's summer season ended, I picked up the phone. After pleasantries, I zeroed in. "What did you find yourself thinking or feeling when the urologist gave you the results of the biopsy?"

"Bummer! It was going to interrupt some things I had planned, like a two-month sabbatical. Prostate cancer in the majority of cases is relatively straightforward. If it'd been pancreatic cancer or lung cancer or those kinds that generally kill, I'd probably have been a lot more concerned. Because it was prostate cancer and they do so many of these operations every year I thought, 'well it's going to be an inconvenience but I've got good insurance and a good doctor,' so I wasn't overly concerned."

"Has this experience changed you at all and if so, in what ways?"

"Well… man… well, I can't… has it changed me?" The question clearly caught him off guard, and it took him a moment to get his thoughts together. "I don't know. I don't think so. Because it's my first surgery and stuff, I think I'm a little more compassionate toward people who have had surgery because I know what it takes out of you. But has it made me a nicer person?

Probably not. I'm not rushing around trying to take care of my life because I think it's going to end. We're only two months out after surgery, so at this point, I'm feeling good about where we're at. Sorry, I know it doesn't make for a good story line."

My turn.

"Well," I began, "let me give you something else to chew on. I've known you for about fifteen years now Steve, but when I talked to you after you received your diagnosis, I was pleasantly surprised. You're a private person who keeps things pretty close to your vest. Perhaps because of that, even though I've known and admired you for a long time, I've never felt particularly close to you. With that call, however, I felt I had been granted entrance into an area of your life that was never open before and, to be honest with you, I felt privileged. Does that make any sense?"

"I guess, I don't know that it was an intentional deal," he responded, quietly.

"I don't think it was. Instead, I think it's just who you are as a person. Early on in our interviews, you described yourself as a person who centers your life on a few very close friends as opposed to many superficial friendships. Since I'm not one of those close friends, there would be no reason for you to be open with me in personal matters. This brings me to another question along the same lines. Knowing how private you are left me wondering if some of the personal questions I've asked in these interviews haven't been a bit challenging to answer."

"Yep," he quickly replied.

Encouraged by his candor, and relieved to be talking about these things, I continued. "Steve, I've got to admit something that's got me smiling right now and something you'll probably find amusing. Every so often this past year I found myself thinking that you might at any time call me up and say something to the effect: 'Well Skip, I'm sorry, but I've decided not to do this after all.'" We laughed. I continued, "I know part of that was my own insecurity, but I asked myself why I might expect you to do such a thing. Here's what I came up with: you're not a person who could be categorized as a 'people-pleaser.'"

"No… yeah," he interjected in agreement.

"One of the people I interviewed said that you're not a person with a whole lot of needs, and another that you're a person who marches to your own drummer. You get a vision, and that's where you're going and if people are on board fine, and if not, that's okay, too. In thinking about all this, I realized that there's a certain security in relating to people-pleasers because you know they don't want to disappoint you. But that doesn't exist for you, so it was a bit unnerving to know that if you decided you didn't want to do this, well, that would be the end of it. In thinking along these lines, I also found myself wondering why—given your private nature—you agreed to these interviews in the first place."

"Well, I don't know that I've ever thought of it," Steve began, "but here's a thought: I feel that I have something to offer those who are starting out in resort ministries. As you know, not many know what we do. Writing about people like us is a great way to encourage others. 'If we can do this, I can say to another person; you can do this—it might not be like anything you've done before, but you can do this.'"

Preparing to wrap up our interviews, I switched gears. "Steve," I began, "Not to be morbid, but I'm wondering how you'd like to be remembered or, put another way, what would you like to see written on your tombstone?"

"Yeah, I've played that game with people before." Then, as if he was standing before a group of people: 'That should be the guiding light of our lives and the vision for our lives, and if that's what we want to be written, how do we operate now to make that happen?'"

Apparently, I just stumbled upon a question used on the motivational circuit. "Well, since you've had some practice responding to this one, you should be all set."

"No, not really," he answered. "I've never done this myself, just made other people do it."

"Gotcha," I said with a laugh.

He went on to respond to my questions.

"I'd like to be remembered as a man of God and someone who enjoyed life—a good husband, father, and son."

It was his following words, however, that took the conversation down an initially confusing, then enlightening road.

"I guess I'd like to be remembered as a 'man of integrity' and 'all of who I am, is just who I am.'"

"What was that again?" I asked. "The first part I got, but not the second."

"All of who I am, is just who I am. The reason I say it that way is that the word 'integrity' comes from the word 'integer' that means one, yet our lives are comprised of many different things and all those things combine to make us who we are. I just want people to say 'that's who he was' and you said that a little while ago. That's just who Steve is: he's not trying to be mean, he's not trying to be ugly, that's just who Steve is, and if you want to know the truth, you'll go to Steve. I'm not going to beat around the bush and lead you to 'pie in the sky by and by.' 'What you see is what you get' is another way to put it."

While Steve's original cancer prognosis *was* good, that soon changed. The prostate cancer itself, a mildly aggressive form, disappeared with the gland's removal, but not before releasing another type of cancer far more dangerous. This new and aggressive cancer continued its slow and lethal growth, surfacing with a fury several months later. Attacking it with ten weeks of daily radiation treatments and months of medications, as of this writing, Steve has been cancer-free for over two years.

By this time, I felt I knew Steve pretty well, but an interview with his boss of many years revealed the limits of my knowledge.

Chapter 17 | STATE STAFF

Steve's success at planting churches and establishing ministries in resort communities was rewarded with additional responsibilities. In 2005, he moved from Aspen to Montrose to open an office in support of the Western Colorado churches of the Colorado State Baptist Convention. In addition, he later became the director of church planting in Western Colorado. As if this wasn't enough, while still the resort consultant for the state, he also ran the program supplying the Southern Baptist churches of Colorado with college summer missionaries.

I was curious. "In all of your work, what brings you the most joy?"

"Leadership Development," came the quick reply. "I like seeing people go 'Ohhhhhhhhhhhh.'"

"The light bulb effect?"

"Yep. I like it when the light bulb goes on and when people say, 'This will help my church,' or 'I never thought about it that way before.' I really enjoy helping pastors and small churches."

Steve loves providing guidance and encouragement. In Biblical language, he enjoys "making disciples," and he's quite good at it. Steve became a member of the state staff in 1981 when he went to Vail and started serving as Colorado's consultant for resort ministries. After leaving Old Snowmass, his focus shifted from laity *and* clergy to almost exclusively clergy, providing them with the same support on a continuing basis that he received from the visits of resort ministry pioneer Chuck Clayton.

Steve's proficiency in mentoring pastors has garnered him the respect and admiration of many. "Steve Hoekstra is a unique and wonderfully gifted minister," says Rev. Mark Edlund, leader of Colorado's Southern Baptists. "In Steve, God has combined a true mountain man and alpine sportsman with a man passionate about his faith, creating a unique missionary to a largely unengaged population. He is responsible for starting churches in Colorado's resort communities, weekly worship services at a majority of Colorado's major ski areas and scores of ministries at campgrounds throughout the Rockies. We view him as the nation's foremost expert in resort ministries. Steve is a special gift to both Colorado Baptists and to me personally."

Steve the Pioneer

No one has helped start more ski resort ministries in the United States than Steve. To find out how he did it, I turned to three people: a resort ministry pioneer, a colleague, and the man he's reported to since 2001.

Chuck Clayton is a first generation resort minister who, before becoming the Southern Baptist's national consultant for resort ministries, started the ministry at Squaw Valley in the '60's and founded Christian High Adventure, a backpacking ministry once active in several states. He suggested four reasons for Steve's effectiveness: his masculine persona, genuineness, mentoring, and consistency with the original vision of resort work.

"Steve is a man's man," said Chuck, "and those around him pick up on his purposefulness and self-confidence. His concern for others is real and genuine, and people sense that. He's been a great mentor to the younger guys who come along and has maintained the vision for resort ministries cast by those of us who pioneered them in the early years."

Pete Owens, a contemporary of Steve's, established the first ski resort ministry at Sun Valley, Idaho, and then went on to serve at Dollywood with Bill Black's Smoky Mountain Resort Ministries.

"What," I asked Pete, "does Steve bring to the table that has made him so effective?"

"Leadership is the first thing that comes to my mind. Steve never went to seminary, but his natural leadership skills, along with his great love for the Lord, driven personality, and sensitivity to God's leading have produced some remarkable results. In addition, after the Southern Baptist's recent exodus from resort ministries, Steve has been extremely influential in keeping them going."

"What comes to your mind when you think of Steve?"

"Just a love for my brother. I went through a very difficult time in my life, and Steve reached out to me. He gave me a simple compliment that ended up validating me at a time that I really needed it. I remarried a gal from Southern Georgia who had difficulty adjusting to the mountain culture of Colorado and then developed health issues that eventually took her life. Steve reached out to us during the whole time. I have nothing but love and gratitude for the man. Of all the people who have impacted my life both professionally and personally, he's among the top three."

Leading Colorado's Southern Baptists since 2001, Mark Edlund has been Steve's boss for well over a decade. Actually, the word "boss" doesn't fit, both because it's hard to imagine Steve being "bossed" by anyone, and because Mark's leadership style is so egalitarian. Mark and Steve first met back in '89 when Mark and his wife were missionaries to Japan. After their first five years, they returned home for a year's furlough, spending a portion of that time visiting churches to talk about their missionary work. As Mark recalls, "Steve found out about us and asked us to come to Vail and share our ministry at their 11 a.m. service. The first time I met him, I found him intriguing. He had a beard and long hair and wore western clothing. After introducing ourselves to each other, my wife and I did our presentation during the worship service, said our thank-you's, and left."

Twelve years later Mark returned to his home state of Colorado—no longer a missionary, but now as a candidate for the state's Executive Director's position.

"Before the Convention voted, they had me do 'listening sessions' around the state. I had a session in Grand Junction and in walks Steve. He was wearing a beautiful long western coat. I recognized him immediately, and we talked briefly. He didn't remember me, but I remembered him and now that he was on the state staff it marked the beginning of our friendship." As Mark was about to discover, there was a lot more behind that beard and western coat than he first realized.

"The first thing I did after becoming the Executive Director was to get to know people. I toured the eleven associations in Colorado, met their leaders, visited their churches and got to know the dreams and goals of their pastors. I asked Steve to show me the five associations he worked with in Western Colorado. We met in Glenwood Springs and piled into his old white truck—at the time it had 'only' 280,000 miles on it—and I spent the next two days with him. Those were two very amazing days. He took me all over the western portion of the state. He knew every inch, nook and cranny, and the pastors he introduced me to were uniformly delighted to see him. As we drove along he'd say 'here's this community, there's no evangelical church here, and we need to get something started,' and he'd tell me the history and folklore surrounding the places we drove by. He showed me the storage unit for Recreational Alpine Adventures, formerly known as the 'RAAT Patrol.' There hung all the sleeping bags, cookware, and backpacks—everything ten to twelve kids would need for six or seven days of outdoor adventures.

"'You're not doing this anymore?' I asked.

"'Well, I just got too old for it. I was fifty-five at the time trying to keep up with teenagers, and it wasn't working for me,' Steve replied.

"'How long did you do it?'

"'About twenty-five years.'

"He told me about the RMRMI that he started and about new resort ministries starting in Colorado and throughout the United States. He told me about the Association of Resort and Leisure Ministers and about his ministry to lift attendants and worship services on the slopes and church services at RV parks. I'd never encountered any of that before and was just amazed. Then he started talking about the churches he had grown and those he had planted: Newcastle, Beaver Creek, Vail, Red Cliff and others. Their number bowled me over.

"He took me to his home, which is a pretty nice house. With all his carpentry and building skills, he took a run-down place and turned it into a beautiful home. After we got back into his truck, he said, 'let me show you the ministry at Snowmass.' We took a back road up to the resort. Grabbing some bags of cookies, he hopped out of the truck and introduced me to Snowmass's Director of Operations, who greeted Steve by name. Then we headed up the slope, and Steve said, 'we're going to have some fun.' He stopped and greeted each lift attendant, calling them by name and giving them a bag of cookies. We then went to the top, where the scene repeated itself, and they greeted *him* by name. This was in the summertime, no less, the off-season. I was in awe.

"At the end of those two days, I found myself asking, 'who *is* this guy?' I was introduced to Steve as the director of Resort Ministries, and that was my tunnel vision of him, but after that trip, I realized he was just an incredible minister and evangelist."

I interviewed Mark knowing that as Steve's "boss," he'd be able to offer a perspective unavailable from anyone else. After spending almost two years interviewing Steve's friends and writing about him, I felt I knew him well. At a conference we were attending, Steve remarked that I probably knew him better than anyone else did. At the time, I may have agreed, but not after talking to Mark. For example, I knew Steve oversaw the Southern Baptist churches in Western Colorado. I didn't know how that occurred. I knew Steve was a carpenter and a mechanic; I didn't know about his other skills. Nor did I know about his involvement with the homeless. Mark started pulling back the curtains, beginning with how Steve came to oversee the churches of Western Colorado—a story that says as much about Mark as it does about Steve.

"Most of our people and services are along the I-25 corridor and after I came on board I sensed that the five associations in the West regarded themselves as the 'ugly stepchild' of the Convention. I was attending an RMRMI conference with Steve in 2005, and we were trying to figure out how we could address the problem. As we talked, there emerged the idea of opening an auxiliary state office in the west. That really resonated with me and over the next couple of days I talked with some of the pastors. Their response was, 'Oh, you'd really *do* that?' So before we left, I said to Steve, 'Well, Steve, I think we'll go ahead, and I'd like you to establish the office and be its director.' In typical Steve fashion, he took it on with a passion. He did a lot of research and decided that Montrose would be the best place, located an affordable office with a reception area and a nice conference room. Janice went to work decorating and turned it into a very welcoming place. We had an opening ceremony, and it's now thought of as the state office on the western side, which was what we were hoping for. A couple of years later we realized that it was impossible for the state D-O-M to supervise an area as large as Colorado, so we decided to divide the job and have two state D-O-M's. The current one kept the six associations in the east, and Steve took the five in the west. At that point, he began reporting directly to me. So of course," Mark continued, smiling, "I proceeded to totally abuse him after he got that assignment.

"Looking back, Steve has done just a great job as director for the West. After the D-O-M positions were eliminated, Steve formed what's called the Western State Coalition. Consisting of moderators elected by each of the five associations, Steve gathers them together on a regular basis to share needs and concerns and plan strategies."

Mark then turned his attention to Steve's skills and hobbies.

"When Steve opened the office in Montrose, he relocated to Cimarron, a small, unincorporated community just east of Montrose. He had been there about a year when I was driving in the area and decided to drop in at his home. He's a humble guy and doesn't brag about himself, so I wasn't prepared for what I was about to see. I said, 'Hey, this looks like a neat place, show me around.'

"He has a large barn and a pretty home with a beautiful view. Half of the barn was for machinery storage, and the other half was his shop. It contained his leather tools, gold-panning tools and several leather projects in the making.

"'What goes on in here, Steve?'

"'Well, I'm a black powder hunter.[15] Most seasons I bring back an elk or at least a deer, and I skin it and tan the hide and make all my leather products out of the hides.' Then he took me into his wood shop.

"'What do you have here?'

"'Well, I enjoy woodworking and making furniture.'

"He showed me some furniture and cabinets he had made, and they were incredibly beautiful. Then we went outside.

"'Let me introduce you to my family,' he said, referring to his animals.

"He always has two cows. He buys them, raises them, and slaughters them in the fall. He called one 'T-bone' and the other 'Tenderloin,' but has since changed their names to 'Hot Dog' and 'Hamburger.' He also had an old and slightly lame mule he used as a pack animal for hunting. He called her 'Edith', and there's an interesting story about her. Sometime after that first visit, I called and asked how he was doing.

"'Awe, I had to put Edith down.'

"'Oh, Steve, how do you do that?' Then, being who I am, 'Does the vet come out and put him down?'

"'No, it's much easier than that. Usually, I use my Colt 45.'

"'Well how do you dispose of the body?'

"'My neighbor has a backhoe,' he said matter-of-factly, 'and I borrowed it to dig a hole, push the mule into it and cover it up.'

"Continuing with the tour of his shop he showed me his mountain man outfit and the costume he wears for Rendezvous gatherings. ' Yeah, I tanned this and made it,' and of course it was a gorgeous outfit with fringe and so forth. He had finished two of them. Then he introduced me to his rabbit-killing cat and showed me the chicken coop that provided them with six eggs a day. He brought me into the house and showed off his wife's pottery and paintings. By the time we were through I had come to understand that yes, he's a minister, but he's also very much a Renaissance man.

"I'll never forget the first time I saw him dressed up in his mountain man outfit as Jedediah Smith. Every year I do an annual report at our state convention. Not wanting to end up as just a talking head, I try hard to be creative. Several years ago, we were meeting at Estes Park, and I gathered my team leaders together and asked, 'Do you guys have any ideas on how I can spice up my report a bit?'"

"'Well,' said Steve, 'how about if Jedediah Smith comes in and does an interview? We could come up with a list of questions he could ask you.'

"'Let's do it,' I responded. I had never seen his routine before, so I didn't know exactly what to expect, but it sounded like fun.

"Standing before the crowd of a few hundred, I started my annual report normally. ' I've got some points I'd like to cover,' I said. Then suddenly, the back door to the conference hall slams open and there's this blood-curdling yell. Everybody jumps up and turns around. Here comes Steve in his costume, striding down the aisle, yelling greetings at people, a black powder rifle slung over his shoulder. Coming right up on stage and still in character, with an accent so thick I could hardly understand it, he starts asking me questions. Both of us are tickled, and the whole audience is laughing so loud they could hardly hear us. Honestly, by the time we ended I was laughing so hard I was near tears."

"Some Would Even Freeze to Death"

By this time, I was well aware of Steve's accomplishments in resort ministries and planting churches, but knew nothing of how he helped the homeless. Mark went on to share a story about Steve that was new to me, even after two years of interviews—a story of preventing death on the frozen streets of a Colorado ski town.

"Awhile back there were a large number of homeless people in the resort town of Glenwood. When winter temperatures plunged below freezing, some would even freeze to death. Steve stepped forward, talked with the town and enlisted the aid of a woman pastor—a single older lady whom he had led to the Lord. Initially, the town provided funding to reserve some hotel rooms for the night. Then, with the town's help, a homeless shelter and feeding station called 'Feed My Sheep' was established complete with bunk beds.[16] The homeless now had a warm place to sleep along with supper and breakfast. Steve isn't involved with it anymore, and it's since become self-sustaining. The city recently picked it up and hired a director, a fine young man. But again that's just Steve: 'How do we address the problem and how do we get it done?'"

Says Mark in conclusion, "I've learned a lot from Steve over the years. As I've slowly got to know him, I've come to appreciate him, love him, and am proud to call him my friend."

Growing churches, planting churches and resort ministries, starting a backpacking ministry, mentoring colleagues, introducing people to Christ, joining others in skiing, hunting, hiking and fishing, administering the Southern Baptist churches of Western Colorado and saving the lives of the homeless—not too bad a record for someone starting out as a twenty-four-year-old farmhand.

Photographs

1980 Hoekstra Family Picture with daughter Holly and son Jake while he was in New Castle, CO, a year before moving to Vail.

Glenda and Marc Wentworth in 1989. They moved to Vail and met Steve in 1983. Glenda had her life-threatening stroke in January of 1993 while Steve was in Estes Park.

Benny McCracken and Steve became close friends after discovering their mutual love of hiking and the outdoors.

Steve in 1997 at the time of our first interview.

Steve and the members of one of his RAAT Patrols during their week-long hike into the wilderness. Steve led these trips for close to 25 years.

Dub and Granddaughter—Dub Chambers was Steve's first pastor after Steve made Christ lord of his life. He and his people had a life-changing impact on Steve's future.

Joe Chambers with his father Dub on one of their many wilderness treks.

Farmer Steve working the farm.

One of many monthly barbecues hosted by Steve and Janice (far right) for the discipleship groups he started at Vail. In the middle is Glenda Wentworth, with her hand resting on the knee of husband Marc. Kevin Erickson is in the third row, third one in from left holding little son who's sitting on the back of the couch.

Steve with Kevin Erickson following an Easter Sunrise service on top of Vail. Kevin was one of the many whose friendship with Steve had a powerful impact on his life.

Steve as mountain man Jedediah Smith in Salt Lake City, Utah during the 2002 Winter Olympics at nearby Park City.

Steve ministering at Snowmass and holding one of the numerous bags of cookies he distributed to workers.

Steve and Janice in 2015. Janice knew on their first date that they'd be getting married.

Brad Lartigue

Chapter 1 | "The Most Beautiful Fish"

Brad Lartigue's visit to the Western Caribbean island of Montserrat was to change his life, but not before it almost ended it.

Known as the "Emerald Isle" for its lush green vegetation and early Irish settlers, the island's popularity peaked soon after its most famous resident, Beatle's producer George Martin, established his recording studio in 1979. When that happened, the formerly quiet island turned into a destination resort for the rich and famous. Elton John, Princess Margaret, Eric Clapton and Sting were among the many walking the tarmac of the island's small airport. In 1982, Paul McCartney and Stevie Wonder flew in to record the smash hit "Ebony and Ivory." It was a decade of glory for the island that had a tragic ending. The first blow came in 1989. Hurricane Hugo ravished the island, causing a quarter-of-a-billion dollars in damage and leaving 11,000 of the 12,000 residents homeless. Then, six years later and just as the island was getting back on its feet, the knockout punch. On July 18, 1995, Soufriere Hills—a once dormant volcano—sprang to life. By the time its tentacles of molten rock stopped flowing and the clouds of gray ash finally dissipated, the entire southern half of the island was covered with a thick blanket of black rock. Homes were (again) destroyed, and the island's capital city of Plymouth turned into a ghost town. A temporary evacuation of the affected area turned permanent. Two-thirds of the islands' population moved away. Post-1995 maps now show a line drawn across the island's midriff, designating the southern half of the island an "exclusion zone" and banning any construction. Volcanic activity continues to this day.

Montserrat's decade of glory and subsequent demise had not yet started when Brad and his six companions arrived in the summer of 1980. Having completed his first year of college, Brad was one of six students selected for an Operation Crossroads Africa medical project. Often cited as a forerunner of the Peace Corps, Operation Crossroad's goals were much the same as its more famous cousin. The purpose of this trip was medical: the six students and their leader would compile and transport emergency medical kits from the island's only hospital to outlying villages. The kits, in the event of a hurricane, would provide the needed emergency supplies until patients could reach the island's distant hospital. After delivering the kits, team members would spend the rest of the summer assisting local doctors visiting the island's scattered population.

Brad's interest in medicine began as a college freshman. Following his father's instructions to become a doctor or a lawyer or as Brad puts it, "some other high profession," he chose medicine, joining the Medical Explorer post (Boy Scouts of America) and volunteering at the local hospital. "I had to wear a blue one-piece uniform with the Medical Explorer patch on it. It was several hours a week of nurse's aide work. I was on the pediatric ward most of the time. I spent one month on the adult ward—pretty much death and dying, and decided to stick with pediatrics."

Traveling alone for the first time in his life, Brad recalls his feelings upon arriving in New York for their three-day orientation: "It was the only time during the trip I felt fearful and nervous. I was in a strange environment, and as we were packing the medical supplies, I thought to myself, 'Oh my gosh, what have I got myself into?'" Missing his family, Brad called home.

"I wanted them to know I was okay, but I also needed to hear their voices. I wasn't going to let on that I was homesick. I told them that I had made it to New York fine, met the rest of the group, and things were going well. It wasn't until I hung up that I got all emotional and the homesickness hit." Fortunately, it didn't last long. The orientation turned into a bonding experience for the small group. By the time they landed on the island, loneliness had given way to closeness; and nervousness, to excitement. Accompanied by their college professor/chaperone, they stepped off the plane not as isolated individuals, but as a tightly knit team. They arrived ready for the adventure of their lives, and they wouldn't be disappointed.

As is common in ethnic melting pots, the different nationalities on the island had their own gathering places. For the Americans, it was a local watering hole. One evening, shortly after their arrival, the team was sitting around a table getting to know a group of young American men. "We're going spear-fishing tomorrow," said one of them, "any of you like to join us?"

Three, including Brad, jumped at the opportunity. "I'll never get this chance again," he thought to himself.

The next morning, carrying masks, fins, and snorkels, Brad and Maureen, another member of the group, walked down to a beach of the black sand common to volcanic islands. The third member of their team had arrived earlier and was already with their hosts about fifty yards from shore.

At the beach, Brad turned to Maureen. Confession time. "I can't swim."

"What?!"

"I can't swim. I really want to do this, but I can't swim."

Recovering quickly, Maureen spoke reassuringly. "Well, you'll be fine. I'll swim right beside you. The water is heavy with salt, and you'll be very buoyant in this stuff. Anybody can swim in this kind of water." It was just what Brad needed to hear. "I had a lot of confidence in her."

Stripping off his t-shirt, Brad donned a mask, snorkel, and fins. The clear water gave him a perfect view of the steep drop-off typical of volcanic islands where five feet out is five feet down. Breathing easily through the snorkel, a beautiful undersea world spread before his eyes. "This is amazing," he thought to himself. Schools of fish swam below him, the colorful ones adding a never-before-seen beauty to the scene. On the right, he could see Maureen's arms rhythmically entering the water. For someone lacking formal swimming lessons and rarely in the water, the ease with which Brad was swimming and the views unfolding before his eyes made for a thrilling experience. "I could do this forever," he thought.

The others were waiting in a circle, treading water and talking. Brad tells what happened next. "We got close to the group and Maureen stopped, so I stopped. Going from a horizontal to a vertical position with nothing to stand on, I began going under. Then I started swallowing water."

Brad couldn't breathe, and began choking. Their backs toward him, the others were oblivious to the life-threatening scene occurring just a few feet away. Brad was drowning, and no one knew it

"What they portray on TV and in the movies, with people shouting and screaming when they're drowning is wrong. You can't shout or scream because you're tensed up; all your muscles are working just to keep you afloat."

Brad went under, and then kicked his way back to the surface, gasping for breath and struggling to keep his head above the water. Glancing in his direction and grasping the scene, an alarmed Maureen darted over. "She was talking to me, trying to get me to relax and to calm down, but I didn't know *how* to calm down."

Brad panicked. His eyes wide as saucers, survival instincts took over. He grabbed at the only thing separating him from a watery grave. "She pushed me away and screamed for help.

"I went under again. I clearly remember being very calm. I started looking around and saw the most beautifully colored fish I'd ever seen in my life. They were all around me. I've never seen anything like it before or since. I don't know how long I was under, but long enough to go pretty deep. The beautiful fish—they were all around me."

Suddenly interrupting Brad's dazzling vision, first one, and then another hand grasped his wrists in jaw-like vices, jerking him upward. Emerging into daylight, coughing up seawater and gasping for breath, Brad felt his arms draped around the shoulders of two of his new friends. After everyone had caught their breath and with the danger over, Maureen shared Brad's confession.

"You can't swim?" exclaimed one of the young men incredulously.

"He did do pretty well in getting out here," Maureen offered in his—and perhaps her own—defense.

His composure returning (for the most part), an embarrassed Brad announced he was returning to the island.

"We'll swim back with you," offered one of his rescuers.

"No, I don't want to ruin your day," Brad replied. "I made it out here okay, and I can make it back. Just keep an eye on me. When I get back to the beach, I'll wave. "I had calmed down enough to put the snorkel on," Brad continued. "They helped me get back into a horizontal position, and I just paddled my heart out until I got back to the beach."

A few minutes later, to several sighs of relief, a waving arm appeared in the distance.

Some people would follow such an experience with the words, "and that's why I don't go near the water anymore." Brad's response, however, was just the opposite. "When I got back to the beach, I had a strong determination to fight this thing. I took off my gear, kept the snorkel on, and went back in to where I could stand up. I was going to teach myself how to float and kept going back to that same spot until I did."

Brad's brush with death taught him two valuable lessons put to good use in his future: first, don't expect drowning people to yell, and second, "when you're in a dangerous situation, the best thing you can do is to relax. If you give way to your fears, you're done."

Years later, in dealing with new and especially threatening situations, the latter lesson still comes back to him. "I try not to get stressed out about things. I had to relax to learn how to swim and now, in marathons and other competitions, there comes a time when I just relax. It's hard to explain how to relax in such intense settings, but you can." It was a lesson that would prove its value on a mission trip the very next summer.

A few weeks later, Brad and his group were taking a break on the nearby island of Antigua when Hurricane Allen struck. On the edge of the storm, Antigua experienced winds of fifty miles an hour—high enough to do some damage, but far less than the 190 mph blasts striking its Caribbean neighbors. While the hurricane was memorable, the permanent mark left on Brad's life that summer had little to do with the weather.

"Experiencing a different culture and a different type of people—seeing the different ways they lived—changed my view of the world. Once on the island, our group went to various churches because our leader wanted us to experience the way other people worshiped. It was uplifting to see people with the same faith so far away from home. I matured a lot. My faith grew, and I left feeling a part of a much bigger Christian family than I had known before. That summer changed my world and it changed my life."

Chapter 2 | GROWING UP A MAN OF COLOR

Brad entered the world on February 10, 1961, in Lafayette, Louisiana, the first of five children born to Rev. Audrey Bradford ("A.B.") Lartigue, Sr., and Anna Marie Lartigue. Both his parents are African-Americans, but Brad and his siblings share four other ethnic heritages: Native American Cherokee and French on their father's side, and Italian and German on their mother's.

St. Matilda's Catholic School in Eunice, Louisiana, provided Brad's first-grade education in 1966. The next year his family moved to Lake Charles, Louisiana, a lower-middle class community of seventy thousand, its ethnic landscape evenly split between blacks and whites and almost as evenly between Catholics and Baptists.

"When we moved to St. Charles, I had to repeat the first grade."

"Why?" I asked, finding it hard to imagine anyone flunking the first grade.

"Well, you have to remember this was back in the sixties. St. Matilda's was upset that I left the Catholic system for the public schools and refused to send my transcript."

"Okay," I replied. "If you repeated the first grade, that means you were a year older than your classmates all through school?" I had heard of kids deliberately kept back by parents who thought it would give them an advantage, so was expecting a similar story from Brad.

"No," Brad replied, "that made me the same age as my classmates."

"What?"

"I started first grade at St. Matilda's when I was five. My dad told them I was smart enough to enter school at age five and pushed it, I mean *really* pushed it. They were against it but decided to give me an interview just to put it behind them. I remember my dad taking me to the school and all these nuns in the room. They asked me all sorts of questions. I must have done okay because they changed their mind and let me enter." Repeating the first grade apparently didn't hurt Brad. In 1979, he graduated with honors from LaGrange Senior High School.

Brad grew up in a close family. When asked to rate their closeness on a scale of one to ten, he responded: "somewhere between an eight and nine." Having grown up in such a warm home, but with no wife and children of his own, Brad created the next best thing: a large surrogate family of brothers and sisters (many call them his "children") and even entire families, all sharing a common faith. Interestingly, the word "family" enters Brad's conversations frequently. He describes his collegiate Baptist Student Union group as a *"family* of young people." On Montserrat, he realized he was part of the "Christian *family."* His initial experiences at Taos ski area were great because "it was *like a family,"* and once the owner of Taos Ski Valley embraced what Brad was doing, "It felt like I was part of his *family."* Finally, in recalling Pres. Jimmy Carter's Sunday sermon at Taos: "I'll never forget what he said. He talked about how the *family* was important."

Dominating Brad's surrogate family are two groups: an extensive network of "kids"—the scores of college students he has worked with over the years—and individual families. I was attending a conference with him a few years ago when one of those families showed up. We were in Lake Tahoe, California, mingling in the hotel conference room between sessions when Brad spotted the family of four coming through the door at the far end of the room. A joyful reunion unfolded. A boy and girl of grade school age rushed forward as Brad bent down to return their hugs. The boy, his proud father bragging about his recent athletic accomplishments, stuck to Brad like glue. Brad later explained that years before, the parents married after meeting in one of his summer programs at Yellowstone.

Brad's present popularity makes a problem in his younger years hard to imagine. He was shy. "My shyness held me back. I remember a friend who was in the high school choir, John Clifton. We had a foursome group of class nerds who did chemistry, math, and choir together. John encouraged me to get out and be more sociable, so in my senior year, I tried to go to more parties. It was nice to have friends like him to pull me out of my shell."

"Did you feel comfortable in the party setting or was it a bit of a stretch?" I asked.

"It *was* a bit of a stretch, but because my friends were there, I was okay with it. When it involved dancing, I got out there and enjoyed myself. When I went to Montana, I was doing weddings and attending the receptions. I didn't want to be the one sitting on the sidelines, so I took country western dance lessons. Now I'm told, 'You're a great dancer!' I go from one dance partner to another, and it helps burn off the calories from the reception food. Partying was hard for me, but it was easy for my siblings who would often sneak out to attend them. I was the good son who always went to bed when he should."

"While we all grew up as preacher's kids, all of us ended up doing something different. Still, we held fast to our faith—a common bond between us. There were differences as we grew up. My brothers were very much into sports: football, basketball, track and running. I didn't do sports. My dad had high academic expectations for me and my oldest sister, who's now a registered nurse. Dad came from the 60's and the Martin Luther King era when education was important, and he passed it on to us. As the oldest, I was expected to set the example, so I couldn't watch TV and stuff like that until all my homework was done."

Another reason Brad abstained from sports was his physique. He was the proverbial "ninety-eight-pound weakling." Not until the end of his senior year of high school did that began to change. "After we got older, my brothers and I did a one-eighty: I got into sports, and they got into indoor jobs. My middle brother is a college recruiter for Upward Bound—a program for underprivileged kids trying to get into college. My younger brother started out in "techie stuff" but has now moved into the oil pipe fitting business. My youngest sister is working for a marketing firm. We have all taken different vocational paths, but the common denominator has always been our faith. We all had our rebellious moments, though not many for me. To this day, we enjoy each other's company and try to stay in touch. I call my parents weekly and my siblings monthly."

Brad's description of his family included warm words of praise for his older sister and middle brother. "Our last big family experience was my parent's fiftieth wedding anniversary. My oldest sister put it all together. She's rather a headstrong person," Brad said, laughing. "She and my dad have the same type of personalities. Because of their stubbornness, they butt heads, but when it comes to family events and putting things together, she's the one to do it. One year, she visited me in Montana during a Christmas week and was determined to have the whole family experience Big Sky in the winter. They've visited me in the summer, but not yet in the winter. When my older sister put together my parent's fiftieth-anniversary celebration, she helped me fly down to surprise them. They walked down the aisle to renew their vows and there I was waiting for them. It was neat seeing their reaction when they saw me. My sister and I stay in touch. And my middle brother? He's the 'glue' that holds the family together—not only the immediate family but the aunts and uncles and extended family." Even in close families, however, there can be hurts and disappointments. "I still have two siblings, the last two, who have never visited me in any of the places I've ministered, even though I've visited them in their homes. It hurts a bit that they haven't been to Montana since I came here in 1990."

Brad describes the differences in his siblings. "We reflect the typical oldest/middle/youngest child syndromes," he states. "I was the one who was more adventurous and did things and made the grades."

Brad embodies many of the characteristics of a firstborn. A February 11, 2009, CBS news report on firstborns pointed out the following: "Newscasters and TV talk show hosts tend to be firstborn or only children. Prominent examples include Walter Cronkite, Peter Jennings, Dan Rather, Ted Koppel, Oprah, Donahue, Geraldo, Arsenio Hall and Rush Limbaugh. Over half of U.S. presidents were firstborns. Clearly, firstborns are natural leaders. They also tend to be reliable, conscientious and perfectionists who don't like surprises. Although firstborns are typically aggressive, many are also compliant people-pleasers. They are model children who have a strong need for approval from anyone in charge."

Another report by the Public Broadcasting System echoed those findings: "Almost all of the U.S. Presidents were either the first-born child or the firstborn son in their families. All but two of the first astronauts sent into space were firstborns, and the other two were 'only children.'" Both the CBS and PBS stories listed characteristics embodied by Brad: he is a natural leader; albeit more of the manager than the loud up-front, "follow me!" type. He is reliable, organized and conscientious, desires the approval of authority figures and needs to please others—common traits of an oldest child.

Brad's response to his father reveals his need for approval from authority figures. A graduate of Grambling College, A.B. Lartigue, Sr. went into teaching and became the principal of Audrey Memorial High School in the Cameron Parish (or "county") south of Lake Charles. "They named the high school for a hurricane in the 50's," says Brad. It's an interesting coincidence that Audrey Bradford Lartigue, Sr. ended up the principal of Audrey Memorial high school." So important was education to Brad's father that he commuted to prestigious Tuskegee Institute (now University) in Tuskegee, Alabama, 530 miles away, to get his Master's in English and Drama. He then earned his doctorate in education, working as a full-time college professor while serving as a part-time pastor.

As important as education was to Brad's father, both parents regard their faith as more important. Having grown up in Christian homes, they passed on this all-encompassing part of their lives to their children. Sunday mornings were hectic times in the Lartigue household. Brad's mother would scurry around to make sure all five of her children were appropriately dressed, their preacher father having left early to prepare for the morning's service. Finally, with everyone ready, their mother shuttled them into the family car for the short trip to the church. Once there, they spent the rest of the morning at church and were always the last to leave, long after the beginning of hunger pangs for lunch.

Brad's mother was also a major influence in his life. While his father contributed to Brad's academic success and can take credit for his decision to go into the ministry, once in the ministry, his mother's influence rose to the surface. "How has she influenced you?" I inquired.

"Her personality—how she approaches people and how she treats people—just a softer, kinder, gentler kind of personality. People compliment me on my hospitality, and that came from her."

Besides hospitality, Brad's mother left her mark on his life in three other ways: singing, a sense of adventure and physical fitness. "My parents both sang, but my mom was the star, even being on TV back in her younger years."

Brad's gift of singing was evident in high school. After joining the choir, he was selected for a special ensemble and then for solos. He credits those solos with erasing his shyness. Currently, he performs in venues from church services and weddings to singing the national anthem at professional sports events. "People say I should make a recording, but I don't want to get caught up in that."

A sense of adventure? Mom had it; Dad didn't.

"Years ago I remember being at an amusement park in California with my uncle. I noticed my dad's reaction to getting on the roller coaster. He was terrified. My mom had already gone on the ride with my aunt and said 'you've got to do this with us—it was fun!' But dad wouldn't."

Besides music, Brad's mother had another love she passed on to her children. "I grew up waking up to my mom doing exercises with Jack LaLanne [TV's first exercise star]. She understood the importance of eating healthy and keeping her weight in check. Recently when a blood test showed signs of diabetes she said, 'That's not who I am.' She changed her diet and at the next exam, there was no sign of it. Those things are still important to her, and they're important to me. I identify with her a lot."

Given his upbringing and his dad's emphasis on education, one might have expected Brad to immerse himself in his college studies and continue on to graduate school. That didn't happen. Instead, his college years would point him in a completely unexpected direction.

Chapter 3 | BSU

Driving to McNeese University from his home on his first day of classes, Brad was on edge.

"McNeese was challenging because I had gone from being with the same people for three years in high school to a new setting with a whole new group of people. It demanded self-reliance and independence." Those traits describe Brad today, but not then. Insecure in his new environment, freshman Brad avoided joining campus organizations and stayed away from extra-curricular activities, music included. "I was nervous. The academic side was the easy part because it was structured syllabus-style. There was no syllabus, however, on how to do life."

Overcoming the insecurity of his first year at McNeese, Brad returned from his summer adventure on Montserrat with two loves: new experiences and volunteering. "Volunteering in the hospital at home and providing those medical kits to the villages on Montserrat—giving back to the community—felt good, and I grew a lot in that area." And Brad grew a lot in another area: from fearing new experiences and meeting new people, he now desired both.

A different Brad started his second year of studies. Now ready for social activities, he was considering a fraternity or professional group when a friend approached him with an invitation that was to have life-long consequences. "Hey Brad, have you ever thought about joining the BSU [Baptist Student Union]? I think you'd really enjoy it. We have a chapel service followed by lunch on Wednesday mornings, why not come?"

Founded in 1925 by the Southern Baptists, BSU (renamed Baptist Collegiate Ministries or BCM in the early 2000's) had chapters on 839 college campuses by 2011. Their purpose is threefold: to lead the college community to faith in Christ, to develop them as disciples and to integrate them into the mission of the church. To this end, they sponsor recreational and social activities as well as Bible studies, retreats and mission trips. While most BSU groups meet on campus, others, like McNeese, own their own buildings.

Located directly across from the campus, the BSU building at McNeese was a short walk for students. Greeting Brad warmly on his first visit was biology student—now dentist—Lee Crawford, along with Betty Gauthreaux, BSU's office manager. They've remained Brad's good friends to this day. Entering the large multi-purpose room, Brad noticed students mingling in the chapel area at the far corner of the room and walked over to join them. The service consisted of a few guitar-accompanied songs, a prayer, a scripture reading and a short message. After the service, everybody filed into the lunch line. Sitting and eating with his new friends, Brad heard enthusiastic talk of BSU events including an upcoming fall conference.

Brad joined his new BSU friends in intramural sports, hikes, camp-outs, and tailgate parties—activities designed both for both their own enjoyment and to build friendships with other students. Such activities created several new and lasting friendships, among them Marshal and Deb Guidry, future financial supporters for decades. Deb recalls those early days:

"We did a lot of BSU stuff together. We went on retreats and to camps and met people from all over the state. Brad is just a great guy—a very strong Christian, great personality, got along with everybody and we always had a lot of fun. When we'd all go out to eat together, there was as much laughing as there was eating."

The BSU drew Brad like a magnet. "I felt that I had found a home," he recalls. While growing up in the church, this was something new. Hiking? Camping? Tailgate parties? This was a Christianity unknown to him, and the friendliness, fun, and sense of adventure of his BSU classmates was irresistible. As Deb recalls, "We made some of our best friends during our college years. We were all concentrating on getting our work done, but we had fun. It was good, healthy, clean fun. It's still hard to find groups of people that aren't into drinking and drugs. We all clicked with each other and had a great time. Those years bring back some wonderful memories. Brad was always up for an adventure. One year, we did a big camping trip to the Buffalo River during the Dec/Jan break—an insane choice because it was freezing cold."

The BSU had another effect on Brad: it changed him from the quiet and shy introvert of his high school years into the still quiet but extrovert of his adult years. I asked him how that happened. "Well, I think it was the students in the BSU who set an example for me. They were all attracted to their faith, but their faith was a lifestyle; it wasn't a part of their life separated from everything else. These people had passions for different things, but they served Christ at the same time. I had never made that connection before. They were a family of young people involved in intramural sports and knocking on doors, giving out Bibles, going to tailgate parties and trying to be a presence for Christ on the campus."

If Brad's experience on Montserrat Island is likened to a bird's first venture out of the nest, then the life now opening up to him was like learning how to fly. From that first BSU meeting, he began to soar.

Changes were also occurring in Brad's vocational plans. In the beginning, following his father's advice to choose a "high profession," he became a premed major, setting his sights on pediatrics. But after Montserrat, his guidance came from another direction. Brad worked in a men's clothing store during his senior year of high school—first doing janitorial work and then, as his talents were recognized, being elevated to a sales position. He developed a close relationship with the store's manager who, as Brad describes it, "became like a father to me." Under his influence, Brad switched majors in his sophomore year from premed to business, a move soon overshadowed by another change in his life.

"When I heard about the BSU fall conference, I didn't know anything about it. Everyone else, however, was so excited about it that I thought it would be a good chance to see what other students around the state were doing. At the time, I didn't know the purpose of the conference; I just knew it would be a time of being with my new friends."

Once there, Brad discovered the conference's purpose was to recruit students for summer missions. "The BSU students had a passion for Christ that led many to go on summer mission trips. It's what they talked about at the fall conference, and that's when things changed for me. Hearing the students share the stories of their summer mission trips, I recalled my experiences on Montserrat. What did I really do to change things for God's glory and not just my own? I was feeling pretty convicted about the things I knew I could have done and didn't. Stories can encourage people to live out their faith, and that's what their stories did for me. In hearing them, I heard God speaking to me. The thing that really got me that Sunday morning was the song 'Wherever He Leads, I'll Go,' and the minister talking about the regrets we'd have if God has called us into missions and we said, "No." Going forward at the end of the service to dedicate myself to summer missions was a tough thing to do, but then I realized no one in this auditorium knows me and I don't know them, so my walking down the aisle was solely to answer Christ's calling."

Brad's exposure to the BSU also affected him athletically. Aided by a growth spurt beginning in his last year of high school, athletics became a new interest. It would eventually become a passion. The BSU was active in intramural sports, and Brad joined their softball team and then began running. Thirty-plus years later, he continues to keep in shape through a careful diet and a life filled with marathons, biking, swimming, hiking, backpacking, skiing, snowboarding, cross-country skiing and most recently—at the age of fifty-four—successfully completing an Ironman "ultimate triathlon."

While Brad's commitment to summer missions was serious, his first assignment was a far cry from the desolate, uncivilized, impoverished and jungle-laced pictures that flash into people's minds when the word "missions" is mentioned. Recalls Deb Guidry, "We all razzed Brad about his missionary assignment that summer. He was going to 'suffer for the Lord' in—of all places—Hawaii! We gave him a bad time about that."

Although the living standards were quite different between Montserrat and Hawaii, there were several similarities between Brad's experiences on the two islands. Both islands were known for their lush beauty, both experiences were as part of a small group (six on Montserrat and five in Hawaii), and both almost took his life by drowning.

Chapter 4 | FROM NERD TO ATHLETE

The BSU president addressed the group at a spring meeting in 1981. "Okay," he said, "we've got applications for summer missions on the back table. Those of you who are going can pick one up." Brad didn't waste any time filling out the paperwork. He expected an assignment somewhere on the east coast, but along with three other students and housemother Cindy Black, Brad ended up in the town of Waikoloa on the island of Hawaii. Sponsored by the church in nearby Waimea, Brad and his small team were the first efforts by Southern Baptists to start a ministry in Waikoloa, efforts that bore fruit a few years later.

Cindy's appointment as the housemother of the group had both an amusing origin and for two of her charges, life-saving consequences. Twenty-five years old and married for just two years, Cindy was in church one Sunday when, at the end of the service, her preacher-husband Bill invited people to come forward and dedicate themselves to spending the upcoming summer on the mission field. Several people moved out of their pews and walked down the aisle. To Bill's surprise, one of them was his wife.

Recalling the event with a mischievous smile, Cindy asks, "What was he going to say, 'no'?" "Looking back on it," she continues, "I can't believe I did it. After being married only two years, I decide to leave my husband for the whole summer. It was so much the working of God because when I called Mike Roberts at the Home Mission Board (HMB) to find out my assignment, he immediately said 'Hawaii' and a few weeks later we were all there." Recovering quickly, her husband Bill gave Cindy his full support.

"I understand Bill visited you for a couple of weeks," I commented.

"Yes, he came for two weeks, and it was really good because in that church if I spent the summer alone they'd be saying, 'Oh no, they're getting a divorce.' He was totally supportive."

Bill's visit was good for Cindy, and it was good for Brad—the beginning of a friendship and a mentoring relationship with Bill that continues to this day. A short time later, Bill and Cindy left their church in Georgia and moved to Gatlinburg, Tennessee, where Bill still ministers to the large, year-round resort population through Smoky Mountain Resort Ministries. His head start in resort work enabled him to blaze a trail for Brad, who took full advantage of Bill's experiences and insights.

Cindy goes on to describe their time in Hawaii. "We were housed in a rented home inside of a planned community. Our outreach primarily consisted of day camps for children, but we also tried to reach out to the community and its residents. On Sundays, the five of us would worship at the church in Waimea about twenty to twenty-five minutes away. We began holding the day camps in the garage of our house. Unfortunately, we found out in that planned community there were regulations against us doing it there. So they gave us the use of the stables, which [when you consider Jesus' birthplace] we thought was very appropriate."

I asked Cindy to recall any stories she remembered about Brad. Her response surprised me. "Of the four students I had that summer, three didn't swim, and Brad was one of them. I had grown up with a pool in my backyard, so when I was in college and had to select a sport, I chose swimming, took the Water Safety Instructor class, and became a Certified Lifeguard. That summer in Hawaii, I had to rescue two of the students from dangerous situations: one from a pool and one from the ocean. Brad was the person I pulled out of the ocean. The waves were big, and he was out over his head. I can't remember whether it was the look on his face or his splashing arms that got my attention—probably the latter, but I swam out to him.

"'What's wrong?' I asked him.

"'I don't think I can make it back.'

"We just talked at first. He was frightened, but he didn't grab at me [he was learning]. Finally, he did the floating thing and with an arm on my shoulder, we just calmly made our way back. It was after that summer that he vowed he was going to learn how to swim, and he did."

Cindy's story was surprising. In all the years I had known Brad—about fifteen by then—and in all the reports I had read about how he fell in love with swimming, this was the first I had heard about a *second* near-drowning experience. I called him up. "Brad," I said, "This is Skip. I just got off the phone with Cindy Black. She said that when you were in Hawaii you almost drowned a second time, and she had to save you?"

"Yeah..." Brad responded hesitatingly, his voice soft and falling.

Oh, so that's it.

Sometimes embarrassment can be a good thing. For Brad, this second brush with death was the "last straw," launching him into a sport that was to become a life-long passion. Immediately upon returning to McNeese, Brad signed up for swimming lessons at the local YMCA. Deb Guidry smilingly recalls his first class.

"We gave him a bad time because he showed up to his first class with flippers. He thought he needed them in order to swim."

Brad explains his decision to take up swimming: "It was an opportunity to experience something I never experienced as a child. I was never pushed into sports. My other siblings did them, but I concentrated on my studies. It was the typical expectation for the oldest child to set the example."

There was, however, another reason Brad learned to swim. It was more than the embarrassment, and more than the desire to make up for lost time while in high school. "The decision to take swimming lessons followed an epiphany: I had an *adventurous* spirit. I never did anything adventurous before Montserrat and Hawaii. While swimming is a basic skill that many learn as children, I didn't, so I decided I'm going to do this thing. I'm going to learn how to swim." Brad "took the plunge" and signed up for swimming lessons, becoming a certified Red Cross Lifeguard and Water Safety Instructor.

"At the time, I thought maybe God is preparing me for a calling that would include swimming, and I could use it to serve Him. I wasn't expecting to excel in it as much as I did."

Swimming was but the first of many of Brad's athletic pursuits. "I thought to myself, I've never done a marathon before. That'd be a great thing to do, so I did it. There are things I won't try because I think they're too risky. I've seen videos on *Outside* magazine where people are climbing mountains with snow and ice, but you're vulnerable in those conditions and at the mercy of the terrain."

Brad accumulated several friends who shared his passion for adventure. "Matt Squires was on a quest to climb the highest points in all fifty states. After a tragic divorce, he joined the Big Sky Volunteer Ski Patrol and the Big Sky Fire Department as a volunteer firefighter/EMT. When he first joined the department, he was an avowed atheist. I had befriended him and known him for a couple of years when all of a sudden, after seeing an ad promising a warm welcome at Big Sky Christian Fellowship, he showed up at church and ended up accepting Christ. It was great to see how his life changed.

"I applaud him for his mountain climbing feats—from the molehills in southeastern United States to a guided climb of Mount McKinley. He had finished his fifty-state climbing quest before I completed my goal of swimming in all fifty states. Mike enjoys rappelling off snow-covered mountains. I'd ski them, but I wouldn't do the rappelling.

"I've become more adventurous later on in life because I've seen there's a whole world of experiences out there and we have only this one physical life to live. I come across as a shy introvert. I don't come across as adventurous. So when people find out that I do extreme skiing, kayaking, snowboarding, rock climbing or my passion, which is swimming, it really surprises them."

While Brad's love of adventure caught fire on Montserrat, "The initial spark," as he explains, "was my first plane ride in high school. It was from Lake Charles to Denver, Colorado with the high school choir. Our director, Mr. Tom Nix, was all about doing tours and concerts, and chartered a Texas Instruments plane to fly us to Denver.

"The difference between my siblings and me is that they haven't traveled outside the United States, and I have. Those trips made a big difference in my life. My world changed after that."

Remembering the stories about his mother, I suggested that she must enjoy hearing of his experiences. "Yes, she does. She identifies with me at that point. My dad is a person who studies and analyzes things, whereas my mother enjoys new experiences. When they were out in Yellowstone, my dad says, 'we're on a volcano, this thing could erupt at any time.' And I said, 'well, yes, I guess it could' and laughed. While my dad would say of Yellowstone, 'this is a dangerous area,' my mom was 'let's go on to the next adventure!'"

Unfortunately, risks often accompany adventures. Brad recounts an experience several years later when he was at Big Sky, Montana. "I knew David from the Bozeman Masters Swim team. I didn't know where his faith was at the time we became friends, but we were getting to the place where we could talk about those things. One day he and his wife went cross-country skiing and ran into an avalanche that took his life. I'll never forget him.

"Then there was Jamie Pierre. He was a strong believer and used his skill as an extreme skier to share the Gospel with his friends. He died because he made the wrong choice to go into a closed area before the ski season. I've lost both of them, and I miss them.

The Pu'u Kahea Conference Center is a twelve-acre estate on the island of Hawaii, built around a three-story white stucco mansion resembling a giant layer cake. The Southern Baptists purchased the estate in 1946 and turned it into a retreat and conference center. Back in the summer of 1981, Brad and his group were serving as counselors and helpers. One evening, sitting around a bonfire with a bunch of campers, "The leader shared a devotional and invited us to commit our lives to the mission field." Brad was among those who responded, making a commitment not just for a summer, but for a lifetime.

Chapter 5 | TAOS

With a need for adventure running in his veins an graduation from McNeese approaching, Brad applied for a two-year resort missionary position. Given his passion for swimming and credentials as a Water Safety and Life Guard Instructor, he assumed God was preparing him for a ministry near the water. He wasn't. In Biblical language, "My ways are not your ways, says the Lord." (Isaiah 55:8) or amusingly stated in contemporary terms, "If you want to hear God laugh, tell him your plans."

"I went to the HMB headquarters in Atlanta that spring for an interview. Before I left, my BSU friend Lee Crawford asked me to look up his friend Chuck Clayton. I did, and we started talking. 'Tell me about yourself,' said Chuck. I didn't know it at the time, but there were several people at the HMB who decided on our assignments and Chuck was one of them." Another was Rev. Bill Lee, his interviewer. As Bill recalls,

"I was greatly impressed with Brad—the way he carried himself and his personality. We had done the usual run of references and life history and experiences. Bill and Cindy Black had contacted me and passed on their experiences with him in Hawaii. One of the things that first struck me was the idea of a black resort minister—what about that! [His surprise is understandable. Primarily for economic reasons, black churches send proportionately far fewer into missions than their white counterparts.]"

At the end of the interview, Brad made sure Bill knew that he wanted to serve in a beach ministry—not that it did any good. After Bill and Chuck had compared notes, they were in agreement. As Brad tells it, "Chuck knew enough about Taos and its ethnic landscape to know I was better suited for the Rocky Mountains than the east coast. After the interview, I received a call saying that I was going to Taos. Taos? I never heard of it."

The ministry at Taos was the dream of local Baptist minister Bob Butler and the Southern Baptist's Director of Missions (D-O-M) for the area, King Sanders. As they thought, planned and prayed, they realized that by combining Taos' winter outreach with a summer backpacking ministry, they could fund a year-round position. They did, and it was offered to Brad. When he accepted, they became his supervisors, meeting with him regularly to provide guidance, support and encouragement.

For housing, Brad shared an A-frame cabin with a young man he met at church. Then, in his second year, he hit pay dirt. An older couple in the church let him use the apartment on the ground level of their large split-level home. "They were Hispanic—Norm and Lilly White. That's where I stayed for the rest of my time at Taos. They are a great, great couple who loved the whole world and warmly welcomed my family when they visited. Their house was big. When others rented the apartment, there was a wrought iron gate at the bottom of the stairway to separate the apartment from the rest of the home, but for me, that gate soon became a doorway. They liked me being there because it gave them a sense of security when they were away. In addition, the people of the church were very supportive, giving me kitchen stuff and everything I needed. Great people—I'm still in touch with some of them to this day."

Brad's feelings upon landing at Taos in the fall of '84 were not unlike those he experienced in New York City on his way to Montserrat. "I was pretty homesick for a long time. It was tough. It took me about a month before I realized I had to get out and be more sociable. Some of the ski crowd were in church, but I didn't even know them. The church had Bible studies I could attend, but they consisted mostly of older folks. I didn't get to know other church members my age until I met the river rafting supervisor for the Bureau of Land Management. His rafting guides were still older than me, but they invited me to their homes for parties where I got to know the ski crowd, the biking crowd, and the river rafting crowd."

In order to build relationships with the employees, Brad secured a job at the mountain. "I took on a part-time job as a Mountain Host. We passed out information at the ticket windows and made sure people remembered where they parked. On-mountain, we coordinated the lift lines and entertained those who were waiting. At the top of the lift, 'body snatchers' had the job of helping those who fell to get out of the way so that the lift wouldn't have to shut down. We'd also serve hot chocolate, report accidents to the ski patrol and help them with sweep at the end of the day. We were auxiliary staff, filling the gaps to keep the guests happy. While I was there, *Ski* magazine voted us the friendliest ski area in America. I continued to work as a Mountain Host while at Taos, and after leaving the mountain for seminary, would return to give them a hand during Christmas vacations, one of the two busiest times of the year."

Establishing a pattern at Taos that would follow him for the rest of his life, Brad focused on developing relationships—relationships with a purpose: "My desire is to help folks realize they're a special creation in God's eyes. When God created us, he touched us with a longing for Him. My greatest hope is that God will use me to help people accept the truth of God's word and recognize their internal longing for Jesus Christ. I don't claim to know all the answers, but that's one thing I do know. That touch from God needs to be fulfilled and can only be satisfied by accepting Christ."

Brad not only established new friendships at Taos, he also expanded his athletic repertoire. Although he knew a lot about swimming, he didn't know anything about skiing. Interestingly, it was his swimming that led to his skiing. As he explains, "When I was taking my Water Safety Instructor and Lifeguard certifications, the other swimming instructors told me that I had a lot of natural balance. 'You'd make a good skier—have you ever tried it before?' Upon arriving at Taos, I tried it and was skiing intermediate terrain the first day. At the end of the season, I took a ten-session local's clinic and ended up on the expert trails."

"When did you become an extreme skier?"

"I consider extreme skiing to be double-black diamonds and the stuff you need to hike into with beacons shovels and probes—terrain such as the North Summit Snowfields at Big Sky and the Big Couloir, along with the gullies and chutes. Taos is a pretty steep mountain and by the time I left I was skiing that kind of terrain." The phrase 'extreme skiing' makes me think of things like jumping off cliffs. Brad has also done that. . once… by mistake. "I ended up in a spot on the mountain where I asked myself, 'Oh no, how did I get here?' I had to jump to get out of it. I'm not big on jumping; I'd rather have both my feet firmly planted on the ground."

Fortunately, such problems didn't present themselves when summer rolled around. Christian High Adventures, a backpacking program founded by Chuck Clayton and designed to introduce teens to the outdoors and to their Creator, was Brad's focus in the summer months. Backpacking was new to him, just one of many sports he would pick up in coming years. Christian High Adventures ministered to kids who were "at risk"—those with horrific home lives which, if not checked, tend to reproduce themselves. Brad explains the program: "We took them out into the wilderness, taught them how to have some time alone with the Bible and with God and introduced them both to the Bible and to low-impact wilderness camping. They were from dysfunctional families, but we cared for them. They came to understand that the limits we set were for their own good. We gave them a sense of family and belonging. The neatest times were when these kids made professions of faith in Christ. That first year there was a girl whose life was so changed that she went back to become a leader in her church and a Sunday school teacher. It was exciting to see how kids respond when they're separated from the modern conveniences of home and are dealing with the basics of life and the challenges of backpacking. My message to them was that their life could be more fulfilling than the ugliness they experienced at home—a message I enjoyed sharing."

Brad was off to a good start at Taos, and it was about to get better.

Chapter 6 | UNFORGETTABLE ENCOUNTERS

Brad spent his first year at Taos becoming acquainted with his new surroundings. Working as a Mountain Host not only endeared him to the mountain's management but also put him on a first-name basis with employees and guests alike. Then, Bob Butler, the pastor at First Baptist Taos who also led on-mountain worship services in a bar, announced his impending departure. To fill the ministry vacuum created by Bob's absence, Brad cancelled plans to work for the mountain that next season.

"After seeing what others like Debbie Wohler and Steve Hoekstra had done with services on the slopes, I approached Ernie Blake, Taos' founder and manager. I told him what other resorts were doing with on-mountain services and that I'd like to do them at Taos. He said, 'Well, this doesn't have to be something in the far future. You're here now, so you have my blessing. Why don't you do it this coming season?'

"I chose a place outside of the Phoenix restaurant [so named because it had literally risen from the ashes on two occasions], a sunny and popular spot on the mountain. Located on the mountain's backside, it had a nice flat area with picnic tables on the snow, giving people the option of sitting for the service while I stood next to a ten-foot high cross." In starting the services on the slopes, Brad had no idea he'd be recruiting a former United States president as a guest preacher.

"President Carter and his wife Rosalyn were coming to Taos to learn how to ski. Their son Chip, who was new to the sport, visited the previous spring, took some lessons, and ended up a skier. Even though Taos is a difficult mountain, he thought it was a great place to learn the sport and talked his parents and family into coming.

"When I heard they were coming I thought, President Carter's a believer, and maybe I can get him to speak at our service. It was tough going from there. I talked to Taos' public relations person. They told me to talk to the head of the ski school, who was assigned as Carter's private instructor. I did, and he said he'd be glad to pass on the invitation. The Secret Service contacted me, set up a meeting and asked about the location of the service, who comes and what the crowd was like. Then they wanted to check out the place for themselves. If the idea was approved, they would set up a face-to-face meeting for me with President Carter."

Unfortunately, the meeting invitation from the Secret Service never came, and as Sunday drew near, Brad began wondering if the whole idea was going to disappear, buried beneath the tidal wave of social invitations and security concerns typically accompanying a former president.

That Friday morning, Brad was working in the corral of a beginner's chairlift, giving people directions and helping them into line when a large entourage suddenly appeared. "It was a pretty big group. Besides the head of the ski school and President Carter, there were all the Secret Service people. The head of the ski school spotted me and said, 'President Carter, this is the person you need to talk to about Sunday, the chaplain Brad.'

"'Oh, great to meet you, President Carter,' I replied.

"'Yes, I got the invitation from you to speak at the service on the mountain and I'll gladly accept. I'd like to do that.'

"'Oh, that's awesome.'

"'Well, what do you want me to speak on?'

"'It's December,' I said, 'and we're approaching the Christmas season. It'd be great if you could have a message relating to Christmas.'

"When the news media hear of that exchange they think it's a pretty big deal that a former president was asking me for advice. I gave President Carter the Christmas story from Matthew, and he agreed to the idea for the message. 'Well,' he said, 'I don't know what my skiing ability will be on Sunday, but I'll work on being able to ski to the service. That's my goal. My goal is to ski there and not to be taken by snowmobile.' It was a good 3-4 minute encounter before he loaded the lift. There weren't a lot of people around, and he was the one to stop and interact with me, so I felt comfortable talking to him.

"When Sunday arrived President Carter's skiing had improved enough so that he *could* ski to the service, but Mrs. Carter had to be brought by snowmobile. A reporter from the *Taos News* and crew from the TV station in Albuquerque were also present. I was going to have President Carter read the Christmas story, but Rosalyn forgot to bring his reading glasses. So I said to myself, 'Wow, this is an opportunity to have both of them speak!' I then asked her to read the Scripture passage that he had chosen, and from there he expounded on it. I'll never forget what he said. He talked about how the family was important and how parents feel attached to their children, and when we're born into God's family, the same attachment exists between God and us—in fact, God loved us enough to send his son to be born and to be our Savior. I thought his message was great. The whole thing was a really neat experience."

Ernie Blake

As Brad looks back on his time at Taos, one man stands out: Taos' founder and general manager, Ernie Blake. "I really enjoyed my time at Taos because it was like a family. It was a mixed culture, a combination of Spanish and Anglo. It was also great having my first resort experience under a resort manager who was initially tentative about my presence, but then became one of my biggest supporters. I'm talking about Ernie Blake, the founder and patriarch of Taos ski area, whose picture still hangs in my home. Everything that happened at Taos had to be approved by him."

"What eased Ernie's anxiety and made him so supportive?" I asked.

"I think the turning point was seeing how I treated people. He told me that he enjoyed how I approached people. I wasn't pushy. He liked the way I greeted people and did things like scraping ice off their boots. He wanted his guests to come back and think of Taos as a fun, family place. He began viewing my ministry as a viable part of the ski area when he saw people's response to the Christmas Eve service. He thought it was incredible. Once he embraced what I was doing, I felt like I was part of his family. We developed a close relationship, and he gave me a free rein in my ministry."

Taos' founder was a legend in the skiing industry. Born in Germany in 1914, Ernie's schooling was in his mother's native country of Switzerland, where she introduced him to skiing. He excelled at this and most other sports and would have easily qualified for the 1936 German Olympic ice hockey team were he not Jewish. It was the beginning of a Nazified Germany, and his life changed dramatically in an encounter with the Gestapo in 1938. It happened at their family home in Frankfurt. As recounted by Ernie's eldest son Mickey Blake,

"The Gestapo showed up to question the family. During the interview, one agent had an earache. My grandmother was a nurse and was able to relieve his pain. Out of gratitude, he told her that they needed to leave Frankfurt immediately."[17]

Ernie's family relocated to the United States. He volunteered for the 10th Mountain Division but they initially rejected him, his German heritage engendering suspicions that he might be a spy. The Army later had a change of mind, commissioned him a Second Lieutenant, and flew him to Europe on the day of the Normandy invasion to serve as an interpreter in General Patton's headquarters. He was with Patton in his drive across Germany in 1945 when they encountered their first Nazi concentration camp.

"That experience always haunted my father," remembers his son Mickey. "I recall on one occasion something I said touched a nerve about those memories; I never saw that look on his face or heard that tremor in his voice at any other time. He said it was the only time he saw General Patton ashen and so upset that he couldn't speak."[18] From this point on, reports Mickey, "Ernie's compassion for his fellow Jews led to generous contributions for Jewish relief both in Israel and worldwide. Ernie, an assimilated Jew who didn't practice his faith, became one of the largest and most consistent contributors to the United Jewish Appeal campaign in New Mexico."[19]

The army put Ernie to work interrogating captured Germans, among them Hitler henchmen Hermann Goering, Wilhelm Keitel, and Albert Speer. To prevent those interrogated from knowing he was Jewish, they changed his birth name, Ernst Bloch, to "Blake."

Following the war, Ernie and his bride Rhoda, whom he met while skiing in Vermont, settled in New Mexico. Ernie went to work for a ski company in Santa Fe, all the while scouting the area for a suitable place to develop a resort of his own. He found it north of Taos. In the beginning, Taos' first trails were so steep that those who skied them won bragging rights. After a while, Ernie added a ski school and developed more moderate terrain for less aggressive skiers.

Brad's friend and mentor Bill Lee recalls a moving encounter between Brad and Ernie. "One of the high points of my ministry was in August of '87. I was in charge of resort ministries across the country. Our Home Missions' magazine wanted to do a story on Brad, so when I went to student week in Glorietta [the Southern Baptist conference center in New Mexico], one of the reporters from the magazine went with me. Joined by the reporter and my mother, we took a day off and went to Taos. Brad met us in town, and we drove up to the mountain.

"We went up to the lodge, vacant in the summer months except for a few workmen doing some remodeling. Once inside Brad said to me, 'I want you to go upstairs with me and meet the guy who founded Taos resort—you ladies will have to wait down here.' And so we climbed the stairs to his private apartment above the main part of the lodge. There sat the diminutive gray-haired, gray-bearded native of Switzerland who had developed this whole resort. The story goes that he and a friend were flying his single-engine plane between Colorado and Santa Fe. He looked out the window, pointed, and said 'right there—we're going to build a ski resort.' So he set about to buy the property and with chainsaw in hand, joined a crew in clearing the land. He was a young man at the time. By the time I saw him, he was getting up in years and near retirement. Brad brought the Bible that Jimmy Carter used on the ski slope and a cassette recording of that service. We began to talk, and it was apparent that this small, Swiss man and this tall African American kid from Louisiana had formed quite a friendship. That touched me. Then at the end of the conversation, Brad gave him the Bible and the cassette recording and they embraced, and they both cried, and I did too. That was a monumental moment. I saw what could happen in people's lives through resort ministries. It remains a vivid memory to this day."

Later that same year, Ernie was inducted into the Skier and Snowboarder's Hall of Fame. Two years after the induction, a victim of pneumonia, New Mexico's skiing legend died at the age of seventy-five.

Chapter 7 | BIG SKY

From his home in Lake Charles, Louisiana, Brad packed his bags, loaded them into his blue 1983 Nissan pickup, and began the six-hour drive to Fort Worth, Texas. Behind him: four years at McNeese University and three at Taos. Ahead of him: three years at Southwestern Theological Seminary.

For majors, Brad selected Christian Education—a telling choice. Those who want to lead churches don't major in Christian Education. It was, however, an understandable preference for Brad, whose leadership style is supportive rather than assertive—a person who shies away from positions of authority. Brad's more comfortable as a team player than a director, his leadership style that of a manager—detail oriented, thorough and conscientious—rather than a CEO motivating people and holding them accountable. Brad firing somebody? It's not going to happen.

During his seminary years, Brad made a point of keeping in touch with friend and mentor Bill Lee. With some amusement, Bill recalls Brad's periodic contacts: "About every six months I would get a note from him or a telephone call. It would go something like this, 'Bill, you *are* going to have a place for me in resort ministries when I graduate?' or, 'Bill, you *are* going to have a place for me when I graduate, I just know it.' And I would say, 'Brad, do you realize how low Resort Ministries is on the budget totem pole?' 'I know,' he would say, 'but you'll find a place for me.'" And he did.

Bill first contacted Brad about Big Sky after Brad's second year of seminary. The "US-2" person appointed to the resort for two years left after one week, and Bill was eager to find a replacement. Unwilling to interrupt his education, Brad declined. After finding a married couple to handle the first half of that two-year assignment, Bill called again a year later, this time when Brad was getting ready to graduate.

"When Bill called me the second time, I had completely forgotten about his offer of the year before. I was in Hawaii on a church choir tour when he called. The hotel's front desk clerk told me I had a message, and when I saw who it was from, it blew me out of the water. I thought, 'Wow—this must be important.' When I reached him, he said, 'I really want you to consider Big Sky. They need someone with experience.' A church in Houston was also interested in me, but I thought Houston—too much concrete—I can't live there. With no other possibilities, I thought, yeah, I'm going to do it."

Brad accepted the second half of the two-year assignment, but even before he settled into his new surroundings, Bill was at work to keep him there. Now in charge of all Southern Baptist resort ministries nationwide, he was in a good position to make it happen. All he needed was the funding. After locating the needed monies and obtaining the necessary approvals, voila!

"We got together something like twenty thousand dollars," says Bill, "turning Brad's temporary job into a new full-time position. I offered it to Brad, and we appointed him in 1991. I've never regretted that decision." While most missionaries have to raise their own support, the Southern Baptist's Home Mission Board was now providing Brad's salary and benefits. He was set for life, or so he thought.

Arrival

After settling into the Spartan accommodations provided for him at the nearby Baptist church in Gardiner (think cot in a Sunday school room), Brad spent the next few days touring Yellowstone, the world's first national park. Awed by the natural beauty of its mountains and forests, he gazed on waterfalls three times higher than Niagara, the park's own twenty-mile long "Grand Canyon," and its unique hot springs and geysers, including the famous Old Faithful.

A few days later, Russ and Amy Dean, the couple Brad was replacing, gave him a tour of nearby Bozeman and Big Sky. The drive to Big Sky snaked along the famed fly-fishing Gallatin River depicted in Robert Redford's movie, *A River Runs Through It*. The final few miles of the journey were a bit deceiving, the gently rolling hills and open spaces giving little hint of Big Sky's 11,166-foot-high Lone Peak, visible only occasionally in the distance. Passing through Big Sky's town center and residential areas, five miles later they entered the community at the base of the mountain, Mountain Village— an area bustling with activity during winter months but a ghost town after the skiers left. Russ and Amy introduced Brad to some of the key people at the resort, inviting several to join the trio for dinner at the 320 Ranch, a rustic and popular lodge listed on the National Historic Registry. Introducing Brad to the area and interrupting their elegant meal that evening was the sound of emergency vehicles responding to a collision. Outside the restaurant, a car had collided . . . with a bear.

The brainchild of former TV news anchor Chet Huntley, Big Sky Resort is, in acreage, the largest ski resort in the United States. While catering to all levels of skiers and snowboarders, most trails are designed for the more advanced, the tram to the top of Lone Peak providing access to some of the steepest and most challenging terrain on the continent.

For a person seeking adventure, and looking for close relationships, Brad had struck it rich. Big Sky and its surrounding mountains easily met his need for challenging adventures, and the isolation of a destination resort insured a close-knit community. Offered a job teaching swimming at the local high school, Brad moved into a condominium in the still-deserted Mountain Village on Labor Day weekend of 1990.

"Moving from a church bedroom into a condo made me feel like part of a community, but with no one around, my initial time at Big Sky was pretty lonely. I did a lot of running and hiking and listening to people telling me things would pick up. Still, it was a tough, boring time. Teaching the kids swimming and having a church community that included me in everything were the two things that got me through those first few months."

Big Sky Christian Fellowship

Brad found a church home in Big Sky Christian Fellowship (BSCF). Established in 1972 as a non-denominational ministry, BSCF spent its first twenty-seven years in need of a permanent home. When Brad arrived, they and the local Catholic congregation were both sharing a local hotel conference room. Finally, in 1993, a group of community leaders and church representatives including Brad came together to construct a house of worship to be shared by the churches of Big Sky. After five years of fundraising and a year of building, Big Sky Chapel was dedicated on Mother's Day of 1999. As of this writing, three churches: St. Joseph's Catholic Mission, All Saints in Big Sky (Episcopal/Lutheran) and Big Sky Christian Fellowship, share the beautiful log and stucco building.[20]

Rev. Gent Cofer was leading BSCF when Brad arrived. Sporting the tall, slim physique of a basketball player, Gent graduated from a Presbyterian seminary and belonged to several other denominations before settling into the ranks of the Southern Baptists. Brad described him in words curiously slow in coming. Indeed, one got the feeling that he never quite found the right ones.

"The most easygoing guy..." he paused, "very gentle, very caring ..." another pause, "very sensitive to people's needs... a gentle giant..." yet another pause, "the best type of personality for a pastor."

"Someone you would feel safe with?" I interjected, trying to help.

"Oh yes, you'd feel free to share anything with him."

Then it hit me. With the exception of the "gentle giant," Brad was not only describing Gent, he was describing himself.

Gent's clearest memories of Brad were when Brad served as a lifeguard at the cancer camps organized by Gent's wife, Diane. Before succumbing herself in 1999, she helped many battle the dreaded disease by founding and directing "For One Another," a cancer support network in Montana.

Following Diane's death, Gent and his two daughters moved out of the area, necessitating a search for his replacement. Two years later, the search ended in the unanimous selection of Doug Timm, a multi-talented man who worked as a builder and construction manager as well as a pastor.

"During the search process," explains Doug, "Brad held things together by serving as Chairman of the Board of Elders. Without him, the church may well have fallen apart."

Firefighter Brad

When the volunteerism bug bit Brad on the island of Montserrat, it didn't let go. As reported by Bill Black, "Brad runs the triathlon in Big Sky. When he's not running himself, I've watched him get up on a picnic table and do a prayer of blessing before the race and then jump down to become one of the volunteers."

The Fire Department also beckoned for Brad's time, though not very subtly. The fire chief had been pressing Brad to join the department for some time, but Brad, his plate already full, kept putting him off. Finally, the chief hatched a fail-proof plan. Besides teaching swimming lessons to residents, Brad also taught Water Safety Instructor classes with their accompanying CPR training. The CPR training is much more realistic when practiced with specially designed dummies. The only such dummies available in the area were at the local fire department, which gave the chief an idea.

"Sure you can borrow the dummies," he said to Brad, "as soon as you join the department." It worked.

Brad's time-commitment as a firefighter was minimal until a new chief arrived. Determined to raise the department standards, he ratcheted up the training requirements. All firefighters were now required to become medical First Responders, followed by training in fire-fighting tactics. Then one of their members upped the ante on his own by becoming the department's first full-time paramedic. With one of their own joining the chief in raising the standards, the rest now set higher goals for themselves. "The paramedic motivated the rest of us to get our EMT certifications," says Brad. After that came the "Firefighter 1" training. When Brad joined the department, it was an all-volunteer force with a couple of paid staff. Today, the Big Sky Fire Department is evenly divided between volunteers and paid personnel. "All of us are both firefighters *and* medical responders," says Brad. "We're not separated into medical and fire-fighting crews as happens in some departments. All of us train in three areas: wildland fires, structural fires, and emergency medicine. Because we are a ski community, about 75% of our calls are for emergency medical care."

Brad grew with the department. He entered as the Chaplain then went on to obtain both his EMT and Firefighter 1 certifications. In 2005, the department honored him as "Fireman of the Year." Several years later, when he was looking for employment in Big Sky, it surprised no one that he dismissed several other possibilities to rejoin the fire department.

A Cross in the Snow

Once at Big Sky, it was only natural that Brad would seek to borrow ideas from his ministry at Taos, including his on-mountain services. Long-time friend and supporter Brock Short tells how the services began at Big Sky.

"Brad went to the mountain management and asked if he could have a service on the hill. The resort management was already very impressed by him, so gave him the okay. Of course, he couldn't have a service without a cross like at Taos." Soon replacing the first cross, a movable six-footer stuck into the snow, a large and permanent fourteen-foot-high log cross became available, donated by a local logging business."

Overcast, with strong gusts of wind, it was not a pleasant November day. Brad, joined by Jason and Tim from the rental shop, hopped onto the gondola (since replaced by a chairlift) for the ride up the mountain. At the same time, a snow cat, its treads biting into the soft snow, roared up the mountain by a different route, a fourteen-foot cross roped onto its short, stubby bed.

"Gee, Brad," said Jason with a smile, "Couldn't you have made arrangements for a nicer day? After all, you've got the connections."

"Sorry, guys" Brad replied, his voice dripping in mock disappointment. "I tried, but when I mentioned your names, all I heard was laughter."

The bantering and joking continued up the mountain. Actually, Jason and Tim were glad to help, feeling somewhat honored to be asked to do something verging on the historic in their little mountain community. It also felt good to help someone who had already helped them in many small ways during the short time they had known each other in the rental shop. Stepping off the gondola a little over halfway up the mountain, they walked over to the small grove of trees where Brad had dug a hole. A few minutes later, the snow cat rumbled up, and the driver hopped out to unload the cross. Brad and his helpers picked up the cross, which weighed close to a hundred-and-fifty pounds, and walked toward the hole. Everything was going fine until they started to raise the top section. It was then that they wished they had taken advantage of the snow cat driver's earlier offer to stay and help. As soon as the top of the cross went up, the wind, gusting up to 30 mph, caught its expansive surface, veering it off course. They tried again, and again. After about thirty minutes, which felt like two hours to their tired and aching muscles, they decided on 'plan B.' They would leave the cross where it was and return on a less windy day. "Okay," said Brad, disappointedly "but before we go, let's give it one more try." They did, expecting more of the same, but got something far different. No sooner had they started to lift the top part of the cross when a particularly strong gust of wind caught it, lifted it out of their hands, and dropped it into the hole. They were speechless.

"Talk about miracles!" said Tim finally.

"I'll certainly talk about this one," responded Brad.

"Guess you've got connections after all," said Jason, smiling.

Brock Short

No ministry survives on the work of the leader alone, and several people helped Brad at Big Sky, Brock Short being the most active. A wealthy lawyer and businessman, Brock and his wife Jane divide their time equally between Big Sky and their home in Tennessee. The Brocks met Brad at church.

"He was helping with the service that day, sang a song and explained his ministry. We invited him out to lunch and have been friends ever since."

Brock is not only a friend, he's a co-worker, often leading the mountaintop services in Brad's absence. "I've had my shares of ups and downs as a lawyer and my share of tough business negotiations as a businessman, but Brad is different than anyone I've ever met—he's just so Christ-like, so genuine and good-hearted. There's no meanness in him, and that's unusual. People who get to know him are often touched by a child-like quality in him that's not thinking of himself first. None of us are perfect, but Brad just touches you as more settled than most."

While Brad and Brock are good friends, it doesn't mean they agree on everything. Brock continues, "Theologically, I'm a pretty liberal and open guy—Brad not as much. I received a good education at Vanderbilt University and law school. I enjoy indulging in studies of comparative religions. I'm from a Native American background, being three-sixteenths Cherokee, and so recently I've been studying Native American religious practices and trying to understand them. I'm looking for points of agreement—different ways in which people try to seek God's kingdom. Brad and I don't always agree on everything and that's okay. When Brad speaks up for the Lord, you can just see his genuineness. Our theological differences don't keep us from sharing in this ministry."

The Race Issue

Don Coverdale is a retired guidance counselor from Boston, Massachusetts. He works weekends as a ski instructor at Sunday River Resort in Newry, Maine, and putting his seminary education to work, conducts weddings and holds services on Christmas and Easter, and he's black. I asked him if he ever ran into racism.

"Occasionally. People would ask me to marry them and then when they found out I was black, abruptly cancel the arrangements. Now I give them my business card—with my photo on it."

I wondered if Brad had any similar experiences. He reflected, "I think I'm the type of person for whom it's not an issue. I know racism is there. I don't know if I ignore it, but it's not been a problem for me. Being in Montana, I really don't think about it at all. The people I socialize with don't bring it up except at times when we might joke about it since Obama became president. Maybe the media sees I'm black and thinks there may be a story there, but I'm recommended for weddings because people have seen me in action.

"I'm reminded of a funny story. A couple from the east coast arranged for a pastor friend to do their wedding at Big Sky Chapel. Then the Big Sky Fire Department received a 911 call from the chapel during the rehearsal. The pastor had a diabetic emergency. As he was being whisked away in the ambulance, the couple asked the responders if there was anyone who could step in and officiate at the wedding the next day. The fire chief said he could call their chaplain and see if he was available, so he called me, and I agreed. When I arrived, the couple took one look at me and were so tickled, I mean really tickled. I didn't know why until after the wedding when this white couple came up and introduced me to their pastor, now recovered from his diabetic emergency. He was a black man. They were just beside themselves and told their pastor friend, 'Hey, you've just been replaced by another black guy,'" Brad said, laughing.

In reflecting on the issue of Brad's race, colleague and good friend Eric Spivey offers the following: "Brad comes from Louisiana and doesn't come from the same part of the country as a lot of us white Anglo ministers. He's always given the racial issue a different face and he's always sort of fit in and made us better."

Being black has even been advantageous for Brad. The media often likes to display their fairness and absence of racism by reporting positively on people of color—a practice that suits Brad just fine.

Chapter 8 | THE VISIT(S)

It was during our tour of ski resorts at the end of my 1997 sabbatical that my wife and I knocked on the door of Brad's second-floor condominium. When it opened, we were surprised to be looking at someone who appeared at least a decade younger than his thirty-six years.

As Brad and I talked that day, I was curious. Sharing one's faith in Christ can be a challenge in the secular environment of a ski resort; at least, it was for me. Wondering if our experiences were similar, I asked how often he talks with people about spiritual things.

"I'd say that every time I walk out my door, the opportunity is there. I work part-time in a ski rental shop. I don't have to do that financially, but I do it to have something in common with them. I think it's easier for them to talk to me because I'm around all week. I have the same experiences they have, but I see things differently. I also respond differently, and sometimes it gets them thinking. They hear about my experience with President Carter and think that's really neat. I have conversations with them on spiritual matters all the time. There is a lot of New Age thinking these days, *but I avoid getting into theological arguments* [emphasis mine]. Arguing can be tempting to those belonging to denominations. Many people I work with wonder why we even have denominations. We don't talk a lot about them here in Big Sky. To be a chaplain is to be available to everyone and not a select group. It's great sharing my experiences with people and hearing theirs, even when they get into some real far-out thinking. I think to myself, 'Wow, how can you think that?' Every other day or so, I'm having conversations with people about spiritual matters. Sometimes I might feel like I should have brought them into a saving relationship with Christ, but then I'm reminded that it's God who saves people, and not me. I try to make myself available so that when they have an encounter with God they'll know who to come to."

Thomas was such a person. The following account comes from the website of Brad's ministry.

"'Brad's a really nice guy,' says Thomas Geithman, a 25-year-old from Milwaukee, Wisconsin, who came to Big Sky to work in construction. 'He likes to do all the same things I do, and he keeps me motivated to do Bible study and come to church. If it weren't for him, I would probably be getting into a lot of trouble around here.'

"Thomas' grandparents were concerned about him when he left Milwaukee, so when they found Brad's ministry online, they asked him to meet with their grandson. 'Thomas loves snowboarding, he loves mountain biking, he loves all the things that many of us love here,' Brad says. 'So I invited him on a bike ride, on a day hike, and to our Twenties Bible Study ministry at BSCF."

"Through their shared interests, Brad got to know Thomas and learned about his struggle with alcohol and the many other decisions that took him down a destructive path.

"'After talking to him and working with him, we were hiking in Yellowstone Park when I asked Thomas if he was ready to rededicate his life to Christ,' Brad says. 'I told him, "Whenever you're ready." Finally, he said he was, and in January of 2007, he was baptized.'"[21]

The Second Visit

Colorado's Keystone Resort was the site of the 2013 gathering of the Association of Resort and Leisure Ministers (ARLM). In preparing to attend, I checked my map. Big Sky was still several hundred miles from Keystone—too far for driving—especially in the winter, but not for flying. Following the three-day conference, I caught the short flight into nearby Bozeman. Brushing a fist-high blanket of new snow off my rental car, I drove an hour to the Whitewater Inn, just three miles from Big Sky and my home for the next four days. The Inn sported a good-sized indoor swimming pool with its own water slide. A few months later, glancing through one of Brad's Facebook posts, I recognized it as the setting for his swimming classes.

After getting settled in the motel, I called Brad to invite him out to dinner. A short time later, I was negotiating the streets of a residential development and pulled into the driveway of a small, dark colored ranch home. Protruding toward the street was an attached single-car garage and in the driveway an aging Jeep Cherokee.

Opening the door, Brad greeted me with a soft and friendly "Hi!" and invited me in. Ahead of me was the living room, which merged into a dining room on the right and a kitchen on the left. Off to the right, a hallway led to a study, two bedrooms and a bath. Awards and certificates of appreciation blanketed its walls together with pictures of those he worked with as a firefighter, EMT, rental employee, swim instructor, ski patroller, and supervisor of summer programs. Just beyond the hallway, a doorway led down to a basement finished with the donated labor of friends, among them Brad's pastor, Doug Timm. At the bottom of the stairs, a bike stand transformed Brad's summer mountain bike into a winter exercise bike. Just beyond it sat the square, chrome framework of a Gold's Gym and behind that, two rows of dumbbells resting on a stand against the wall. Of the three young men renting space from him that winter, one of them occupied the basement bedroom and the other two—preferring economy over privacy—threw their sleeping bags on a large king-sized bed in what would normally have been the family room.

We ended up at Olive B's for dinner—an Italian restaurant chosen by Brad because "it's fairly new and I haven't been there yet." A quaint and stylish building, the wooden door opened into a tunnel-like hallway, its dark wood paneling reminding me of an old English tavern. Framed at the end of the hallway, an attractive blonde-haired woman in her early twenties stood behind the host's podium. Her pleasant smile when she saw me turned into an ear-to-ear grin when she saw Brad. "I'll be able to come to your service," she said excitedly.

"I taught her to swim," Brad explained in a quick aside. As they began talking, amidst the din of numerous conversations in the busy restaurant, I heard Brad say, "We're part of God's family." Mentioning names of her friends, Brad continued, "They're sons and daughters in God's family, and God wants us to be living with him forever. We're going to be together for eternity."

The above comments may sound like preaching, but they weren't. Brad's soft and gentle voice turned them into words of comfort and reassurance, her nodding indicating that he was getting through. Our waitress approached, ending the conversation, but before following her, Brad went behind the podium, and putting his arm around the girl's shoulder, gave her a warm side hug.

Doug Timm

In a phone interview months before my visit, Doug Timm, the pastor of BSCF, offered to take me skiing if ever I came to Big Sky. Recalling his thoughtfulness, I called him before arriving. The next morning, dressed in skiwear and carrying a helmet, ski boots and (much to my chagrin) only one glove, I walked out of the motel toward Doug's waiting car. "We'll have to drop by the house and get your skis," he announced. Then, much to my relief, "I've also got another glove you can use."

Doug Timm is not your usual pastor, which made him a great fit for Big Sky. Of average height, his thick gray hair shows only minimal signs of receding from a high forehead. Rimless rectangular glasses are almost invisible above a set of thin lips and slightly down-turned nose. He exudes the energy of a person twenty years younger and flashes an easy smile that can quickly turn into a mischievous grin around friends. The position of pastor, which can so easily consume a person's life, didn't consume his.

"I'm not a full-time pastor, even though I could be. I work 30 hours a week. I like to keep in touch with people out in the real world, so I design and build homes, teach skiing and go on mission trips to Haiti. My wife and I have a wonderful life and ministry here in Big Sky. We teach believers, reach out to unbelievers, and have a lot of Bible studies, which makes for a dynamic church."

Doug and Brad's leadership styles are vastly different. Some leaders are the aggressive out-front types leading the charge and shouting, "Follow me." Then there are those who feel more comfortable working behind the scenes. The first type is Doug; the second, Brad. When the church was between pastors, Brad was the one who procured other preachers and guided the church in its search for new leadership. Becoming the new pastor himself was never a temptation.

Doug describes himself as having a heart for "the dopers and drinkers and losers and oddballs—the people that others reject. I got a call from a lady," he continues, "who said her nephew was getting a job as a lift attendant at Big Sky. He wasn't a Christian, and neither were his parents, but she saw our ministry online and wondered if I'd drop by and visit him. I said I'd be glad to, looked up his address and knocked on his door. The door opened into a cloud of marijuana smoke. In the doorway was her nephew and in the background, three guys playing video games. I introduced myself as the pastor of Big Sky Christian Fellowship, said that his aunt had asked me to look him up and asked if I could come in. I spent the next hour playing video games. By the time I was ready to leave, all of them had agreed to come to church. After saying my good-byes, I stepped out onto the balcony and saw this tall guy weaving toward me, the all-too-familiar scent of marijuana wafting around him.

"'What are you doing here?' he half-asked and half-demanded.

"'I'm the pastor of Big Sky Christian Fellowship,' I replied, 'I've just been visiting with the guys in that apartment, and they're all coming to church this Sunday.'

"'That church stuff is bulls--t.'

"'No it isn't,' I countered, 'The God who created you loves you and sent Jesus to die on the cross for the forgiveness of your sins so that you could live with him forever.' He flipped me off and walked away.

"A few weeks later, I was at the Costco in Billings, Montana, a couple of hundred miles away, with Jeff, a good friend and church member. This tall, good-looking guy in a shirt and tie walked toward me and greeted me as if he obviously knew me.

"'Do I know you?' I responded.

"'I met you on the balcony of an apartment complex a couple of months ago. After I got back to my place, I began wondering if what you said was really true—that God really did love me and that Jesus had died for me. I figured I didn't have anything to lose by giving it a try, so I asked God to come into my heart.'

"God did," said Doug, "and since then he had left Big Sky and secured a full-time job with Costco. As we were leaving, my friend Jeff chided me.

"'What kind of a pastor are you? You lead this guy to Christ in thirty seconds and then don't even remember him!'"

Skiing Big Sky

Arriving at the drop-off area in front of Big Sky's main lodge, I moved our skis and poles to a nearby ski rack while Doug parked the car. When he returned, we shouldered our equipment and headed to the lodge, the stinging cold of a zero-degree day increasing our appreciation for the puff of warmth coming from a nearby fire pit. The glass doors of the lodge opened into a mall-like atrium lined with shops. At the far end was the locker room, and after pulling on our ski boots, we grabbed our skis and poles and headed out to the lifts. "What kind of terrain do you ski?" asked Doug as our four-person chairlift made its way uphill.

"Blues and Blacks," I responded, referring to intermediate and expert trails.

"Okay," he said, "we'll stick to the blues."

That's fine, I thought. I don't mind sticking to the easy trails on my first visit. Actually, I was relieved. My fear was that we were going to ski the death-defying double-black diamond chutes off Lone Peak, specifically the Big Couloir. Brad, Brock, and Doug had all skied this treacherously steep slope, and I had nervously prepared myself for such an invitation, even watching YouTube videos of others skiing it. I finally made up my mind that if they asked, I'd go, but I wasn't looking forward to it, so when Doug said we'd stick to the blues, I breathed a sigh of relief. Nothing to worry about, I said to myself. For the most part, we did ski the blues, then we stopped at the top of a black diamond run—moguls in the foreground, trees in the background.

"You okay with this?" Doug asked.

"Yep," I said, lying. After five years of trying, I had briefly mastered the trees and bumps a few years before but hadn't skied them since. Down we went, and once in the trees, down I went (fortunately only once). Even though he was still recovering from the complications of surgery that almost took his life, Doug negotiated the bumps and trees effortlessly.

Following a few more runs, we headed for the cafeteria and lunch. Doug saw a small group of young people who were a part of his church—two of them Brad's renters—sitting at one of the long, school-cafeteria-like tables. We joined them, and the conversation soon turned to Brad. Said one of his renters, "I asked him if we could use his outdoor hot tub and he said we could, but that he'd have to charge us extra to cover the cost of electricity."

Heads nodded in recognition. Brad's reputation for frugality was well earned.

The second renter mused aloud, "I wonder what he'd say if I told him I'd like to invite some friends over for a hot tub party."

"He wouldn't say anything at the time," replied the other, smiling. "He'd be very quiet, then awhile later, he'd just come up to you and say, 'I don't think that would be a good idea.'" Smiles of recognition with some accompanying chuckles swept over the table.

Heading back to the slopes and approaching the lift, Doug recognized a young couple from his church and invited them to join us. "Now *that's* a good example of building relationships by just doing what you love doing," I thought.

The Next Day

Saturday afternoon I joined Brad at the cross-country ski center. It'd been awhile since I'd been on "skinny skis," and thinking we'd be skiing together, I didn't like the idea of slowing him down. Then, a friend of his skied up, coming off one of the expert trails. After exchanging greetings, Brad invited me to join them.

"Go for it," I said to them, relieved. "I'm heading for the beginner terrain."

Brad invited me to meet him that evening at the town's hockey rink for the annual game between the present high school team and the veterans of past teams. Night had fallen when I drove to the lighted area just off the center of town and located the small parking lot near the announcer's booth. The below-zero temperatures resulted in a small crowd of onlookers huddling in the darkness near the protective wooden waist-high wall surrounding the lighted rink. Brad appeared a few minutes later.

"Come over here," Brad said, "I want to introduce you to someone." We made our way through the thin crowd and Brad walked up to a man in his eighties wearing a Detroit Red Wings jacket. The ease with which they talked suggested a long friendship. "Marty, I'd like you to meet my friend

Skip who's visiting from New Hampshire. Skip, this is Marty Pavelich [former four-time Red Wing All-Star player in the 1950's and a member of the Hockey Hall of Fame]."

Church on the Slopes

Lone Peak, framed by the windows up front, made a beautiful view for those of us sitting in the pews of Big Sky Chapel on Sunday morning. Unfortunately, the sun's glare all but hid the praise band and speaker on the platform below. Some spotlights would sure come in handy, I thought. Following the service, Brad and I joined the others downstairs for a potluck supper. His service on the mountain didn't give us time to linger, and people were still eating when we left.

After riding up the four-person chairlift, Brad and I hopped off at the top and skied over to a small cluster of pine trees providing the backdrop for the fourteen-foot-high cross. Grabbing a small podium hidden among the trees, Brad placed it in front of the cross, and we waited for folks to arrive. No one appeared, but at ten below zero, that wasn't surprising. Then, just about the time we were thinking of leaving, "Hi!" said a cheerful female voice, her smile appearing from the only part of her face not covered. Brightening the morning for both of us was our hostess from Olive B's. There was a quick exchange of greetings and then Brad, propelled by the morning's frigid temperatures, launched into the service. He read a scripture passage, shared a three-minute devotional and closed with prayer—a mercifully short experience. Explaining that she wanted to get in a couple of runs before heading off to work, our lone attendee bid us good-bye. Tough cookie, I thought to myself, the only thing I want to do is get into a warm lodge.

I was looking forward to attending Brad's normal twenty-minute service, but having picked the wrong day, I asked him to describe it as we drove back to the church to pick up my car.

"Well, the first thing I do after setting up the podium is to attach my iPod to the portable sound system, so music is playing when people arrive. As they ski up, I introduce myself and mingle until the service begins.

"I start the service by asking people where they're from—it's a lot of fun, and sometimes I see if we can span the country from coast to coast. I also ask how long they've been skiing Big Sky and if this is their first time at the service. After a couple of songs and a prayer, there's a short five-minute message, and then I sing a solo accompanied by my iPod. People don't expect it, but they enjoy it. We don't take a formal offering, but I've had some amazing responses when I tell folks we're self-funded, even pastors from other denominations coming up to me after the service and asking, 'can our church support you?'

"Our traditional closing is singing 'The Trees of the Fields,' an audience participation song with people clicking their ski poles together [or stomping their feet if they're snowboarders]. When the song comes to 'and all the trees of the field clap their hands,' we get a lot of attention from people on the nearby chairlift ['what are they doing?']. Then I wrap up with the doxology. I love the doxology. When I climb a mountain I don't just want to say, 'Oh what beautiful scenery,' I want to have a moment to realize that it's God who has created all of this and praise Him. When some of my summer kids go on trips without me, they take videos of themselves doing the same thing."[22]

Brad doesn't keep attendance figures, but pegs the average at between 15-20, with 10-12 in the colder months and 30-35 in March. Sometimes he meets people while skiing or riding (snowboarding) on the mountain and invites them to the service. "I ran into this elder (leader) from another church the other day, and he said, 'I'll be there' and he came with his son and it was just amazing to see them. Little things like that have been very encouraging this season. A couple of girls from Brazil showed up at our service last week.

"'We've only got 15 minutes before we have to leave and get back to work,' they said, 'but we wanted to come for at least that.'

"I invited them to our young adult Bible study," Brad said. "They need to get some spiritual support, or the party scene around here will do them in."

Doug invited us over to his house that afternoon to join a few others for cheese and crackers. Doug and Brad have become good friends over the years and share a close working relationship. "I've told him things I haven't even told my own parents," Brad once confided.

Reaching into the refrigerator, Doug was talking about the seasonal renters he had referred to Brad and subjected Brad to the kind of kidding often used by men to express their affection.

"Ah, come on, you know if I hadn't sent those guys over, you wouldn't have anyone renting from you this season," Doug said, grinning mischievously.

Brad looked down at the counter. He wasn't smiling. "That's not the way it happened," he replied, softly.

I smiled at an obviously irritated Brad, imagining similar scenes playing themselves out on frequent occasions. While close, their personalities are polar opposites, and I can easily imagine them occasionally getting on each other's nerves. One of their major differences is how they share their faith with others.

Chapter 9 | DIFFERENCES

Both Brad and Doug are committed followers of Christ who want to lead others to him, but they go about it in two entirely different ways. Part of it is their personalities. Brad is quiet and laid-back while Doug is gregarious and outspoken. Brad enjoys supporting people while Doug enjoys leading them. Brad shares his faith when the other person is receptive while Doug enjoys sharing Biblical truth regardless of people's openness, trusting that at some point it will bear fruit. Doug talks about their theological differences: "Brad and I are probably at opposite ends of the theological spectrum. I believe that the Bible is the word of God and is understandable. Brad's much more latitudinarian in that he sees the validity of a kind of New Age approach to life."

"What's 'latitudinarian' mean?" I asked.[23] "I've got three degrees and forty years in the ministry, but I haven't heard that one before."

Laughing, Doug responded, "We learned that in seminary. It means you don't believe in absolute truth but that there may be all kinds of truths, and they may be contradictory. It's the prevalent view today. It's the liberal's approach to the Bible: you can believe one thing, and I can believe another, and we don't have to talk about which one is objectively correct because truth is subjective. I'm not rigid, cold, or hateful, but I just read things and they make sense, and they're clear. Jesus says, 'I am the way and no one comes to the Father but by me,' and those things are just basic. I understood those things when I was ten years old. I'm not angry and not harsh, but there are certain philosophical and logical realities. It seems to me that Brad can hold contradictory or conflicting views simultaneously. That's a summary of my theological differences with Brad. I love the guy to death. I spent time with him yesterday, but there are times I scratch my head and wonder if he's really thinking clearly about the implications of his theological latitudinarianism."

"What's the topic that leaves you scratching your head?" I asked.

"Salvation—the doctrine of salvation by faith alone—I think that's our primary difference. He can hold different views at the same time, which I cannot. I'm not saying that I'm angry, or rigid, or a fundamentalist nut, I'm just saying either Jesus is the only way to heaven, or he's not. But Brad would say 'well, Jesus is a way to heaven, but if you're sincere, and you try hard and you confess your sins to a priest, that counts, too.' He doesn't think in theological categories, terms, postulates, or proposals; he is just a big-hearted, warm and accepting one-of-a-kind guy. I've never met anyone exactly like Brad. He's definitely the least theological person I've ever met."

"Whew!" I thought to myself, "I didn't know Brad believed those things." He doesn't.

Brad's reaction to the above words, a mixture of hurt, disappointment and uncharacteristic anger, clearly indicated something was amiss. But how could Doug, who has known and worked with Brad for so long, misunderstand him? Doug's own words provide a clue. Brad is "relational, not theological." Brad's basic beliefs are conservative, and they're Christian, but they're not something he would debate with anyone, especially someone like Doug, for whom questions about beliefs are of supreme importance and their answers clearly revealed in Scriptures. That's why in all the years they've known each other, they've never sat down and discussed Brad's beliefs. In the absence of such a discussion, Doug's take on Brad's theology comes solely from what he hears Brad saying. Inevitably, some of those conclusions will be accurate, and others not.

In painting an accurate picture of Brad, I'm indebted to Doug for describing him as "relational; not theological." It's because Brad is relational that he impacts people's lives *and* their relationships with Christ. Conversely, it's because he's "not theological" that someone like Doug can so easily misread him.

When Doug labels Brad as a "liberal" however, he's probably revealing more about himself than about Brad. No, Doug isn't a "fundamentalist nut," nor is he harsh, cold or condemning, but he's still a fundamentalist in the *best* sense of that word, one who emphasizes and strives to be true to the fundamental beliefs of the Christian faith. Furthermore, he places considerable importance on an accurate grasp of those beliefs. One can't help but sense his frustration that Brad doesn't do the same. By Doug's definition, Brad *is* a liberal, but as the word is *commonly* used, he's not. For example, how many liberals do you know who can't stop talking about Jesus?

Is Brad a "New Ager?" Not the Brad I know, but because Brad is "relational; not theological," I can easily imagine why Doug would think so. Picture this scenario: because right beliefs are so important to Doug, he questions the eternal destiny, or salvation of a person who belongs to a church embracing some unbiblical beliefs. However, because one's *relationship* with God is of supreme importance, Brad disagrees. A theological Doug then concludes that Brad is defending that church's erroneous beliefs. Doug is as intelligent as they come, and calling Brad "relational" is right on, but what Doug doesn't understand is how Brad's desire for relationships affects his response to non-believers. Doug doesn't understand it because he would never back off from proclaiming Biblical truth for fear of damaging a relationship. Right beliefs are that important. Therefore, when he sees Brad looking for points of agreement and ignoring heretical beliefs, he doesn't see Brad trying to build a relationship. Instead, by not challenging those heresies, he sees Brad agreeing with them. If this misunderstanding of someone he's known for so long says anything about Doug, it shows how focused he is on right beliefs.

Of course, it's impossible to separate a person's beliefs from his relationship with Christ. Right beliefs lead to a right relationship, and a right relationship leads to right beliefs. The strength of Doug's approach, as evidenced in the life of the young man on the balcony, is that inherent in the Gospel message is the power to change people's hearts. If there's any potential shortcoming in Doug's approach, it would be equating salvation with having the "right answers." The strength of Brad's approach is that the vast majority of those who convert to Christianity do so as the result of their relationships with other Christians. If there's any potential shortcoming, it would be the reluctance to challenge a person's erroneous beliefs *after* they've become a Christian. Fortunate is the person who has both a Doug and a Brad in their life.

Different ways of viewing the Bible also contribute to Doug's misunderstanding of Brad. Where Doug sees things in black-and-white, Brad sees the grays. Doug would say, "The Bible says it; I believe it; that settles it," while Brad would likely respond, "I, too, believe the Bible, but sometimes there's more than one way of looking at a passage." As an example of how seriously Doug takes a literal interpretation of the Bible, he once had a rebellious teenaged son on his hands. The Bible says that those who can't control their own families have no business being in charge of a church (1 Timothy 3:4). Faced with that passage, Doug resigned from a successful and growing church and moved the family to Hawaii where he worked as a contractor. He didn't return to the ministry until after things were straightened out with his son, who is now a successful attorney.

"Are there any other ways in which you'd describe Brad?" I asked Doug.

"He loves people. He loves ministry—a good-hearted, 'I'm your buddy' kind of fellow—very relational, not very theological. Brad is both unique, and in some areas, very limited. If he was a staff guy in a big church, he would be the minister of visitation or congregational care. He's not an upfront dynamic speaker, but he's really good one-on-one with people. He's built relationships with people that have spanned decades, and not all of them have been easy nuts to crack. Some of them are irreligious people, but he's somehow linked up with them and has helped them in their spiritual journeys. He is not confrontational and in that respect, he and I are quite opposite. I like to talk to someone, get to know them, introduce them to

Christ and press them for a decision. One of my gifts is evangelism. I like to bring people to Christ, particularly those from different backgrounds and nationalities—druggies, total losers, goofballs. I like to explain the Gospel to them. I like to reach out to them, befriend them, and bring them into the family of God. Brad, on the other hand, is not a proclaimer of the Gospel as much as he is a nurturer of people. He can connect with very unusual people, older and younger. He has a very broad presence. My ministry is more one of proclamation. When people are troubled or alone or thinking of suicide, they will go to Brad rather than me because Brad is a more relationally centered kind of guy.

"When God first established His church he chose a wide variety of people, all with different gifts, to build up, to encourage and to strengthen believers, and to explain the Gospel to unbelievers. Brad has been the founder of our church, and if it wasn't for Brad, I don't think we'd have a church. There were just a handful of people when I came here twelve years ago, and Brad was one of them. I just love the guy. I think he's a gem. When you read the depictions of people in the Bible, fearful or angry or whatever they were, you just smile and ask: 'how could the Lord use people like that and like us to do his work,' but he does, and he gets the glory. Brad is a great tribute to the Lord's work and a great contributor to the overall work of the Gospel. The Lord uses different kinds of nets for different kinds of fish. Brad gets close to people that I couldn't even get near because of our different personalities. He's just a good, good friend."

Chapter 10 | MOUNTAIN EMPLOYEE

When Brad started his ministry at Big Sky, he followed in the shoes of his predecessor by working in the mountain's rental shop. "The bottom line was building relationships with the employees. The structured part of my job was serving as chaplain, leading the Easter Sunrise and Christmas Eve Candlelight services and handing out bags of cookies for employees at Christmas. The focus of our ministry, however, wasn't the skiers; it was the employees. Working for Big Sky opened the door for close relationships with other employees. Assistant rental shop manager Jeff Bell was one of them.

"Back then it was neat," says Jeff. "The rental shop was a hangout for all of us who worked there. Some of us had nicknames, and after we got Brad up on a snowboard that first season, we started calling him the 'Shred Chaplain.' He had a hard time learning the sport in the beginning, but besides me, there was a snowboard instructor named Faith, who worked upstairs, and another rental shop employee named Bob and we all banded together to teach him how to ride. It took him a little while to get the hang of it, but he's been doing it ever since."

"How would you describe Brad's relationship with the other employees?" I asked Jeff.

"He's really close to everybody. He's a great friend, and if you need any help, advice, or somebody to talk to, he's always there, at least, he's always been there for me. He's a genuine guy and a great worker."

"When you think of Brad, what memories come to mind?"

"It was his first season up here. We all wear nametags and Brad's read: 'Mountain Chaplain.' Some guests were renting skis, and one of them asked, 'What does that mean? What do you do, worship the skis?' And I explained to them, 'No, he does a worship service up on the mountain every Sunday.' They got quite a kick out of that." I asked Jeff whether the guest made the comment kiddingly or mockingly. Perhaps still trying to protect his friend, he assured me it was just good-natured kidding, but that's not how Brad remembers it. "At the time," said Brad, "I was trying to decide whether to accept the full-time position that Bill Lee was offering me. That was a tough decision. I was wearing my nametag, and someone made a flippant (read "mocking" or "sarcastic") remark. Jeff Bell, who worked with me at the rental shop, came to my defense." That simple act of friendship on Jeff's part sealed Brad's decision.

"It was then that I decided to stay in Big Sky."

Brad and Jeff have been friends ever since. In 1995, Brad officiated at Jeff's wedding. "It was such a great experience," says Jeff, "that we asked him to perform my daughter's wedding in 2002." In the years since their marriage, three boys and an adopted daughter from Bulgaria have joined Jeff's family. "Brad baptized all of our boys as well as our adopted daughter. We moved away to Boise, Idaho for five years and we stayed connected the whole time. He contacts us by email or phone and does a good job of keeping in touch."

"Any other memories of Brad at Big Sky?"

He laughed, and then said, "When he first started snowboarding we would give him a hard time because he would always have such a tight schedule, and he still does. He always has everything laid out and is very organized, but we were a bunch of ski bums. Sometimes on a powder day, he'd say, 'well, I've got to do this,' or 'I've got to meet with so-and-so.' We would give him a hard time, 'Oh come on, let's just take one run,' but he'd always beg off."

"What influence has he had on your spiritual life?"

"He's helped me a lot. If I'm up at Big Sky on a Sunday, and we didn't go to our own church, my boys and I would always go to Brad's service. He's helped me make worshipping God a priority on Sundays."

Ski Patrol

Even before the 2013 merger with adjacent Moonlight Basin made Big Sky the largest ski resort in the country, its 3832 acres still made it one of the biggest. That tremendous amount of terrain mandates a large ski patrol For Big Sky, this meant a roster of two hundred: seventy-five paid and one-hundred-and-twenty-five volunteer patrollers.

With years of experience in teaching CPR and certified as an EMT, it was easy for Brad to transition from the rental shop in 2000 to join Big Sky's volunteer Ski Patrol. "The medical training opened the door, but after twelve years I just felt it was time to move on—I loved the people I met at the rental shop. Several ended up attending our services on the mountain, and the same thing happened with the ski patrol. The reaction I got from most of the patrollers was, 'Oh great; now the chaplain is a part of our team.' My presence added something new. For instance, when we had bad accidents or an unexpected death, it gave them a level of comfort to know there was someone available to take care of the victim's family. The conversations I used to have with rental shop employees were now conversations with lift operators or patrollers holed up in a lift shack waiting for the next call. I had more spiritual conversations with ski patrol because I was one of them. I'm no longer on the patrol, [his tenure lasted seven years] but to this day, I'm still invited to their end-of-the-season parties. The first time I showed up and the paid staff saw me, it wasn't, 'what are you doing here?' but rather like I belonged."

Fellow patroller "Jimbo" Humphries spoke for many during Brad's tenure on patrol when he said, "Brad does a fine job for us on Ski Patrol. His services are well attended and he's respected by the guests and everyone in the community. He's a true all-star here at Big Sky."[24]

Dean Hall, one of the female patrollers, describes an amusing encounter with Brad. "A funny thing happened with Brad at one of our banquets. Of course, all the patrollers know me and when one of them walked by me and grabbed my butt, I let out a shriek. That kind of stuff goes on all the time, and the guy who did it is a really good friend, but he continued walking as if nothing had happened and when I turned around the only person I saw was Brad. 'I didn't do it!' he exclaimed with a look of horror on his face. You should have seen him—I'll never forget it—he was just shocked. I knew he didn't do it and told him so, but I got a pretty good laugh out of it."

Big Sky's ski patrol was open to Brad not only because of his medical skills, but also because he's an expert skier/snowboarder. A testimony to his competence comes from conquering the treacherous Big Couloir—a chute off Big Sky's Lone Peak. As one experienced ski instructor told me, "I've never skied it. I make it a point of not skiing anything that could kill me."

Says Brock Short, "Getting to it is probably more dangerous than skiing it because you're on the exposed ridge of this mountain—a lot of rock. You're walking on these rocks in your skis, and part of it is side slipping. Often there are 60 mph winds that can blow you off the mountain if you're not careful, so it's pretty intimidating just getting there. Once you arrive, you're looking down a 52-degree pitch into a chute that's only 10-20 feet wide bordered by high rock walls. At the end of the chute is a big dogleg to the left and at the dogleg is a large boulder. If you fall, it's not going to shoot you out at the bottom; you're going right into that boulder. One mistake could very well be your last, so you'd better be at your best to do it. When you look down it, there's no easy way down. All you see is this chute with the high rock walls on either side. It's like you're looking down a mineshaft. I've done it with Doug and Brad, and we're doing a lot of praying when we get there.

"The three of us consider ourselves 'cautious extreme skiers,'" continues Brock. "Of course, we want to ski—that's why we're all here—but at the same time we have a duty to others to do it as safely as possible. We're trying to be an example because some who come out to ski this kind of terrain don't belong there. Doug and I are certified ski instructors, so we spend a few days a week instructing. Our focus now is on doing things safely and being prepared.

Never drink when you're skiing and wear pads on your elbows and knees in case you have to self-arrest [stop yourself after you've fallen]. We're trying to pass that along to help keep people alive."

Brad enjoyed his work in the rental shop and on ski patrol, especially for the friends he made, but he still had no contact with hundreds of employees. He wondered, "How can I pass on God's love to them? There's got to be a way, even something small." He was giving it a lot of thought, trying to come up with something. Then one day, he was talking with his friend and mentor Bill Black. As Bill recalls,

"We were just a couple of years ahead of Brad, so rather than reinventing the wheel, we'd say, 'Here's what's going on in our life and ministry and here's how it works.' Brad always took what we were going through and adapted it to fit Big Sky. For example, we put together gift bags of homemade cookies that we gave out to employees. Brad took that idea and used it in a way that got him known all around the mountain. He built it into something much bigger than we ever did." "Much bigger" is right. When the program ended with Brad's temporary departure in 2009, he was distributing over 900 bags at Christmastime. With 3-4 cookies in every bag, that was a lot of cookies coming out of the ovens of churchwomen in Montana, Louisiana, and Texas.

As people got to know Brad, both at Big Sky and during summers at Yellowstone, he received invitations to officiate at weddings, one of which was a life-changing experience for the person helping him conduct the service. Just as God used a visiting preacher's musical talents to awaken Dann Masters to the possibility of merging ministry and music, so he used Brad to bring together the discordant callings in another man's life.

Joe Beckler

While Joe Beckler grew up in the thriving metropolis of Atlanta, Georgia, his family's roots lay in the mountains of Northern Georgia. Exploring these mountains and forests as a youth, Joe quickly fell in love with the beauty of his untamed surroundings. Their allure took up a permanent residency in his heart.

After finishing seminary, Joe began his pastoral career as the Pastor of Discipleship at Dunwoody Baptist Church, a large, multi-staffed church in the northern part of Atlanta. Everything was fine on the outside. He was doing a great job, and both the church's staff and the congregation admired and respected him. On the inside, however, the ground was shifting.

"I wanted to reach those who shared my love for the outdoors. The church structure, however, was getting in the way. Outdoor folks are another culture—they are actually another people group, and just as overseas missionaries need to understand the different ethnic and tribal groups to which they're sent, we need to understand how to reach the outdoor culture, a culture whose numbers are increasing in the south. Those folks would rather be in the outdoors than sitting in church having somebody talk to them for thirty to forty-five minutes. For them, church services are downers. They'd much rather be up in the mountains. That's what was going on inside of me when I met Brad."

"So Brad was an example of someone reaching the outdoor culture?" I asked.

"Yeah, he was really cool. I knew of him through friends but didn't meet him until we were officiating together at a wedding. At the time, I was trying to figure out my next step. I was feeling that God wanted me to move on, but couldn't figure out how I could merge my love for the outdoors with reaching people for Christ. All this was going on when I met Brad. It was great. I just sat there and listened while he shared his story. We talked on the phone the next day, Sunday, and I had a strong feeling that this was my answer; this is what I should be doing with my life.

"The Monday morning after the wedding ceremony, I walked into my church office super early. I was walking around the office praying and reading Scripture and all of a sudden I was overwhelmed, literally overwhelmed. I just sat there and felt the fire in my belly. I knew this was it. I remember saying, 'This is what I'm called to do. Wow!' I felt so relieved. It was one of those defining moments. I felt called to the outdoor culture, and that was going to be my platform for sharing the Gospel. I had no idea how I would do it, but God gave me an example in Brad. Before meeting Brad, that calling didn't make sense, but when I saw what he was doing I was excited about the possibilities."

After staying another year to help his church through a change of leadership, Joe resigned from Dunwoody and moved to the resort community of Durango, Colorado. His goal? To start a new church. As he was settling in, a local minister approached him. As Joe relates it, "Without knowing anything about my connection with Brad or my yearning to reach out to the outdoor culture, he said he was leaving the area and had a ministry at Purgatory Resort (now Durango Ski Mountain). Would I want to take it over? I said, 'are you kidding me?'" Joe went on to establish a thriving and growing church with a vibrant outreach to both the college and resort community. Known as Restoration Community Church, he presently serves as its Executive Pastor.

"I think the greatest thing about Brad," Joe continues, "is that he became one with the people in that resort community. He was on Ski Patrol, and he was working in the rental shop, and he was a fireman, and he had all these natural connections and 'oh, by the way, I'm a Jesus follower, and I lead chapel services and do weddings and pastor in a ski resort community.' Those connections are important in that culture. You have to think of not pastoring a church as much as pastoring a community. Brad would show up in the ski shop, and people would say, 'we know him, and we love him because he loves us. And oh yes, he's a missionary.'"

Brad lived in Big Sky during the fall, winter, and spring. His summers, however, were quite different in Yellowstone National Park.

Chapter 11 | YELLOWSTONE

Taking advantage of college students' availability during the summer months, the Southern Baptists created their "Christian Innovator" ministry. Students would work at popular summer resorts, make friends with their coworkers, and then sponsor activities to nurture those friendships in hopes of leading them to Christ. Brad was in charge of the Yellowstone Christian Innovator Ministry, whose participants became his "kids' for the summer. For many, their connection with Brad would continue for years and even decades to come.

After hosting the Innovator's in Yellowstone for nine years, the Baptist church in Gardiner temporarily closed its doors, leaving the ministry in need of a new home. In consultation with the area's D-O-M, First Baptist Church of West Yellowstone agreed to become the new host church beginning in the summer of 2000.

The handoff wasn't a smooth one. For the next four years, Brad tried to cope. "My biggest frustration was the feeling of "not belonging." I felt more like a summer tenant than a part of the church." By the time house parents Vi and Butch Riek arrived in 2004, "Brad was pretty discouraged," says Vi.

"Brad didn't feel close to the pastor of this new church, or to its people," Vi explained. "We knew how he felt because when we arrived, the pastor didn't show up for several hours and then we didn't see him for several days. Brad was complaining that he hadn't even invited him over to his house for dinner, and so I said, 'Have you invited him over to your home?' 'Well, no' Brad replied."

West Yellowstone's pastor, Benny McCracken, may be legally blind, but lives a very active life, doing everything but driving a car. Benny mentioned to the Rieks, "Brad is up at Big Sky. The skiing's great, but he's never offered to help me or anybody from the church to ski there."

"We started talking to the people in the church," said Vi, "and found out that the problem was that they didn't know Brad and had seen him only once or twice even though their church was supposed to be sponsoring the ministry. So we told him, 'Brad if you want them to be your friends, you're going to have to do a little better and do a little differently.'" Fortunately, Brad was open to the advice. What he discovered was that both he and Benny were expecting the other to take the first step.

Brad and Benny never did have dinner together. Instead, they did something far more important. One of the people Brad voiced his frustrations to was his ministry supervisor, David Howeth, the D-O-M for Southwest Montana. David suggested a meeting in Benny's home between the three of them and drew up an agenda. He then guided the meeting as they looked at the needs of the Innovator ministry and drew up a written understanding of the host church's involvement. Caught up in numerous other summer responsibilities, Benny hadn't been aware of Brad's frustrations or the unmet needs of the Innovators. For him, the meeting was enlightening; for Brad, it was relieving. For both, it broke the ice to begin a life-long friendship.

"Benny and I learned that we both loved the outdoors; we were just enjoying it separately. When I heard he was legally blind, I couldn't imagine him hiking, backpacking and climbing mountains. How wrong I was! As soon as I found out he could do these things, I invited him on our backpack and overnight trips."

Benny happily shared with his people the agreements they reached that day and how their church could be of help. He then introduced his congregation to Brad and the Innovators. The church responded with open arms.

Butch and Vi's relationship with Brad had its amusing moments. In response to my question about their first impressions of Brad, Vi said, "Excuse me for laughing, but Brad was a southerner, and we're from Alabama. When we first got there, I told him that we didn't shake hands we hugged. I said, 'Look, Brad, if we're going to work together, you're going to have to learn how to hug people.' If you've known Brad for long, you know that he's a real germaphobe. He didn't want anybody to touch him."

"You'd shake hands with him, and he'd pull out his sanitary stuff and wash it off," added Butch.

"But after that first year," continued Vi, "we didn't have any problem—we just gave him a hug. Now it's pure habit."

"So you trained him," I replied.

"Yes, and you know it's interesting. Wherever we serve, we run into people who know Brad. We were in southern Alabama at the state office wearing our Yellowstone Christian Innovator shirts, checking to see if they needed help in their state parks. The guy behind the desk, noticing our shirts, turns to us and asked, 'do you know Brad?'"

"How would you describe Brad to someone who *doesn't* know him?" I asked the now routine question.

"He's very self-assured. You're not going to be in a conversation with him very long before he brings up Jesus. He's funny sometimes—we still tease him about the hand washing—but he's taught all of us that it's pretty important. He's very careful about everything he eats and stays away from fructose. One day we made some potato candy. You boil a potato, peel, mash it, and put powdered sugar in it. You then roll out the dough, spread it with peanut butter, make rolls out of it and cut it into little pieces. Many times when there were desserts, Brad would fuss about it, but eat it anyway. This time, when he tasted the potato candy, he couldn't get enough of it. I'd tell him, 'Brad, there's a whole lot of sugar in those,' and he'd say, 'I know, but it tastes so good!'"

Vi's next story says as much about her as it does Brad.

"The Innovator ministry always had a summer retreat about mid-summer. For several years, it was up on Beartooth Mountain. In preparing for it, I told Brad: 'Brad, I'm not sleeping on the ground.'

"And he said, 'but Miss Vi, you've got to.'

"And I replied, 'Brad, you didn't understand me. I'm not sleeping on the ground.'"

'But you'll have to because you have to go up to the mountain with us, and we all stay in tents.'

"I said, 'One more time, Brad, I'm not sleeping on the ground.' Another couple who was with us had just had a hip surgery, so it would be difficult for them, too. We had a Nissan Sentra we could sleep in. Anyway, Brad just fussed up until the time to go."

"He said: 'Miss Vi, I've got an air mattress. You can do that!' And I said, 'Brad, I'm not sleeping on the ground.'"

"When we got up there, we took the air mattress and put it in the back of the Sentra and Butch and I slept in the car. He kept talking to me about sleeping on the ground, and I said, 'Brad, I'm not sleeping on the ground. Let me explain it to you. I'm not sleeping on the ground. I can't get off the ground if I'm on the ground. If Jesus wants me to sleep on the ground when I get to heaven, I'll sleep on the ground when I get to heaven, but not 'till then.'"

Then Vi addressed Brad's frugality. "Brad was tickled pink when we went up to the Beartooths with him because it was a National Forest campground and we have a senior citizen pass that gets us in for half-price. 'We get to camp for half-price!' he exclaimed.

"He always had a hard time with us on the picnics we held for everyone during the summer, because we always spent too much money on food," said Butch.

"But those kids ate really well," added Vi, triumphantly.

On a more serious note, Butch continued with his reflections on Brad. "One of the first things that impressed me when we met Brad was that he tries to stay in touch with anyone who has ever worked for him. I thought that was phenomenal!"

"A lot of them keep in touch through Facebook," adds Vi. "Brad thinks that all of the Innovators are his children. He is so close to them that they're like his own. Quite a few of them have returned and stayed with Brad, spending a week with him. His heart is as big as the world. It's amazing. They're his kids, and his home is open to them. He's as strong a Christian as I've ever known. A few Innovators gave misleading information on their applications—they were either not involved in a church at all or were immature in their faith, but we saw them grow and change under Brad."

Butch added, "I don't know if anybody has kept any records, but for a lot of the Innovators, it was their first mission trip. After working with Brad, however, it wasn't their last. Some returned five and six times, and several are now serving as missionaries in other parts of the country. I'm not saying that Brad is the only reason or even the primary reason, but I know he made a significant contribution. Brad wouldn't tell you this, but if all his Innovators who became full-time missionaries were to get together, it'd be quite a testimony."

And how does Brad view his ministry to the Innovators?

"I've been an uncle and a big brother to these former students and performed many of their weddings," says Brad. Some have even gone on to be missionaries. For me, the Innovator ministry is the most successful thing I've ever done."

Mike and Amy Whitlark

Brad kept in touch with Michael Whitlark long after his tours as an Innovator in 1993 and 1995. Following Michael's marriage, they and their two sons and daughter have become one of Brad's closest surrogate families. "They're like a younger brother and sister to me," says Brad.

Mike tells how they became friends. "When I was in the Innovators, student housing was all spread out. My schedule was such that I only saw Brad about three times during the summer since I worked on weekends and that's when most of the group activities took place. At the end of that first summer, everybody else had left. Brad looked me up and invited me to join him on a hike up Lone Peak at Big Sky. It was a bonding experience. He's a man who's easy to talk to and very guileless. When I came back in 1995, my schedule was like everyone else's with the weekends off, and I saw a lot more of him. He's a very open person, and it doesn't take long until you feel close to him."

"One of the things about Brad," added Mike's wife Amy, "is that he has an instant rapport with people from all walks of life. People with colorful personalities immediately get along with him and respect him."

"Why do you think that is?" I asked.

"Because he seems genuinely excited to meet you," responded Mike.

"He's not judgmental," said Amy. "He has a memory for the minutest details of people's lives."

"I wonder how he does that," I mused aloud.

Amy replied, "If you've ever been in his house you'll see the walls and shelves covered with pictures and objects that evoke memories of people and events. There's a story behind everything hanging on his wall."

"Brad's very organized," continued Mike, "and I'm just the opposite. When I visited him early on, I'd take things out and put them where they didn't belong, and he'd look at me and say, 'what are you doing?' Later, he'd make a joke out of it. He's very orderly."

"Tell him the story of the spoon," Amy said with a laugh.

Mike continued: "He has a specific spoon he uses for his cereal every morning. Somebody gave it to him. Once when we were visiting, some people had been in the house before us and had mislaid his spoon. He just about went crazy looking for it when breakfast time came. He couldn't eat his cereal without that spoon."

"It was a decorative spoon," added Amy, "a little more so than the others, but that was THE spoon he ate his cereal with every morning. He was almost hysterical when he couldn't find it."

"Others have mentioned his penchant for cleanliness; did you find him that way?" I inquired.

"Oh yes," responded Mike. "You don't borrow his sleeping bag. I remember once we wanted to use his sleeping bags and crawl into them for a group picture and he thought for a moment and said, 'I consider sleeping bags a personal item.'"

Amy recalled some more recent memories.

"When we were renting from him last summer, he'd come over from Missoula to spend time with us. Our kids love him. He's like an uncle to them. He took us all on a long hike and would carry each kid on his back for hours at a time. Our kids adore him."

"One thing we learned about Brad," Mike continued, "is that whenever we visit him, we need to remind ourselves that we're on 'Brad time.' If you want to get up first thing on a winter's morning and hit the slopes you can forget it. Brad will have this to do and take care of that, and you're not going to be skiing until 11 a.m."

"Speaking of skiing," said Amy, "he loves teaching people how to ski and has all the patience in the world. Maybe that's because he learned later in life. Many people learn when they're young, but he was in his twenties."

"Another thing about Brad is that he doesn't like it if you're out of shape," Mike laughed.

"He'll make fun of you," Amy added, a smile in her voice.

"I remember our hike up to Electric Peak," said Mike. "It was an overnight trip. I was so tired I just collapsed over this rock. But Brad had told me earlier that he had taken a group of girls up to the top. I said to him, 'girls?' and he said 'yep' and so I thought if a bunch of girls could do it there's no way I wasn't going to make it.

"Brad is also very resourceful. He'll always have the latest and greatest technology. You wouldn't think working for a non-profit that he'd be up on these things, but he is. He was using Prodigy when it first came out."

Chapter 12 | ARLM

Emotional isolation, as mentioned earlier, is a common phenomenon among resort ministers, particularly those whose ministries aren't extensions of a local church. The concerns and challenges faced in the resort environment are often very different from those experienced by regular church pastors. While those leading local churches spend the greatest part of their time relating to church members—people with whom they share a common faith and a common focus, resort ministers spend much of their time relating to the unchurched in a secular environment bereft of both faith and focus. If that wasn't enough, some church pastors regard their resort colleagues with suspicion ("how do they earn their salary by skiing all day?"), envy ("wish I could do that and get paid for it"), or disparagement ("how can their work be all that important when their numbers are so small?"). Of course, the Southern Baptists didn't do themselves any favors by labeling such outreaches "Resort and *Leisure* Ministries." Taken from a heightened academic interest in the subject of leisure back in the nineteen-eighties, this synonym for kicking back and doing nothing paints a picture at complete odds with a job that taxes energy levels, challenges creative abilities and strains one's emotional resources.

Steve Hoekstra's Rocky Mountain Resort Ministry Institute was an effective response to the isolation experienced by resort clergy. Some started his three-day institute with thoughts of quitting, but within those three days decided to stay. Steve's secret? He simply gathered them together for mutual support, encouragement and training. In the early 1990's, seeking to provide on a national level what Steve was providing regionally, Southern Baptist resort ministers (there were about four hundred at the time) received an invitation to join the newly formed Association of Resort and Leisure Ministers (ARLM). With the denomination underwriting much of the cost of their triennial gatherings, attendance at ARLM conferences averaged 125-150, similar to the National Resort Minister's Conferences they replaced. In their first decade-and-a-half, ARLM was going strong.

Eric Spivey served as president of ARLM when Brad was the Vice President of Membership. I placed a call to Eric for his reflections on Brad.

"The thing I love about Brad," said Eric, "is that he has this personality that just draws people to him. It doesn't matter who it is. It could be anyone from denominational leaders to students, to people in the rental shop. Wherever he is, his laid-back attitude just draws people. He's kind, considerate, and not over-bearing. He makes you feel like you've known him a long time even though you may have just met him. He doesn't take himself too seriously, and he doesn't have a big ego. Professionally, he's on the cutting edge of finding creative ways to do resort ministry—he's the kind of person you want to spend time with, and when you do, you always learn a lot."

Another colleague Brad met through ARLM is Lynn Davis, the director of a resort ministry in Ocean City, Maryland.

"Brad's very enthusiastic about everything—especially his ministry in Big Sky. We came to know each other by just sitting and talking. Like me, he's one who would stay up late at ARLM conferences to talk about things and openly share what was going on. He's very transparent, letting you know up front where he stands on things, what disappoints him and what makes him happy. He's very friendly, which is important in a ministry among the transient. You have to be the one taking the initiative to meet people, and he's always had that kind of personality."

Speaking of Brad's personality, there are some who experience him as an extrovert, and others who know him to be an introvert—the reason? According to the Myers-Briggs Personality Inventory, which Brad took, on a continuum between introvert and extrovert, he is almost in the middle, only slightly over the line on the extrovert side. In other words, he enjoys almost equally his opportunities to relate to others as well as time spent alone. Because he's an extrovert, he enjoys staying in touch with people. Because he's an introvert, he also needs solitude, which is why it's easy for him to work alone instead of skiing with others.

"The people here in Big Sky really love you," I said to Brad during my visit in 1997. They enjoy talking to you and being around you. Why do you think that is?"

"I don't know; maybe it's just because I'm an easy person to talk to. I like to keep my responses positive. I don't like to say that I'm busy all the time. Not until you experience the loss of something do you realize that life is so precious you don't want to take anything for granted."

"What happened to make you realize that?" I asked.

"It was having memorial services for people who abuse themselves through drugs and alcohol. You wonder how they could do that in such a beautiful place as this. I try to provide a role model that would discourage them from destroying their lives in such ways. My hope is that they'd see reflected in me the fulfilling life available through a relationship with Christ."

I was curious. Statistics reveal that most people come to faith in Christ through a relationship with another Christian. I thought this was simply because an ongoing relationship affords more opportunities to talk about spiritual issues. However, when I asked Brad about the connection between relationships and sharing one's faith, his response pointed to something much deeper. "If you have a *relationship* with people, they can see you're not just preaching to them; you're living it. They can see the difference a relationship with Christ makes in your life."

Brad then went on to refer to his "life verse"—appearing on his stationery, in his emails and often heard from his lips. "For me, the scripture that helps me build relationships is, 'Jesus grew in wisdom and stature and in favor with God and men' (Luke 2:52). God came in human form in Jesus Christ so that he could experience what it's like to be human and we, in turn, would know what it's like to be totally in God's will. When we look at the life of Christ and see him growing 'in wisdom,' we're taught to be wise about the things around us. To 'grow in stature' I view as Christ being a physically fit person. I don't picture him in a chariot, or riding a horse, but always walking and doing something physical, so I equate stature with physical fitness. To grow 'in favor with God' is to grow spiritually in a relationship with God the father. To grow 'in favor with mankind' is to develop relationships that make a difference in people's lives."

It's no coincidence that Brad identifies with this verse. Its few words chronicle not only Jesus' growth; they describe his own.

Poster Boy

"By the time Brad came into ARLM," explains Lynn Davis, "people like Bill Black and I had gone through the process of being featured in mission videos and magazines, and it was fun seeing Brad's enthusiasm about it. Our attitude had become, 'Oh, do we have to do an interview again?' but those things excited Brad. It was fun watching him. He loved being on the front page of a magazine or being videotaped, etc., and he brought the old perspective back. Resort Ministries treated him like a cover boy of sorts, and he loved it. We called him the 'Poster Boy' of resort ministries because it seemed like he was always the one to get the most publicity. If anyone was to get into a missions magazine or a denominational magazine, it was going to be Brad. If there are many missionaries in the magazine, Brad's going to be the one on the cover. We were just joking about that on Facebook. With all the Easter sunrise services, Brad's was the one that appeared on a TV newscast."

Bill Black agrees. "Brad has always been our poster child. Whenever we needed to stay out of the limelight, we'd call on Brad. If we needed somebody that would be the face of Resort Ministries, Brad was it. Do you know the story about him getting President Carter to speak at one of his worship services? That's just a Brad classic."

In July of 2014, Brad traveled to California to enter a half-Ironman competition in preparation for the full one in September. There were twenty-three hundred entrants. The local paper got a head shot of one of them swimming across the lake, eyes protected by goggles, head turned sideways, left arm cocked and pointed fingers ready to enter the water.[25] Twenty-three hundred entrants to pick from, and they chose Brad.

"You're known as the Resort Ministry's 'Poster Boy' because of all the publicity you get. Does this publicity come to you, or do you seek it out? For this year's Easter sunrise service, did the TV crew just show up or did you call the station suggesting they might enjoy covering it?"

Brad laughed. "They showed up. I remember getting an email from the PR guy at Big Sky. He asked me to tell him about the service and I realized that he had never been before. I said we're having it at the top of the lift because some people will be on foot and they'll be allowed to ride down. That's when he said a TV crew from Bozeman wanted to attend."

Brad's love of publicity is undoubtedly encouraged by at least two factors: the generation he belongs to and being single. A generation ahead of Brad, Lynn Davis points to the age factor.

"Recognition makes those in my generation extremely uncomfortable. I don't enjoy doing interviews and being in front of the camera, but Brad's generation—those born in the sixties, seventies and later—love it. I had to do the state mission offering video, and they came down and did a whole day of filming. I'm not really good at telling our story, but my daughter and son-in-law just ate it up. I had *Capitol News*, a national newspaper, come in and do a story on the international kids we help and I invited my son-in-law and another kid to help—they just loved it. I answered the questions and was polite, but I think they do a better job. Because I'm the veteran, the news media wants to talk to me, but I don't like it. My son, who is in Brad's age group, just loves it and thinks it's a lot of fun. Maybe if I was exposed to such publicity when I was younger, I'd be less reticent today. If my program aired on *Capitol News*, I would never tell you—if you happened to see it that was okay, but I'd never tell you. Brad, on the other hand, would have Facebooked everybody telling them he was going to be on it."

Single

Brad's enjoyment of publicity is also a by-product of his singleness. For those who have families awaiting them at home, good news such as, "Honey—I just got a promotion!" is something one looks forward to sharing. But Brad isn't married, so who does he tell? He tells his friends, colleagues, and surrogate family. Publicity simply makes that easier.

I asked Brad why he was single.

"I don't know. It wasn't planned that way. I've gone through the emotional and hormonal changes that bring about the desire for companionship. I've also had times when it's felt great to be free. My desire to follow God's plan in physical relationships has kept me from succumbing to the type of romantic relationships common in today's world. When I was in Rome, Italy, and at Vatican City with the Montana family who invited me there for their son's ordination, I spent three weeks at the Vatican's seminary as a guest. I went to their prayers and devotionals and ended up feeling a kindred spirit. I thought, "Wow, I could easily have become a priest, perhaps this is another avenue of ministry." Then I recalled the things in the Catholic Church I don't agree with. Still, it made me ponder how my life could have been different. I met some priests who, sadly, had issues with alcohol, but there were others who were athletic and had a great sense of humor—something they didn't lose when they become priests. I identified with them, and being celibate I've been called to something similar—I'm a Baptist priest!" Brad says, laughing.

Long-time friend Mike Whitlark commented on Brad's trip to the Vatican, "It was a very important trip for Brad. Outside the Catholic Church, the single life is undervalued. There are some advantages to being single that aren't recognized by many."

"I don't know why I've remained single," Brad continues, "perhaps it's just my personality or loving my lifestyle and the freedom to come and go as I want. I've been on dates, but never a long-lasting relationship. I once had some friends who told me about a lady who had the same interests and said you have to meet her. We met, but we were so much alike it just wasn't going to work. She was from Atlanta, Georgia, but really shouldn't have been in the south—she loved backpacking and the mountains too much.

"I've been on EHarmony, and I've got an account on Christian Mingle, but I just look at it occasionally."

As satisfied as he is in being single, one cannot help but catch a note of wistfulness in Brad's next words.

"I do weddings for couples. There are some amazing couples with beautiful relationships and at times I'm drawn to that and say to myself, that's so awesome! Then there are times when I think about what my life would be like if I had a wife and children and yes, it would be different. I know people who have great lives with their families, but I see others who have great lives as single people.

"At times, I've struggled with being single in a ski area. I'm comfortable with it, but there are a lot of times when I like to get out and socialize. Unfortunately, the social atmosphere here is often incompatible with my relationship with Christ. When I enter a room, I'm always the one that brings up spiritual subjects. There are times when I wish I was just like everyone else, but I am who I am, and I can't change that. I was once in a Christian singles ministry, and I could just relax and be myself. It was very enjoyable. Of course one of the advantages in being here as long as I have is that there are a lot of folks with whom I'm comfortable enough to confide my fears and joys and frustrations."

"On the whole," I added, sensing the conversation ending, "would I be correct in saying that God has given you a fulfilling life as a single person?"

"Yes, at this point, I'm very fulfilled. Whenever I need companionship, I have any number of friends I can turn to for company and emotional support. It also helps to have others sharing my home, such as my present renters."

From this writer's perspective, if there is anyone whom God has called to the single life, it's Brad. While there's little doubt that he could be a good husband and father, it's hard to imagine what his ministry would be like if he *were* married. One thing's for sure—he wouldn't have the emotional energy and time to nurture the friendships that now fill his life. Brad without those friendships would be a very different Brad, and for many of those friends, life without Brad would be a very different life.

Chapter 13 | THE WINDS OF CHANGE

As the summer of 2008 ended, Brad could look back upon eighteen years of a personally rewarding ministry at Big Sky. A valued and much-loved member of the community, Brad was not only the resort's chaplain, he also served as a fireman, swimming instructor, mountain employee, and part of the leadership of Big Sky Christian Fellowship. Big Sky was his home; it was where he belonged, and all that was about to change.

Both Barrels to the Chest

In May of 2008, Brad received a call from his new boss, the Executive Director for the Southern Baptist Convention of Montana.

"Brad, this is Fred Hewett calling from the Convention. We haven't met yet, and I'll be in Bozeman on Wednesday the twenty-first. I'd like to get together with you over lunch if you're free that day… oh, good… you pick the place."

Brad chose Dave's Barbecue, a local favorite, and one of a chain of two hundred in the Midwest. With barn-high ceilings, knotty pine interior, chandeliers made out of deer antlers, and lacquered pine tables, the ambiance was more "old west" than Midwest. Brad was looking forward to meeting his new boss and telling him about his ministry, which he assumed was the reason for the call. It was—in part.

Fred Hewett took over as the new Executive Director of the Montana Southern Baptist Convention with an impressive background of strengthening and planting churches. In the two years he led Morningside Baptist Church in Atlanta, it grew from 50 senior adults to 165 people of all ages. In his eighth and final year of starting "Church in the Farms" in West Palm Beach, Florida, 650 people were attending Sunday morning worship and 92 people were baptized. On a larger scale, Fred served as Church Planting Coordinator for a 10-state/two-nation region stretching from Texas and Louisiana to Canada. A strong and aggressive leader, his philosophy of ministry was as powerful as it was simple: the Church exists to advance the kingdom, and this occurs when strong churches start new churches. He was just what the Montana State Convention needed at the time, and just what Brad didn't. With two entirely different personalities and approaches to ministry, conflicts between Fred and Brad were inevitable, and they weren't long in coming.

As Fred prepared for their meeting, he asked others, "So, what has Brad accomplished in the time he's been at Big Sky?" He heard, "Well, he's established this ministry at the mountain and is active in the community. He holds services in the winter for skiers and is a member of his church's leadership, helping lead their young adult Bible study and participating in their worship team. He also leads the Innovator ministry at Yellowstone during the summer months."

"Okay," Fred replied, somewhat disappointed at no mention of programs to disciple and train new believers or launch similar ministries at other mountains. "Who's his pastor? I'll give him a call and get his input."

"Well," his friend responded, "He's a member of Big Sky Christian Fellowship. It's not a Southern Baptist church." "It's not?" Fred exclaimed in surprise. This was unheard of in Fred's world. A missionary sponsored by the Southern Baptist denomination supporting and helping to lead a non-Southern Baptist church? What's going on? The picture wasn't encouraging, but Fred had faced bigger challenges. He was certain he could find a way to integrate Brad into the state convention's goal of strengthening the Southern Baptist churches of Montana. He was now *very* interested in talking to Brad, even hoping that such a conversation would produce news of heretofore unknown activities he *would* approve of. Without knowing it, Brad was already off to a bad start with his new boss. His failure to contact Fred before their upcoming meeting made it all the worse.

"I was Brad's new boss," said Fred, "and Brad had not taken the initiative to contact or interact with me at all, to say, 'Fred, you're my new boss, welcome to Montana, I'd like you to come down here to see what God's doing with my ministry here.' There was nothing."

As they sat down to lunch, Brad was looking at a man older than him by ten years, of muscular build, his fair complexion topped by a head of dark brown hair and sporting a gray mustache and chin beard. Following opening pleasantries and after placing their orders, Fred looked at Brad and asked, "so, tell me what you do... just what is it *that* you do?"

"His condescending tone took me aback," said Brad. Being the poster boy of resort ministries for almost two decades, Brad was expecting an invitation to share about his ministry, not a challenge to its value. That wasn't Fred's intent, and upon learning how he came across, he replied,

"I'm a strong personality, kind of bold and brash, but you know, to come in with a tone of condescension? I would not. I simply needed to learn from this young man who had shown no effort to contact me or invite me into his ministry. I was taking the initiative to sit down and say, 'Hey, share with me your ministry.'"

At that point, there were a couple of things that Fred didn't know about Brad. First, while Brad had come a long way in overcoming the shyness of his youth, in dealing with male authority figures, it remained. He would never take the initiative to call up his new boss—Fred or anyone else—and invite them to Big Sky. Brad viewed the role of an authority figure to reach out to him, not vice-versa. Secondly, from such authority figures, Brad had a pronounced need for affirmation and encouragement—a need that was about to go unmet.

"My job is to share the Good News of Jesus Christ with those at Big Sky in the winter and Yellowstone National Park in the summer," Brad began. He then went on to describe his life at Big Sky and the summer Innovator ministry at Yellowstone, being careful to highlight the successes and stories of those people who came to faith in Christ.

"When I heard that," said Fred, "it let me know that Brad and I had an entirely different view of what his ministry should be. We were on two different tracks."

Non-verbal communication is easy to pick up, and while Fred didn't mean to convey his disapproval, it was obvious to Brad. As Fred told me later, "I had to pick a lot of it out of him. He was not very forthcoming and I threw him many questions. The more questions I asked; the more he began to withdraw. He would not share with me, 'here's what we're doing and here's what we're all about.' After a while, I began to understand what he was doing and how he was operating, and I wanted to go back and rethink how to approach him. I had already made up my mind about one thing, however, and I needed to tell him."

"Brad," Fred started, "things are changing in Montana. I'd like you to work more closely with the state office, so from now on you'll be working as a state staff missionary. I want you to feel part of this team and come to our staff meetings. For the time being, continue with what you're presently doing and we'll be in touch."

Brad was quite satisfied with his present job description, so Fred's announcement was unsettling. He didn't know what was in store but figured worst-case scenario he'd just be adding some state responsibilities to his plate. He could handle that. As Brad saw the future, Fred's announcement appeared as a small storm cloud on the horizon. A squall—a small shower, no problem. That cloud, however, would move more quickly than expected, and be larger than he anticipated. When it hit, Brad wasn't dealing with a small squall; he was experiencing a hurricane.

A few months later, with the summer behind them and only a few leaves left on the trees, Fred called Brad to set up a second lunch meeting for October 18. This time, Brad—born and raised in Louisiana—chose a personal favorite, Café Zydeco, Bozeman's only Cajun restaurant.

For the past eighteen years, the Southern Baptists had supported Brad at Big Sky. He was raised the son of a Southern Baptist minister, served in their summer programs, graduated from one of their seminaries, and accepted their call to resort ministries. "I had been doing what I had been doing and loving it for eighteen years," Brad recalls. He earned a reputation for effectiveness and creativity and in the view of many, acquitted himself well at both Taos and Big Sky. But that's not how Fred saw it.

For Fred, "the Church" is not an individual acting alone to advance the kingdom, it's a body of believers banded together for that purpose. "I'm a strong church, bride-of-Christ man," explains Fred. "I believe that ministry belongs to the church as an expression of a local body of believers, not the church universal in which each person is a member, but as a gathered body of believers." In other words, what Brad was doing by himself was so far outside Fred's paradigm of ministry as to be irrelevant. Fred focuses on kingdom building through the church—and for Brad as a Southern Baptist Missionary that meant a Southern Baptist church.

A compassionate man, Fred's disapproval of Brad wasn't personal, but professional. To Brad, evangelism was individual—he built relationships. For Fred however, evangelism was a function of the church—he built churches—congregations of believers. Going forward, Fred wanted to employ Brad to strengthen the Southern Baptist churches of Montana. He wanted to draw him in; not cast him out. That was his intention, and Brad would eventually embrace it, but that day at Café Zydeco, the message that Brad was about to hear wasn't conciliatory: it was traumatizing.

"Brad, I've been doing a lot of thinking on how we can use your gifts and talents to strengthen our churches," Fred started. "As I mentioned the last time we met, there are going to be some changes. I have problems with the way you've been doing ministry because you're not doing it in a way that strengthens our churches. You should know that there's no longer any place in the Montana Southern Baptist Convention for you to be doing resort ministry as a single individual. We need you to start doing it through our churches—from being a lone ranger to being part of a team."

For Fred, this was not a firing; it was simply a change in Brad's job description—something people should expect with a new boss. For Brad, however, whose style of ministry had been acceptable for almost two decades, it may as well have been his termination notice.

"I was blown out of the water," Brad recalls. "I felt as if somebody had taken a shotgun and emptied both barrels into my chest."

The fact that Brad was in a state of shock helped him maintain his composure during the rest of the conversation as Fred went on to describe the state's new emphasis on strengthening churches.

As soon as a traumatized Brad walked out of the restaurant, he got on the phone. "I called a friend of mine. I was shaking uncontrollably; I was so upset and nervous. I felt like I had just been hit by a Mack truck."

After eighteen years of receiving nothing but affirmation and support from his superiors, Brad was now told that what he had been doing was wrong. In the space of a single meal, he had gone from famous to infamous, from poster boy to miscreant. Years later, Brad would look back upon these life-changing encounters with Fred with a sense of appreciation, "He was the catalyst in getting me to where I am today." At the time, however, he was stunned.

While Brad understood Fred's strategy, that knowledge provided little comfort, and in the next two weeks, he entered into the deepest depression he had ever experienced. He continued to function, but gone was the joy, the zest, and the energy that was typically Brad.

Playing the Hand You're Dealt

Fortunately, Brad belonged to a supportive church and community, not to mention his wider fellowship of resort ministers. As the shock wore off, he came to understand Fred's thinking and accept his reasoning. After a lot of prayer, Brad accepted his new role and decided to make the best of it.

Hoping to duplicate in Montana the work that Steve Hoekstra accomplished in Colorado, Montana's Southern Baptist leadership appointed Brad "Resort Ministry Strategist." It seemed like a logical idea: make use of Brad's skills to advance their focus on strengthening the local church, uniting Brad's expertise with the church's needs.

Brad re-adjusted his sights and embraced the new direction. He sat down with Steve Hoekstra and shortly after, an optimistic and upbeat Brad stated, "I've got an opportunity to influence churches in two great national parks, Yellowstone, and Glacier. I went and talked with Steve Hoekstra and after that conversation feel I can encourage pastors and people to look at the missionary opportunities in their own communities. What we've done at Big Sky and Yellowstone can be replicated in other resorts. We need to get people out of the pew and involved in the lives of others." Brad was not only on board with the state's new emphasis on building up churches—he was excited about it.

Unfortunately, the idea of duplicating Steve's accomplishments had no chance of succeeding. For a mover and shaker like Steve Hoekstra, such exploits were natural. But Brad wasn't a mover and shaker. He was, in the language of recent brain research, an "adaptor."[26] He had no "fire in the belly" for starting ministries all across the state. Rather, he had a "hearth in the heart" for the people of Big Sky. As much as Brad wanted to succeed in his new responsibilities, it wasn't going to happen. Conversations with Steve would give him Steve's ideas, Steve's experiences and Steve's encouragement, but they couldn't give him Steve's drive and Steve's aggressiveness. Steve Hoekstra was made for such challenges; Brad wasn't.

Brad encountered the same obstacle that first stopped Steve: you can't motivate pastors whose plates were already filled with other responsibilities. Most of those approached by Brad were already heavily involved in traditional forms of outreach. When Steve ran into this problem in Colorado, his response was to back off. He waited until a new pastor appeared and then provided him with the training, encouragement, and guidance necessary to establish a successful ministry. Steve, however, had the time to sit back and wait for the new pastors to appear; Brad didn't. In Colorado, there were other responsibilities to keep Steve busy, but this was Brad's *only* responsibility. The pressure was mounting. Seen as a means of invigorating their local churches, Montana wanted such outreaches *yesterday*.

To enable him to concentrate on his state duties, Brad received orders to shed his responsibilities at Big Sky and Yellowstone and turn them over to local churches. While catching him by surprise, Brad saw the request as a good thing for two reasons: first, it was encouraging to know these ministries would be continuing; and secondly, if anything were to happen with his state position, he knew he could always return to them.

While Brad was dealing with the changes at Big Sky, the concessionaire running the retail outlets at Yellowstone notified him that a downturn in the economy meant they could no longer hold jobs for his Innovators. Brad and Benny McCracken put their heads together. They decided to focus their ministry on the town instead of the park, with the church providing housing and supervision.

That summer at their annual national gathering, Southern Baptists established the Great Commission Resurgence Task Force (GCR) for the purposes of revitalizing and starting churches around the country. Their first task was to engage in an exhaustive study and present their recommendations at next year's conference. Those recommendations were to have a dramatic impact on both Brad's ministry and resort ministries nationwide.

Brad's Yellowstone Christian Innovator Ministry would include several firsts that following summer of 2009. It would be their first time working outside the park, their first time living outside the park, their first time supervised by a local church, and their first life-threatening tragedy.

Chapter 14 | "One Killed on I-90."

I-90 was clear and dry on July 31, 2009, as three brothers and a friend, all Innovators, drove back to Yellowstone from Glacier National Park. The drive was long—three-hundred-and-fifty miles— but it was worth it. Besides the brothers' reunion with relatives visiting Glacier, the sweeping vistas and cloud-covered peaks of the park stunned the North Carolina brothers and their twenty-year-old friend Steve Myerson from Alabama. Nothing in their home states could compare to such sights.

Driving the Jeep Cherokee for the last leg of the journey was Steve, described by his campus minister as "an intelligent young man; a strong believer from a strong family who has been one of our key leaders the past couple of years."

Next to Steve, Roger Fordane rode shotgun. Claiming the back seat were Roger's two brothers, Don and Jason. A University senior, Jason was an All-American track star rated thirteenth in the nation and a three-time Academic All-American with a 3.63 grade-point-average. Jason's track coach recalls him as "… A kind of goofy kid with a great sense of humor. He was one of those kids with whom you could have an adult conversation. I enjoyed him, not just as an athlete, but as a person."

The foursome had been on the road for five hours. The day was clear, hot and sunny. Soon after they started, the air conditioning broke down, so they rolled down the windows for the little relief it provided. Exhausted by the hectic weekend and drugged by the heat, Don and Jason unbuckled their seatbelts, propped their feet on each other and dozed off. They had just left Belgrade, Montana on their way to Bozeman, ten miles away. It was four in the afternoon.

Don's ear, pressed against the seat cushion, absorbed the rhythmic hum of the Jeep's tires on the smooth pavement. Suddenly the sound changed, replaced by the bone-jarring vibration of a rumble strip and then, silence. Jolted awake, Don yelled just as the Jeep continued drifting off the highway to the right, sideswiping a large highway sign. Alerted by Don's yell and the scraping sound of metal against metal, Steve instinctively jerked the wheel hard left—too hard. The Jeep's wheel hit a ridge of new asphalt, catapulting it into the air and then down on its side, the start of a corkscrewing rollover. Across two lanes, the Jeep pitched end over end and side over side, the laws of gravity and momentum holding it in its clutches with disastrous results. To those inside, the Jeep's ceiling became the floor and the floor the ceiling again, and again, and again. Don and Jason flew out of the Jeep's back windows and down onto the highway, the momentum bouncing their limp bodies along the burning hot asphalt like rag dolls.

"When I went out the window, it was like an out-of-body experience, looking down and seeing all this happening," recalls Don.

The Jeep finally came to rest on the grass in the median strip, the driver's side sinking into the soft earth and the passenger side pointing to the sky, a hunk of metal looking more like an abstract sculpture than a vehicle.

Don awoke in a fetal position, straddling the broken white center line, the hot pavement burning his cheek.

"'I've got to get out of the road,' he recalls saying to himself, 'and I tried to move, but the pain was so great I just gave up. I cried out for help, but everything was so still and quiet. I was afraid, and then I remembered the others. I looked around and saw the Jeep, smoke and steam coming out of it. It lay on the driver's side, demolished. Then the most amazing thing happened. The passenger door swung open and Roger stumbled out. I saw it all in slow motion. The hinges on that door were so bent by the collision there was no way he could have opened it by himself. I asked him about it later, but he remembered nothing.

"After seeing Roger emerge, a sense of peace came over me. He came over and appeared to be all right, just a cut under his eye. When he saw my injuries, he raised his hands into the air and then down to his head, shaking it and crying, 'Oh God, Oh God!'

"After asking how he was doing, I asked about Jason. He didn't know about Jason and went to check. As soon as he left, the pain took over. Besides my other injuries, the road rash on that hot pavement made me feel like I was on fire. 'I'm going to die,' I thought. Then I looked up into the clear blue sky, and I saw an image of Christ—an image I'll never forget. His face was bloody, and I thought, 'He's been here before,' and then a peace came over me. I knew I was going to be okay."

Roger's cuts and bruises marked him as the only one escaping without serious injury. Don suffered a compression fracture in his lower back and a dislocated knee, besides severe lacerations and abrasions—injuries requiring three operations at Deaconess Hospital in Bozeman. The seatbelts worn by Roger and Steve kept both in the car and enabled Roger to walk away almost unscathed, but Steve, the driver, wasn't so lucky. A fractured vertebra in his neck and accompanying spinal cord swelling left him temporarily paralyzed. The muscles and ligaments in his neck were torn, an artery going through his neck was pinched shut, a fractured skull left him with a concussion and two bruised lungs required a ventilator to keep him breathing. Fortunately, there wasn't any brain damage; unfortunately, the same wasn't true for Jason.

The next morning's headlines shouted, "1 Killed on I-90."

As it turned out, the newspaper had accurately reported the information provided by the Montana State Police. However, in the confusion of three accidents within a period of two hours, even state troopers can make mistakes. Because of a couple of Good Samaritans, Jason didn't die at the scene.

Traveling a few minutes behind the Jeep, a husband and wife—both physicians—were also returning from Glacier. Coming upon the accident, they pulled over to help. Discovering that Jason wasn't breathing, the husband started CPR, spelled by his wife, until ambulances—delayed by the other accidents—finally arrived. After the paramedics took over and before leaving the scene, the husband took out a piece of paper, wrote down his name and phone number, and gave it to Roger.

Jason's injuries, while not fatal, remained life threatening. He suffered a fractured pelvis, two collapsed lungs and, most seriously, brain damage from both a lack of oxygen and a severe diffuse axonal injury (DAI—damage to the nerve axons in the brain caused by a rapid acceleration or deceleration within the skull).[27] A helicopter rushed both Steve and Jason to St. Vincent's Healthcare in Billings, Montana.

Unable to reach Jason's parents, hospital officials in Billings called his older brother Travis in St. Louis. They needed to know: did he want them to keep Jason on life support?

At the hospital, surgeons placed a shunt in Jason's brain to decrease the potentially fatal brain swelling, and a catheter to monitor his intracranial pressure (ICP).

That night Travis arrived from Missouri followed by his parents from North Carolina and Steve's parents from Alabama. Prayers were going up for healing for all three and for a miracle for Jason. Medical personnel were doing everything possible but feared the worst.

News of the accident flashed around the country, indeed around the world. Family and friends, including an uncle and his congregation in Thailand, acquaintances, and even total strangers began bombarding the gates of heaven with prayers for the boys and a miracle for Jason.

"That first night the doctors told us that he was essentially gone," wrote Travis on Jason's Caring Bridge website. Their negative prognosis was justified. Some months later a neurosurgeon told the family: "We rate brain injuries on a certain scale. Of all the possibilities, Jason suffered probably the worst."

Jason lay in the hospital bed, a clear plastic breathing mask over his nose and wires and tubes protruding from underneath the sheets. His small cubicle in the ICU hummed with the whish-clicking of the life-sustaining ventilator and the beeping of monitors whose digital displays flashed numbers both reassuring and frightening.

Returning home from West Yellowstone, Brad noticed his answering machine blinking. Dialing the number, he talked with the chaplain at Deaconess Hospital in Bozeman. The news left him stunned.

"I was very distraught. The first thing I did was to head for the chapel to pray. I needed to calm my nerves."

A calmed but still shaken Brad drove to the hospital in Bozeman. He was relieved to see Roger in such good condition, but Don was still in the operating room. With Don inaccessible and Roger okay, Brad headed for Billings. On the way, he called Doug, Brock and others, telling them what happened and asking them to get people praying. Steve and Jason were both in surgery when Brad arrived but they soon ended up in the ICU. Brad traveled between their two bedsides, praying for each and providing what comfort he could to the rapidly growing collection of family and friends.

Both the Fordane and Myerson families commenced their respective vigils, alternating between bedside and waiting room, with occasional trips to the chapel and cafeteria and, for the Fordanes, frequent trips to Billings to visit Don. Steve's condition was serious (both he and Jason were listed in critical condition) and his paralysis scary, but he was likely to survive. Jason's prognosis was not so positive.

"They told us that each brain injury is different," said Don. "No two are alike, so it was just a matter of waiting to see what happened."

While Brad invested himself in bringing comfort and support to the boys and their families, others mobilized to support Brad. As reported by friend and mentor Bill Black, "When the accident occurred, I called Jeff Wagner at the North American Mission Board (NAMB), and I said either you're going, or I'm going, and you're paying for it, but someone is going to be with Brad right now. Jeff couldn't go, so I went there for a week or so. Brad was still sitting in the ICU, and his summer missionaries were at a total loss, so I got one of our state employees, and we worked with Brad's staff to cover the work in West Yellowstone. I also took charge of Brad a little bit: 'you need to sleep right now, and you need to eat this right now,' which is the same thing that Eric Spivey did for me when we had a death in our own ministry. At that point Brad earned high honors with me on several fronts: the way in which he ministered to the victims, sought God's guidance, cared for the families, facilitated God's healing, handled his own grief, and accepted the support offered by me and others."

Jason soon supplied a reason for hope. Two days after the accident, although still comatose, he responded to voice commands, at least occasionally. By the fourth day, his lungs had improved enough so that they could remove his chest tube. The next day, both his intracranial pressure and blood pressure returned to normal. Six days after the accident, the neurosurgeon reported small but encouraging increases in his responsiveness and visual tracking.

The Glasgow Coma Scale is a medical measurement of a person's level of consciousness. Normal is fifteen. Ten days after the accident, Jason was hovering between a four and a five.

"Brain injuries have a life of their own," one of Jason's nurses explained to the family, "no one knows with certainty what the outcome will be."

On day twelve, family and friends gathered in Jason's room for a time of worship and prayer—think church in a hospital room. "We were praying for his eyes to open," wrote Travis. "There was a real sense of God's presence. Then Jason opened both eyes and began to move his lips! I bent down, and I know he was trying to tell me he loved me."

A month after the accident, Roger reached into his pants pocket to find the slip of paper bearing the name and phone number of the physician who administered CPR to Jason at the scene of the accident. He called.

"All the time thinking that Jason had died, when he heard that he was alive he started weeping," said Don. He couldn't believe everyone survived. That was a pretty cool miracle." A miracle indeed—the mortality rate for severe DAI's like Jason's is 50%.[28]

On day thirty-nine, three days after Jason's transfer to a rehab hospital in his hometown of Raleigh, the family posted, "Jason is in a 'persistent vegetative state' (PVS)—slightly better than a coma. He appears to be awake but is not yet conscious. We were told awakening from a coma normally happens in tiny baby steps, and the PVS could be as far as he goes."

The days that followed were a mixture of discouraging complications and encouraging improvements. Jason developed shingles, began biting his tongue and losing weight in spite of a high caloric intake. On the positive side, his responsiveness increased, his eyes opened, and he was tracking and sometimes responding to verbal commands.

Jason is "minimally conscious," Roger posted on their Caring Bridge web site two months after the accident. Encouraged by this hopeful development, family and friends attacked Jason's injuries with renewed vigor. As further shared on Caring Bridge, "We began assaulting Jason's senses daily—strong scents to smell, colored flashcards to look at, describing pictures to him, talking out math problems, rubbing weird things on his skin, even putting flavored drops in his mouth. Three times a day we do 'command response' tests that target all different areas of his body. We log everything, looking for patterns in how he responds."

Jason's level of consciousness, however minimal, was cause for great joy. Of those suffering from a severe DAI, over ninety percent never regain consciousness.[29]

The efforts and prayers of family and friends finally paid off. On day sixty-nine, posted on their web site were the words, "JASON IS FOLLOWING COMMANDS FOR US!"

"Seeing this gave me the chills," said Roger, "and the nurses in the room said the hair literally rose on their arms."

Jason's breathing improved and they removed the tracheostomy tube. On day ninety-three, Steve walked into his room and was shocked to hear Jason say, "Hi, Steve." It would be several weeks before he spoke again, but on day one-hundred-and-twenty-two, November 29, Jason went home. Back to a familiar environment and surrounded by a lot of sensory stimulation, his level of alertness increased dramatically. Seventeen days after coming home, he began using his index finger to answer "yes" and "no."

Then, on December 25 came the "Christmas miracle." As described by the family, "Jason began smiling for long periods of time and broke out laughing at some familiar and humorous video clips. The most amazing and confirming part of this miracle was that the boys observed Jason laughing at the parts he used to laugh at. This is such a huge breakthrough because up until now Jason has not displayed any emotion besides looking sad or in pain. We felt for the first time that Jason was truly present instead of just seeing the shell of his body."

After watching several videos of Jason on YouTube, I spoke with Don, now five years after the accident.

"I saw a video of Jason doing paintings with his feet. What are his present limitations?"

"He's a spastic quadriplegic,"[30] replied Don. "One doctor said it's like the body wants to go back into the fetal position. Cognitively, he's pretty much all there. His way of communicating is with his foot, so if you have an alphabet board, he can spell out a sentence. When I discovered that Jason could finally communicate, I asked him if he could remember the accident. He shook his leg free for us, and I said 'could you spell out what you remember?' He spelled out 'I saw nails, I saw Jesus; it was awesome.'"

Chapter 15 | MISSOULA

Shrinking state resources for resort ministries and word of their impending defunding demoralized Southern Baptist resort ministers around the country. From a normal attendance at the ARLM national conferences of 125-150, in 2009 at Branson, Missouri, those figures fell to 65.

What was happening to resort ministries in 2009 had its origin almost twenty years prior. Beginning in the early 1990's, financial pressures hit most church denominations. Income was no longer keeping up with needs. Liberal denominations were dealing with two causes: rapidly declining memberships and reduced giving by those who remained. Conservatives viewed this as the inevitable consequences of exchanging the Gospel for a more socially acceptable agenda. A few years after the turn of the century, however, the unthinkable happened. Membership in the Southern Baptist Convention, a denomination that *had* remained true to the Gospel and Biblical values, began declining. While nowhere near the double-digit losses of their liberal neighbors, any loss by Southern Baptists was unacceptable. Their response? Start new churches. As one person amusingly put it, "it's easier to make new babies than to raise the dead." State staffs around the country were already cutting back due to decreased financial support, and where possible, some states were directing savings toward church planting.

In the summer of 2010, the Great Commission Resurgence Task Force reported back with their recommendations. The Southern Baptist's national gathering endorsed all of them, sending them to the agencies affected for their approval and comments. The longest list of recommendations appeared before the trustees of the North American Mission Board (NAMB). All were approved. The dye was cast. To free up monies for planting new churches, all resort ministries sponsored by the Southern Baptist's NAMB would be defunded by the end of 2011. Attendance at ARLM's 2011 conference in Las Vegas dropped to forty-five. In 2013, their last conference at Keystone, Colorado, would draw only thirty.

I was present when Brad received the Resort Minister of the Year award at Branson in 2009, and thought it strange that he went forward, accepted it, and returned to his seat without cracking a smile or saying a word. I hadn't yet started interviewing him and realized only later that the recent accident involving his Innovators and word of the likely defunding of resort ministries had left his secure and predictable world in chaos. It was about to get worse. In November of 2009, denominational officials summoned him to a special meeting at their state headquarters in Billings. "We'd like you to move from Big Sky to Missoula. There's room in our building for you to share an office. Missoula's a much better location for your travels around the state and your presence in the office will integrate you more closely onto our state staff team."

The thought of leaving his home of almost twenty years was "another kick in the chest," recalls Brad. He was tempted to resist, and declare, "Enough!" "I could have been stubborn and refused, but I wanted to be a team player, so I went along with it."

A team player he was, but once again, a very depressed one. The grief he was dealing with was the same as losing a loved one, but in this case, it wasn't just one person, it was an entire community, which over the past eighteen years had become his family.

"I struggled. I really, really struggled with leaving," recalls Brad. "What kept me calm was just praying for the people who were making the decisions. Prayer helped me to relax and go with the flow. It took me a couple of months to get over the depression. I had never been that depressed before; I never knew what it felt like. Now I can identify with someone who's depressed. I'm not so quick to simply say 'oh, you'll get over it.'"

Brad's move from Big Sky also upset his neighbors.

"He was very much a part of the community," says Dean Hall, "and I think it was devastating when he was transferred. He also taught swimming at Orphis School, and people lost out when he left. He was such a positive influence; very levelheaded and respected by everyone. People missed him. I don't know if his superiors realized what a help he was. Many of the kids at Big Sky are there to party—you won't get them into church, but Brad was a steadying influence on them. I know he made a difference."

Handoff

With the mountain ready to open for skiing, it was time to pass the baton. "I was planning on asking the church to take over my ministry," explained Brad, "but before I could do that, Brock Short came to me. He and his wife Jane came up with the idea of creating a Big Sky Chaplain's Association."

"Brad wanted to keep the ministry going," explains Brock, "so my wife and I offered to make that happen. We formed the Chaplain's Association consisting of myself, my wife Jane, Brad, Taylor Kissel and Doug Timm, our senior minister. While I'm the chairman, Brad and Doug provide the guidance, and that's worked very well."

Still wanting to offer church services to their guests, the mountain agreed to provide lift tickets for the chaplains and Brad offered to come up once a month—no small commitment considering it was a three-and-a-half-hour drive.

As noted by Lynn Davis, "He exhibited extreme faithfulness in making his monthly trip to Big Sky. Don't forget; he was the denominational poster boy before feeling like an outcast. He went from the pinnacle to the basement; it was very difficult."

Brock earned the gratitude of many by overseeing the services for the next two winters, yet it wasn't the same. "Almost every time I covered the service for Brad, people always asked about him," reports Brock. "Returning guests would say, 'well, we're glad you're here, Brock, but where's Brad?' He has endeared himself to so many people. As you get to know him, you realize he is a very special person, and I have come to know him quite well over the years. He has come to stay with me in Nashville, and we have run the Country Music Marathon together. We have hiked, and we have sailed together. The best way I can explain Brad is to say, 'He's the real deal.' A lot of us try. I am a man of the people, and I have had my shares of difficulties. I am also a lawyer, and I have had my share of tough business negotiations. But Brad is a just a different person than anyone you will ever meet. He is just so Christ-like, so genuine and good-hearted. There is no meanness in him at all, and that is unusual. None of us is perfect, but Brad just touches you as more settled than most, the "real deal" is how I can best describe him. His kindness runs deep, and it's genuine. He believes deeply—and feels it—and it's contagious."

While far from pleasant, Brad's move to Missoula had its redemptive aspects. "I made connections with people that I'm still in touch with today," he says. "It was awesome."

In an email in the fall of 2013, Brad refers to one of them. "I just had a GREAT day yesterday with one of the young men that I am currently mentoring. His name is James Farmer. We met in October of 2010 when I was in Missoula, a meeting we regard as a 'divine appointment.' I would not have met him if I had not moved—evidence that God's hand is in everything.

"James has a dynamic story of his own—a twenty-four-year-old who had just overcome a drug addiction when we met. God has done some amazing things in his life and since we began the mentoring he has matured greatly in his relationship with the Lord."

James Farmer

"You met Brad when he moved to Missoula?" I asked James.

"It was kind of crazy how we met," he responded. "My mom met Brad the year before at a church in Manhattan, Montana. Discovering that he was into outdoor stuff, and knowing that was something I really liked, she said, 'I wish you could meet my son.' That was it. Because Brad was still in Big Sky, there was no 'here is his phone number, give him a call.' She just wanted us to meet.

"God made it happen. It was crazy. We met at a Bible study in Missoula. It was the first church I had gone to on my own. Before that, I had gone my own way and walked down some paths that weren't very productive. I was just coming back to God and found this church through a friend. Brad was in one of the Bible studies and we kind of hit it off."

"Did you know who he was when you first met?"

"No, I didn't. Awhile later, I was telling my mom about him. She was surprised and told me about meeting him at that church in Manhattan."

"How has Brad helped you?"

"He's a great example for me. Brad is one of the most outwardly focused people I know, and it was very important to him that I have that relationship with God. I was a person who was always questioning—I don't take things at face value, and very few pastors or Christians allow me to question things before becoming defensive and snapping at me. But Brad listened to me and even encouraged me to ask questions."

"Any other ways he helped?"

"The biggest thing for me was that he went about doing what he loved to do while all the time trying to build relationships. He was not one kind of person in church and another kind of person when he was out hiking or swimming. He was all the time doing what he loved to do but at the same time doing what was important to him, and that was building relationships."

"What were some of the things you did together?"

"He taught me how to swim—I wasn't a swimmer before that, and we'd run together. I was into running before we met. We also did yoga. I had been taking classes and said, 'Okay, you taught me how to swim, so I'm going to teach you one of my sports.' He's been doing it ever since and loves it."

"Any stories that come to your mind about Brad?"

"I lived with these guys when I was in Missoula—four of us in a two-bedroom apartment. Those guys were far from clean; our place was a mess and our bathroom absolutely disgusting. If you know Brad, you know he's a germaphobe. One day he shows up with a pair of gloves and cleaning equipment and cleans our entire bathroom, it must have taken him two hours. Wouldn't take anything for it. That's just the kind of person he is."

"The most important thing you've picked up from Brad?"

"Life's all about relationships. Most importantly, it's about a relationship with Christ."

Chapter 16 | RELEASED

Unfortunately, Brad did not do as well motivating churches as he did inspiring individuals. Attempts to start new outreaches went nowhere, stymied by overcommitted pastors and congregations already involved in other programs. Providing ample footage for Brad's video camera, however, were several churches already active in campgrounds, ski resorts, state fairs, parades, and community festivals. If he couldn't motivate those who weren't interested, at least he could encourage and recognize those who were.

On May 17, 2011, Fred called Brad and asked him to come to his office in Billings. When Brad arrived, Fred handed him a letter from NAMB.

"Your position won't be terminated immediately," said Fred, "but long-term, you need to be looking for a new job." Fred went on to mention a couple of job avenues Brad might explore, both of which involved giving up resort ministries and moving out of the area.

The letter cited a termination date of December 31.

Expecting to hear an account of further discouragement and depression, I asked Brad how he felt when he read the letter. His response took me by surprise.

"It was different this time. I didn't feel like the bottom had dropped out or that I'd been shot with a shotgun. You know how I felt? I felt released."

"Really?" I exclaimed, not quite believing my ears.

"Yes. I realized I had been finding my security in the financial support and the sense of belonging I received as a Southern Baptist missionary. Now, none of that—the feeling of belonging or the financial support—was important. I went through those past two years as a team player because that's where my security was. However, when he handed me that letter and said that it was all ending, I thought, 'Great! It's finally happened. Nothing I can do about it, so let it be. I am done playing this game.'"

"What changed between those first two meetings with Fred and this one almost three years later?"

"I re-evaluated my calling. I'm definitely called to be a missionary. That won't change just because I've lost my funding. As I see it now, man's decision called me away from Big Sky and moved me to Missoula. That was man's choice, but God used it for his glory, and I absolutely enjoyed it. It took me almost two-and-a-half years to realize where my heart is. I now feel much more secure in following God's leading and embracing my missionary calling."

"So the May 17th letter released you from what you had to do and let you follow your heart and God's calling?"

"I've never thought of it like that before, but that's exactly how I felt. People I've known for years wanted to come alongside me. 'We want to support you after the funding dries up,' they'd say. This meant more to me than a termination letter. It meant a lot to hear those kinds of things and to receive the support of the state D-O-Ms who were with me through this whole thing. They said to go back to Big Sky and raise my own support.

Brad and his team of supporters incorporated as Big Sky Resort Ministries (BSRM), receiving their non-profit status from the IRS in April of 2013. As of this writing, BSRM is providing about $500/month or almost 20% of Brad's total support.

"For two-and-a-half years, I did what man wanted me to do. Now I could do what God wanted me to do. It felt great."

Homecoming

"When I returned in September," continued Brad, "the Big Sky community welcomed me with open arms. They had always embraced me, supported my ministry, loved me and missed me when I was gone."

Brad received several offers of employment, but he returned to the group he had grown close to, with their ambulances and glistening red fire trucks. Unfortunately, it didn't last long. When training for 911 calls was added to the firefighting and medical training, the time demands jeopardized Brad's ministry. At the end of the ski season, he resigned, agreed to continue as the department chaplain, and went looking for another job.

"How about driving bus for us?" asked Ron Downer, the Bus Supervisor for Big Sky School District. The invitation was on the table when Brad first returned, but he dismissed it for the Fire Department. Now, however, it just might work. If only he could get the needed hours, the "no evenings and no weekends" schedule would fit beautifully with his ministry. Mastering an inch-thick manual and passing the written exam, Brad borrowed a school bus to finish his commercial driver's license exam and became Big Sky's newest school bus driver. Adding two or three nights a week of custodial work (the hours were flexible) gave him the hours qualifying him for medical benefits as well as supplying the needed income.

"Mr. Downer wants me to put in more hours," Brad said at the time, "but I told him, 'I need more time in the evenings for ministry. I don't want to spend all my time in the school.' My evenings would all be busy if I took on extra hours. Working more hours isn't the point. The point is to have enough to support myself until I see where God is leading me ministry-wise."

The adjustments Brad was making to stay in Big Sky didn't go unnoticed by the local population.

"People wanted to know how I was making it when the Southern Baptist Convention terminated my support, and when they found out that I was working as a bus driver and janitor to stay in Big Sky, they were impressed."

Moonlight Basin

With only half the acreage, Moonlight Basin, adjacent to Big Sky, has long been the little sister of the two resorts. Sharing the same mountain, Moonlight skies the north side of Lone Mountain and Big Sky, the south. When Brad first moved to Missoula, Brock Short, who also works as a part-time ski instructor at Moonlight, started lobbying Moonlight's management. The goal? To hold services in a setting similar to Big Sky's. After Brad returned from Missoula, the management agreed and on July 19, 2013, a cross—similar to the one at Big Sky—appeared on the slopes of Moonlight Basin. With crosses identifying worship areas at both Big Sky and Moonlight, Brad points out a hidden blessing in being at Big Sky.

"Privately-owned resorts have their advantages. At Whitefish Mountain, the local American Legion had put up a statue of Jesus as a memorial to the veterans who served in the war. Now a group is trying to get it removed because it's on Forest Service land. With things like that happening in other parts of the country, I really appreciate being at Big Sky. Here, that cross may create controversy, but the support of resort management and second-home owners ensure that it won't go anywhere."

Soon after giving their okay for the services, in October of 2013, Big Sky purchased Moonlight Basin, the combined 5750 skiable acres now making it the largest ski resort in the country.

Summers

Upon his return to Big Sky, Brad initially worked with the summer Innovators in West Yellowstone as a consultant. Following the nationwide defunding of Innovator ministries in 2103, his summers have changed.

"Summers now consist of co-leading the church's 20's Bible Study group that's held in my home and leading at least two backpacking trips in the Big Sky/Yellowstone National Park area. Between May and October, I'll have seven to twelve weddings and am continuing to teach swimming. I'm also under contract with the Big Sky Community Corporation for both group and private lessons from June through August. This summer [2016], I plan to do three triathlon events: one Olympic distance, and two half-Ironman's. Such a mixture of ministry and athletic events has been the norm since 2014.

"Bradford, you're an Ironman."

Outside of "Christian" and "relational," if there's any other word that describes Brad, it's "athletic." A colleague, Eric Spivey, mentioned this attribute when I asked him for his reflections on Brad.

"Brad's a unique man," says Spivey. "People who have been to Yellowstone always speak very highly of him including some of his former house parents whom I talked with—he's just so relational. He also pushes himself physically. Every time we talk he's pushing himself—running, biking and cross-country skiing."

The importance of sports in Brad's life is obvious in two emails he sent to me in the summer of 2013:

"Well, I've got an hour's drive to Hebgen Lake for a Laser Dinghy Sailboat Regatta starting at 1 p.m. Hope I can remember what I learned last weekend about my Sailboat Clock!!

"Sorry for the delay in my reply. I'm teaching swimming lessons this week in the mornings till about 1 p.m. This weekend is my two-wedding weekend. Then, I'm off to Whistler, Canada with two friends from Bozeman, who are competing in the Ironman competition where I will be a volunteer at the race. I'll be on the road from Aug. 21-27th, then I'll be back to my school schedule on Aug. 29th with after-school swim lessons and part-time custodial work three nights a week. I've had an amazing summer and am looking forward to more adventures in ministry!"

Brad accompanied two friends to Whistler because one of them was going through some marital challenges. As hoped, Brad was able to help his friend during the trip, but it wasn't only his friend who benefited from their time together.

"They posted me at the finish line," said Brad of the Ironman competition, "and when people came across, I'd help them with anything they needed: water, the massage table, or perhaps medical help. One guy said: 'come over here, I want to have my picture taken with you—you're the first person to congratulate me after I crossed the finish line.'" Brad went on to explain an unusual tradition at Ironman competitions: "When you come across the finish line, they don't just announce your time over the loudspeakers. Instead, you'll hear the pronouncement: 'John, you are an Ironman!'"

Not surprisingly for those who know Brad, the "Ironman bug" bit him, too. Shortly after his return, he started training for the competition to be held the next year at Lake Tahoe. As race day approached, to the disappointment of its 1754 entrants, a nearby forest fire filled the air with so much smoke that race organizers were forced into a last-minute cancellation. While a major letdown, Brad wasn't about to give up. He set his eyes on the next year's *Ironman Lake Tahoe 2015* and started his training six months in advance. Curious, I looked up the suggested training regimen for first-timers. It was grueling. By the time they compete, first-time Ironman competitors are running 18 miles, biking 100 miles and swimming 2.5 miles a week for an event described by Ironman founder John Collins as, "Swim 2.4 miles, bike 112 miles, run 26.2 miles and BRAG FOR THE REST OF YOUR LIFE."

Brad explained his routine: "I couldn't always follow the suggested schedule because I didn't have a nearby swimming pool, so I usually went to Bozeman once a week for a long swim. Once Lake Levinsky's ice broke, and it warmed to 50 degrees [still crazy cold], I'd ride my bike up to Big Sky *Mountain* Village from the Big Sky *Meadow* Village [approximately a 1,000-foot gain in elevation] carrying my wetsuit in a small backpack. Once I completed the 6-mile ride to the lake, I would don my wetsuit and neoprene swim cap [much warmer than a traditional swim cap] and try to swim a mile in this small cold-water lake, giving me at least two swims per week. In a typical week, I felt great if I could swim, bike and run at least twice, providing six workouts per week for the six to seven months before race day."

On September 20, 2015, following months of training and after sixteen-and-a-half grueling hours, Brad crossed the finish line to the longed-for words from the loudspeaker, "Bradford, you are an Ironman!"

As Ironman competitions go, Lake Tahoe gained a short, but well-deserved reputation as one of the most difficult in North America. Due to the exceptionally cold water for swimming and the demanding six-thousand-foot climb for biking, the inaugural race in 2013 saw an unacceptable 20% DNF (Did Not Finish) rate among entrants. With word spreading and 2014's race canceled because of the smoke, the 2015 race was void of the usual professional entrants and down over three hundred registrants from 2014. Race organizers had enough. Following 2015's race, instead of announcing next year's schedule, they announced the cancellation of all future competitions at Lake Tahoe.

Brad refers to his race time (he finished 941st out of a field of 1423) as "not great." However, having completed a competition that over 450 dedicated and highly trained participants couldn't even finish, not only is his time an accomplishment, but for a 54-year-old man, it IS "great."

Community Chaplain

A few months after visiting Brad at Big Sky in January of 2013, Doug Timm resigned, leaving a pastoral vacancy at BSCF. Brad was among those serving on the search committee.

Hundreds of miles away, Rev. Brian Van Eps, serving as Pastor of Adult Discipleship for a 3000-member church, was in a conversation with his Senior Pastor and mentor. "Well," said the Senior Pastor, "have you decided yet what you want to be when you grow up? People love you here, and you're doing a great job, but I feel it's time for you to move on and take over a church of your own somewhere."

"It was amazing," said Brian. "He didn't know it, but my wife and I were having the same conversation at home." Soon after, a friend of theirs called. "There's this little chapel up at Big Sky, and they're looking for a pastor. You ought to check it out—I think you'd be a great fit." Brian and his wife Lori just looked at each other. She grew up on a farm 45 minutes from Big Sky, and her parents and extended family were still there. Also, with their engagement taking place in the Soldier's Chapel at Big Sky, the town had a special place in both their hearts. Following talks and a Skype-enabled interview with the search committee, in January of 2015, Brian accepted the position. The Van Eps moved to Big Sky. Within a year, the church's exploding attendance forced BSCF to construct a building across the street for their growing Sunday school program. As of this writing, the chapel itself is thinking of enlarging the building to accommodate their growing numbers.

After hearing Doug Timm's assessment, I was curious how BSCF's new pastor viewed Brad and called Brian to ask him.

"Brad is the heart and soul of a lot of things that go on in Big Sky. He drives the bus for the school and does some janitorial work. It's not the most glamorous job, but Brad loves driving the bus because he loves the kids. He's able to minister to them and their families and views all of this as part of his mission to the community."

When Brad accepted the position at Big Sky, in July of 1990, it's unlikely he expected to spend the rest of his ministry at a destination ski resort tucked into the Gallatin Range of the Rocky Mountains. However, by all appearances, this is *exactly* what he's doing. After some serious soul-searching following his temporary move to Missoula, Brad concluded that God had called him to the community of Big Sky. In the same way that a couple may suddenly realize their friendship is heading for the altar, Brad came to realize that his heart was wedded to the people of Big Sky. A destination resort with a population of 2300 and located forty miles away from the nearest city, Big Sky residents share a love for the outdoor activities offered in their scenic wonderland. Most ministers are called to a church, but Brad's call is significantly different: he's called to a community.

"When I think of Brad," said Brian, "I'm reminded of Jesus' parable of the talents. Those who had invested what they received heard the words, 'well done, good and faithful servant. You have been faithful over a little; I will set you over much'(Matthew 25:14-30). One doesn't have to look far to see the evidence of Brad's faithfulness at Big Sky."

Harbor

Candice Brownmiller spent several seasons crewing on sailboats and dolphin watching boats. During that time, Harbour Town was by far her favorite port. The amenities it offered, the friends she had made and its quaint beauty combined to give her feelings of joyful anticipation whenever she stepped off the ramp and onto the pier. In searching for a name for her new son, it just made sense. It would be different, but it was right. To avoid difficulties arising from its unique spelling, she dropped the "u." Her son would forever be known as "Harbor."

Everybody loved the boy with the different name. In a community catering to the adventurous and athlete-prone, he shined. He started skiing at the ripe old age of two, with many other sports exerting their magnetic pull on his over-abundance of energy.

A cold is probably the most frequent illness children experience, so Candice wasn't that worried when her five-year-old son arrived home from school with the sniffles on the first Monday of January in 2015. She made a mental inventory of the cold medicines available in their home in case it got worse. Harbor went off to hockey practice and returned, feeling a little bit worse than when he left. The sniffles soon turned into a sore throat and then a fever set in. "He was a healthy as a horse then just got a bad cold," she explains. When the cold didn't let up, and his breathing became labored, she sought medical help.

"Yep," said the doctor, "he's got croup, and there's nothing we can do." The diagnosis was accurate and for the vast majority of sufferers, the disease would have run its course without incident. Unfortunately, Harbor wasn't among the vast majority.

With a gasp, Harbor took his last breath at 1:30 on Friday morning. In a panic, Candice called 911. Paramedics arrived and got him breathing again, but it was too late. Tests performed later at the hospital revealed that the lack of oxygen had left him brain dead.

"While we were at the hospital and unsure of the prognosis, we would call Brad, and he would pray for everyone over the phone," said Candice, choking back tears. "That Sunday Brad turned his regular service on the mountain into a huge prayer service for Harbor. The hospital had a chaplain, and he would come in and pray with us, but it wasn't the same. We would call Brad, and we'd put the speaker next to Harbor's chest so he could hear him pray."

"They kept Harbor alive for several days while they prepped him for organ transplants. After he passed away that following Friday, we had a Celebration of Life for him. Brad was among those who spoke, and he also led a prayer."

Candice then told of Big Sky's outpouring of love and generosity. The community not only raised enough money to cover Harbor's hospital and funeral expenses, but they also provided Candice with an income for the time she had to take off work. After all the bills were paid, Candice talked to the man in charge of the "Neighbors Helping Neighbors" account, a non-profit entity set up to help people like Candice. "It's a Christian organization," she pointed out. "I spoke to him, and he backed me in using the money for travel. I attended a couple of yoga retreats in India and visited some friends in Hawaii."

As we talked about Brad, I mentioned his recent Ironman competition. "We're so proud of him," Candice replied. Our call was ending when she asked, "Is there anything else you'd like to know?" I responded with my routine question: "How would you describe Brad to someone who doesn't know him?" From Candice however, I received an answer unlike any other.

"He's the heart and soul of our community; he embraces everyone."

Photographs

A young Brad Lartigue with former president and Mrs. Jimmy Carter following the service at Taos in December of 1986. Pres. Carter delivered the message and Rosalynn read the scripture.

Brad in his lifeguard attire in 1990. After two near-drownings in his college years, Brad developed a passion for the sport, goin on to become a certified Lifeguard and swimming instructor.

A family picture of Brad's parents and siblings in 2015 at the family home in Louisiana. They remain a close family, with weekly and monthly calls keeping them connected.

Yellowstone Christian Innovator Ministry 2005

The Big Sky Fire Department in 2009, shortly before Brad left and moved to Missoula. As were all firefighters, Brad was ceretified as both an EMT and a Firefighter. In 2005, he was honored as Firefighter of the Year.

Doug Timm served as the pastor of Big Sky Christian Fellowship from 200 until 2013

Brock and Jane Short remain two of the most active participants and supporters of Brad's ministry.

A 1994 picture of the cross marking the chapel area at Big Sky.

"Shredder Chaplain." Brad on his snowboard. Continuing to both ski and ride, he frequently favors the board.

"Bradford, you are an Ironman!" Brad completing 2015 Ironman competition at Lake Tahoe, CA, a course so difficult 26% of contestants didn't finish.

After his denomination stopped funding Resort Ministries, Brad took a job driving bus to stay at Big Sky.

As 6-year old Harbor lay unconscious in the hospital, Brad turned that Sunday's service into a prayer service for him. The unusually large attendance was an indication of the community's love for this young boy.

Endnotes

1 Wilkerson, David, John L. Sherrill and Elizabeth Sherrill. *The Cross and the Switchblade.* New York: Jove, 1962.

2 Several years later he surprised me at a conference we were attending. "You did a good job at Sugarloaf."

3 http://ski-patrol.net/wordpress/

4 http://www.fallscreekok.org/index.php?id=8 "History." *Falls Creek.* Baptist General Convention of Oklahoma. Web. 12 Jan. 2016.

5 Weiser, Kathy. "New Mexico Legends: The Birth of Angel Fire." *Legends of America.* 2015. Retrieved from http://www.legendsofamerica.com/nm-angel-fire.html.

6 http://www.newmexico-demographics.com/angel-fire-demographics

7 Ibid.

8 Jet Cadets for Jesus--a Bible club patterned after scouting with different caps and sashes for various age groups and badges awarded for memorizing Bible verses.

9 Christian High Adventures is an outdoor adventure program for youth fourteen and over consisting of a week of backpacking or white water rafting. Hosted by Southern Baptists in North Carolina and Virginia, it began in 1976 and ended thirty-six years later in 2012.

10 The golf pass ended and restrictions placed on the ski pass after the privilege was abused by a "Rev" with no church.

11 U.S. National Library of Medicine, National Institutes of Health, PubMed Central archive of biomedical and life sciences journal literature, "Living at high altitude and reisk of sudden infant death syndrome," Kohlendorfer, Kiehl, Sperl; Arch Dis Child 1998;79:506-509. Retrieved from http://www.ncbi.nlm.nih.gov/pmc/articles/PMC1717761/pdf/v079p00506.pdf.

12 Smith, Lorin. "The House Church Movement." *House Church Basics*. Retrieved from http://www.housechurch.org/basics/lorin_smith.html

13 "House Church Movement Keeps Growing." *Koinonia House*. April 26 2011. Retrieved from http://www.khouse.org/enews_article/2011/1768.

14 Note: Interestingly, Crossroads Church in Aspen, formerly known as First Baptist Church, has since employed this very approach to ministry. At this writing they have seven active house churches with another in the planning stage. While these house churches are offshoots of an already-established church, their success validates Steve's original vision. He had the right idea; he was just too early.

15 "In simplest terms, 'traditional black powder hunting' is an ever-changing mix of America's rich pioneer heritage, the old-style arms from the black powder era and fair-chase hunting. As you can see, the name embraces the sport's three major elements, tradition, black powder and hunting, but as with any sport, the guiding principles form a framework that defines a philosophical outlook that sets traditional black powder hunting apart from all other outdoor pursuits." Neely, Dennis, "Unlocking the Secrets of the Past." 2011. Retrieved from http://traditionalblackpowderhunting.com/.

16 "Feed My Sheep." *Clear Path Productions*. 2011. Retrieved from http://www.YouTube.com/watch?v=Bs85_jULTow.

17 Bell, Lance. "Ernie Blake, Taos Ski Pioneer." *Legacy*. 23: 1, March 2009. Retrieved from www.nmjhs.org/mar-09-low.pdf.

18 Ibid.

19 Ibid.

20 www.bigskychapel.com

21 "Ministry Team." *Big Sky Ministries*. *Retrieved from* http://bigskyresortministries.com/ministry-team/ .

22 The words of the doxology are: "Praise God from whom all blessings flow, praise Him all creatures here below, Praise him above, ye heavenly hosts, Praise Father, Son and Holy Ghost."

23 https://en.wikipedia.org/wiki/Latitudinarian Wikipedia *Latitudinarian* was initially a pejorative term applied to a group of 17th-century English theologians who believed in conforming to official Church of England practices but who felt that matters of doctrine, liturgical practice, and ecclesiastical organization were of relatively little importance.

24 From "Resort Minister Spotlight on BSRM web page http://bigskyresortministries.com/ministry-team

25 https://www.facebook.com/photo.php?fbid=10154395450925440&set=a.10 150556058365440.676904.520750439&type=1&theater

26 Kosslyn, Stephen and Miller, G. Wayne. "A New Map of How We Think." *Wall Street Journal.* WSJ Oct 20, 2013. Retrieved from http://www.wsj.com/articles/SB10001424052702304410204579139423079198270

27 Unlike brain trauma that occurs due to direct impact and deformation of the brain, DAI is the result of traumatic shearing forces that occur when the head is rapidly accelerated or decelerated, as may occur in auto accidents, falls, and assaults. Wolf J.A., Stys P.K., Lusardi T., Meaney D., and Smith, D.H. (2001). Traumatic axonal injury induces calcium influx modulated by tetrodotoxin-sensitive sodium channels. *Journal of Neuroscience.* 21 (6): 1923–1930 at https://en.wikipedia.org/wiki/Diffuse_axonal_injury

28 Severe DAI, which has a mortality rate of 50%, occurs when there is an extensive disruption of axons in the white matter of the central nervous system. People who emerge from coma usually do so in the first 3 months after injury, but many of those who live remain in a persistent vegetative state. http://nursing.unboundmedicine.com/nursingcentral/ub/view/Diseases-and-Disorders/73573/all/diffuse_axonal_injury.

29 Wasserman, Jeffrey R., and James G. Smirniotopoulos. "Diffuse Axonal Injury Imaging." *Medscape.* Oct. 2013. Retrieved from http://emedicine.medscape.com/article/339912-overview.

30 Spastic Quadraplegia is the most severe form of cerebral palsy, and is generally caused by brain damage. Among the four types of brain damage causing the condition is insufficient oxygen to the brain. http://en.wikipedia.org/wiki/Spastic_quadriplegia